Private Antitrust Litigation

MIT Press Series on the Regulation of Economic Activity

General Editor
Richard Schmalensee, MIT Sloan School of Management

1   *Freight Transport Regulation*, Ann F. Friedlaender and Richard H. Spady, 1981

2   *The SEC and the Public Interest*, Susan M. Philips and J. Richard Zecher, 1981

3   *The Economics and Politics of Oil Price Regulation*, Joseph P. Kalt, 1981

4   *Studies in Public Regulation*, Gary Fromm, editor, 1981

5   *Incentives for Environmental Protection*, Thomas C. Schelling, editor, 1983

6   *United States Oil Pipeline Markets: Structure, Pricing, and Public Policy*, John A. Hansen, 1983

7   *Folded, Spindled, and Mutilated: Economic Analysis and U.S. v. IBM*, Franklin M. Fisher, John J. McGowan, and Joen E. Greenwood, 1983

8   *Targeting Economic Incentives for Environmental Protection*, Albert L. Nichols, 1984

9   *Deregulation and the New Airline Entrepreneurs*, John R. Meyer and Clinton V. Oster, Jr., with Marni Clippinger, Andrew McKey, Don H. Pickrell, John S. Strong, and C. Kurt Zorn, 1984

10   *Deregulating the Airlines*, Elizabeth E. Bailey, David R. Graham, and Daniel P. Kaplan, 1985

11   *The Gathering Crisis in Federal Deposit Insurance*, Edward J. Kane, 1985

12   *Perspectives on Safe and Sound Banking: Past, Present, and Future*, George J. Benston, Robert A. Eisenbeis, Paul M. Horvitz, Edward J. Kane, and Goerge G. Kaufman, 1986

13   *The Economics of Public Utility Regulation*, Michael A. Crew and Paul R. Kleindorfer, 1987

14   *Public Regulation: New Perspectives on Institutions and Policies*, Elizabeth E. Bailey, editor, 1987

15   *Deregulation and the Future of Intercity Passenger Travel*, John R. Meyer and Clinton V. Oster, Jr., with John S. Strong, José A. Gómez-Ibáñez, Don H. Pickrell, Marni Clippinger, and Ivor P. Morgan, 1987

16   *Private Antitrust Litigation: New Evidence, New Learning*, Lawrence J. White, editor, 1988

Private Antitrust Litigation
New Evidence, New Learning

edited by
Lawrence J. White

MIT Press
Cambridge, Massachusetts
London, England

This book was set in Times New Roman by Asco Trade Typesetting Ltd., Hong Kong, and printed and bound by Halliday Lithograph in the United States of America.

Library of Congress Cataloging-in-Publication Data

Private antitrust litigation.

(MIT Press series on the regulation of economic activity; 16)
1. Antitrust law—United States.   2. Actions and defenses—United States.
I. White, Lawrence J.   II. Series.
KF1657.P74P75   1988   343.73'072   87-22557
ISBN 0-262-23131-X   347.30372

Contents

Series Foreword   ix

Foreword   xi
Robert Pitofsky and Steven C. Salop

Preface   xv

I
OVERVIEW AND DATA

1
Private Antitrust Litigation: An Introduction and Framework   3
Steven C. Salop and Lawrence J. White

2
**The Georgetown Project: An Overview of the Data Set and
Its Collection**   61
Paul V. Teplitz

Discussion

Commentary on the Data Base of the Georgetown Study   82
Thomas J. Campbell

**Detrebling versus Decoupling Antitrust Damages:
Lessons from the Theory of Enforcement**   87
A. Mitchell Polinsky

Comment on the Salop-White and Teplitz Papers   95
F. M. Scherer

Comment: The Counterfactual and Legal Reform   99
Warren F. Schwartz

Comment   102
Joe Sims

II
THE OPERATION OF THE LITIGATION SYSTEM

3
The Costs of the Legal System in Private Antitrust Enforcement   107
Kenneth G. Elzinga and William C. Wood

4
Settlements in Private Antitrust Litigation   149
Jeffrey M. Perloff and Daniel L. Rubinfeld

5
**Equilibrating Tendencies in the Antitrust System, with Special
Attention to Summary Judgment and to Motions to Dismiss**   185
Stephen Calkins

Discussion

Comment   240
Ernest Gellhorn

Comment   244
Walter A. Schlotterbeck

Comments on the Operation of the Antitrust System   246
John De Q. Briggs

Comment: Critical Factual Assumptions Underlying Public Policy   252
Joseph F. Brodley

III
SPECIAL ISSUES IN ANTITRUST LITIGATION

6
**A Comprehensive Analysis of the Determinants of Private
Antitrust Litigation, with Particular Emphasis on Class Action
Suits and the Rule of Joint and Several Damages**   271
George J. Benston

7
Private Antitrust Cases That Follow on Government Cases 329
Thomas E. Kauper and Edward A. Snyder

Discussion

Comment: Settlement Incentives and Follow-on Litigation 371
Roger G. Noll

Comment 379
Charles B. Renfrew

Comment 381
Lawrence A. Sullivan

Comment 385
Thomas B. Leary

IV
POLICY IMPLICATIONS

8
Policy Implications of the Georgetown Study 389
George E. Garvey

9
**The Georgetown Study of Private Antitrust Litigation: Some
Policy Implications** 399
Ira M. Millstein

10
Private Antitrust Enforcement: Policy Recommendations 407
Donald F. Turner

Discussion

Comment: The Policy Implications of the Georgetown Data Set 410
William F. Baxter

Comment on the Policy Implications of the Georgetown Study 412
Harvey J. Goldschmid

Comment: Proposed Changes in Private Antitrust Enforcement,
Policy Implications   416
Emory M. Sneedon

Luncheon Address

Let's Fix Only What's Broken: Some Thoughts on Proposed
Reform of Private Antitrust Litigation   419
Peter W. Rodino, Jr.

Conference Participants   425

Legal and Corporate Donors to the Georgetown Project   427

Index   429

Series Foreword

Government regulation of economic activity in the United States has grown dramatically in this century, radically transforming the economic roles of government and business as well as relations between them. Economic regulation of prices and conditions of service was first applied to transportation and public utilities and was later extended to energy, health care, and other sectors. In the early 1970s explosive growth occurred in social regulation, focusing on workplace safety, environmental preservation, consumer protection, and related goals. Regulatory reform has occupied a prominent place on the agendas of recent administrations, and considerable economic deregulation and other reform have occurred, but the aims, methods, and results of many regulatory programs remain controversial.

The purpose of the MIT Press series, Regulation of Economic Activity, is to inform the ongoing debate on regulatory policy by making significant and relevant research available to both scholars and decision makers. Books in this series present new insights into individual agencies, programs, and regulated sectors, as well as the important economic, political, and administrative aspects of the regulatory process that cut across these boundaries.

Most regulatory programs are operated primarily or exclusively by a single government agency. Antitrust policy is an important exception in two respects: the U.S. antitrust laws are enforced by two government agencies (the Department of Justice and the Federal Trade Commission), and private parties can also file antitrust cases. In recent years there have been at least ten times as many private cases as government cases. Critics have argued that because successful plaintiffs are entitled to three times the actual damages they have suffered, there are too many private antitrust cases filed. Yet, although government antitrust enforcement has been frequently studied, almost no empirical work has heretofore been done on private enforcement—in large part because of a lack of data.

The Georgetown project on private antitrust litigation began with the laborious compilation of detailed data on over 2,000 private antitrust cases. This book contains a set of revealing analyses of those data, along with commentary and discussions of implications for antitrust reform. This work should be of interest to students of the judicial system and its operation, as well as to those with particular interest in antitrust policy.

Richard Schmalensee

Foreword

Private enforcement of the antitrust laws and the payment of mandatory treble damages and lawyers' fees to successful plaintiffs have been important features of U.S. antitrust enforcement ever since the Sherman Act was passed in 1890. In recent years this aspect of antitrust enforcement has become controversial.

During 1975 to 1980 an average of almost 1,500 cases per year were filed, with successful recoveries occasionally in excess $100 million. Increasingly, concern was expressed about the treble damage "bonanza," vocalized by a wide range of the scholarly and political spectrum. It was claimed that many of these lawsuits were of little merit and were instigated in the hopes of generous settlements and generous attorneys' fee awards. Further many critics claimed that the fear of private treble damage actions deterred companies from taking risks in areas near the uncertain line defining legal behavior, for fear of becoming the targets of enormous private actions. As a result innovative manufacturing, organizational, and distributional techniques were not adopted.

Others, however, claimed that private antitrust enforcement had served the country well and that the treble damage remedy was essential to compensate adequately the victims of anticompetitive behavior for the risks and burdens of antitrust suits and to deter wrongdoing in an area where detection of violations and successful enforcement were far from certain.

While there was no lack of debate on policy issues, there was a striking absence of hard empirical data about the costs and benefits of the present system. It was against this background of conflict and uncertainty that the Georgetown private treble damage project was initiated. A few experienced antitrust lawyers in Washington, including Joe Sims, Howard Adler, Thomas Long, and Martin Connor, initiated the project. With the special help of Jeffrey Kessler, financial support was sought and received from a large number of corporations (listed at the end of this volume) that believed that the absence of data hampered any assessment of the private antitrust enforcement system. Finally, an advisory committee of prominent lawyers and academics was established to oversee the project, with Robert Pitofsky serving as chair.

The preliminary design of the project was carried out in the summer and fall of 1983 by Thomas Krattenmaker, Steven Salop, Lawrence White, and the advisory committee. Lawrence White was selected as the research director of the project, and Cambridge Research Institute was selected to develop the data collection methodology and to carry out the data collection itself. The project designers hoped to collect extensive information about the private antitrust litigation system generally, so as to provide background information about litigation activity, including information on the types of cases brought, the cost and duration of litigation, and the outcomes of the cases. They also hoped to provide data that would allow researchers to infer some of the effects of proposed changes in the rules governing private antitrust litigation.

The data collection effort involved two phases: First, a considerable amount of data was collected from the dockets of all antitrust cases filed between 1973 and 1983 in five selected districts. Second, the parties (or their attorneys) were surveyed in an attempt to collect additional information on settlement terms and legal fees. Unfortunately, this second survey provided only limited additional information.

The project commissioned a number of prominent scholars to analyze the prominent issues underlying proposals to reform private antitrust litigation, using the data collected by the project to inform their analysis. Their research was presented at a conference held in November, 1985. This volume contains the papers prepared by those researchers, comments prepared by discussants, and policy commentary by other invited speakers.

The paper by Steven Salop and Lawrence White (chapter 1) presents an analytic framework for studying private antitrust litigation, sets out the policy issues, and provides an overview of the data collected by the project. They argue that the economic incentives of potential defendants to undertake questionable conduct are related in complex ways to potential plaintiffs' incentives to sue and to the parties' mutual incentives to settle rather than to proceed to trial. Paul Teplitz's paper (chapter 2) discusses the data collection effort and the nature of the data collected. He provides the reader with a sense of the docket and survey information underlying the summary data presented.

Kenneth Elizinga and William Wood (chapter 3) analyze the cost of the antitrust litigation system. They compare the cost of litigation to the size of settlements and awards in an attempt to gauge the degree to which the system compensates victims of antitrust violations, as opposed to the effectiveness with which the system deters antitrust violations. They find that jury trials last considerably longer than cases tried by judges and that price-fixing cases last longer than cases involving other antitrust issues. Jeffrey Perloff and Daniel Rubinfeld's paper (chapter 4) focuses on settlements. These authors analyze the incentives of litigants to settle and then use the data generated in the project to make rough predictions of the effect of reducing the damages multiplier on settlement behavior. They conclude that reducing the multiplier likely would reduce the settlement rate and thus increase the overall social cost of litigation. Stephen Calkins' paper (chapter 5) analyzes the reaction of the legal system to the treble damages remedy with regard to motions to dismiss and motions for summary judgment. Calkins concludes that courts have compensated for the apparent harshness of the treble damages remedy by disposing of relatively more cases prior to trial.

Thomas Kauper and Edward Snyder (chapter 7) analyze those cases that followed on government cases. The prototypical follow-on case is a price-fixing case. The authors find that fewer of these cases are dismissed and more settled. Of those that were tried, however, the plaintiff win rate did not exceed the win rate in independently initiated cases. George Benston's paper (chapter 6) focuses on multiparty cases. He analyzes the effects of class actions, joint and several liability, and various claim reduction reform proposals on deterrence and the incentives to settle. This paper is largely theoretical, but it may suggest methods of analyzing the rich data set on multidistrict litigation collected by the project.

The final section of this volume focuses on three policy commentaries prepared by George Garvey, Ira Millstein, and Donald Turner. These authors draw quite varied conclusions from the data and the analysis of the primary researchers.

Where do we go from here?

In the policy session at the conclusion of this conference, several participants expounded the view that the private treble damage system is not out of control. Private antitrust litigation generally does not appear to be excessively expensive, to consume a large amount of judicial resources, or to result in inappropriate recoveries. They argued that any significant reform proposal would damage a system that is fair and useful, particularly during periods when government antitrust enforcement is lax and pro-business. But other participants in the policy session thought that the present system unduly encourages frivolous suits and deters efficient behavior, and they suggested a variety of ways to reform private enforcement. One problem, however, is that few of the critics of the status quo could agree on a single policy of reform.

As this book goes to press, the Reagan administration has proposed restricting the treble damage remedy to lawsuits alleging antitrust overcharges or underpayments (i.e., only for price-fixing cases), with single damages applying in all other situations. The proposal also would provide automatic prejudgment interest on actual damages. At least for the immediate future, that proposal will be the focal point of serious debate.

The only thing that appears clear at this point is that treble damage reform has moved to center stage and that its supporters and critics are digging in for a period of spirited dispute. All participants, pro and con, should find a substantial amount of useful material in the volume.

Robert Pitofsky and Steven C. Salop

Preface

On November 8 and November 9, 1985, a group of leading antitrust academics, practitioners, and government officials attended a conference at Airlie House, Virginia. The conference, held under the auspices of the Georgetown University Law Center, was the culmination of a two and a half year effort to plan, collect, and analyze a new data base on the enforcement of the antitrust laws through private litigation. This volume represents the edited papers and comments presented at that conference.

As with any effort of this magnitude, multiple thanks are due to many parties: to the corporate donors (listed at the end of this volume) whose donations funded the project; to the law firms and corporate legal departments (also listed at the end of this volume) who donated paralegal time to permit collection of the data that lay at the heart of the project; to the advisory board members who provided counsel in shaping both the broad scope and many of the details of the project; to the law firm of Jones, Day, Reavis & Pogue, which devoted resources to the project, and to Margaret Stuart Staudinger of that law firm, who provided administrative assistance; to Georgetown University Law Center, which provided resources and a home base for the project, and to Kitty Hackett of the Law Center, who handled many of the day-to-day details of the conference; and to Robert Pitofsky, whose firm leadership and good sense guided the project successfully from its beginnings until the appearance of this volume, marking the project's conclusion.

Lawrence J. White

I

OVERVIEW AND DATA

Private Antitrust Litigation: An Introduction and Framework

Steven C. Salop and Lawrence J. White

1.1 Introduction

Concern has been mounting about the nature, volume, and consequences of private antitrust litigation.[1] Surprisingly, there has been little systematic study of private antitrust litigation that could illuminate these questions. Only two previous research efforts tried to collect systematic data on private antitrust litigation,[2] and the data collected and questions explored by those two studies were relatively limited. The Georgetown project on private antitrust litigation was formulated and designed to expand the available knowledge in this area and to inform the antitrust policy debate.[3]

In this chapter we first provide an overview of the data collected by the project. Second, we set out a framework for analyzing litigation in general and private antitrust litigation in particular. Third, we return to the data and explore the ways in which the statistical patterns of private antitrust litigation illuminate our framework. Finally, we offer our conclusions.

1.2 An Overview of the Data

Private suits have been the predominant form of antitrust litigation for at least 40 years. Table 1.1 provides data on all U.S. government and private antitrust cases filed since 1941. During this period private cases have consistently outnumbered government cases. Until 1965, with the exception of a "spike" in 1962 due to the electrical conspiracy follow-on cases, the ratio of private to government cases tended to be 6 to 1 or less. From the mid 1960s until the late 1970s the absolute and relative number of private antitrust cases grew, reaching a peak of 1,611 cases in 1978, while the ratio of private to public cases exceeded 20 to 1. In the 1980s, however, both the absolute and relative numbers of antitrust cases have declined, and the private to public ratio has fallen to the 10 to 1 range.

The Georgetown antitrust project collected data on all private antitrust cases filed from 1973 through 1983 in five federal districts: the Southern District of New York (Manhattan), Northern District of Illinois (Chicago), Northern District of California (San Francisco), Western District of Missouri (Kansas City), and Northern District of Georgia (Atlanta).[4] These

Table 1.1   Antitrust cases commenced, 1941–1984

Fiscal year	U.S. government cases	Private cases
1941–1945	181	297
1946–1950	256	529
1951–1955	197	1,045
1956–1960	317	1,163
1961	63	378
1962	74	2,005
1963	77	380
1964	83	363
1965	49	472
1966	48	722
1967	55	543
1968	59	659
1969	57	740
1970	56	877
1971	70	1,445
1972	94	1,299
1973	72	1,125
1974	64	1,230
1975	92	1,375
1976	70	1,504
1977	78	1,611
1978	72	1,435
1979	78	1,234
1980	78	1,457
1981	142	1,292
1982	111	1,037
1983	95	1,192
1984	101	1,100

Sources: Stelzer (1983); CCH *Trade Regulation Reports*, no. 647 (October 31, 1984), p. 3.

district courts were chosen to provide breadth and depth to the sample; the years were chosen to provide sufficient historical perspective. The project culled all relevant data from the docket files on these cases and mailed a follow-up survey to all of the parties or their attorneys on both sides of these cases. This latter survey yielded a limited amount of data on legal fees and settlements.[5]

There were 2,357 usable cases in the sample: 398 cases that were consolidated into 19 multidistrict litigations (MDLs)[6] and 1,959 non-MDL cases.[7] These cases were approximately one-sixth of all private antitrust cases filed during these years. The cases span the range of antitrust, from the *Folding Carton* cases to *Berkey* v. *Kodak* to *Grandma's Foods, Inc.* v. *Mother's Cake & Cookie Co.* Because the MDLs are difficult to describe quantitatively and less complete information was available for them, much of our discussion focuses on the 1,959 non-MDL cases. Where appropriate, however, we also provide relevant data from the MDLs.

Table 1.2   Identities of plaintiffs and defendants, by major economic sector, with 1978 GNP for comparison

	Plaintiffs	Defendants	GNP in 1978 by sectors
Agriculture, forestry, and fisheries	1.1%	0.4%	3.0%
Mining, petroleum	0.5	0.9	2.6
Construction	2.0	1.3	4.7
Manufacturing	24.1	44.3	24.6
Transportation, communications, and utilities	6.2	6.6	3.7
Wholesale trade	18.8	10.0 ⎫	17.2
Retail trade	19.9	5.7 ⎭	
Finance, insurance, and real estate	5.8	11.2	13.8
Services	14.8	12.5	12.5
Governments	2.3	2.0	12.1
Trade organizations	0.7	3.0	—
Labor unions	0.4	1.6	—
Individuals	5.3	0.4	—
Rest of world	—	—	1.0

The Parties

The average number of named plaintiffs per cases was 2.1; the median was one. In only 32 percent of the cases did the number of plaintiffs exceed one; in only 9.8 percent of the cases did that number exceed three. The average number of named defendants was 4.8; the median was three. In 32.1 percent of the cases there was only one defendant; in 11.1 percent there were ten or more.[8] Intervenors were rare: they appeared on the plaintiff's side in only 1.6 percent of the cases and on the defendant's side in 2.0 percent of the cases; in 2.8 percent of the cases the intervenor was "other."

In many of the cases the primary business activity of plaintiffs or defendants could be identified by SIC code. Table 1.2 reports the percentages of identified plaintiffs and defendants by major economic sector and, for comparison, those sectors' contributions to GNP in 1978. The table illustrates the substantial overrepresentation of manufacturing firms among defendants, the substantial overrepresentation of wholesale and retail trade firms among plaintiffs, and the underrepresentation of finance, insurance, and real estate firms among plaintiffs. The MDL cases reinforce this pattern: in 11 of the 19 identified MDL cases, accounting for 313 of the 398 underlying cases, the defendants were firms in the manufacturing sector.[9]

The data do not indicate the relative sizes of the litigants. But casual observation of the names of the parties indicates that the defendants were

Table 1.3 Antitrust statute violation alleged in complaints

Sherman Act, section 1	74.9%
Sherman Act, section 2	46.5
Sherman Act, unspecified	7.4
Clayton Act, section 2	18.1
Clayton Act, section 3	11.1
Clayton Act, section 7	6.1
Clayton Act, section 8	0.6
Clayton Act, other sections	26.0
Clayton Act, unspecified	6.3
Other antitrust claims	14.3
Other, nonantitrust statutes	18.6
No information	4.7

Note: Percentages total more than 100 percent because a complaint may contain more than one allegation.

Table 1.4 Illegal practices alleged in complaints

	Primary allegations	Combined primary and secondary allegations
Horizontal price fixing	15.7%	21.3%
Vertical price fixing	3.5	10.3
Dealer termination	4.4	8.9
Refusal to deal	12.0	25.4
Predatory pricing	3.1	10.4
Asset or patent accumulation	2.5	5.6
Price discrimination	5.0	16.4
Vertical price discrimination	1.7	5.8
Tying or exclusive dealing	9.6	21.1
Merger or joint venture	2.6	5.8
Inducing government action	0.5	0.8
"Conspiracy"	3.0	5.9
"Restraint of trade"	4.3	10.0
"Monopoly" or "monopolization"	3.7	8.8
Other	8.6	8.9
No information	25.2	13.4

Note: Percentages total more than 100 percent because a complaint may have more than one allegation.

Table 1.5 Illegal practices alleged in complaints, consolidated into horizontal, vertical, and other allegations

	Primary allegations	Combined primary and secondary allegations
All horizontal allegations	27.7%	52.8%
All vertical allegations	31.2	71.6
All other allegations	23.0	31.3
No information	25.2	13.4

Note: Percentages total more than 100 percent because a complaint may have more than one allegation. Allegations are as classified in chapter 7 by Kauper and Snyder.

much more likely to be familiar "Fortune 500" names than were plaintiffs. The sectoral pattern of the litigants in table 1.2 reinforces this notion, since firms in the manufacturing sector tend to be larger than firms in other sectors. We are quite confident that plaintiffs tended to be much smaller than defendants.[10]

Type of Case

Table 1.3 shows that the Sherman Act was cited most frequently in complaints. Less than one-fifth of cases involved Robinson-Patman (Clayton Act, sec. 2) claims; only 6 percent involved section 7 of the Clayton Act. Most complaints also contained language indicating the specific types of illegal business practices alleged. Table 1.4 indicates that horizontal price fixing was the most frequent primary allegation, followed by refusal to deal. When primary and secondary allegations are combined, refusal to deal was the most frequent, followed by horizontal price fixing, tying or exclusive dealing,[11] and price discrimination. Table 1.5 consolidates allegations into horizontal and vertical categories and shows that vertical allegations outnumbered horizontal allegations.

Most complaints provided enough information so that the business relationships of the parties could be determined. Table 1.6 shows that the largest group of plaintiffs was downstream business entities—dealers, business customers, franchisees, and licensees—suing their suppliers. The next largest group was competitors suing each other.

Table 1.7 cross-tabulates the business relationships of the parties and the alleged illegal practices, indicating a reasonable consistency between the two. Thus dealers are overwhelmingly the parties who allege illegal dealer terminations; competitors are the main parties who allege predatory pricing; dealers are the main parties who allege vertical price fixing. A surprising number of cases, however, involve competitors' alleging an illegal

Table 1.6 Plaintiffs' business relationships to defendants, as indicated in complaints

Competitor	36.5%
Dealer	27.3
(of which terminated dealer)	(9.9)
Customer company	12.5
Franchisee	1.6
Licensee	1.3
Final customer or end user	8.7
Supplier	5.6
Employee or former employee	3.5
State or local government	1.4
Other	12.7
No information	13.8

Note: Percentages total more than 100 percent because a complaint may involve more than one business relationship.

refusal to deal. In addition competitors' challenges to mergers outnumber those by suppliers, dealers, or customers by a factor of 2 to 1.

Process

We now turn our attention to some of the process aspects of the cases. We restrict ourselves to the 1,802 cases in which all legal activity was completed, the files were available, and a last docket entry date was known. Table 1.8 shows that the average case lasted slightly over two years, the median case lasted less than a year and a half,[12] and 38.8 percent lasted less than a year. The average case involved 70 docket entries and 2.9 judicial orders. The average docket file was about eight inches thick. Because these data include cases from recent years (in which, by definition, only the shorter cases had terminated), we also examined the process aspects of terminated cases that had been filed before 1980. Table 1.8 demonstrates that this added time perspective—which allowed more of the longer cases to complete themselves—meant slightly longer cases, more depositions, and thicker files. The MDL cases, not too surprisingly, involved more effort. They averaged 5.7 years in duration and 968 docket entries per consolidated case.

These process data are consistent with the limited amount of publicly available data on private antitrust suits. The *Annual Reports* of the Director of the Administrative Office of the U.S. Courts for 1973 to 1983 show that the median length of private antitrust suits terminated each year ranged from 13 months to 23 months, with the median of the annual medians at 17 months. This is virtually identical to the median of 16.6 months shown in

Table 1.7 Cross-tabulation of business relationships and alleged illegal practices

	Hori-zontal price fixing	Vertical price fixing	Dealer termi-nation	Refusal to deal	Pred-atory pricing	Asset accumu-lation	Price discrim-ination	Vertical price discrim-ination	Tie; exclusive dealing	Merger; joint venture	Induce govern-ment action	Con-spiracy, restraint, monopo-lization	Other	No infor-mation	Total
Competitor	141	68	36	214	138	77	141	53	161	82	10	240	83	18	1,462
Dealer	105	112	159	211	56	19	138	68	165	19	2	125	30	5	1,214
Customer company	85	39	8	102	23	13	63	17	55	11	0	44	10	3	473
Franchisee	3	3	6	9	6	1	12	3	23	1	0	5	3	0	75
Licensee	2	1	1	3	1	2	0	0	12	0	0	25	2	0	49
Final customer	97	4	0	25	7	6	29	4	35	6	0	39	13	3	268
Supplier	23	8	3	35	10	3	23	4	20	4	1	25	15	2	176
Employee	10	3	4	18	8	8	6	3	11	6	1	15	15	1	109
State/local government	13	0	0	1	0	3	0	0	0	2	2	9	3	1	34
Other	48	14	6	59	4	11	15	14	39	10	3	86	55	7	371
No information	13	2	2	2	4	3	6	2	10	1	0	20	3	228	296
Total	540	254	275	679	257	146	433	168	531	142	19	633	232	268	4,527

Note: The totals of the cross-tabulations total more than 1,959 because individual cases can have more than one type of business relationship and/or more than one alleged business practice.

Table 1.8   Process aspects of cases

	All terminated cases		Terminated cases filed before 1980	
	Average	Median	Average	Median
Length (months)	24.9	16.6	27.9	18.8
Number of docket entries	70	35	75	36
Depositions noticed by plaintiffs	3.1	0	3.3	0
Deposition noticed by defendants	2.5	0	2.8	0
Number of judge orders	2.9	2	3.0	2
Number of magistrate orders	0.4	0	0.5	0
Thickness of docket file (in inches)	8.2	3.0	8.5	3.5

Table 1.9   Primary outcomes of cases

	All cases		Cases filed before 1980	
	Number	Percentage	Number	Percentage
Settlements[a]	1,436	73.3%	1,117	77.7%
Judgment for all or some plaintiffs	54	2.8	47	3.3
Judgment for all or some defendants	137	7.0	115	8.0
Judgment for some plaintiffs and some defendants	1	0.1	0	0.0
Case still pending or on appeal	114	5.8	15	1.0
Transferred or remanded to state court	109	5.6	78	5.4
Consolidated	40	2.0	19	1.3
File missing and/or outcome unknown	68	3.5	46	3.2
Total	1,959	100.0	1,437	100.0

a. Broad definition of settlement, including dismissals.

table 1.8. The same data also show the stock of private antitrust cases pending each year to be roughly twice the annual flow of new cases, which implies an average length of about two years—again quite consistent with table 1.8. Thus the data in the Georgetown sample appear to be representative of private antitrust suits generally.

Finally, the median length of private antitrust cases is appreciably longer than the median length—nine months—of other cases in federal courts.[13]

Outcomes

We now focus on the primary outcomes of the full non-MDL sample of 1,959 cases.[14] Table 1.9 shows that almost 75 percent of the cases settled, if we use a broad definition of settlement;[15] another 10 percent reached final judgments of some kind; and the remainder of the cases were still pending, had been transferred or consolidated, or had unknown outcomes.

Table 1.10   Percentage distribution of cases in which final disposition is known

	Broad definition of settlement[a]		Narrow definition of settlement[b]	
	Terminated cases	Litigated cases	Terminated cases	Litigated cases
Settlement	88.2%	—	70.8%	—
Judgment for all or some plaintiffs	3.3	28.1%	3.3	11.3%
Judgment for all or some defendants	8.4	71.4	25.9	88.4
Judgment for some plaintiffs and some defendants	0.1	0.5	0.1	0.2

a. Includes dismissals in settlements.
b. Includes dismissals in judgments for defendants.

Table 1.10 focuses solely on those cases for which the final disposition was known. When a broad definition of settlement is used, over 88 percent of the cases settled. Plaintiffs prevailed less than 30 percent of the time in the remaining cases.

This definition of settlement may be too broad. A number of the cases in the "settlement" categories, especially "dismissed," may have been true victories for the defendant. Unfortunately, there is no definitive way of ascertaining the true outcome.[16] As an attempt at a narrower definition of settlement, table 1.10 also shows the percentage outcomes when all dismissals are counted as victories for defendants rather than as settlements. Under this narrower definition of settlement a substantial majority of the cases still were settled, but the plaintiff win rate drops substantially, since many more cases are now counted as defendant victories.

The "truth" probably lies somewhere between these two definitions of settlement, but we have no way of knowing where. Accordingly, where appropriate, subsequent analysis will employ both definitions.

Only 106 cases—5.4 percent of all cases—went to trial. The average number of days of trial was 11.4; the median was six days. Of these cases 22 cases settled or failed to reach a final judgment. In the remaining 84 cases plaintiffs prevailed in 28 cases (33 percent).[17]

These settlement and judgment outcomes can be compared with outcomes reported elsewhere. Using data for 1964 to 1970 provided by the Administrative Office of the U.S. Courts, Baxter (1980, 17) found that 82 percent of antitrust cases settled and plaintiffs prevailed in only 15 percent of the cases that were litigated to a final judgment. Unfortunately, the criteria used by the Administrative Office for classifying cases were not reported, so exact comparisons with the Georgetown data are not possible.

The settlement rates indicated by the two alternative definitions in the Georgetown sample, however, bracket the rate reported by Baxter, as do the Georgetown sample's plaintiff win rates.

By contrast, for a sample of 770 civil cases of all kinds terminating in 1978 in five federal district courts, Grossman et al. (1982), using criteria similar to our broad definition of settlement, found a settlement rate of 72 percent. Priest and Klein (1984) report that plaintiffs prevailed in 53 percent of a sample (819 cases) of cases decided in U.S. District Court in Cook County, Illinois, during 1959 to 1979. It appears that antitrust cases have higher rates of settlement and that antitrust plaintiffs prevail in a lower percentage of judgments than is true generally in federal district courts.

Monetary Awards or Recoveries
Information is available on the monetary awards (recoveries, excluding legal fees) made to plaintiffs in 42 of the non-MDL cases.[18] The average award was $7 million, but this is skewed upward by the very large award of $276 million in *Litton* v. *AT&T*.[19] If that case is excluded, the average award was $393,000, and the median award was $154,000. Because these awards occurred during a decade that experienced significant price inflation—the general price level more than doubled between 1973 and 1983—we have also converted the awards into 1984 dollar equivalents, using the Consumer Price Index. Excluding *Litton*, the average award was $456,000 in 1984 dollars, and the median was $194,000.[20]

The MDL cases are a second source of information on awards. Of 18 completed MDLs, 12 had information on judgment or settlement awards to plaintiffs. The awards ranged from $250,000 to $218 million. The average award for the 12 MDLs was $44.5 million. These 12 MDLs represented 337 underlying cases, so the average recovery per underlying case was $1.6 million.

Settlements
To obtain more information on settlements and legal fees, the project mailed questionnaires (which promised confidentiality for individual responses) to all of the parties—approximately 9,000—on both sides of all of the cases in the sample. Unfortunately, only 7 percent responded, and less than half of those provided usable information.

The responses contributed only meager settlement information. Only 71 parties provided information on the monetary amounts of settlement payments, with most of the responses coming from defendants. For this limited sample the average settlement amount was $1,244,000, but this average was sharply skewed by one large settlement of $50 million. Without this settlement the average was $547,000, and the median was $50,000. When the series is transformed into 1984 dollar equivalents, the average is $676,000 without the large settlement, and the median is $50,000. The responses provided even less information about the nonmonetary terms of settlements, and accordingly, we cannot conclude much more about the settlement terms.

Costs

Data on the legal costs of the parties in these cases are not, for the most part, available. Because most cases are settled, usually no public record of legal costs exist in these cases. Furthermore, even where plaintiffs win judgments and are entitled to receive legal fees, the data are not always readily available.

This study generated two sources of data on litigation costs. First, in some of the case records legal fees and court costs are awarded to one party or the other, either as part of a judgment or as part of a settlement. Second, the follow-up questionnaire to the parties yielded some additional data on costs. We use both data sources in the following discussion.

The ratio of litigation costs to monetary recoveries, either through judgment awards or settlements, is a statistic that is frequently cited as a measure of the efficiency of the antitrust litigation system as a mechanism for compensating victims. We believe, however, that antitrust litigation should be viewed less as a compensation mechanism and more as a means of deterrence. Hence we place little normative value on this ratio. Moreover the ratio ignores the value of injunctive relief or other nonmonetary gains to the plaintiff. Nevertheless, because of the widespread interest in this ratio, and because we will provide positive content to these data in section 1.4, we present the available data in table 1.11. The last line of table 1.11 provides comparison data from an earlier study (Kelly 1972) of antitrust judgments for 1904 to 1972.

Though the data are sparse, the award data from the Georgetown sample indicate that the cost ratio is in the range of 10 to 20 percent in cases in which awards were made. This finding is consistent with the Kelly data. The ratio of costs to settlements, however, appears to be appreciably higher. Also, though not reported in the table, the underlying cost ratios for each category exhibit a pattern of smaller ratios in cases in which the recoveries or settlements are larger.

Table 1.11   Ratios of legal fees to plaintiff recoveries

	Number of cases	Average ratio	Median ratio
Non-MDL cases[a]	12	20.2%	16.8%
MDL cases[a]	11	8.3	10.2
Combined cases	23	8.4	12.4
Settlement[b]	55	20.3[c]	110.0
Kelly sample[a]	47	6.5[d]	21.0

a. The ratio of plaintiff legal fee award to monetary judgment award.
b. The ratio of reported defendant legal fees to moneys paid in settlement.
c. With the exclusion of one large settlement, the average ratio is 85 percent.
d. With the exclusion of one large award, the average ratio is 11.7 percent.

We now turn to efforts to measure the legal costs per case. Although 48 cases in the docket survey listed legal fee awards in a useful manner, these 48 cases were not typical of all cases in the sample. These cases lasted appreciably longer (an average of 43.6 months), and they involved appreciably more legal effort. Accordingly, simple extrapolation of the average or median fees of these cases would not be appropriate. Statistical efforts to relate the fee awards to the characteristics of the cases that produced them—for example, number of plaintiffs and defendants, length of case, type of allegations, number of docket entries—did not yield satisfactory results.

Instead, we focused on the cost information from the questionnaire survey. These data suffer from potential problems of response bias, but our analytic methods control for at least part of this problem. There were 184 instances in which the respondents provided usable data on the legal costs of their participation in their antitrust case. Since these costs covered a period of a decade, we converted them into constant dollar (1984 dollar) equivalents.[21] There were 151 responses for which the conversion could be made. For these 151 responses the average legal costs per party (in 1984 dollars) were $194,000,[22] and the median was $59,000.

Examination of the cases that generated these legal costs indicate that they were atypical: they lasted longer and involved more legal effort. Accordingly, we used ordinary least squares regressions to relate fees to the characteristics of the cases. Unlike our efforts with legal awards data, the larger sample size and diminished problems of multicollinearity in this sample yielded more consistent results. Table 1.12 provides the equation that yielded the best, and quite reasonable, fit to the data.[23] This method of analysis corrects for some of the possible response bias in the data. Although the respondents were involved in cases that, on average, were

Table 1.12   Ordinary least squares regression explaining respondents' legal costs

LC = Legal costs of questionnaire respondents (in thousands of 1984 dollars)

NDE = number of docket entries in case

NJO = number of judge orders

NP = number of named parties on respondent's side of case

$$\log(LC) = 1.74 + 0.58 \log(NDE) + 0.27 \log(NJO) - 0.42 \log(NP)$$
$$\qquad\qquad\quad (3.60) \qquad\qquad (1.28) \qquad\qquad (3.37)$$
$$\bar{R}^2 = 0.23, n = 118$$

Note: Numbers in parentheses are t-statistics.

bigger and more costly, we have used the relationships among the variables to estimate the costs that parties in smaller cases were likely to incur.[24]

The coefficients from the equation and the average values of the number of docket entries and judicial orders for the entire sample of cases yield a predicted average cost for a sole plaintiff or defendant of about $75,000 per case, with lower amounts per party if there were other parties on the same side of the case.[25] Accordingly we estimate that the average total legal costs per case (for both sides combined[26]) were in the range of $200,000 to $250,000.[27]

The average cost of an antitrust case (corrected for the general level of inflation) does not appear to have increased over 1973 to 1983. A time trend introduced into the regression reported in table 1.12 was not significant, and examination of the median duration and median number of docket entries for the cases filed in each year yielded no apparent upward time trend.[28]

Our cost estimate of $200,000 to $250,000 per case translates into an estimate of around $250 million per year for all private cases filed in recent years. We are aware of only one previous estimate of aggregate antitrust costs for private litigants: Reich's (1980) estimate of $2.1 billion for 1979 for all private antitrust legal costs, including counseling, negotiating, and defense against government cases. The equivalent figure would be $3.3 billion in 1984 dollars, but Reich's estimate encompasses many antitrust functions and activities that ours does not.

Initial Conclusions

Although there was significant absolute and relative growth of private antitrust litigation in the 1970s, the wave crested in the late 1970s and has since receded. Plaintiffs continue to allege a wide variety of statute violations and illegal practices. But the "interminable" case is a rarity. The average case lasts for only slightly more than two years, and the typical (median) case lasts for less than a year and a half. The overwhelming majority of cases settle. Plaintiffs prevail about 28 percent of the time when cases go to judgment—11 percent if dismissals are counted as defendant victories. Furthermore the costs of litigation do not appear to be crushing. The current total annual costs of private antitrust litigation are probably in the range of $250 million.[29]

More questions however, remain unanswered. Why are settlement rates so high? Do they represent efficient economizing of legal fees or successful extortion by plaintiffs? Why are plaintiff success rates in antitrust cases below those of plaintiffs in other federal cases? Is there a relationship between settlement patterns and plaintiff success rates? How does the treble damages remedy affect all of this? What would be the consequences of a change in the treble damages remedy or in other legal rules?

To shed further light on these questions, we establish a framework for analysis in section 1.3 emphasizing the economic incentives that the legal framework creates for the parties' behavior with respect to law violations, suits, legal expenditures, and settlement. We then turn to further data analysis in section 1.4.

1.3 An Analytic Framework[30]

Private litigation is part of a larger overall system consisting of four distinct phases: the business conduct of potential litigants, the suing decisions of potential plaintiffs, the settlement offers of the litigants once a dispute has arisen, and the litigation strategies and expenditures of both parties if settlement cannot be reached. These various phases and the parties' decisions are interdependent. For example, a potential defendant's business conduct decision depends on the likelihood that the potential plaintiff will sue, the likelihood that a suit can be settled at low cost before trial, the cost of defending the case, the likelihood of loss at trial, and the penalties consequent to loss. Which practices are pursued or abandoned, which disputes lead to suits, which suits are settled, and which go to trial depend on the actions of the adversaries and their perceptions and reactions to each other.

By altering the economic incentives of the parties, antitrust rules influence the costs and likelihood of alternative outcomes and thus influence the parties' decisions. For example, by increasing the returns to successful plaintiffs, the treble damages remedy increases the likelihood that injured plaintiffs will sue over questionable conduct, as compared with, say, single damages. This increased likelihood of suit, as well as the higher penalties that a losing defendant faces, in turn reduces the potential defendants' incentives to engage in the conduct. Other rules governing fee shifting and legal standards can be examined in a similar way.

In this section we briefly explore the economic incentives that arise in the antitrust litigation system.[31] By examining the parties' mutually reactive incentives, the effects of changes in antitrust rules can be predicted more accurately. We focus on the parties' economic incentives because we believe these incentives are central to their actual decisions. Indeed, any belief in the efficacy of deterrence through civil penalties ultimately rests on such a belief in the primacy of economic incentives.

The Incentives to Violate and to Sue

If litigation were inexpensive and outcomes were easy to predict in advance, virtually all litigation would be eliminated. This paradoxical result can be derived from an analysis of the parties' incentives and perceptions. If the defendant anticipated that he would be sued for his conduct, that the plaintiff would prevail, and that the penalties would be prohibitive, then the defendant would not carry out the conduct that would lead to suit. Only in those instances in which the potential defendant anticipated that he would not be sued, that the suit would fail, or that the penalties were less than the gain from the conduct would the defendant undertake business conduct that might lead to litigation. Of course, if outcomes were easy to predict, a plaintiff would only sue in those instances in which he anticipated success at trial.[32] In those instances, however, the defendant, anticipating such success, would forego the business conduct that would lead to such a case, if the penalties were greater than the gain from the conduct. Thus there would be no litigation.

Of course, litigation is expensive and filled with risks and uncertainties. Under these circumstances the parties must base their decisions on uncertain expectations about the eventual outcomes rather than on anticipations that are certain, and they must weigh expected litigation costs against potential awards. As a result litigation does sometimes occur.

From the litigating parties' perspective, uncertainty can encompass the exact location of the substantive legal standard, the evidence that will be introduced, and the fact finder's interpretation of this evidence. Each party not only faces uncertainty about these issues but also is unsure about his adversary's perceptions of these risks. This translates into three sources of uncertainty for the defendant in calculating the likelihood that his business conduct will be enjoined and penalized: the likelihood that the plaintiff will detect a potential antitrust violation, the likelihood that the plaintiff will initiate a suit, and the likelihood that a suit will succeed if one is initiated.

The plaintiff must estimate his likelihood of success in deciding whether to initiate a suit.[33]

The parties' decisions, uncertainties, and litigation costs are interdependent. The parties' reactions to each other's perceptions and decisions are fundamental to analyzing both their incentives to violate and to sue and also the roles of uncertainty and of legal fees in this determination. For example, the uncertainty faced by the defendant is complicated by the fact that he must estimate the behavior of the plaintiff, who faces uncertainty himself. Whether the plaintiff initiates suit will depend on his perceptions of the likelihood that he will prevail at trial. Thus the defendant faces uncertainty not only about the law but also about the plaintiff's own uncertain estimates. A similar point can be made with respect to litigation expenditures. Consider a situation in which a potential defendant believes that the plaintiff is unlikely to sue because high legal fees would make suit uneconomical once the plaintiff takes into account the possibility that he may lose at trial. In this instance even if defending a suit would be expensive and would mean potential exposure to large damages, the potential defendant could conclude that the relevant business conduct could be safely undertaken.

The Expected Value of Litigation   Antitrust litigation ultimately is a financial proposition involving stakes and costs. The stakes of the litigation are the sum of the likely damages award and the dollar equivalent of the likely injunctive relief if the suit goes to trial and judgment. The costs include the lawyers' fees, expert fees, and executive time expanded on the litigation.

Given these uncertain costs and benefits, the parties can calculate (at least roughly) the economic value, net of costs, of alternative courses of action. These net expected values consist of four components: the benefit (or harm) of the business conduct at issue, the potential award, the costs of litigation, and the likelihood that the plaintiff prevails. Thus the defendant's net expected value of undertaking questionable business conduct is comprised of his benefit from the conduct less the expected financial exposure arising from a suit. That expected exposure consists of the defendant's likely legal fees plus the potential damages award, discounted by his perception of the probability that the plaintiff will not sue and the probability that he will sue but the defendant will prevail. Similarly the potential plaintiff's net expected value of suit is the sum of the expected damages award and the value of injunctive relief, multiplied by his subjective probability of winning, less his estimated litigation expenditures.[34]

This analysis has the following general implications: A plaintiff is more likely to bring a suit when his perceived probability of success is greater, when his litigation costs are lower, and when his rewards from success are greater. Potential defendants are more likely to be deterred from conduct that may lead to an antitrust complaint when the probability that a potential violation will be detected is greater, when the probability that a suit will be initiated is greater, when the probability that the plaintiff will prevail is greater, when the defendant's litigation costs are higher, and when the potential exposure from an award of damages is greater.

This analysis also provides a general prediction about the effect of eliminating the treble damages remedy. By reducing the plaintiff's expected award, detrebling reduces the expected value of suing. Thus cases that would be expensive to litigate or have a low probability of success would be discouraged. As a consequence potential defendants would be less deterred from questionable business conduct for two reasons: they are less likely to be sued, and they face lower penalties if they lose.[35]

The docket data collected by the project can illustrate this approach. It appears that initiating an antitrust suit was a rational strategy for the average plaintiff who persisted to a final judgment. As was discussed in section 1.2, plaintiffs won 28 percent of the cases that continued to final judgment. In cases in which we had information on awards, the average award was $456,000 (in 1984 dollars), excluding *Litton*. The ratio of plaintiff's litigation costs to awards was in the range of 10 to 20 percent. If we use the latter figure, the average plaintiff's net expected value was $62,000.[36]

Similarly, the average defendant who was sued in these cases faced an expected financial exposure of $244,400, given that a suit was initiated and pursued to a final judgment.[37] Whether undertaking the business conduct that led to these suits was rational depends on the benefit of the conduct to the defendant. More important, it depends on the fraction of the actual number of violations that were detected and led to suits. Imperfect detection and foregone suits can reduce the defendant's true financial exposure dramatically. For example, if the defendant's conduct only brings forth a suit 10 percent of the time, then the defendant's expected exposure falls to $24,440. Because, by definition, there are no data on "undetected violations," we cannot estimate the true financial exposure.[38]

The "Laffer Curve of Litigation"   By increasing the plaintiff's recovery in the event he succeeds, a treble damages remedy increases the likelihood that a potential plaintiff will initiate a suit. The higher penalty and the increased likelihood of suit, in turn, reduce the potential defendant's incentives to

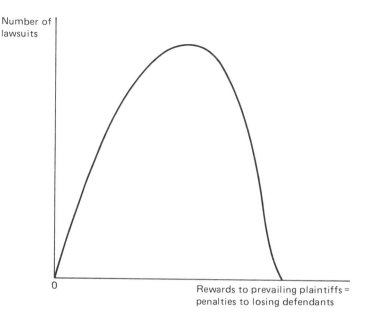

Figure 1.1   The Laffer curve of litigation

undertake such questionable conduct. As a result the number of violations will fall. This is an obvious result.

Somewhat less obvious, however, is the effect of the treble damages remedy on the level of overall litigation activity—that is, on the number of suits initiated. Although the number of violations will fall, the number of suits could rise rather than fall.[39] This is because the treble damages remedy, compared with a single damages remedy, increases the incentive for plaintiffs to initiate suits for the remaining violations.

We might illustrate the interdependence between the number of suits, the number of violations and the damages multiplier with the following aphorism: If the courts awarded no damages (a damages multiple of zero), there would be a large number of violations but no suits, because plaintiffs would have no incentive to sue;[40] if the damages multiple were huge (e.g., octuple damages), there would be (virtually) no suits because defendants would be unlikely to violate the legal standard; with an intermediate multiple, there are violations and suits. This Laffer curve of litigation is illustrated in figure 1.1.[41]

A similar analysis would show the effect of legal fees. For violations where suit would require relatively high plaintiff's legal fees, plaintiffs are less likely to sue. Because suits are less likely, however, potential defendants have a greater tendency to violate the legal standard. Thus the overall number of suits in this area may be higher or lower than for violations where plaintiff's fees generally are smaller.

This analysis has an important implication for the interpretation of litigation activity data: data on the number of suits initiated, when viewed in isolation, are insufficient to draw conclusions as to the effectiveness of deterrence and the extent to which violations are being committed.[42] A low level of complaints may be the consequence of a high level of deterrence and few violations, or it may indicate a low level of deterrence because of insufficient incentives to initiate suits.

The Effects of the Location of the Legal Standard   The location of the substantive legal standard is another influence on the rates of violations and suits. A more lenient standard is likely to lead to fewer violations for two reasons: First, conduct that was previously a violation would now be legal. Second, the incentive for a potential defendant to violate is reduced, because the more lenient standard permits him legally to get "closer" to his more preferred, but illegal conduct. Thus the net gain from violation is reduced.[43]

With the number of violations reduced, the number of suits also will be smaller. These results only occur when the new standard is well defined. As we explain later, the *transition* to a more permissive legal standard may create greater uncertainty about the exact location of the legal standard and could induce greater suits, until the uncertainty is reduced.

The Effects of Uncertainty   Litigation is a risky business. The parties face uncertainty both over the likelihood that a trial will occur and the outcome at trial. This uncertainty is compounded because these likelihoods depend on the actions of the other side—decisions that both depend on the adversary's own interpretations of these uncertainties and that are themselves interdependent. Litigants can, however, partially reduce the uncertainty that they face by exchanging legal arguments and evidence with the other side and by gathering additional evidence and undertaking additional legal and economic analysis (at additional cost).[44]

Litigation uncertainty varies generally according to the type of litigation at issue and specifically according to the particular facts of the case being litigated. As a general matter, simple cases probably involve less uncertainty than more complex ones because the former have fewer issues to predict. The more fact dependent is a case, the less likely are the parties to be able to know the strength of their adversary's case before trial and thus the less certain would be the predicted outcome. Thus per se cases probably involve less uncertainty about liability than rule of reason cases.[45]

Some antitrust policy changes might affect the degree of uncertainty. A discretionary damages multiple increases uncertainty, as does a rule of joint and several liability. Uncertainty also might be increased during transitional periods culminating in a new legal standard.

Uncertainty affects on the plaintiff's willingness to initiate suit, the defendant's willingness to engage in potentially illegal behavior, and the ability of the parties to reach a settlement. In this section we discuss the first two, leaving the effect on settlement behavior for later.[46]

Greater uncertainty over the outcome at trial may make the defendant either more or less aggressive in his business conduct.[47] The defendant's most profitable conduct represents a balancing of two conflicting tensions. On one hand, the defendant may choose the conservative strategy of moving his conduct farther away from the standard. In this way the defendant is less likely to be held liable even if the court adopts a very restrictive approach to the law and the facts.[48]

On the other hand, the defendant may choose a more aggressive strategy, because uncertainty reduces the causal nexus between the conduct and the likelihood of the outcome: even if the defendant's conduct violates the standard, he may still escape suit or prevail at trial; alternatively, liability may still attach even if he does not violate the standard. Therefore the defendant will have less incentive to avoid violations at the margin when his choice of conduct has less effect on the likely outcome.[49]

Uncertainty also affects the incentives for potential plaintiffs to sue. To the extent that the potential plaintiff is risk averse, uncertainty reduces his incentive to sue by increasing the overall variance of the returns from this strategy. However, uncertainty has effects in the other direction as well. In many cases the plaintiff's damage award is higher for conduct that is more egregious. For example, damages in price fixing cases rise with the size of the cartel overcharge. In contrast, the plaintiff's legal fees generally are the same, regardless of the margin by which he loses.[50] As a result greater uncertainty (e.g., as to the extent of the violation) can increase the upside return (the potential damage award) while holding the downside losses (the legal fees) the same. In these cases the plaintiff's expected return and thus his incentive to sue is increased.[51]

Economizing on Litigation Costs   The costs of litigation can enter the analysis in a number of ways. For example, even if the potential defendant were sure that he would prevail in the end, it might be more economical to alter his business conduct slightly than to bear the expenses of litigation until he is exonerated. In those areas of the law where litigation is most expensive, the incentive for the defendant to undertake conduct that induces litigation is reduced. Similarly in those areas where suits are most expensive for plaintiffs, potential plaintiffs' incentives to sue are reduced, leading to a reduction in deterrence.

The costs of litigation also create incentives for the parties to economize on these costs, by limiting expenditures unilaterally and by settling suits before the trial and appeals process is completed. Finally, they give plaintiffs (and defendants) a potential weapon of extortion: the threat of forcing litigation costs on one's adversary in order to induce a favorable settlement. We turn to these issues next.

Incentives to Settle

The vast majority of cases, possibly as much as 88 percent in our sample, settle before trial. Additional disputes are settled even before a complaint is filed. This results from strong incentives shared by both parties: settlement avoids the costs and uncertainty associated with further litigation. Given these benefits, it is not surprising that most cases are settled. Indeed, the more interesting question is why any cases continue to trial.

The basic logic of the settlement process is demonstrated by the following analysis:[52] suppose the two parties agree on the amount of money at stake (and no other considerations concern either side), and they agree on the *probability* that one side or the other will prevail at trial, so that they are in agreement as to the *expected* monetary value of the case. A settlement payment by the defendant to the plaintiff of an amount that is in the vicinity of this expected monetary value would allow both parties to save the litigation expenses of a trial. Thus, on an expected value basis, both parties would be better off with the settlement.

For example, if both parties agreed that the plaintiff had a 30 percent chance of obtaining an award of $1 million and if a trial would cost each side additional legal fees[53] of $50,000, any settlement above $250,000 would be more beneficial to the plaintiff than continued litigation; similarly any settlement below $350,000 would benefit the defendant.[54] Therefore our analysis would predict a settlement in the $250,000 to $350,000 range.[55] In general, the logic of the example indicates that the possibilities for a mutually acceptable settlement agreement increase as the costs of prospective litigation rise, as the defendant's estimate of the plaintiff's prospects increases or the plaintiff's estimate falls (when each has become relatively pessimistic about his own prospects), or as the separate costs to the defendant of a loss at trial rise (e.g., the defendant may fear that a loss at trial will spur other suits by other plaintiffs).

Why, then, would the parties fail to settle? First, disagreement about the likely outcome from continued litigation may prevent settlement. In particular, when the parties each are relatively optimistic about the outcome of the case, they may be unable to reach agreement despite the prospects of large savings in legal fees and the elimination of the uncertainty of trial. To alter our previous example slightly, if the plaintiff thought the likelihood of a decision in his favor was 50 percent, while the defendant thought it was only 10 percent, then no settlement would be possible. The plaintiff would demand at least $450,000, while the defendant would offer no more than $150,000.[56] Thus no settlement would occur.[57] Similar settlement problems would arise if the parties agreed on the probability of winning, but each was relatively optimistic about the size of the likely damage award.

Second, settlement may fail because of the parties' separate concerns about the outcome of this case (or of this settlement) on other litigation. The plaintiff may be concerned about maintaining credibility as a serious litigant in other suits; the defendant may worry that news of this settlement may attract other plaintiffs primarily motivated by the prospects of a settlement.

Third, if settlement (as well as a plaintiff victory at trial) would enjoin a challenged business practice that provides greater gains to the defendant than it causes losses to the plaintiff, the defendant will be more reluctant to settle and more willing to take his chances at trial. This would be the case where the defendant derives efficiencies from the practice, where the plaintiff can pass on the costs to other parties, or where third parties not involved in the suit are injured.

Fourth, bargaining techniques designed to get a somewhat better share of the benefits may lead to a breakdown in negotiations. For example, if each party makes a "final" settlement offer in the hope of squeezing the other side's share, bargaining may end without agreement.[58]

This analysis of settlement has important implications for observed patterns of settlements, trials, and outcomes, for policy, and for nuisance suits.

Observed Patterns of Settlements, Trials, and Plaintiff Win Rates   Our analysis indicates that settlement is not a matter of animal spirits. Rather, the likelihood of settlement—and hence the likelihood of trial as well—is related to the characteristics of the case and of the parties in the ways just

Table 1.13 Influences on settlement rates and on observed plaintiff win rates

Variable	Effect on settlement	Effect on observed plaintiff win rate
Increased relative plaintiff optimism as to his probability of prevailing	−	+
Increased relative plaintiff optimism as to award	−	+
Increased trial costs	+	−
Increased defendant follow-on costs from loss at trial	+	−
Increased defendant differential loss from injunctive relief	−	+
Increased defendant differential cost of settlement consequences	−	+
Increased stakes (if plaintiff is relatively optimistic)	−	+
Increased stakes (if plaintiff is relatively pessimistic)	+	−

Source: Salop and White (1986a, app. D).

described. The observed settlement and trial rates are endogenous to the litigation system, rather than exogenous.

Accordingly, the cases that proceed to trial are not a random sample of all suits. Rather, they are a selective sample of cases in which one or more of the factors just discussed causes one party to reject offers that the other side finds acceptable. This principle applies regardless of permissiveness of the legal standard or the inclinations of the fact finder.

This selectiveness has direct implications for the observed plaintiff win rate in cases that proceed to trial: plaintiff win rates also are endogenous to the litigation system and are influenced by the same causal factors that affect settlement rates. For example, if the defendant is especially concerned that a loss at trial will have adverse consequences for other cases, the settlement rate will consequently be relatively high, and the plaintiff win rate will be relatively low for those few cases that fail to settle and proceed to trial. Table 1.13 summarizes the application of this logic to the other variables that affect settlement and observed plaintiff win rates at trial. The analysis predicts that variables that tend to increase the settlement rate tend also to decrease the observed plaintiff win rate at trial, and vice versa.

Priest and Klein (1984) show that there is a direct relationship between the tendency of cases to settle and the tendency of cases of the same type, when they proceed to trial, to yield a plaintiff success rate that approaches a specific level that is determined by the factors listed in table 1.13. If the parties' stakes in the case are symmetric, this level would be 50 percent.[59] Their analysis focuses largely on the effects of the parties' prediction errors. Cases that are "easy" tend to settle because they are less likely to exhibit the requisite disparity in relative optimism that prevents settlement. If the parties' prediction errors were relatively large, there would be few such "easy" cases, the settlement rate would be low, and the plaintiff win rate would approximate the average of the overall distribution of disputes around the decision standard. As the parties' prediction errors narrow, the number of "easy" cases increases, and the settlement rate rises concomitantly. Moreover the remaining "hard" cases that go to trial will yield an average plaintiff win rate determined only by the distribution of these "hard" cases, as discussed earlier. [60]

Uncertainty also may have an effect on settlement patterns. Greater uncertainty about the procedures and likely outcome at trial may make settlement less likely, because greater uncertainty means that the parties are less likely to share common expectations about their chances. For this reason cases often settle immediately after a judicial order or the filing of papers with the court, as the added information reduces the parties' uncertainty and brings their expectations closer together. In addition a more uncertain legal standard leads to fewer of the "easy" cases that are more likely to settle. These effects of uncertainty suggest that there will be different settlement rates for different classes of cases, since some types of cases may have inherently more uncertainty than others.[61] Uncertainty also might be increased in the short run during a period of transition when it is not clear what approach the courts will take toward a particular type of case.

These predictions concerning the effects of increased uncertainty have been based on the assumption of that the parties are risk neutral. If the parties are risk averse, greater uncertainty has the opposite effect, pushing them toward settlement, because settlement provides certainty and replaces an uncertain outcome. Accordingly, when risk aversion is taken into account, the net effort of greater uncertainty on settlement rates may be in either direction.

Policy Implications The analysis above indicates that higher stakes may either decrease or increase the prospects for settlement. If the parties each are relatively optimistic, higher stakes magnify the effects of optimism and reduce the likelihood of settlement. By contrast, if the parties each are relatively pessimistic (but other considerations are blocking settlement), higher stakes magnify the effects of pessimism and increase the likelihood of settlement.

An increase in the damages multiple clearly raises the stakes of a case. But, as this logic indicates, we cannot make any simple predictions regarding the effect of the higher multiple on settlement rates.[62] Similarly a change from a specific mandatory damages multiple to a discretionary damages multiple would likely increase uncertainty and as a result affect settlement rates.

Automatic fee-shifting rules that make a losing party liable for the litigation costs of the winning adversary add to the effective stakes of a case and affect settlement negotiations for two reasons: First, to the extent that a litigant believes that his adversary is going to pay his prospective legal costs, he has less incentive to economize on these costs.[63] Second, rather than being sunk costs that play no role in prospective decision making, litigation costs incurred prior to the settlement negotiations also will be paid by the losing adversary. From our previous analysis, because the effect of higher stakes on settlement rates is ambiguous, the effect on settlement of fee shifting rules is ambiguous.[64]

Finally, as Polinsky and Rubinfeld (1985) demonstrate, the prospect of settlement as an alternative to a final judgment both raises the expected returns to a plaintiff contemplating suit (thus increasing the incentive to sue) and decreases the expected loss to a defendant in the event of suit (thus increasing the incentive to violate). In essence the prospect of settlement has effects similar to a decrease in litigation costs.[65] Thus the prospect of settlement alters the fundamental cost-benefit calculus determining the defendant's expected value of violating the law and the plaintiff's expected value from suing.

Nuisance Suits and Extortion by Litigation   The possibility of economizing on litigation costs by settling can have adverse effects on the legal system when one or both parties use the threat of costly suit as a mechanism for inducing an adversary to submit to a costly settlement. At the extreme, even if a defendant knew that he surely would prevail at trial, he would be willing to settle for some amount that is less than his anticipated litigation expenditures rather than pay the cost of defending himself at trial. Knowing this vulnerability, a potential plaintiff might have an incentive to file suit as a means of simple blackmail.[66]

Extortion by litigation has limits. First, the defendant may choose to fight, realizing that, otherwise, the blackmailer will return, perhaps repeatedly. Second, unless the plaintiff has a reasonable chance of success, the threat of litigation will not be credible; if the defendant realizes that the plaintiff is bluffing and will fold his case in the event that defendant does not pay, the blackmail attempt will fail. Thus absolutely frivolous suits are unlikely to force a settlement, irrespective of the cost of a successful defense. Third, anticipating this problem of extortion, the courts have discretion to make plaintiffs who file frivolous claims liable for the defendant's expenses. Because legal fees form the basic financial incentive to pay the blackmail, this sanction restricts the credibility of the plaintiff's threat.[67]

Extortion may not be limited to nuisance suits by plaintiffs, of course. Both the defendant and the plaintiff can threaten the other side with increased litigation expenditures, by creating additional issues of fact or expanding document requests, so as to force a more favorable settlement. As a general matter, extortion tactics are more credible when the adversary's costs can be raised *relative* to the increase in the extortionist's own costs. It is not entirely obvious which side has the overall advantage.[68]

The possibility of extortion settlements makes the interpretation of our data more difficult. In section 1.2 we noted that the aggregate settlement rate in antitrust cases is higher than the rate in ordinary civil litigation. This might suggest that antitrust is a well-functioning system economizing on costly litigation to the parties' mutual benefit. Once the possibility of extortion is added to the analysis, however, a high settlement rate may imply that antitrust is a blackmailer's paradise. A decline in the settlement rate may be a negative indicator that aggregate litigation costs have increased, or it may be a positive indicator that the rate of extortion has fallen.

The Determination of Litigation Expenditures

Litigation expenditures are themselves the result of the interaction of the parties' economic incentives. Each litigant has the incentive to increase his expenditures at the margin in order to increase somewhat his likelihood of prevailing at trial. Of course, to the extent that both parties spend more, the expenditures may cancel one another, leaving the same probability of success that would have occurred at a lower level of effort. It is often difficult, however, for the parties to limit their expenditures.

These incentives imply that, on average, cases with greater stakes will have greater expenditures by both parties.[69] Because a given increase in the likelihood of prevailing translates into a greater dollar increase in value in larger cases, each party has an incentive to spend more in larger cases in what may turn out to be a futile attempt to gain an edge over its adversary. For example, the large stakes in class action antitrust cases have the effect of raising litigation expenditures. Our sample illustrates this point: the MDL cases lasted longer, involved much more legal effort, and yielded much higher legal fee awards than did non-MDL cases. Expenditure levels also vary with the complexity of the case, the court's procedural rules, and the allocation of the burden of proof. Diminishing returns, in terms of the effect of extra expenditures on the increased probability of winning, probably set in faster in simple cases than in complex ones. The court can hold down total expenditures with indirect restrictions, such as an insistence on a tight trial schedule and a limitation on the number of material issues, as well as direct restrictions on depositions and discovery.

Not only does the determination of litigation effort add another layer of complexity to the analysis, but it also has a number of important policy implications. By raising the stakes in the litigation, the treble damages remedy tends to increase litigation expenditures, thus reducing somewhat the expected benefit of the treble damages remedy to plaintiffs.

For complex cases, however, achieving outcomes that reflect correct results generally requires extensive and expensive litigation. The resolution of the complexity makes the extra expenditures socially efficient. The treble damages remedy has the effect of raising the plaintiff's stakes sufficiently to make such inherently complex litigation worthwhile. If the treble damages remedy were eliminated across the board, its effects would not be uniform. Instead, potential plaintiffs would be deterred more from bringing complex cases than from bringing simple ones. Stated another way, rule of reason cases may require the treble damages remedy to finance the information gathering necessary for the rule. Moreover the additional litigation expenditures induced by treble damages may increase the accuracy of the outcome reached in the litigation by increasing the amount of information provided to the fact finder.

The increases in litigation expenditures induced by the treble damages remedy also may have the effect of altering the relative advantages of plaintiff and defendant in the litigation. Depending on the procedural and substantive rules (including the relative burdens of proof), stripped-down, low cost litigation may favor one side, whereas extensive, high cost cases may favor the other.[70] Thus the damages multiple may affect the likelihood that the plaintiff prevails at trial, which will in turn have further effects on plaintiffs' incentives to sue and defendants' incentives to violate.

Policy Implications
Up to this point our analysis has focused on a positive analysis of the economic incentives of the parties involved in antitrust litigation and the interaction among those incentives. In this section we take a more normative approach, setting out the determinants of economically efficient legal

rules and then applying those ideas to evaluating the treble damages remedy and a number of other policy proposals.[71]

If litigation were costless and outcomes were prefectly predictable in advance, it would be relatively easy to specify the economically efficient legal standard and the appropriate penalty for violating that standard. The standard would be set at a level to induce economically efficient business conduct. The sanction for violating this rule would be set equal to the harms inflicted on others as a consequence of the conduct. If there were no uncertainty, that rule perfectly would induce defendants to undertake the efficient level of business conduct, thereby deterring all illegal conduct while avoiding any deterrence of efficient conduct.[72]

Because outcomes are uncertain and litigation is expensive for the courts and the parties, the problem of defining efficient legal rules and penalties is more complex. The analysis must take into account the costs to the parties of litigation, the costs to the court of administering the case, the possibility of errors in assessing liability and damages, and resulting social cost of those errors. This creates a series of trade-offs that the policymaker must balance in trying to determine the "optimal" level of deterrence that minimizes the sum of these costs.

A fundamental conflict exists between the costs of carrying out the litigation process and the costs of error. Erroneous determinations of liability and damages can be reduced by gathering additional evidence and more carefully analyzing the evidence and the legal and economic policy issues involved. However, this type of careful analysis is expensive, as it involves expert witnesses and extensive discovery. The policymaker or the court must balance these different types of costs in determining efficient rules and procedures. For example, the choice between per se rules and the rule of reason involves precisely these cost tradeoffs.

Conflicts may also exist among different types of errors.[73] A very restrictive rule will reduce the incidence and social cost of inefficient conduct, since less of that conduct can slip past a more restrictive net. However, unless the fact finding and analytic process is perfect, a highly restrictive rule sometimes will also erroneously assess liability on efficient conduct that is not anticompetitive; in addition other potential defendants will be deterred from engaging in conduct of uncertain legality. Instead, they may opt for safety by overcomplying (choosing conduct that is farther from the efficient level) to reduce their financial exposure from a possible suit. A highly permissive rule can have the opposite effects. Thus, in establishing legal rules, policymakers and the courts face a problem of balancing the social costs of erroneously deterring truly competitive efficient conduct with the costs of erroneously encouraging truly inefficient conduct.

In principle, it is possible to define a set of rules that minimizes the sum of these costs of legal process and legal error. However, finding even the "second-best" solution to this optimization problem is difficult because much of the analysis is ambiguous and the data are either unavailable or imperfect. In addition various substantive and procedural rules interact so that the effects of one rule may either reinforce or offset the effects of another.

In the rest of this section we evaluate the efficiency of the treble damages remedy and other policies in light of this general normative analysis and the analytic framework developed earlier.[74] This discussion presents an overview and is not intended to provide a full cost-benefit analysis of these issues.

The Treble Damages Remedy   A damages multiple in general, and the treble damages remedy in particular, affects the degree of deterrence and the costs of participating in and administering the legal process. A multiple damages remedy is frequently justified as a way of establishing a rough equality between the inefficiencies caused by anticompetitive conduct and the level of damages awarded and also as a way of offsetting the effects of imperfect detection of potential antitrust violations. In addition the treble damages remedy has conflicting effects on litigation costs and on the likelihood of errors.

Anticompetitive conduct harms its victims by wasting resources through inefficient conduct and by transferring wealth to the perpetrator. For example, the harm to consumers from horizontal price fixing consists of the sum of the "deadweight loss"—the loss in net value of the quantities *not* purchased—due to the restraint of output below the competitive level and the "monopoly overcharge" extracted from consumers. Optimal deterrence of violations requires that the violator be liable for the total harm to others caused by his conduct. This requires compensation for both the inefficiency and the transfer of wealth. Unfortunately, the calculation of damages usually includes only the transfer of wealth, not the inefficiency. For example, victims of price fixing are compensated for the monopoly overcharge but not for the deadweight loss. Moreover, to the extent that some victims are not parties to the case, compensation of only those victims who are parties understates the aggregate injury caused by illegal conduct.[75] And, to the extent that true (opportunity cost) interest, levied from the onset of the violation, is not part of the damages calculation, the true injury is understated.

If measured damages understates the total injury, potential violators will be underdeterred. One rough solution to this underdeterrence would be to increase the defendant's financial exposure by giving victims a multiple of the measured damages. A more precise version of the rule would tailor the multiple on a case by case basis to a rough approximation of the degree to which measured damages underestimates the actual harm in that case.

This clearly is an imperfect solution. First, to the extent that the multiple is intended to compensate for a deadweight loss, an alternative would be to include the deadweight loss explicitly in the calculation of damages.[76] Second, the plaintiffs in the case who receive the damages generally are not the same as the group who are undercompensated. By awarding all of the damages to the former, the treble damage remedy may distort their incentives to initiate suits. Third, additional deterrence created by the fear of government antitrust suits should also be included in the calculation. This does not imply that the treble damages multiple is either too high or too low, only that the problem of calculating the optimal multiple is complicated and contains a number of important components.

An additional standard justification for the treble damages remedy is its effect in offsetting imperfect detection and conviction of antitrust violations. For example, even if defendants were liable for all the harms their conduct caused, they would discount their financial liability accordingly if they perceived that they would be sued only 10 percent of the time. The result would be underdeterrence of violators. By this reckoning a trebling rule would perfectly offset a detection, suit, and conviction rate of one-third by reestablishing equality between financial liability and harm caused.

A damages multiple has a further benefit with respect to the detection of violations: by raising the return to potential plaintiffs, it leads to a greater channeling of resources toward detection and suing. By raising the detection and litigation rate, deterrence is increased.

Finally, the outcome of litigation can have spillover effects, by establishing precedents that are valuable for other plaintiffs or other defendants. A damages multiple can help align the private incentives of the litigants with the value of their litigation actions to others.

The analysis becomes far more complex when uncertainty is explicitly taken into account. As discussed earlier, uncertainty about the outcome of litigation might lead to underdeterrence or overdeterrence. In either case the damages multiple can be used to offset the distortion. This result can be seen most clearly in "close" cases where uncertainty has the effect of reducing the nexus between the defendant's conduct and the likelihood that the conduct will be detected and enjoined. Under these circumstances uncertainty tends to lead to underdeterrence as the defendant perceives that moving his conduct slightly over the line will have little effect on the likelihood of liability. A damages multiple can offset this possibility. By raising the defendant's exposure in the event of conviction, the difference in defendant's *expected* costs between efficient and inefficient conduct can be magnified to the level that would have obtained if there were no uncertainty.

This last result leads to a counterintuitive policy implication: contrary to the frequent assertion that treble damages should be reserved for conduct that clearly violates the law, our analysis implies that treble damages should be reserved for the close cases where it is necessary to magnify deterrence by increasing the nexus between the defendant's conduct and his financial exposure.[77] As a policy matter this suggests the need for a damages multiple in difficult, rule of reason cases rather than in per se cases.[78]

The damages multiple also has an effect on the process costs of the antitrust system, increasing the resources put into detection. The resource issue, however, is quite complex. A damages multiple has a number of effects on the costs of litigation, some leading toward higher costs and others toward lower costs. When the interaction between increased costs of litigation and reduced costs of errors are taken into account, it is not clear that higher costs should be condemned.

First, a high damages multiple encourages plaintiffs to initiate suits. This obviously raises costs by encouraging litigation. However, the Laffer curve of litigation implies that the total amount (and cost) of litigation may not rise. To the extent that violations are deterred by the damages multiple, the aggregate number of suits may fall rather than rise.

Second, a high damages multiple has an uncertain effect on settlement decisions. It may either encourage or discourage good-faith settlements; it surely encourages forced settlements arising from extortion. To the extent that good-faith settlements are discouraged and forced settlements are encouraged, the costs of litigation are raised.

Third, a high damages multiple increases litigation effort and expenditures in those cases that are not settled. Further, these increases in litigation expenditures may alter the parties' relative advantages. Plaintiffs probably gain a strategic advantage from a high multiple in rule of reason cases, while defendants probably benefit in cases where controverting the plaintiff's case is sufficient to prevail. This change in strategic position will have further effects on the incentive to sue and to violate the legal standard initially.

Fourth, a high damages multiple reduces the cost of errors in assessing liability and damages, because it increases litigation effort. To the extent that the parties gather more evidence and provide the court with more analysis, the court will be better equipped to decide the case correctly. Thus the twin costs of erroneously deterring business conduct and erroneously permitting inefficient conduct will be reduced.

It is surprising that this last point has been given so little attention in the debate over the treble damages remedy. It can be a significant effect, and it relates closely to debate over the use of per se rules in antitrust cases. Consistent with the previous discussion of deterrence, it suggests that treble damages would be more appropriate for rule of reason than for per se cases. This result, though contrary to the common policy prescription that treble damages be reserved for per se offenses, has a strong logical base: per se rules generally are criticized because they tend to lead to errors, since the court ignores considerable information that might be provided on the likely effect on competition of the questionable conduct. In contrast, by allowing the court to examine that information and by requiring the parties to provide greater analysis of the effect of the conduct on competition, the rule of reason tends to reduce the error rate and the cost of errors.

A high damages multiple supports the rule of reason by providing plaintiffs and defendants with the incentive to gather the necessary information. In the absence of a damages multiple, plaintiffs may not have the incentive to expend the necessary resources to pursue rule of reason cases. This may reduce their suing rate, leading to the adverse effects on deterrence discussed earlier. Alternatively, as is discussed toward the end of this section, it may lead courts to return to the use of per se rules to compensate for the procedural disadvantages that plaintiffs would otherwise face.

A Variable Damages Multiple   The previous discussion suggests that the optimal multiple varies across different classes of antitrust violations. An examination of different types of cases would likely reveal substantial variation in the detection rate, burden of proof, likelihood of extortion, strategic advantages of litigation spending, error rate, and degree to which actual harm exceeds measured damages. This suggests that efficiency might be increased by mandating a different multiple for different classes of violations, with the multiple varying in accordance to the complexity of the case, whether it raises per se versus rule of reason claims, or whether the conduct is overt or covert.[79] For example, the multiple for "garden variety" price fixing with no colorable efficiency claims might be increased to quadruple, sextuple, or beyond.[80]

Two other considerations, however, argue against adding variation to the damages multiple. First, as a substantive matter, variation increases the uncertainty faced by the parties. Uncertainty over the multiple would be one more source of disagreement to deter settlements.[81] Second, it is ironic that on pure efficiency grounds the most egregious violations might deserve a somewhat lower multiple. Because these violations are often the easiest to detect, a high multiple would not be necessary to offset difficult detection.[82] From the perspective of public acceptability, this would be an unfortunate side effect.

One other damages remedy worthy of consideration has been given less attention: "decoupling" the plaintiff's gains from the defendant's penalties. We have already noted that the private damages remedy has two simultaneous direct effects: deterrence, and an incentive for plaintiffs to invest resources in detection and litigation (with corresponding litigation investments by the defendant as well). Any simple change in the damages multiple affects both. One way to break this linkage would be to "decouple" the plaintiff's gains from the defendant's penalties.[83] For some classes of cases—perhaps per se cases or egregious violations where extensive plaintiff effort is not warranted—the penalty levied on the losing defendant could be higher than the reward received by the successful plaintiff.[84] But some cases might call for the reverse: where a plaintiff's case establishes a new legal doctrine, fairness considerations might call for a lower penalty for the losing defendant,[85] while the positive spillover effects of the case for other plaintiffs would call for a higher reward for the plaintiff. A greater flexibility in penalties and rewards would allow a finer tuning of the balance between deterrence and process costs.

Automatic Fee Shifting   Full fee shifting (the "British rule") may discourage frivolous suits and extortion by plaintiffs, since a defendant with a high probability of winning at trial would not have to settle just to save litigation costs; he could persist to trial with reasonable confidence of prevailing and collecting legal fees from the losing plaintiff.[86] This benefit is not guaranteed, however, because a plaintiff may avoid paying the defendant's legal fees by dropping the case before final judgment.[87]

As our preceding analysis indicates, an automatic fee-shifting rule has other effects. It may either discourage or encourage settlements. Fee shifting also encourages greater litigation expenditures by the parties. Further it requires the use of greater judicial resources in determining fee reimbursement. Finally, full fee shifting would increase the incentives for potential defendants to violate by reducing their expected legal costs of defending a suit. Because of these shortcomings a direct attack on the problem of frivolous suits—for example, through higher sanctions for frivolous suits—would be preferable to adoption of the "British rule."

Payment of Interest on Awards   In general, damages awards should include interest (at the defendant's true opportunity cost rate) from the onset of the damages arising from the violation. The interest rate should compensate the injured party for the time value of the money foregone as a consequence of the violation. Payment of interest (especially at true opportunity cost rates) also has the desirable property of reducing the strategic advantage to the defendant of adopting delaying tactics.

Spiller (1986) has noted one possible drawback to the payment of interest accruing from the time of violation: a plaintiff might have an incentive to delay bringing suit, since delay would push the plaintiff's costs of litigation farther into the future, while the payment of interest on the damages would fully compensate him for the delay in the payment of damages. To the extent that the social inefficiency caused by the violation is not captured by the damages claimed by the plaintiff, such delay is inefficient.

In practice, however, delay by the plaintiff is unlikely to be a problem. The plaintiff's fears that documents might disappear or memories fade, plus the jockeying among attorneys for priority of position in multiparty cases, would surely override the incentive for delay in virtually all instances.

Other Legal Standards   A variable damages multiple might be justified as a means of offsetting poorly designed substantive or procedural legal standards. Although antitrust rules are substitutable to some extent, the use of the damages multiple to compensate for, say, inefficient liability or standing rules is probably unwise because changing the multiple would create a variety of other effects that then would require further adjustment. There seems to be little reason to control the overall system indirectly or covertly when a direct change in the inefficient legal standard is an alternative. Similarly efforts to compensate for inappropriate damages multiples through adjustments in other procedural and substantive rules are likely to create inefficiencies and anomalies in the legal system.

The Judiciary as Participants

The judiciary is also an important party to litigation because they control the rules that guide the litigants' behavior.[88] Since the antitrust laws are quite broad and general in their language and the relevant legal standards encompass a number of important dimensions—activities that constitute a violation, standing to sue, measurement of damages, applicable multiple of damages, burden of required evidence, and so on—judges have considerable discretion to affect outcomes through their interpretations. Courts may have their own views about proper antitrust rules. Thus, if the Congress changes a law or if a body of interpretation of one dimension of the law turns out to have unexpected consequences, the judiciary may modify its interpretations of other dimensions of antitrust rules.

This process may have been occurring recently.[89] As the potency of the treble damages remedy has come to be recognized in the years since the *Bigelow*[90] decision and the electrical conspiracy cases, the courts may have been trimming plaintiffs' powers and strengthening defendants' powers in the other dimensions, so as to regain the desired overall balance.[91]

This hypothesis has an important implication for antitrust policy: if the antitrust laws were changed significantly (e.g., eliminating treble damages) and the judiciary were to perceive a loss of the proper balance, we would expect to see offsetting judicial modifications. For example, if the damages multiple were to be reduced for some types of cases, we might well find that judges subsequently would ease the criteria for standing, for withstanding a defendant's motion for summary judgment, or for presenting evidence of injury. This is a prospect that should be weighed carefully in considering legislative changes in the antitrust laws.

1.4 Further Analysis of the Data

Having established a framework for antitrust analysis, we now return to an examination of the antitrust data base for further insights and inferences.

The Temporal Pattern of Suits

As table 1.1 indicated, private antitrust litigation peaked in the late 1970s. We suspect that the recent decline in private filings has been, at least partially, a consequence of the new antitrust interpretations of the late 1970s.[92] These changes shifted substantive standards and increased the burden on plaintiffs. Since the new antitrust interpretations were not aimed at traditional, "smoke-filled room" horizontal price fixing, the greatest relative decline in private suits should have been in cases alleging other illegal practices, such

Table 1.14   Frequency of alleged statute violations by year of filing

	Number of cases in sample	Sherman, section 1	Sherman, section 2	Clayton, section 2	Clayton, section 3	Clayton, section 7
1973 and before	209[a]	77.5%	48.3%	22.0%	16.7%	7.7%
1974	214	82.7	57.9	19.2	14.5	5.1
1975	205	76.1	52.7	23.4	12.7	6.8
1976	234	77.4	47.4	14.5	12.8	5.6
1977	220	73.2	45.9	15.9	10.4	8.6
1978	190	72.6	46.3	23.2	10.5	5.8
1979	165	71.5	44.2	19.4	10.3	6.1
1980	134	73.9	38.8	14.2	6.7	5.2
1981	168	66.7	42.3	14.9	7.1	6.5
1982	108	72.2	38.0	13.0	2.8	4.6
1983	112	75.9	36.6	14.3	10.7	2.7
All cases	1,959	74.9	46.5	18.1	11.1	6.1

a. One case was filed in 1969, and two cases were filed in 1972.

as vertical restraints or predatory pricing. Most of these other practices do not constitute violations of section 1 of the Sherman Act but rather are violations of section 2 of the Sherman Act and/or section 2 of the Clayton Act. Therefore the largest relative decline in private filings also should have been in cases alleging violations other that section 1 of the Sherman Act.

Tables 1.14 and 1.15 support these predictions. The percentages of cases alleging a section 1 violation or horizontal price fixing has remained relatively constant since 1973, whereas the percentage of cases alleging other statute violations or other illegal practices declined during this same period. The tables also demonstrate that the percentage of cases alleging a violation of section 2 of the Clayton Act or alleging vertical price fixing, dealer terminations, refusal to deal, or price discrimination peaked in 1978 and 1979 and then declined rapidly.

We suggest that the legal changes of the late 1970s caused the declined in the number of private suits for two reasons: First, the changes represented a liberalization, legalizing some previously illegal behavior and reducing the net gains to firms from violating the antitrust laws. Second, the changes imposed increased burdens on plaintiffs, reducing the probability that they would sue over any given suspected violation. Though the latter effect would likely lead to more violations (and therefore possibly to more suits), the net effect was a reduction in the number of suits.[93]

Table 1.15 Frequency of alleged illegal practices, by year of filing

	Horizontal price fixing	Vertical price fixing	Dealer termination	Refusal to deal	Predatory pricing	Price discrimination	Tying or exclusive dealing
1973 and before	24.4%	16.3%	9.1%	26.3%	12.4%	23.4%	29.2%
1974	25.7	13.6	12.1	28.0	9.8	18.7	26.6
1975	20.5	7.3	11.7	25.4	10.2	20.0	29.8
1976	28.6	8.5	7.7	21.4	10.7	14.1	19.2
1977	17.3	7.3	6.4	21.8	11.4	17.7	18.2
1978	18.9	15.8	10.0	34.7	11.6	14.7	18.9
1979	18.2	13.3	11.5	33.9	13.3	21.8	19.4
1980	17.2	4.5	8.2	26.1	9.7	13.4	15.7
1981	19.6	7.1	10.1	24.4	8.3	10.1	16.7
1982	23.1	8.3	4.6	15.7	7.4	9.2	12.0
1983	32.1	8.0	2.7	15.2	5.4	9.8	17.9
All cases	21.3	10.3	8.9	25.4	10.4	16.4	21.1

Note: Primary and secondary allegations are combined.

Table 1.16 Settlements and judgments: percentage of cases settling and percentage of judgments favorable to plaintiffs, by year of filing

Year that case was filed	Broad definition of settlement[a]		Narrow definition of settlement[b]	
	Settlement as a percentage of terminated cases	Percentage of judgments favorable to plaintiffs	Settlement as a percentage of terminated cases	Percentage of judgments favorable to plaintiffs
1973 and earlier	83.6%	32.3%	71.7%	17.0%
1974	83.3	15.6	72.6	9.6
1975	92.8	57.1	73.2	15.4
1976	85.6	26.7	66.8	11.4
1977	89.5	30.0	72.8	11.5
1978	86.1	21.7	65.1	8.6
1979	94.0	41.7	71.6	13.2
1980	91.0	25.0	72.3	8.1
1981	89.9	20.0	72.6	6.2
1982	91.0	14.3	68.4	4.0
1983	92.7	66.7	73.8	8.2
All cases	88.2	28.1	70.8	11.3

a. Includes dismissals in settlements.
b. Includes dismissals in judgments for defendants.

Settlements and Judgments

The analysis in section 1.3 demonstrated that settlement rates and plaintiff win rates are endogenous to the litigation system and indicated the types of relationships that one should expect. The Georgetown data allow us to explore these propositions in further detail.

First, the overall pattern of settlements and plaintiff win rates shown in table 1.10 supports the hypothesis that antitrust defendants have more at stake (e.g., precedents for other trials and relationships with other dealers or customers) than do plaintiffs. The vast majority of cases are settled, regardless of the definition of settlement. More important, plaintiffs win far less than half of the remaining cases. Antitrust defendants appear to be careful and conservative in deciding which cases should go to a judgment.

Table 1.16 reports the time series of settlements and judgments. The data utilizing the broad definition of settlement indicate a rising trend in settlements, even if the cases filed after 1979 are excluded,[94] but the plaintiff win rate has not approached a specific value. The data utilizing the narrow definition of settlement fail even to indicate the rising trend of settlement rates. Accordingly, these time series data are inconsistent with a progressive reduction in the litigants' prediction errors. Of course, the late 1970s were a period of major new antitrust decisions, which introduced a new set of possible litigant prediction errors. Therefore it is likely that our time series spans too short a period and antitrust law is not stable enough to capture the effects predicted by Priest and Klein (1984).

Table 1.17 reports the settlement and judgment data arrayed by major categories of statute violation, alleged illegal practice, and business relationship among the litigants.[95] Unfortunately, no clear picture emerges. In some categories (e.g., tying) the data utilizing broad definition of settlement suggest one pattern (below average settlement rate, below average win rate), while the data utilizing the narrow definition suggest another (above average settlement rate, above average plaintiff win rate). In other categories (e.g., vertical price fixing; predatory pricing; suits by competitors, customer companies, or suppliers) both definitions support our hypothesis: when settlement rates for that category deviated in one direction from the overall average rate, plaintiff win rates for that same category deviated in the opposite direction from the overall average rate. For yet other categories (e.g., price discrimination), though both definitions indicate a consistent pattern, that pattern does not support our hypothesis.[96]

Costs

Table 1.11 presented data on the ratio of litigation costs to moneys transferred in settlements and awards. We now reexamine those data with the help of our analysis in section 1.3.

Our discussion of the settlement process indicates that settlements should involve payments by defendants to plaintiffs that are roughly equal to the money at stake multiplied by the perceived probability that the plaintiff would prevail if the case were pursued to a final judgment. Under most circumstances these payments will be considerably less than the payments received by the plaintiffs who persist to successful judgments in equivalent cases. At the same time settled cases should involve less litigation expenditure than similar cases that are litigated fully, since an important motivation to settle cases is to reduce litigation expense.

A comparison of the ratio of litigation costs to moneys transferred in settlements with the same ratio computed in fully litigated judgment awards to successful plaintiffs should therefore reflect the expected plaintiff success rate and relative savings from avoiding extended litigation (including trial). The plaintiff win rate in the data sample was between 11 and 28 percent, depending on how dismissals are treated. The regression reported in table 1.12 indicates that litigation costs bear roughly a square root relationship to the number of docket entries in a case. For the narrow

Table 1.17 Settlements and judgments: by alleged statute violation, alleged illegal practice, and business relationships

	Broad definition of settlement[a]		Narrow definition of settlement[b]	
	Settlement as a percentage of terminated cases	Percentage of judgments favorable to plaintiffs	Settlement as a percentage of terminated cases	Percentage of judgments favorable to plaintiffs
Alleged statute violation				
Sherman, section 1	87.7%	27.9%	70.7%	11.8%
Sherman, section 2	88.6	27.4	71.7	11.0
Clayton, section 2	91.0	34.5	73.4	11.4
Clayton, section 3	84.9	26.7	71.4	14.0
Clayton, section 7	92.5	37.5	74.8	11.2
Alleged illegal practice[c]				
Horizontal price fixing	84.2	24.6	68.3	12.3
Vertical price fixing	88.5	19.0	72.5	8.0
Dealer termination	86.2	43.5	74.5	23.8
Refusal to deal	85.6	25.4	68.6	11.6
Predatory pricing	92.9	23.1	77.6	7.3
Price discrimination	88.9	34.4	73.0	14.1
Tying or exclusive dealing	87.7	28.9	72.2	12.7
All horizontal	88.5	23.8	72.2	9.8
All vertical	86.9	27.9	72.3	12.7
Plaintiff's business relationship to defendant				
Competitor	91.1	20.8	73.4	7.4
Dealer	86.2	23.9	69.8	11.1
Customer company	92.0	5.9	77.9	2.1
Final customer	86.6	26.3	74.9	10.9
Supplier	96.9	25.0	74.4	4.5
All cases	88.2	28.1	70.8	11.3

a. Includes dismissals in settlements.
b. Includes dismissals in judgments for defendants.
c. Combined primary and secondary allegations.

definition of settlement the ratio of docket entries in settled cases to docket entries in fully litigated cases was 0.62; for the broad definition of settlement, the comparable ratio was 0.50. The square root relationship of costs to docket entries thus suggests that the litigation costs of settled cases were 70 to 80 percent of those of fully litigated cases.

Accordingly, we would expect that the ratio of litigation costs to moneys transferred would be appreciably higher for settlements than for judgment awards.[97] The data in table 1.11 are consistent with this prediction.

Stakes

Our framework indicates that the stakes of a case are likely to be an important determinant of the resources expended and the case's eventual disposition; parties involved in cases with higher stakes should be willing to spend more money to litigate them, and the awards to successful plaintiffs should be higher. Our analysis in section 1.3 indicated, however, that the effects of higher stakes on settlement patterns are ambiguous.

There is no perfect measure of the true stakes of a case. In the absence of a better measure, we assumed that the stakes were equal to the damages specified in the complaint.[98] All damage claims were adjusted for inflation (using the CPI of the year that the case was filed). The average damages claim (in 1984 dollars) was $41 million; the median was $1.4 million.

First, we tried to relate the initial damage claims to the amount of legal effort expended on the case.[99] This effort suggests that the damage claims of a case appear to be, at best, a very weak determinant of the legal effort subsequently expended on it.[100]

Second, we compared the initial damage claims with the subsequent awards received (for cases in which both were present), but we found no positive correlation.[101] For a small sample (32) of questionnaire responses for which settlement payments could be linked with initial damage claims, we found a significant positive correlation when the variables were converted into logarithms. The magnitude of the relationship was larger than for any other variable; a doubling of the damage claim was associated with a 34 percent increase in the monetary settlement. Unfortunately, though, the level of explanatory power was relatively low ($R^2 = 0.17$).

Third, to discover the effect of damages claims on settlement patterns, we examined the relationship between the initial damages claim of a case and its subsequent disposition. Unfortunately, no clear pattern emerged. Using the broad definition of settlement, we found that the average settled case had substantially higher initial damage claims than the average case that went to judgment; using the narrow definition of settlement, however, we found exactly the opposite.[102] And the median damage claim for all categories was virtually identical. Consequently the question of the empirical effect of higher stakes on the disposition of antitrust cases remains open.[103]

Accordingly, from these tests it appears that the initial damage claim of an antitrust case is, at best, a weak proxy for the true stakes of a case.[104]

Countersuits

In 47 cases (2.4 percent of all cases in the sample) the antitrust claim was a counterclaim—that is the plaintiff in the case at hand was also a defendant in a prior suit. These cases were significantly different from the average case in the sample: they were shorter in length (20.6-month average,) had fewer docket entries (51 average), and involved fewer depositions.[105]

Countersuits could arise in a number of ways. First, if a manufacturer cuts off a dealer, the dealer may refuse to pay for goods already delivered, the manufacturer may sue for payment, and the dealer may counterclaim on antitrust grounds. Second, one party, A, may believe that he is the victim of an antitrust violation by a second party, B, but does not believe that the stakes are high enough to warrant a suit. If A is brought into court (for whatever reason) by B, however, A finds worthwhile the raising of the antitrust claims in a countersuit. In this scenario some of the fixed or joint costs of litigation are already incurred in the primary suit, so the marginal costs of the counterclaim are lower. Third, the antitrust counterclaim may be a "strike" or nuisance suit, designed to pressure the plaintiff in the primary suit to settle. Fourth, it may be an effort to transfer the suit from state court to federal court.

The first scenario is not consistent with the plaintiff profile of these antitrust countersuits; surprisingly, the plaintiffs were more likely to be competitors or suppliers and less likely to be dealers or customer companies than was true for the other antitrust suits in the sample.[106] The second scenario is more consistent with this pattern. Unfortunately, we can think of no satisfactory way of testing the third or fourth scenarios against our data.

To the extent that the second scenario is prevalent, the process characteristics of the counterclaim cases provide some indications of the kinds of *extra* cases that would be brought if legal costs for plaintiffs were to decline or if the damages multiple for the plaintiff were to rise. These cases would be shorter, involve less effort, and by inference, involve lower stakes.[107] We cannot calculate any magnitudes, but the direction is clear.

Cases That Were Not Primarily Antitrust

In 424 cases (21.6 percent of the sample) the paralegals examining the court records concluded that the central issue in the suit was not an antitrust issue. These may well have been cases that fit one of the criticisms of the treble damage remedy offered by Areeda and Turner (1978, 150): "Ordinary tort and contract claims are transformed into antitrust complaints." If the criticism is valid, the antitrust allegations raised in these cases should parallel tort and contract claims.

The pattern of allegations in these cases is consistent with this prediction. The plaintiffs were less likely to allege horizontal price fixing, predatory pricing, or price discrimination and more likely to allege refusal to deal and dealer termination than was true in the other antitrust cases in the sample.[108] Further, if these really were "ordinary tort and contract claims," we would expect that, absent the antitrust claim, they would have much shorter lives than the true antitrust cases. Grossman et al. (1981) found that the median length of contract, tort, and business law cases in federal court was around nine to ten months. By contrast, the median length of these "noncentral" cases in the Georgetown sample was 15.4 months—much closer to the median length of the remaining antitrust cases. Thus, if these cases truly were ordinary tort and contract cases, the existence of the treble damages remedy increased the length of the cases and induced more litigation than otherwise would have occurred, as we predicted in section 1.3.

1.5 Summary and Conclusions

Private antitrust litigation continues to be an important component of antitrust enforcement. Over 1,000 cases are filed annually. The cases, as indicated by the project sample, encompass a wide variety of allegations of statutory violations and illegal practices. The cases terminate, on average, after slightly more than two years. The bulk of the cases are settled. Of those that reach a final judgment, plaintiffs prevail 28 percent of the time; if dismissals are counted as defendant victories, plaintiffs prevail only 11 percent of the time. Legal fees for these antitrust cases (for both sides together) probably total $200 to $250 million per year.

As we pointed out in section 1.3, legal costs are only one of the cost components of the larger antitrust litigation system. The other cost components are the costs of anticompetitive behavior that the antitrust laws are supposed to deter, the costs of the efficient behavior that may also be deterred when legal lines are drawn incorrectly, and the costs of legal error

Through the collection of the project data base we have been able to observe only litigation and its costs. We cannot, unfortunately, directly observe deterrence or undetected violations. We presume that most suits are filed in response to perceived violations, though nuisance suits may also be present. It is impossible, however, to observe the undetected violations or the detected violations for which potential plaintiffs decided that suit was not worthwhile. We do not even know whether a violation actually occurred in the bulk of the cases that are settled. Only for the cases in which the plaintiffs receive a final favorable judgment—about 3 percent of all private antitrust cases, or about 35 cases per year—can we conclude that violations have occurred. Indeed, even in some of these cases, the courts may have convicted an innocent defendant.

We can observe some of the external signs of deterrence. Beckenstein et al. (1983) found that many companies had instituted compliance programs over the previous decade.[109] The Georgetown project's survey found additional evidence of companies' instituting compliance programs as a consequence of defending an antitrust suit.[110] But compliance programs are only external indicators. They are no assurance of the absence of violations.

This inability to observe violations, compounded by the fact that all our observations on litigation take place in an environment of treble damages (i.e., we have no observations on environments of doubled or quadrupled damages), makes predictions of the consequences of changing the treble damages remedy extremely difficult.[111] If one believes in deterrence, then one must believe that a decrease in the damages multiple would lead to more violations.[112] But predicting the magnitude of the increase in violations, their character, or their consequences requires much more information.[113]

Nevertheless, we believe that our analysis, supported by our observations from the Georgetown sample, indicates the basic principles that should guide any consideration of antitrust policy changes:

1. Incentives matter. This is, by now, the economists' cliché. Nevertheless, it is true and important. The incentives created by the legal system affect business behavior, and they affect the ways in which the potential and actual parties to a suit choose to sue, litigate, and settle their dispute.

2. Costs matter. All of the costs of litigation system should be taken into account when any policy change is considered. Most policy changes inevitably involve trade-offs of reductions in one category of costs (e.g., process costs) against increases in another category of costs (e.g., error costs).

Careful consideration should be given to the types and terms of these trade-offs.

3. Litigation involves the mutual actions and reactions of both parties to a dispute, and a complete understanding of the litigation process must encompass this simultaneous system and its complexities. For example, as our framework indicated, the interaction of plaintiff suits and defendant violations makes impossible an a priori prediction of the effect of a change in the damages multiple on the volume of suits.

4. The parties' perceptions of uncertainty about outcomes may reinforce or undermine the deterrence created by penalties, depending on how the uncertainty interacts with the other features of the litigation system. Any assessment of the deterrence effects of penalties should include an analysis of uncertainty.

5. The proper delineation of substantive legal lines is important for minimizing the costs of the antitrust litigation system. Modifying other aspects of the litigation process, such as the criteria for standing to sue or the treble damages remedy, to compensate for perceived improper locations of substantive legal lines is surely a second-best remedy. Such second-best remedies could have unintended side effects that discourage meritorious suits. It would be better to modify the substantive legal lines.[114]

6. Automatic fee-shifting rules affect incentives to settle as well as incentives to bring suit. Losers-pay-winners'-fees rules may discourage or encourage settlement, depending on the other characteristics of the cases. To the extent that they do discourage settlement, automatic fee-shifting rules have perverse consequences, because settlements economize on scarce legal and judicial resources. Modification of fee shifting rules to deal with perceived problems of frivolous or nuisance suits is, again, surely a second-best remedy. A better approach would be to strengthen directly the penalties against frivolous or nuisance suits.

7. Modifications in the treble damages remedy would have many ramifications. A decrease in the damages multiple would decrease deterrence, and violations would increase. Despite the decreased incentives to sue in any given instance, the increased number of violations might yield an increase in the number of suits. With lower stakes, there would probably be fewer nuisance suits, less legal effort would be expended on most suits, and complex cases would be less likely to be litigated.[115] The effects on settlements cannot be predicted a priori.

Because the elements that should enter the calculation of the appropriate damages multiple are varied and complex, a variable multiple should be considered. Judges could be given discretion as to the appropriate multiple. The status quo, treble damages, should be the norm (since many of the arguments advanced in section 1.3 point to the need for a multiple in most cases to compensate for imperfect detection and the disparity between allowable damages and true social costs), but the judge should be able to modify the multiple upward as well as downward. Legislated guidelines could indicate the considerations (along the lines suggested in section 1.3) to guide the court. For example, higher multiples might be applied to cases of covert action,[116] to more complex cases,[117] or to both, so as to reduce the costs of error. Lower multiples might be applied to cases with the opposite characteristics. We recognize that the introduction of a discretionary multiple would increase uncertainty for the parties; nevertheless, we believe that the gains in flexibility are worth the costs.

Consideration also should be given to decoupling the penalties and rewards.[118] Successful plaintiffs would receive a different multiple than would be paid by losing defendants. If plaintiffs received a lower multiple than that paid by the defendants, deterrence would be maintained, while the incentives for nuisance suits would be reduced. As noted in section 1.3, however, some circumstance might call for the opposite. A combination of a discretionary multiple and decoupling seems worthwhile.

8. Settlement is the overwhelmingly dominant outcome of antitrust litigation. But most settlements currently need not be made public, nor are they. This level of secrecy makes a more complete assessment of the antitrust litigation system difficult. It also means that anticompetitive agreements arising from settlements may go undetected. A requirement to make antitrust settlements public would remedy the problems just noted, but would discourage some settlements. Also it may not even be enforceable, since the parties might publicly settle by simply dropping the suit and then arrange a separate and private agreement, which (if subsequently challenged) they would claim had no relationship to their settling of the suit. The costs and benefits of a requirement of this type should be carefully weighed.

9. The judiciary is likely to have the last word in determining the net effect of any legislated changes in the antitrust laws. This is true not only because of the judges' direct role as interpreters of the changes but also because of the judges' ability to make modifications in other aspects of the antitrust laws so as to maintain or achieve their notion of the proper overall impact.

The private antitrust litigation system is complex indeed and deserves further study and debate. We do not claim to have a monopoly on wisdom in this area (which, under some judicial interpretations, might be deemed a violation of section 2 of the Sherman Act—or even of section 1, since this chapter is a joint venture). We do, however, believe that our analysis and conclusions are sensible and should help focus and guide that debate.

Notes

The authors would like to thank Thomas Krattenmaker, A. Mitchell Polinsky, F. M. Scherer, and John Siegfried for their helpful comments on an earlier draft and Linda Canina for her research assistance on this project. This chapter is a slightly modified and abbreviated version of Salop and White (1986a).

1. For example, see Breit and Elzinga (1974; 1985), Elzinga and Breit (1976), Baumol and Ordover (1985), and the articles cited in Garvey (1984).

2. See Posner (1970) and NERA (1979).

3. For more details on the history of the project, see White (1985).

4. The only exception is that most of the 1982 cases and all of the 1983 cases in the Southern District of New York were omitted because access to these files could not be obtained.

5. Further details on the data collection effort are provided in chapter 2 by Teplitz.

6. Information on ten MDLs was not available.

7. The number of non-MDL cases analyzed in this chapter is slightly larger than the number analyzed in the other chapters in this volume. We were able to use additional information from a few cases that arrived too late to be included in the data base sent to other researchers.

8. This count of named parties substantially overrepresents the actual numbers of relevant parties per case. If "Mary Jones" and "Robert Jones" both were named as plaintiffs in the same case, they were counted as two parties; if a defendant company, its officers, and its subsidiaries were named, each was counted separately.

9. Where we could identify the business activities of both plaintiffs and defendants in cases, we calculated a "who sues whom" matrix. The matrix indicated that a disproportionate number of suits involved firms in the same sector suing each other. In addition a disproportionate number of suits came from firms downstream in the distribution chain suing their suppliers, including the suppliers of financial services.

10. Data compiled by Perloff and Rubinfeld in chapter 4 reinforce this view.

11. Allegations of tying or exclusive dealing constitute a higher fraction of all cases than do allegations of a Clayton Act, section 3, violation. This is true because tying claims involving services must be brought under the Sherman Act rather than the Clayton Act.

12. The median is less affected by a handful of very long cases that would tend to raise the average.

13. See the *Annual Reports* of the Administrative Office of the U.S. Courts for years 1973–1983. See also Grossman et al. (1981).

14. Some cases also had secondary outcomes; for example, the plaintiff may have won a judgment on the major issues, but the parties settled on minor issues.

15. The data base categorizes all cases into one of nineteen possible outcomes. As a broad definition, we labeled as "settlement" any outcome that fell into the following categories: dismissed pretrial on motion, pretrial stipulation and order, pretrial withdrawal, settlement, statistically closed, dismissal by court, dismissal for other reason, and settlement after judgment.

16. The parties may have negotiated an agreement and then asked the court to dismiss the case, or they may have contested the dismissal motion. The former would properly be called a settlement, the latter a win for the defendant. The data, however, do not allow us to distinguish between the two.

17. These trial data are puzzling. They seem to imply that plaintiffs prevailed about 24 percent of the time on cases that were decided on pretrial motions—an unbelievably high percentage. It appears, however, that some of these pretrial judgments favoring plaintiffs were actually settlements—involving a substantial payment to the plaintiff—that were subsequently entered in the court records as a judgment. Thus the substance of the outcome is probably still correct, though the exact characterization may be slightly off. Another problem of characterization occurs when cases settle *after* a judgment is issued by a court at the pretrial or trial stage. These cases also are classified as settlements. There probably is no entirely satisfactory way to characterize these cases.

18. A larger number received awards, but the information is not available in some cases.

19. 586 F. Supp. (1983).

20. In addition defendants received awards in 31 cases. In most instances these appear to be payments on counterclaims, probably for money due on shipments or contracts that were suspended at the time of suit.

21. There is no readily available price index for legal fees. We used a component of the CPI—services less rent—that correlated reasonably with the starting salaries of leading law firms, as reported in the *National Law Journal* for 1978–1984. We were unable to find a more satisfactory index. We used the terminal year of each case as the date to which the cost index should be applied. To the extent that the expenses were incurred in earlier years, our method understates these constant dollar costs. If we had applied the index instead to the filing year of the case—which on average was two and a half years prior to termination—the constant dollar costs would have been one-third larger.

22. Attorneys' fees were 85 percent of this total.

23. The time duration of the case and the total number of depositions were also tried but did not yield results that were as satisfactory. Also a dummy variable for whether the party was defendant or plaintiff was tried, but it did not yield significant results. The dummy variable, though never significant, always indicated slightly higher costs for plaintiffs. Finally, one formulation that included the thickness of the docket file as an explanatory variable yielded an estimate of a *marginal cost* per party of approximately $5,000 per inch of file!

24. We have not, though, corrected for the possible response bias stemming from the fact that over 80 percent of the respondents to the questions concerning legal costs were defendants. If defendants, who tend to be larger than plaintiffs, tend to use larger law firms, who in turn tend to have higher billing rates, our data may overestimate actual costs. It is interesting to note, however, that in our sample plaintiffs tended to have slightly higher legal costs than did defendants.

25. If we use the coefficients from the equation in table 1.12, a lone party involved in the *median* case had costs of $45,000, and the minimum cost of involvement was $5,700.

26. As noted earlier, the number of named parties overstates the number of true parties. We use the number of named parties in our regression to estimate the costs per respondent, and then we use the number of true parties to estimate the total costs per case. We estimate that there were, on average, slightly more than one true plaintiff and slightly more than three true defendants per case.

27. The estimate of the average cost per case is not appreciably different from the estimate of $280,000 per case provided in chapter 3 by Elzinga and Wood. These costs do not include the

opportunity costs of executives' time on both sides nor the time of inside counsel. They also do not include the costs of counseling and of efforts that did not lead to cases. These cost estimates can be compared with those reported by Trubek et al. (1983). For a sample of approximately 800 civil cases of all kinds terminating in 1978 in five federal district courts, they found that the median legal cost per party was just under $2,500; in 1984 dollars this figure would be around $4,400. For our sample the median legal cost per party was about $28,000. But the median stakes in their sample were $15,000. The true stakes in antitrust cases are difficult to determine (see section 1.4), but they are surely a good deal higher. Thus it is not surprising that legal costs in antitrust cases are also a good deal higher.

28. If anything, the median case appears to have become slightly shorter and less complicated. However, the inflation correction series that we used to convert the legal fees into current dollar equivalents—the CPI component of all services less rent—tended to rise slightly faster (about 1 percent per year) than the general rate of inflation (as measured by the overall CPI). On balance the cost of a typical case probably rose at about the same rate as the general price level.

29. Plaintiff costs are probably about a third of this total, or $80 to 100 million per year. For comparison, the annual budget of the Antitrust Division of the U.S. Department of Justice is in the range of $45 to 50 million. The Division's responsibilities, however, encompass amicus briefs, regulatory filings, legislative review, and decree review, as well as litigation.

30. This framework draws on a large number of sources cited later in this chapter. Other broad approaches are found in Becker (1968), Posner (1972), Ehrlich and Posner (1974), Becker and Stigler (1974), Landes and Posner (1975), and Schwartz (1980).

31. Formal demonstrations of some of the propositions advanced are found in Salop and White (1986a, app. A–D).

32. For the purposes at hand we ignore the possibility of settlement, which is discussed in the following section.

33. As is discussed in more detail later, the possibility of settlement is also an uncertain proposition.

34. The requirement in antitrust cases that a losing defendant must pay a winning plaintiff's litigation costs alters the expected value calculus of each party; the plaintiff would discount these litigation costs by his perceived likelihood of success, and the defendant's expected exposure would be increased by those costs multiplied by his perception of the plaintiff's likelihood of success.

35. This prediction assumes that detrebling would have no effect on litigation costs, and it ignores the possibility of settlements. These effects can complicate the analysis significantly.

36. This is calculated as follows: The plaintiff had a 28 percent chance of winning $456,000. His legal expenses were 20 percent of $456,000, or $91,200. Because winning plaintiffs do not have to pay their own legal expenses, the plaintiff expected to pay these legal expenses only 72 percent of the time. Thus we have $62.0 = 0.28 \times 456 - 0.72 \times 91.2$. (If we instead used the 11 percent win rate that counts dismissals as defendant victories but used the 10 percent ratio of costs to awards, we would still find that initiating a suit was rational.) This figure *understates* the expected benefit, of course, since the financial value of injunctive relief and the possibility of a pretrial settlement have not been included. As Polinsky and Rubinfeld (1985) demonstrate, the possibility of a pretrial settlement improves the expected return to the plaintiff and reduces the expected loss to the defendant as well.

37. This is calculated as follows: The defendant faced a 28 percent chance of liability for the $456,000 award and plaintiff's legal fees. He also faced his own legal fees, which we assume were also $91,200. Thus we have $244.4 = (0.28)(456 + 91.2) + 91.2$.

38. With enough data one could develop similar expected value calculations for specific kinds of cases and/or before and after crucial legal decisions.

39. A formal demonstration of this result is provided in Salop and White (1986a, app. A) and White (1987). At some point penalties get high enough so that the decrease in violations is so severe that the number of suits must fall.

40. This analysis does not take into account the situation where the benefit to the plaintiff of an injunction during the pendency of trial outweights the costs associated with bringing and trying the suit.

41. This curve is named after the equally obvious curve relating tax revenues to average tax rates, often attributed to Arthur Laffer. It has an equally obvious ambiguity: we do not know whether the current state of the legal system is located on the rising or falling position of the curve.

42. This caution was largely ignored by Landes and Posner (1979) and Snyder (1985).

43. The existence of this second effect is proved rigorously by P'ng (1985). It has an interesting normative implication: since some defendants may be induced to engage in less egregious behavior, a more lenient standard could lead, on average (or in aggregate), to behavior that is less extreme. For example, if the national speed limit were increased from the current 55 miles per hour to 60 mph, the average speed of motorists might actually *decrease* if there were a large enough number of motorists who currently travel 65 mph (risking detecting and penalty) but who would find a legalized 60 mph to be a satisfactory second-best alternative. Whether this result could occur would depend, among other things, on the penalty structure.

44. As we discuss later, this increases the likelihood of reaching a mutually acceptable settlement as well.

45. Almost all cases involve uncertainty as to damages.

46. We draw heavily here on Calfee and Craswell (1984).

47. The trial outcome may be uncertain for a number of reasons, including the parties' uncertainty over the legal standard, the facts of the case, or the court's interpretation of the standard or the facts.

48. This strategy is yet more likely if the defendant is risk averse and if the likelihoods of detection, liability, and a large damages award are highly sensitive to the degree to which the defendant's conduct diverges from the legal standard.

49. The following numerical example illustrates how uncertainty can reduce deterrence. Suppose that the damage award from violating a legal standard is $100 and that the detection rate is 0.5. For simplicity, litigation costs are ignored. In this case a defendant who would derive a benefit of $45 from violating the rule would be deterred by the expected financial exposure of $50. Suppose uncertainty arises because the fact finder may misconstrue the conduct. In particular, suppose that 10 percent of the time the conduct exceeding the standard would be erroneously permitted and 10 percent of the time conduct below the standard would be erroneously penalized. In this case, the defendant's expected financial exposure from exceeding the standard falls to $45; that is, the probability that his conduct is detected and he is penalized is 45 percent = 50 percent × 90 percent. In addition he now faces expected costs of $5 even if his conduct does not exceed the legal standard because that conduct may be detected (with probability of 50 percent) and penalized (with a probability of 10 percent); 5 percent = 50 percent × 10 percent. Thus the *additional* exposure he faces from deliberately exceeding the standard is reduced to $40 ($45 − $5). As a result, if the defendant would derive a benefit of $45 from exceeding the standard, he would no longer be deterred.

50. In some extreme circumstances, defendants may be able to recover their legal costs from plaintiffs who bring "frivolous" suits under Federal Rule of Civil Procedure 11. It is a rare event, however.

51. Also, if plaintiffs deliberately provoke violations or behave strategically with respect to purchases from businesses who they believe may be violating, then uncertainty may affect their behavior. For a discussion of this strategic behavior, see Breit and Elzinga (1974; 1985), Elzinga and Breit (1976), Salant (1984), and Baker (1985).

52. See Salop and White (1986a, app. D) for a more rigorous analysis. Our discussion here follows the logic found in Gould (1973), Baxter (1980), and chapter 4 by Perloff and Rubinfeld.

53. Only the prospective legal costs matter. Costs incurred prior to the "settle or proceed" decision are sunk and should not affect the prospective decision, unless the payment of those costs is affected by the decision (e.g., when there is fee shifting).

54. The plaintiff's expected return from going to trial is 30 percent of the $1 million award, or $300,000, less his legal fees of $50,000, for a total of $250,000. The defendant's expected exposure from going to trial is the 30 percent probability of the $1 million award plus his legal fees of $50,000, for a total of $350,000.

55. This assumes risk neutrality and no fee shifting.

56. The plaintiff's expected return from trial is 50 percent of $1 million less $50,000 in costs, for a total of $450,000; the defendant's expected exposure is 10 percent of $1 million plus $50,000, for a total of $150,000.

57. Sufficiently risk-averse parties, however, might settle.

58. This failure of the Coase theorem is no different from failed negotiations over the sale of a piece of land to a developer that leads to inefficient land use or a failed labor negotiation that leads to a mutually detrimental strike.

59. See also Baxter (1980, 16).

60. Our analysis in the text is clearly compatible with the Priest-Klein (1984) approach, and many of the factors that we analyze are discussed in the Priest-Klein article. Their emphasis on the error reduction process appears more suitable for interpreting time series data for a specific type of case. Our emphasis is more suitable for cross-sectional analysis across different types of cases.

61. For example, if a case is more fact dependent, the parties may be less likely to know the strength of their adversary's case before trial. Similarly, if juries are inherently less predictable fact finders, the settlement rate should be lower for jury trials.

62. The analysis is complicated yet further by the fact that higher stakes are likely to induce greater litigation expenditures, as is discussed in later in this section.

63. See Braeutigam et al. (1984).

64. See Shavell (1982b) and Simon (1984) for earlier treatments of the question.

65. See the basic model presented in Salop and White (1986a, app. A).

66. See Shavell (1982a) and Rosenberg and Shavell (1985), but see also Mennell (1983).

67. It appears, however, that the use of this sanction is relatively rare. Federal Rule of Civil Procedure 11 is the source of this sanction.

68. The plaintiff has the clear advantage of being able to initiate suit at low cost and being able to drop the suit at any time, though this latter ability may reduce the credibility of his threats. Moreover the requirement that he prove his case first is at least a partially offsetting disadvantage. In addition a court can probably detect and penalize frivolous suits more easily

than frivolous defenses. A further issue is the plaintiff's ability credibly to increase the defendant's relative costs. The tactical advantage likely varies with the type of litigation. For example, the plaintiff may have an advantage in per se cases and the defendant the advantage in rule of reason cases. Finally, to the extent that any eventual award does not include true (opportunity cost) interest, the defendant gains from any litigation tactics that produce delay.

69. A formal demonstration of this proposition is provided in Salop and White (1986a, app. B).

70. For example, in a rule of reason case in which the plaintiff has a heavy burden of proof to withstand a motion for summary judgment, matched increases in litigation expenditures by both parties would probably tip the balance in favor of the plaintiff. In other cases the advantage may flow to the defendant. For example, in a price-fixing case, matched increases in the use of econometric experts to critique and reformulate estimates of damages would probably reduce the credibility of the typical plaintiff's study.

71. A formal model is provided in Salop and White (1986a, app. C).

72. See Landes (1983).

73. Further discussion is found in Posner (1972) and Ehrlich and Posner (1974).

74. For further discussion on setting damage awards in antitrust cases, see Easterbrook (1985).

75. Similar problems arise in setting the compensation level for illegal exclusionary behavior aimed at rivals. The rivals are compensated for the additional costs caused by the use of inefficient inputs. If damages are based on lost profits, however, there may be no compensation for the consequent injury (caused by the restricted output and higher prices) to consumers, if the latter are not parties to the case. See Salop and White (1986b). For a different analysis of this "passing on" problem, see Easterbrook (1985). We should note that part of the lost profits may be a monopoly transfer of wealth to input suppliers who are not parties to the case.

76. This calculation would be easier if the victims are firms rather than consumers. In this event most of the deadweight loss represents the higher price for alternative inputs that are less cost effective.

77. The standard analysis generally is based on two independent lines of argument. First, egregious conduct far from the line separating legal from illegal behavior generally entails greater social cost; this would imply greater damages, although not a greater multiple. Second, it is unlikely that such conduct could be undertaken unintentionally; thus a damage multiple acts like a punitive damages rule for intentional violations. Our analysis does not negate these arguments. Instead, it adds a third argument that cuts the other way. The fact that a case is close and hard to decide need not imply that the behavior, if found to be illegal, is less deserving of punishment.

78. In further discussion later, we provide a second, independent argument in favor of assessing a damages multiple in rule of reason cases, based on the added complexity and expense of dealing with such cases.

79. If the damages multiple were made variable, the initial legislative change could specify the multiple that should apply to each class of case, or complete discretion could be left to the courts. Under this discretionary approach the appropriate multiple would be resolved and developed in an evolutionary fashion on a case by case basis. A somewhat analogous method is currently used for calculating attorneys' fees in class action cases. If the court controlled the damages multiple, it would have the ability to use the multiple to induce the parties to litigate efficiently. An evolutionary approach would allow the courts to learn from experience in using this new tool. In addition to the general benefits that come from a case by case approach, a discretionary multiple would be a particularly good way to handle the need for a high multiple

in complex cases to finance the necessary litigation costs that prevent judicial error. It might be difficult to define in advance, as a general matter, which cases are most likely to be complex. For example, even some price-fixing cases become very complex and expensive.

80. This recently appeared to be the view of the Antitrust Division of the U.S. Department of Justice. See Rule (1985). Or as one of our colleagues, Thomas Krattenmaker, remarked, "For covert price fixing the only question is what comes after 'octuple.'"

81. On the other hand, the extortion-minded plaintiff's lawyer with even a minimal threat of octuple damages would become a dangerous threat. The possibility of bankruptcy, causing firms to become judgment proof, would put a limitation on the effectiveness of a variable damages multiple.

82. It is not true, however, that the most egregious violations would necessarily have the lowest multiple. By itself, egregiousness would tend to increase the multiple.

83. Schwartz (1980, 1981) has also suggested this as a possible change in the treble damages remedy. See also Landes and Posner (1975) and the discussion by Polinsky at the end of part I of this volume.

84. The difference between the penalty and reward could go into general federal tax revenues; or it could be devoted to a special fund to help cover the administrative costs of the courts. To an extent, the focus of public enforcement on per se rules creates a decoupling process, though it is not an explicit aim of government policy.

85. This is similar to the principle that the Department of Justice uses in deciding to bring civil antitrust cases rather than criminal cases when it tries to establish new legal doctrines.

86. For analyses that point in this direction, see Shavell (1982a) and Rosenberg and Shavel (1985).

87. This still appears to be true, despite a recent strengthening of rule 11 of the Federal Rules of Civil Procedure.

88. The Congress and the executive branch are clearly also parties in a larger political system.

89. This point is raised by Garvey (1984). See chapter 5 by Stephen Calkins.

90. *Bigelow* v. *RKO Radio Pictures, Inc.*, 327 U.S. 251 (1946).

91. The Supreme Court's decision in *Illinois Brick Co.* v. *Illinois*, 431 U.S. 720 (1977) and *Matsushita Electric Industrial Co.* v. *Zenith Radio Corp.*, 54 LW 4319 (1986), might be interpreted in this fashion.

92. See, for example, *Continental T.V.* v. *GTE Sylvania*, 433 U.S. 36 (1977), *Brunswick Corp.* v. *Pueblo Bowl-O-Mat*, 429 U.S. 477 (1977), and *Broadcast Music* v. *Columbia Broadcasting System*, 441 U.S. 1 (1979). Also during this period the Areeda and Turner (1975) predatory pricing rule was widely adopted.

93. It is frequently alleged that the decrease in private antitrust activity is also related to a decrease in federal government prosecutions, since a decrease in the latter would mean fewer "follow-on" opportunities. As table 1.1 indicates, government activity actually increased in the early 1980s. But a significant fraction of these cases were price-fixing prosecutions of highway contractors, which frequently had few follow-on cases. For more discussion of the relationship between private and government litigation, see chapter 7 by Kauper and Snyder and Joyce and McGuckin (1985).

94. The cases filed after 1979 may present a deceptive picture. A larger fraction of these cases were still pending at the time of the data collection. Of those that had terminated, one would expect that a high fraction would settle, and of those that had reached judgments, a large fraction would be decided on pretrial motions, where defendants would be expected to prevail if a judgment was reached.

95. We should add one caveat to these data: our allegation data were taken from the initial complaints. It is possible that by the time the cases settled or reached a final judgment, some of the claims had been dropped or others added.

96. It is noteworthy that plaintiffs had comparatively high win rates in dealer termination suits. One would expect that defendants in this type of case would have higher stakes than plaintiffs. Unlike most plaintiffs in these cases, the defendants would be concerned about the effects of a loss on their relationships with other dealers and hence would be reluctant to allow cases with favorable prospects to reach final judgment. Accordingly, one would predict that plaintiffs would have a low win rate. It may be true that defendants were even more concerned that information about settlements would leak out to other dealers and lead to a rash of "me too" suits. Conversely, suits by customer companies had very low win rates. We have no easy explanation for this result either.

97. Suppose that the settlement amount S were equal to the expected value of the money transferred πH, where π is the plaintiff's expected win rate and H is the money that the prevailing plaintiff would receive; or $S = \pi H$. Let c denote the litigation costs prior to settlement negotiations and c' be the subsequent litigation costs if settlement fails. The ratios of litigation costs to money transferred in settled cases and in fully litigated cases must therefore have the following relationships:

$$\frac{c}{S} = \frac{(c + c')}{H} \cdot \frac{1}{\pi} \cdot \frac{c}{(c + c')}.$$

If $c/(c + c') > \pi$, the cost ratio for settled cases must exceed the cost ratio for fully litigated cases. As the text indicates, $c/(c + c')$ appears to be in the range of 0.7–0.8; π is in the range of 0.11–0.28 (depending on the definition of settlement). Therefore one would expect the cost ratio for settled cases to be three to seven times higher than the cost ratio for fully litigated cases.

98. Only cases that named damages in the complaint were used in the analysis that follows. There were 807 such cases.

99. Trubek et al. (1983) found that the stakes of a case were a significant determinant of the amount of legal effort.

100. From the docket data we chose the length of the case, the number of docket entries, the total number of depositions noticed by both sides, and the number of judicial orders as alternative measures of legal effort. For the 368 cases in which all the requisite data were available, initial damage claims did not correlate positively with these measures. However, when all the variables were converted into logarithms, damage claims did correlate positively (and significantly) with length of case and with the number of docket entries. The explanatory power of the correlations, however, was weak (in each case, $R^2 = 0.04$), and the magnitudes of the relationships were quite low: a doubling of damage claims was associated with only a 3 percent increase in the length of a case or a 5 percent increase in the number of docket entries. Further for a far smaller sample—72 cases in which damage claims were available from the docket survey and legal costs were available—we found a significant positive correlation between damage claims and legal costs when both were coverted into logarithms. However, the explanatory power was again low ($R^2 = 0.07$), and the magnitude of the relationship was relatively small, with a doubling of damage claims associated with only a 17 percent increase in legal costs.

101. For this test the nominal values of damage claims and awards were used.

102. The average damage claim for the settled cases (broad definition) was $50 million (in 1984 dollars); the average claim for cases that went to a final judgment was $12 million. For the narrow definition, the figures were $35 million and $67 million, respectively.

103. In addition we computed an ordinary least squares regression in which the disposition of a case (settlement = 0; judgment = 1) was the dependent variable and the damage claims and alleged statute violations were independent variables. No significant relationship was found. We did not employ logit or probit analysis; we doubt that such analysis would have changed these results.

104. This conclusion was echoed in the remarks at the conference by a number of practicing attorneys.

105. The average number of judicial orders in these cases, though, was the same as for the overall sample.

106. The plaintiff percentages for these countersuits (with the percentages for the entire sample in parentheses, for comparison) were competitors, 54.5 percent (36.5 percent); suppliers, 13.1 percent (5.6 percent); dealers, 15.2 percent (27.3 percent); and customer companies, 2.2 percent (12.5 percent).

107. This assertion does not contradict our earlier claims that a higher damages multiple tends to lead to longer cases and more legal effort. An increase in the damages multiple has the following two effects: it raises the stakes for cases that would have been filed anyway, and it causes more marginal cases to be filed.

108. The allegation percentages for these "noncentral" cases (with the percentages for the entire sample in parentheses, for comparison) were horizontal price fixing, 11.1 percent (21.3 percent); predatory pricing, 7.8 percent (10.4 percent); price discrimination, 13.4 percent (16.4 percent); refusal to deal, 31.6 percent (25.4 percent); and dealer termination, 11.1 percent (8.9 percent).

109. See also Beckenstein and Gabel (1983).

110. Only 287 defendants responded to a survey question asking about antitrust compliance programs. Of 111 who had had a program in effect, 3 indicated that they modified it as a consequence of defending the suit; of 70 who indicated that they had not had a program, 14 initiated one as a consequence of the suit.

111. To use an analogy, the task is similar to that of trying to judge the effectiveness of the local police and prosecuter in combating crime, when one can only observe the prosecutions initiated and the convictions eventually obtained but cannot observe the underlying volume of crimes committed nor even learn the details of the plea bargains that settle most prosecutions.

112. We cannot predict, however, whether the number of suits would increase or decrease.

113. The model in Salop and White (1986a, app. A) could be used for such predictions if we knew the relative distributions of violations.

114. There is widespread disagreement across much of the legal profession (and some of the economics profession) about the wisdom of the legal lines that have been drawn in many areas of antitrust law. There are few dissenters to the propositions that "smoke-filled-room" horizontal price fixing is anticompetitive and socially deleterious and thus should carry heavy penalties to deter it or that mergers in highly concentrated industries with high barriers to entry should be discouraged. Beyond those points, however, agreement dissolves. Partly, the disagreements involve the efficiency consequences of certain practices—tying, exclusive dealing, full-line forcing, vertical price and nonprice restraints, price discrimination, and predatory pricing—and their ability to create or enhance market power. Partly, the disagreements involve the size of markets, ease of substitutability in supply and demand, and ease of entry (and hence the likelihood of anticompetitive effects occurring, even if they are possible). And partly, the disagreements involve the noneconomic questions of whether upstream entities simply should or should not be able to dictate terms of sale to downstream entities. It is no accident that those who believe that judicial interpretations of the Sherman and Clayton

Acts in these areas are inhibiting efficient business practices are also those who are most concerned about the inhibiting effects of the treble damage remedy.

115. Even with a lower multiple of damages for past harms available to prevailing plaintiffs, injunctive relief against future harms (an important factor in many injured plaintiffs' calculations) would still be present. We suspect (following our argument in section 1.3) that if a lower multiple of damages were available to plaintiffs, judges would be more prepared to grant preliminary injunctions to plaintiffs. See also chapter 5 by Calkins.

116. To compensate for reduced probabilities of detection.

117. To finance the litigation.

118. See the discussion by Polinsky at the end of part I in this volume.

References

Areeda, Phillip, and Donald F. Turner. 1975. Predatory Pricing and Related Practices under Section 2 of the Sherman Act. *Harvard Law Review* 88 (February): 697–733.

Areeda, Phillip, and Donald F. Turner. 1978. *Antitrust Law*. Boston: Little, Brown.

Baker, Jonathan B. 1985. The Effect of Private Antitrust Damage Remedies on Resource Allocation. Stanford Law School, Law and Economics Program. Working paper no. 22 (October).

Baumol, William J., and Janusz A. Ordover. 1985. Use of Antitrust to Subvert Competition *Journal of Law & Economics* 28 (May): 247–266.

Baxter, William F. 1980. The Political Economy of Antitrust. In Robert D. Tollison, ed., *The Political Economy of Antitrust: Principal Paper by William Baxter*. Lexington, Mass.: Lexington Books.

Beckenstein, Alan R., and H. Landis Gabel. 1983. Antitrust Compliance: Results of a Survey of Legal Opinion. *Antitrust Law Journal* 52 (Spring): 459–516.

Beckenstein, Alan R., H. Landis Gabel, and Karlene Roberts. 1983. An Executive's Guide to Antitrust Compliance. *Harvard Business Review* (September–October): 94–102.

Becker, Gary S. 1968. Crime and Punishment: An Economic Approach. *Journal of Political Economy* 76 (March–April): 169–217.

Becker, Gary S., and George J. Stigler. 1974. Law Enforcement, Malfeasance, and Compensation of Enforcers. *Journal of Legal Studies* 3 (January): 1–18.

Braeutigam, Ronald, Bruce Owen, and John Panzar. 1984. An Economic Analysis of Alternative Fee Shifting Systems. *Law and Contemporary Problems* 47 (Winter): 175–185.

Breit, William, and Kenneth G. Elzinga. 1974. Antitrust Enforcement and Economic Efficiency: The Uneasy Case for Treble Damages. *Journal of Law & Economics* 17 (October): 329–356.

Breit, William, and Kenneth G. Elzinga. 1985. Private Antitrust Enforcement: The New Learning. *Journal of Law & Economics* 28 (May): 405–445.

Calfee, John E. and Richard Craswell. 1984. Some Effects of Uncertainty on Compliance with Legal Standards. *Virginia Law Review* 70 (June): 965–1003.

Easterbrook, Frank H. 1985. Detrebling Antitrust Damages. *Journal of Law & Economics* 28 (May): 445–468.

Ehrlich Isaac, and Richard A. Posner. 1974. Economic Analysis of Legal Rulemaking. *Journal of Legal Studies* 3 (June): 257–286.

Elzinga Kenneth G., and William Breit. 1976. *The Antitrust Penalties: A Study in Law and Economics*. New Haven: Yale University Press.

Garvey, George E. 1984. *Study of the Antitrust Treble Damage Remedy*. Report of the Committee on the Judiciary, U.S. House of Representatives, 98th Congress, 2nd Session (February).

Gould, John P. 1973. The Economics of Legal Conflicts. *Journal of Legal Studies* 2 (June): 279–300.

Grossman, Joel B., Herbert M. Kritzer, Kristin Bumiller, and Stephen McDougal. 1981. Measuring the Pace of Civil Litigation in Federal and State Trial Courts. *Judicature* 65 (August): 86–113.

Grossman, Joel B., Herbert M. Kritzer, Kristin Bumiller, Austin Sarat, Stephen McDougal, and Richard Miller. 1982. Dimensions of Institutional Participation: Who Uses the Courts and How? *Journal of Politics* 44 (February): 86–114.

Joyce, Jon M., and Robert H. McGuckin. 1985. Assignment of Rights to Sue under *Illinois Brick*: An Empirical Assessment, EPO discussion paper no. 85-6. Antitrust Division, U.S. Department of Justice (April 9).

Kelly, Kevin K. 1972. Attorneys' Fees in Individual and Class Action Antitrust Litigation. *California Law Review* 60:1656–1682.

Landes, William M. 1983. Optimal Sanctions for Antitrust Violations. *University of Chicago Law Review* 50 (Spring): 652–678.

Landes, William M., and Richard A. Posner. 1975. The Private Enforcement of Law. *Journal of Legal Studies* 4 (January): 1–46.

Landes, William M., and Richard A. Posner. 1979. Should Indirect Purchasers Have Standing to Sue under the Antitrust Laws? An Economic Analysis of the Rule of Illinois Brick. *University of Chicago Law Review* 46: 602–635.

Mennell, Peter S. 1983. A Note on Private versus Social Incentives to Sue in a Costly Legal System. *Journal of Legal Studies* 12 (January): 41–52.

National Economic Research Associates, Inc. 1979. A Statistical Analysis of Private Antitrust Litigation: Final Report. Prepared for the American Bar Association Section of Antitrust Law (October).

P'ng, I. P. L. 1985. Liability, Litigation, and Incentives to Take Care. Mimeo.

Polinsky, A. Mitchel, and Daniel L. Rubinfeld. 1985. The Welfare Implications of Costly Litigation in the Theory of Liability. Mimeo.

Posner, Richard A. 1970. A Statistical Study of Antitrust Enforcement. *Journal of Law & Economics* 13 (October): 365–419.

Posner, Richard A. 1972. An Economic Approach to Legal Procedure and Judicial Administration. *Journal of Legal Studies* 2 (June): 399–458.

Priest, George L. 1985. Reexamining the Selection Hypothesis: Learning from Wittman's Mistakes. *Journal of Legal Studies* 14 (January): 215–243.

Priest, George L., and Benjamin Klein. 1984. The Selection of Disputes for Litigation. *Journal of Legal Studies* 13 (January): 1–55.

Reich, Robert B. 1980. The Antitrust Industry. *Georgetown Law Journal* 68: 1053–1073.

Rosenberg, D., and S. Shavell. 1983. A Model in Which Suits Are Brought for Their Nuisance Value. *International Review of Law and Economics* 5 (June): 3–13.

Rule, Charles F. 1985. Testimony before the Committee on the Judiciary, U.S. Senate, Concerning S. 1300, Joint and Several Liability in Antitrust Litigation. July 19.

Salant, Stephen W. 1984. Private Enforcement of Penalties against Price Fixing. Mimeo.

Salop, Steven C., and Lawrence J. White. 1986a. Economic Analysis of Private Antitrust Litigation. *Georgetown Law Journal* 74 (April): 201–263.

Salop, Steven C., and Lawrence J. White. 1986b. Trebel Damages Reform: Implications of the Georgetown Project. *Antitrust Law Journal* 55: 73–94.

Sarris, Valerie. 1984. *The Efficiency of Private Antitrust Enforcement: The "Illinois Brick" Decision.* New York: Garland.

Schwartz, Warren F. 1980. An Overview of the Economics of Antitrust Enforcement. *Georgetown Law Review* 68: 1075–1102.

Schwartz, Warren F. 1981. *Private Enforcement of the Antitrust Laws: An Economic Critique.* Washington, D.C.: American Enterprise Institute.

Shavell, Steven. 1982a. Suit, Settlement, and Trial: A Theoretical Analysis under Alternative Methods for the Allocation of Legal Costs. *Journal of Legal Studies* 11 (January): 55–81.

Shavell, Steven. 1982b. The Social versus the Private Incentive to Bring Suit in a Costly Legal System. *Journal of Legal Studies* 11 (June): 333–339.

Simon, Marilyn J. 1984. Product Quality and the Allocation of Legal Costs. EPO discussion paper no. 84-8. Antitrust Division, U.S. Department of Justice (May 22).

Snyder, Edward A. 1984. "Defensive Effort" and Efficient Enforcement: An Application to Antitrust. Ph.D. dissertation. University of Chicago (June).

Snyder, Edward A. 1985. Efficient Assignment of Rights to Sue for Antitrust Damages. *Journal of Law & Economics* 28 (May): 469–482.

Spiller, Pablo T. 1986. "Treble Damages, Limited Liability and Optimal Suing Time. *Research in Law and Economics* 8: 45–56.

Stelzer, Irwin M. 1983. Procedures for Private Antitrust Enforcement in the United States. Presented at the Second Oxford International Antitrust Law Conference, Queen's College, Oxford (September 12).

Trubek, David M., Joel B. Grossman, Austin Sarat, William L. F. Felstiner, and Herbert M. Kritzer. 1983. The Costs of Ordinary Litigation. *UCLA Law Review*, 31 (October): 72–127.

White, Lawrence J. 1985. The Georgetown Study of Private Antitrust Litigation. *Antitrust Law Journal* 54: 59–63.

White, Lawrence J. 1987. Litigation and Economic Incentives. *Research in Law and Economics*, forthcoming.

Wittman, Donald, 1985. Is the Selection of Cases for Trial Biased? *Journal of Legal Studies* 14 (January): 185–214.

2

The Georgetown Project: An Overview of the Data Set and Its Collection

Paul V. Teplitz

This chapter has two purposes. First, it describes the data collection process for the Georgetown antitrust project. Second, it presents a selection of summary statistics from the data, along with a brief discussion of the underlying phenomena that they represent.

2.1 The Data Collection Process

Selection of Cases in Sample

Between 1,000 and 1,500 private antitrust suits are filed each year in the United States. Activity is highly concentrated, however, in a few key districts. The Georgetown sample included all private antitrust suits filed during an 11-year period, 1973 to 1983, in the most active three districts—the Southern District of New York (New York City), the Nothern District of Illinois (Chicago), and the Northern District of California (San Francisco)—plus all those filed during the same years in two other districts selected as being representative of "grass roots" antitrust activity: the Western District of Missouri (Kansas City) and the Northern District of Georgia (Atlanta). In total, the five districts had approximately 2,900 suits during this period, as shown in table 2.1, representing roughly one-fifth of all private antitrust suits filed in the United States during these same years. The cases were identified from the computer files of the Administrative Office of the United States Courts (AOUSC) in Washington, D.C.[1]

Collection of Information from Court Records

Field data collection was performed under the supervision of Cambridge Research Institute (CRI) in the five federal courthouses and Federal Records Centers by paralegals whose time was contributed by local law firms and corporate legal departments in the five selected cities.[2] Most of this work was conducted during the summer and fall of 1984.

The paralegals examined the docket sheets and available file material on each of the cases and filled out a ten-page questionnaire.[3] Depending on the course of events in a case, this could involve answers to as many as 174

Table 2.1   Number of suits in the Georgetown sample

New York City	905
Chicago	885
San Francisco	789
Atlanta	169
Kansas City	126
Total	2,874

questions, which required an average of about fifty minutes of a paralegal's time. Large or complex cases often required much more effort, however, and a few cases took several days to analyze.

The practical problems of collecting this information proved to be far more difficult than anticipated. The problems arose from two main sources. The primary factor was the complex (and sometimes seemingly convoluted) nature of the cases themselves. Cases rarely occurred in the classic *A* v. *B* format of law school cases or law review articles. More often the cases had multiple plaintiffs suing multiple defendants on several claims, with the defendants suing on one or two counterclaims, frequently transferred to (or from) other districts, often consolidated with other cases, with different outcomes on the various claims, and with different outcomes for different parties. All of these strands were woven together in the chronological case docket, with no separation by claims or by parties. Often it required a careful reading in context to determine which rulings were associated with which motions. The thorniest problems involved ascertaining some of the cases' outcomes. Courts (and parties) often used euphemisms to make a defeat appear less humiliating, such as "motion for denial of the Section 1 claim is granted" (essentially, case dismissed) or gave partial "victories" to both sides. In such cases, with these items often buried in the midst of several pages of densely typed docket sheets, the amount of time required to puzzle out the true nature of a case could become substantial. Also the opportunities for errors in classification increased for the same reasons.

This inherent "messiness" of the cases, particularly the issue of multiple claims and multiple outcomes, makes certain lines of inquiry impractical. For example, most effects to interpret the pretrial "drift" of a case (e.g., by analyzing the nature of motions filed and the court's rulings on them) lead to ambiguous or statistically unsupportable results.

In addition to the complexity of the cases themselves, a wide variety of logistical and mechanical hurdles arose, which created significant sources of delay, cost, and (most important) unusable data. The following are some of the more important such problems:

1. Docket sheets (which are essential as guides to the case files) are kept in the courthouses; the rest of the case files are kept in Federal Records Centers, generally 15 to 20 miles away.

2. Case file is completely missing, whereabouts unknown.

3. Important parts of files are missing, such as opinions or complaints.

4. Files may be unavailable when requested because (a) they are in judges' chambers, (b) their files are in circuit court, (c) they are in transit (the 15 to 20 mile "transit" from the courthouse to the Federal Records Center often takes several months, particularly in New York), or (d) they are kept under seal.

5. Many of the Federal Records Centers provide little space to work.

6. Files must be requested 24 to 48 hours in advance; if work proceeds slowly, unfinished cases must be returned at the end of the day and a new request filed, with attendant delays.

7. Photocopying in Federal Records Centers costs $.50 per page and often requires a long wait. (In some instances we paid for an outside service to bring in its own machine, set up, and make the copies.)

8. Cases are not stored by docket number but by an unrelated "accession" number, which must be separately looked up and which contains errors.

9. There is no standardization to the "shorthand" used by court clerks to describe motions, rulings, and the like; the resulting variations, plus frequent typing errors, make interpretation difficult.

The net result of the survey of court records was partial or complete information for 2,554 cases, which were classified roughly into 1,946 "individual" cases and 613 cases that were subsequently grouped into multidistrict litigation (MDLs).

Not all information on each case was equally available. Basic "vital statistics" about the filing of a suit were almost always available, but information about some of the subsequent history was often incomplete or missing altogether. Many topics, such as the parties' sizes and lines of business, were simply not well covered in the court documents. Some cases were filed and then apparently abandoned by the parties. Others were settled or dismissed on stipulation with relatively little information surfacing in the public record. Table 2.2 gives, as a rough indication, an index of the completeness with which the ten pages of the questionnaire were filled out.

Table 2.2 Court questionnaire completeness

Page	Subject matter	Completion index[a]
1	Civil cover sheet information	96.5
2	Parties and lines of business	68.5
3	Counterclaims; business relationship	72.4
4	Products/markets at issue; statutes	81.1
5	Alleged practices; damages and relief	74.4
6	Measures of litigation effort	79.2
7	Motions, counterclaims, and dismissals	31.1
8	Outcomes and awards	19.6
9–10	Appeals, settlements, costs, and comments	20.3

a. Index is the number of responses divided by the total number that would have occurred if all information had been fully available. These indexes should be used only as a rough guide, however, as many questions would be left blank in the normal course of events. For example, a case with no appeals to higher courts would show a low "completeness" rating for pages 9–10.

Collection of Information from Parties and Lawyers

Court files capture only the official portions of a lawsuit's history. They reveal little about the amounts of money spent for lawyers' fees and other expenses, and they often explicitly exclude information about the nature of settlements. To gain information about these aspects of private suits, CRI sent a two-page questionnaire to all locatable parties or their attorneys in all cases for which usable court information had been gathered.[4] In total, this represented 9,049 requests, or about 4.4 parties per case.

As with the court records survey, a series of mechanical and logistical hurdles was encountered, of which the following were most important:

1. Law firm names that have changed or named partners that have established independent firms.

2. Companies that have been merged into larger corporations.

3. Law firms or companies that are no longer locatable (e.g., either out of business or absorbed into other entities).

4. Names misspelled, particularly for lawyers, sometimes creating ambiguity with other attorneys with similar names.

5. Lack of standardization in case names and "shorthand" designations used by the courts, requiring separate lookups and prompting some puzzled telephone calls from survey recipients.

The requests were mailed from January through mid-March of 1985, and most responses had been received by the end of June, though a few responses continued to arrive as late as early 1986.[5] A total of 609 mail responses were received in time for tabulation, but many of them indicated only that the information was unavailable or would not be disclosed. After subtracting these responses plus duplicates and other unusable information, the number of usable responses remaining was 315.

As with the court questionnaire, not all items on this survey were answered with the same frequency. In general, the questions about numbers of lawyers and measures of company effort were answered most often, and questions about fees and particularly about settlements were often left unanswered.

Possible Sources of Error or Bias in the Surveys

Any survey as comprehensive and complex as this one is subject to possible errors and bias. The largest source of error, we believe, was the study's size, which required participation by many people and therefore introduced the possibility of variability in their work. Extensive efforts were made, however, to train the 26 paralegals who gathered the information from court records and to standardize their approach to the raw data.

A second source of variability arose at the stage of coding the court questionnaires for computer entry. Again, however, extensive efforts were made to standardize and to review and edit the data.

Because cases take several years to be resolved, cases filed toward the end of the sample period will have less information than cases filed earlier. In New York this pattern was exacerbated by a particularly large number of 1982 and 1983 cases for which the files were missing, in judges' chambers, or in transit to the Federal Records Center. The sample includes only 11 out of 152 cases that were fied in New York during those two years.

The mail survey to lawyers and parties was also subject to variability because respondents could misunderstand questions or arrive at different interpretations of some items, such as antitrust compliance programs. However, the questions were kept brief and straightforward to help avoid such difficulties, and the responses do not suggest any particular problems with the questions.

Another possible bias in the mail survey is the relative weighting that is given to responses from defendants, who responded in slightly greater proportion than plaintiffs, and from parties or attorneys who participated in multiple suits. One company, for example, provided responses to 18 suits, and to the extent that these suits were not representative of a cross section of the sample, the survey results could contain a bias.

2.2 A Summary Review of the Cases

With 174 possible items of information about each case on the court questionnaire and 21 separable items on the lawyers' survey, a thorough description of the data in this brief chapter is not practicable. Instead, in this section, we shall "browse" through the data, so that readers can gain a feel for the nature of the cases. In the next section we shall focus on a few, selected aspects of the cases in more detail. (*Except where noted, all of the following discussion excludes MDL cases.* These cases are highly situational in nature and by their sheer size would overshadow the general patterns.)

General Information
Information from the civil cover sheets of the cases is presented in table 2.3. The balance among districts matches more or less the proportion of suits filed in these districts. The heaviest weights among years filed was in the mid-1970s, reflecting the higher intensity of private antitrust litigation during those years and the unavailability of case files from the most recent years.

By far the majority of these cases were original proceedings, and their reason for being in federal court was their antitrust aspect. Class actions were demanded in 14 percent of the cases and juries in 59 percent. Interventions by third parties were rare.

On average there were 2.2 named plaintiffs and 5.0 named defendants. Proper interpretation of these numbers, however, requires some adjustments, such as the listing in some suits of companies and their officers separately. We found in preparing the lawyers' survey that there were, on average, 4.4 parties per case (versus the 7.2 parties suggested by the civil cover sheet listings).

One concern in the responses to the lawyers' survey was an evident bias in favor of defendants and in favor of larger cases. Only 26 percent of the responses came from the plaintiffs' side of the cases, whereas a random sampling based on the preceding numbers of parties per case would suggest 31 percent. Also, it was evident in reading the names of the parties who responded that large cases were somewhat overrepresented (on both sides).

Parties and Nature of Suit
Table 2.4 summarizes ten major characteristics of the parties and of the suits. One striking observation from this exhibit is the wide disparity in sizes between plaintiffs and defendants, more than 100 : 1. Only 27 cases in the sample included this information for both sides of the same case, but

Table 2.3 Civil cover sheet information

A. Districts ($N = 1,946$)

Atlanta	7%
Chicago	29%
Kansas City	5%
New York	34%
San Francisco	25%

B. Year filed

Year filed	Number of cases	Fraction of sample
72	4	0.2%
73	204	10.5
74	211	10.8
75	207	10.6
76	230	11.8
77	220	11.3
78	189	9.7
79	162	8.3
80	133	6.8
81	168	8.6
82	107	5.5
83	111	5.7
		100.0%

C. Jurisdiction

Federal question	87%
Diversity of citizenship	4%
Other, or no information	9%

D. Origin

Original proceeding	86%
Removed from state court	3%
Transferred from another district	2%
Other/no information	9%

E. Diversity of citizenship

Plaintiffs	4%
Defendants	6%

F. Jury demand

By plaintiff	59%
By defendant	2%

G. Class action demand

By Plaintiff	14%

H. Number of named

	Plaintiffs	Defendants
1	68%	32%
2	16%	18%
3	5%	14%
4	3%	7%
5	2%	5%
6–10	3%	12%
Over 10	3%	12%

I. Number of interventions

Plaintiff side	Defendant side	Other
1.5%	2.1%	3%

Table 2.4 Parties and nature of suit

A. Sizes of the parties

	Plaintiffs	Defendants
Number for which size was given	70	166
Median annual sales	$1,000,000	$230,000,000
Average annual sales	$27,600,000[a]	$2,865,700,000

B. Was this a countersuit?

Yes   2.4%

C. Business relationship of plaintiff to defendant

	Primary	Secondary
Competitor	30%	7%
Dealer, agent, distributor	25	3
(of which, terminated distributor)	(10%)	
Corporate customer	10	3
Final customer	8	1
Licensee	4	3
Supplier	3	2
Stockholder, employee	3	1
Other	5	1
Insufficient information	12	—

D. Geographic markets at issue (where specified)

United States	41%	
U.S. region	19	
Pacific	13%	
East north central	12	
Mid-Atlantic	10	(Includes multiple mentions)
South Atlantic	5	
Other	6	
Specific metropolitan area	16	
Specific state	15	
Specific country	4	
Worldwide	3	
Other	5	

E. Antitrust statutes allegedly violated

Sherman Act, section 1	75%	
Sherman Act, section 2	47	
Sherman Act, unspecified	7	
Clayton Act, section 2	18	
Clayton Act, section 3	11	(Includes multiple mentions)
Clayton Act, section 7	6	
Clayton Act, other or unspecified	33	
Other antitrust statutes	14	
Nonantitrust statutes (e.g., contract)	19	
Antitrust not a significant issue in the opinion of the paralegals	22	(Overlaps above mentions)

Table 2.4 (continued)

F. Alleged illegal practices

	Primary	Secondary
Horizontal price fixing	17%	6%
(of which, "naked cartel")	(0.6)	
Refusal to deal	14	11
Exclusive dealing or tying	12	10
Price discrimination	8	9
Vertical price fixing or squeeze	5	5
Dealer termination	5	4
Other horizontal offenses		
(e.g., merger, predation, asset accumulation)	13	16
Other vertical offenses		
(e.g., vertical price discrimination resale price maintenance)	3	4
Other	12	18
Missing information, indeterminate	11	—

G. Year alleged practices began (if given)

1965 or earlier	9%
1966–1970	16
1971–1975	38
1976–1980	31
1981–1983	6

H. Damages claimed in the complaint

Number that named a specific amount	815
Median amount	$945,161
Average amount	$26,959,000

I. Other relief requested

Cease and desist from joint action	32%
"injunctive relief" (unspecified)	14
Requirement of dealing	5
Attorneys fees	5
Change in dealers' restrictions	5
Treble damages	5
Pricing changes	5
Costs	4
Other (wide range)	15

Table 2.4 (continued)

J. Industries of the parties

	Plaintiffs	Defendants
Agriculture, mining, construction	2.9%	1.8%
Automobile, retail or wholesale	2.9	—
Automobile manufacturing	0.6	2.1
Business services	3.2	3.2
Chemicals	1.7	4.3
Electrical, electronic equipment	1.6	4.3
Entertainment	4.1	3.6
Finance, insurance, real estate	4.3	6.3
Foods and beverages	8.8	7.9
Franchising	0.4	3.3
Governments	1.7	0.8
Households, individuals	4.4	—
Manufacturing, n.e.c. (diverse)	13.8	23.4
Membership organizations	0.9	3.9
Oil and gas extraction, refining, distribution	3.8	3.8
Retailing	—	3.4
Services (wide variety)	5.2	3.4
Transportation, utilities, communication	5.3	5.9
Wholesaling	11.4	5.7
Other and unknown	14.2	12.9

a. Excluding two firms at $10 billion (L. M. Ericsson) and $18 billion (Mobil Oil Corp.).

that small group tends to confirm the *David* v. *Goliath* pattern suggested by the overall averages. (The average ratio among the 27 cases was over 300 : 1.) Also a reading of parties' names further confirms the widely held notion that plaintiffs usually are small companies and defendants large ones.

The United States, or large parts of it, was the geographic market at issue in most suits, and the product markets spanned a wide range.

Horizontal price fixing was the most common allegation, in 17 percent of the cases, although a broad range of other offenses were also mentioned. Compared with popular perceptions, a relatively small number of cases involved dealer terminations—only 5 percent. However, a closer reading of the case materials suggest that *partial* terminations—in such forms as denying certain product lines or use of certain trademarks —may be a more frequent cause of action. These cases most often alleged refusal to deal, exclusive dealing, or patent/trademark/franchising issues.

Measures of Litigation Effort

Although there is a widespread notion that antitrust cases are more expensive and complex than most litigation, a significant portion of them are, in fact, relatively modest in their costs and amounts of formal litigation activity. Table 2.5 presents summary information on twelve measures of litigation effort. Some important highlights supporting this observation are as follows:

1. The typical thickness of case files was less than three inches; only 3 percent of the cases exceeded 36 inches.

2. a substantial majority of cases was handled by a litigation team (per client) of only one or two lawyers with no help from paralegals, economists, or other consultants.

3. The average amount of time spent by companies' executives on the cases (if mentioned at all) was only about 30 hours.

4. Typical costs (per client) were about $48,000 for lawyers' fees and other disbursements. (Because of a suspected bias in survey responses, this number is probably higher than a full cross section would show.)

A comparison of formal litigation activity between plaintiffs and defendants tends to show a slight leaning toward more activity by plaintiffs:

1. The average litigation cost per client reported by plaintiffs was $109,000 versus $45,000 for defendants.

2. Among plaintiffs who chose to record depositions, the average number was 4.2 depositions versus 3.2 depositions noticed by defendants.

3. Similarly, among parties who recorded interrogatories or requests for documents, plaintiffs issued slightly more than did defendants.

As with many economic phenomena there tended to be a concentration of activity in a small, select group of cases. As mentioned earlier, 3 percent of the cases had over 36 inches of case pleadings, but these 3 percent of cases had almost 10 percent of all pleadings. In the lawyers' survey the top 10 percent of cases represented 66 percent of all parties' costs reported.

Intermediate Outcomes during the Suits

Table 2.6 summarizes several indicators of formal litigation activity that occurred as the cases proceeded toward resolution. The most significant of these were voluntary withdrawals and dismissals of parties that occurred in almost half of the cases. Most of these dismissals were granted in conjunction with settlements. The incidence of partial dismissals (e.g., one defendant among several) was relatively rare in these non-MDL cases.

Table 2.5 Measures of litigation effort

A. Number of docket entries

1–10	12.8%	
11–20	15.8%	
21–30	12.8%	
30–40	11.5%	
41–50	7.3%	
51–100	18.2%	
101–200	13.0%	
Over 200	8.6%	3 cases exceeded 1,000 entries
Average	72.5	

B. Thickness of case file

Under 3 inches	50%
3–12 inches	36%
Under 12–36 inches	11%
Over 36 inches	3%

C. Number of amendments to the complaint

None	72%
1	22%
2	4%
3 or more	2%

D. Depositions recorded in the docket[a]

	Plaintiffs	Defendants
None	48%	49%
1	12%	17%
2	7%	9%
3–5	13%	13%
6–10	9%	6%
Over 10	11%	7%
Average	4.2	3.2

E. Interrogatories by[a]

	Plaintiffs	Defendants
None	46%	48%
1	27%	28%
2	14%	11%
3–5	10%	9%
Over 5	3%	3%

F. Request for production of documents by[a]

	Plaintiffs	Defendants
None	43%	51%
1	30%	28%
2	13%	10%
3–5	10%	8%
Over 5	4%	2%

Table 2.5 (continued)

G. Litigation team size (from lawyers' survey)

1 lawyer	18.2%
2 lawyers	36.5%
3–5 lawyers	38.3%
6+	6.9%

H. Others on litigation team (from lawyers' survey)

Accountants	8.4%
Economists	10.6%
Paralegals	25.6%
Consultants	5.3%

I. Executive participation (from 142 cases of any participation)

1 person deposed	30%
2	24%
3–5	30%
6+	17%
Average	3.2
1 person testified	12%
2	8%
3–5	8%
6+	1%
Average	0.7

J. Hours of executive time (225 mentions of any significant time—from lawyers' survey)

0–25 hours	43%
26–50 hours	18%
51–100 hours	20%
101–200 hours	13%
Over 200 hours (up to 5,000)	6%
Case occupied board time	23 instances

Inside litigation team (79 mentions of any inside team)

1 lawyer	76%
2 or more	24%
Included paralegals	30%
Included clericals	37%

K. Parties' costs (where costs are given)

	Plaintiffs	Defendants
$0–5,000	18%	9%
5,001–10,000	4%	7%
10,001–20,000	7%	16%
20,001–50,000	15%	22%
50,001–100,000	4%	18%
100,000–200,000	15%	10%
Over $200,000	37%	18%
Median	$109,000	$45,000

a. While practices seem to vary, depositions, document requests, and interrogatories are usually not entered into court records unless they are contested or placed in the record specifically for use in pleadings or at trial.

Table 2.6   Intermediate outcomes during litigation

A. Voluntary dismissals of

	Plaintiffs	Defendants
None	52%	50%
All on same side	48%	47%
One of several on same side	0.5%	3%

B. Motions for sanctions

Occurred in 6.2% of cases
Average sanction requested was $8,623.
Sanctions were granted or partly granted in 2.2% of cases

C. Number of court rulings by (other than scheduling and mechanics)

	Judges	Magistrates
None	5%	84%
1	33%	7%
2	23%	3%
3.5	24%	4%
Over 5	15%	2%

D. Pretrial motions[a]

	Plaintiff	Defendant
Summary judgment or involuntary dismissal		
Number filed	70	306
Percentage won	28%	61.1%
Lack of jurisdiction, improper jurisdiction, improper venue, or lack of standing		
Number filed	—	220
Percentage won	—	36.4%
Failure to state claim		
Number filed	24	323
Percentage won	29.2%	54.5%
Partial summary judgment, no substantial claim, or no issue of fact in dispute		
Number filed	45	145
Percentage won	15.6%	43.4%
Dismissal of counterclaim		
Number filed	21	—
Percentage won	33.3%	—

a. Some motions include multiple requests and are double-counted in this tabulation.
Percentage won includes motions that were partially granted.

Motions for summary judgment or dismissal for such reasons as lack of standing occurred in 11 percent of the cases. As table 2.6 shows, such motions originated most often with the defendants; moreover defendants tended to achieve more success with these motions than did plaintiffs.

Measures of Case Outcomes

As with other types of litigation, relatively few antitrust suits ever go to trial—only 5.4 percent in this sample. The rest were settled, dismissed, or disposed of on motions. Cases that did go to trial, however, reflected in their lengths the more complex nature of antitrust litigation. The median trial lasted 5.4 days, and the average was 11.4 days.

Table 2.7 presents six indicators of case outcomes, including a characterization of the outcome based on a synthesis of the case record. Settlements and pretrial stipulations and orders (which often represent settlements) accounted for a substantial majority of the known outcomes. Dismissals or withdrawals represented the next most frequent outcomes, and only a small fraction (4 percent of cases with known outcomes) resulted in judgment for plaintiffs.

In order to dig further into the cases that end by an action of the parties (settlements or stipulations and orders), we made several attempts to characterize the presettlement direction or drift of the case by examining motions, depositions, and similar factors. No clear answers emerged.

Awards, Settlements, and Other Relief

As can be seen in table 2.8, damage awards to plaintiffs occurred in 44 cases, or 2.3 percent of the sample. However, awards to defendants (usually on counterclaims) occurred in 29 cases (1.5 percent)—sometimes the same cases.

Relatively few settlements divulged their monetary terms—67 in all. Except for class actions, where the amounts were part of the official proceedings, most of the publicly recorded settlements were small. The median was approximately $24,000. Settlements disclosed in the confidential questionnaire were substantially larger, with a median of $50,000. Even at this level, however, the settlements were surprisingly small in relation to the damages claimed—in effect only a few percent.

2.3 Further Analysis of Costs and Payoffs

This section takes up in more detail the questions of how much parties spend and how much they receive from antitrust suits, using information

Table 2.7   Measures of case outcomes

A. Incidence of trials

Cases that reached trial   5.4%

Of these 106 trials, lengths were

1 or 2 days	22%
3–5 days	25%
6–10 days	24%
Over 10 days	30%

Average 11.4 days

Median 5.4 days

B. Judgments by the court

For plaintiffs	3.5%	3 cases were "some" plaintiffs
For all defendants	10.1%	
For some defendants	1.3%	

C. Basis for judgment

Motion	6.2%
Jury verdict	1.8%
Court trial	1.7%
Other	3.6%

D. Class action status (excludes MDL cases)

Requested	14%
Certified	3%
Certification status appealed	0.3%

E. Appeals (total number of appeals = 140)

Original ruling upheld fully	72%
Upheld in part	9%
Reversed without new trial	8%
Remanded	11%

F. Best characterization of case outcome

	Primary outcome	Secondary outcome
Pretrial stipulation and order	39%	8%
Settlement or settlement after judgment	11%	1%
Dismissed pretrial on motion, dismissal by court, or dismissal for other reasons	19%	4%
Judgment for all or some plaintiffs	3%	1%
Judgment for all or some defendants	6%	3%
Transferred, consolidated, or remanded to state court	8%	2%
Pending, or outcome otherwise unknown	9%	4%
Pretrial withdrawal	4%	1%
Other	1%	1%

Note: Some cases involved judgments for both sides.

Table 2.8   Court awards and other relief

A. Sizes of awards

	To plaintiffs	To defendants
Number of cash awards	44	29 predominantly on counterclaims
Average size	$380,903[a]	$291,946
Median size	$153,416	$50,894
Top 10 percent of awards	98% of total	78% of total

B. Other relief awarded

	Number of instances
Cease and desist from joint action	6
Access to patent or trademark	2
Changes in pricing	2
Reinstatement of dealer	2
Other (wide range)	27

C. Interest awarded

Number of awards   32   Amount usually not stated

D. Attorneys fees awarded

Number of awards	51[b]
Average amount	$166,239[c]
Median award	$24,160
Top 5 awards	74% of all awards

E. Costs awarded

Number of awards	196
Median award	$3,182
Average award	$9,954
Maximum award	$241,815
Top 13 awards	63% of all awards recorded

F. Settlements (from court records)

Number of cases with recorded settlements   254[d]   (11.5 percent of all cases)

Number with dollar amount revealed   67
Ranges from $−33,580[e] to $8.1 million

Median settlement	$23,997
Average settlement	$450,938

G. Settlements (to plaintiffs, from lawyers' survey)

0–10,000	26%
10,001–25,000	15%
25,001–50,000	14%
50,001–100,000	11%
100,001–300,000	12%
Over 300,000	23%
Median	$50,000
Maximum	$50 million

Table 2.8 (continued)

H. Settlements to defendants: (from lawyers' survey)	

Average = $442,000
Median = $35,000
Maximum = $2 million

I. Other settlement provisions (from lawyers' survey)

Price changes	5 mentions
Merger stopped	2
Patent access	5
Agreement to purchase/sell/etc.	14
Admission to trade association or league	4
Dismissal of lawsuit	80
Other, e.g., counterclaims dismissed	51

J. Factors leading to settlement (from lawyers' survey)

Evidence from discovery	81 mentions
Court rulings	55
Projected legal costs	89
Projected damages	46
Settlement of other parties	27

Note: The amounts shown are amounts paid or received at the time and are not adjusted for subsequent inflation.
a. Excluding one outlier of $276,000,000 (*Litton* v. *AT&T*).
b. Actually a total of 68 awards were made, some offsetting each other.
c. Excluding one outlier at $5.6 million.
d. Note that many dismissals and terminations also represent settlements.
e. Negative number indicates settlement or countersuit.

from the lawyers' survey linked with the court records for the same cases. This discussion will refer to *costs per party* and reflect the actual costs paid at the time. (We have not tried to adjust these costs for inflation.) In only a handful of instances did we receive responses from more than one party in the same case. Awards and settlements, in contrast, were most often reported *per side*, and always so in the court records.

Parties' Legal Costs

As with many other aspects of the sample, legal costs tended to be concentrated in a relatively small portion of the cases. Legal costs followed the classic "80-20 rule" familiar to economists—that is, the top 20 percent of the cases accounted for about 80 percent of all reported costs. (The top 10 percent of cases accounted for 66 percent of all costs, and their average cost per case was almost $1.3 million.) When these 20 percent top-spending cases are excluded, the average spending per party among the remaining 80 percent of cases was $48,500.

On average, plaintiffs reported slightly higher spending per party

Table 2.9   Average legal costs per party

	Plaintiffs	Defendants
Top 20 percent of cases	$737,300	$801,000
	(5)	(30)
Remaining 80 percent of cases	$83,900	$41,500
	(22)	(120)

($205,000) than did defendants ($195,000). When adjusted for the larger average number of defendants, however, most of the reported costs in these suits were spent by the defense side. Although the sample sizes are small, table 2.9 indicates that plaintiffs spent more per party in the smaller cases, but defendants spent more in the largest cases.

The pattern of legal costs by district revealed that costs in New York were more than 60 percent above the overall average. New York cases represented a disproportionate share (more than half) of the high-spending group. When legal costs were classified by defendant's industry, oil and gas cases cost more than twice the overall average. (This was not a "New York" effect, as the frequency of survey responses from oil and gas cases in New York was about average.)

A final comparison of legal costs relates to the nature of alleged offense. Although many observers associate such issues as predatory pricing and horizontal price fixing with "big" antitrust cases, vertical price fixing and exclusive dealing emerged in this sample as the most costly suits to pursue. Such a pattern might result from a tendency of defendants to settle horizontal price-fixing cases earlier than they settle other kinds of cases.

Plaintiffs' Awards and Settlements

The size of plaintiffs' awards and settlements tended to increase with the time duration of the case. In cases that lasted over four years and a payment was received, the average payment was almost $600,000. By contrast, in cases that lasted less than six months, the average payment was less than $100,000. This is a predictable pattern, since one would not expect parties on either side of a lawsuit to pursue the case for a long time if the stakes were small in proportion to the cost.

Similarly there were larger payoffs to plaintiffs in cases with larger numbers of defendants: payments of almost $600,000 in cases with five or more defendants, but payments of less than $200,000 in cases with one defendant. By way of contrast, no consistent pattern was found for payoffs according to numbers of plaintiffs.

The classification of average payoffs to plaintiffs according to defendants industry revealed that plaintiffs tended to receive much higher payments—more than twice the average payoff—when the defendant was in manufacturing. Either U.S. manufacturers are guilty of more severe antitrust violations than firms in other sectors, or there is something in the litigation process that leads to their paying larger awards and settlements than other firms. One explanation, of course, is the "deeper pockets" theory, but the number of firms for which we had annual sales was too small to permit any efforts at a direct correlation.

Finally, the average payoffs to plaintiffs classified by nature of offense or statute allegedly violated showed that horizontal price fixing and Sherman Act violations yielded above average payments.

2.4 Summary

The Georgetown project has produced a rich set of empirical data, against which many hypotheses can be tested. However, this brief review has also shown that, like many empirical studies, examination of evidence tends to stimulate as many new questions about antitrust litigation as it answers.

In concluding, we offer two observations that relate to the study as a whole. First, in some respects there are indications of a "two-tiered market" in private antitrust litigation. As we noted at the outset, this discussion has excluded MDL cases because, in size and many other respects, they appear to be a world apart. Even within these non-MDL cases, the high degree of concentration of spending and payoffs suggests that justice is far more costly—or rewarding—for a select few parties than for the majority.

Second, the legal profession is not an easy environment in which to conduct research. We have already noted some of the obstacles in assembling a coherent picture of cases from court records. But, further, the response to the lawyers' survey was disappointingly small. Despite its ABA endorsement, plus telephone calls and follow-ups, this survey drew only a 3.5 percent usable response. Policy research would be greatly facilitated if ways could be found to gain better support from the rank and file of the profession.

Notes

1. The designation of nature of suit, for purposes of recording in the AOUSC files, is made by the local clerk of the court at the time a suit is filed. To the extent the clerks erred in these classifications, or judged wrongly on ambiguous suits, the sample could contain suits that were not really antitrust cases and omit some that were. As a cross-check, we asked the paralegals who conducted much of the field work in this study for their independent assess-

ment of whether the suit was truly an antitrust case. Although 22 percent of the sample involved nonantitrust matters "dressed up" as antitrust by plaintiffs, only a handful of cases proved to be true misclassifications.

2. The law firms and corporate legal departments that donated paralegal time are listed at the end of this volume.

3. The questionnaire that the paralegals filled out is available from the author or the editor.

4. The questionnaire is available from the author or the editor.

5. One month after the initial mailing, a follow-up request was sent to all recipients who had not yet responded.

Commentary on the Data Base of the Georgetown Study

Thomas J. Campbell

The Irresistability of Drawing Some Conclusions from Numbers

It is frequently in the nature of a researcher to analyze whatever data are available. Occasionally, however, the data are insufficient in number and quality to allow statistically significant conclusions. In such a situation the appropriate application of statistical tests for reliability will indicate to a reader that the results under study could have occurred by chance. Certain parameters are set in advance for how unlikely an event must be before we are willing to reject the possibility that it was the product of chance. A common standard is 1 chance in 20, or 5 percent.

However, this approach is often ignored in the application of social science to law. Following a rule much like "admitting evidence for whatever probative value it may have," lawyers have a tendency to rely on "point estimates" in empirical research. It is too hard to admit that the evidence gathered in an empirical study may simply not offer us reliable bases for conclusions. Such an admission would run contrary to lawyers' instinct that surely the evidence must be worth *something*. But it often is not.

The foregoing is a plea for statistical rigor in working with the Georgetown data base. Too many statements in the papers, and virtually all of the discussion, ignored this plea. I urge the reader of any of the papers presented in this volume to pause at any statistical conclusion that is presented and ask whether the author has provided an adequate confidence level for that conclusion. I now turn to specific points where the statistical warrant may have fallen a bit short of the conclusions suggested.

The Small Numbers Problem

The Georgetown data base was drawn from two sources: a search through dockets, and questionnaires to antitrust litigants. The former produced 1,946 usable cases; the latter 315. In order to perform any analysis, these numbers must be broken down into categories, and it is there that the problem of inadequate sample size surfaces.

For example, of the 1,946 cases, only 19.6 percent reported information on outcomes and awards. If a researcher is analyzing these approximately

380 cases according to some criterion with, say, five categories (e.g., manufacturing, distribution, transportation, financial, other), the numbers in each category may well become too few to allow reliable distinctions between group averages. Thus, whereas 1,946 cases sounds like a large number, they may well be too few to answer a question such as, do awards tend to be higher in distribution than in manufacturing?

A small numbers problem surfaces in many other areas as well. There are 254 recorded settlements, of which only 67 have dollar amounts. Only 106 cases went to full trial. Once again, each category becomes even thinner when meaningful subclassifications are attempted.

Subcategories containing small numbers of cases (the "small cell size" problem, in statistical jargon) are common in this data base. Yet the Salop-White and Teplitz papers continually provide data and draw conclusions without considering sample size or statistical significance. For example, consider the Salop-White statement, "In the remaining 84 cases [of those that went to trial], plaintiffs prevailed in 28 cases (33 percent)." This is a correct characterization of *this* sample, with 84 data points. What does it tell us about who wins antitrust in general? To establish a 95 percent confidence interval around 33 percent, with 84 observations, we would have to be willing to go as low as 23 percent or as high as 43 percent. Suppose Salop-White had said, "of final judgments at trial, as many as 43 percent might be for the plaintiff." Would that not have sent a very different message to the reader? Yet it is an equally valid statement from the data reported.

There are two solutions. The first is to demand of every paper analyzing these data, whether in this symposium or in subsequent years, that confidence intervals be provided around all point estimates. This suggestion, I know, will not be followed. Having made the initial caveats, researchers will continue to rely on point estimates, "for what they are worth." The 33 percent plaintiffs' victory figure will remain in the reader's minds, not the confidence interval from 23 percent to 44 percent.

The second suggestion is to obtain more data. It is a tired stereotype of doctoral dissertations to conclude with a call for more data. But if the Georgetown study were to be doubled, preferably by recourse to dockets from different districts, virtually all of the small numbers problems I have been identifying would be resolved. Hence this is not a call to obtain all information potentially relevant—the dream of any social science researcher. It is a narrower request that if the present Georgetown study were to be replicated, much more powerful conclusions could be drawn.

Biases

Adequacy in numbers of cases is a separate problem from the representativeness of those cases that were reported. This latter problem surfaces most directly with the information obtained from the survey of litigants. I suspect that parties asked to assist in a survey of information dealing with the treble damage remedy in antitrust will know that the information will likely be used to lower the damage multiple or leave it alone. Increasing to quadruple damages is not in the offing. Plaintiffs therefore would have no incentive to assist in the creation of this data base. It is no surprise that defendants answered the survey far more frequently than plaintiffs, as Teplitz explicitly observes.

A separate point compounds this problem. The preponderant majority of cases from the litigants' survey involves cases in which only one side, usually defendant, have replied. Given the fact that the parties knew the uses to which this survey would be put, information from one side alone simply should not be trusted. Plaintiffs have an incentive to give information indicating the present system is working well; defendants have an incentive to give information that the present system is fraught with delay, expense, and unfairness. Each side has an incentive to distort. Unless we disregard cases in which only one side has replied, there is no adequate check against this risk.

A less draconian response would be to trust information only in neutral categories, where there was no obvious reason to distort. The problem is to define what is truly neutral. The size of the defendant firm might appear to be a neutral fact; yet, if one anticipates the likely political arguments in favor of detrebling, defendants might prefer to portray themselves as smaller rather than larger. Contrary arguments could also be constructed: showing antitrust defendants to be large could substantiate the description that treble damages leads to harrassment of large companies simply because they are large. That there are potentially conflicting biases, however, does not guarantee that they will cancel each other and produce a single body of accurate information. It only guarantees that the results are not trustworthy.

An alternative suggestion would be to accept only counterintuitive results drawn from the survey data. For example, consider the reported information on costs. Salop-White note that defendants did not incur significantly greater costs than did plaintiffs. All of the defendants' incentives would be to report exceptionally *high* costs to defending antitrust actions. Hence this result seems contrary to defendants' bias. Even this conclusion is not free from doubt, because of the bias of plaintiffs. Plaintiffs could have been engaged in strategizing on their own. A finding that antitrust litigation was costlier for plaintiffs than for defendants would defuse one major argument against detrebling. Hence plaintiffs would also have an incentive to exaggerate their costs. Possibly they were bolder in doing so than defendants, and that strategem, rather than the truth, yielded the observed result. The problem is simply that one cannot assume the subjects of the survey were ignorant of the uses to which it would be put.

Ambiguous Categorization

As paralegals went through dockets, they were asked to categorize claims according to a list of 12 types. Four of these categories contained conjunctions: "horizontal price-fixing *and* market allocation by horizontal competitors," "asset accumulation *or* patent accumulation," "exclusive dealing *or* tying," "vertical price fixing *or* squeeze" (emphasis added).

I see no need for conjunctions. Could not four additional categories have been added, so that each category would be relatively unambiguous? The latter two examples show the danger of the combinations that were used. A researcher without access to the underlying docket sheets would have no idea whether a case involved a vertical price fix or a vertical price squeeze. Yet these are substantially different forms of conduct. The former violates Sherman, section 1, and, with the modifications from *Monsanto Co. v. Spray-Rite Service Corp.*, 104 S. Ct. 1464 (1984), remains per se illegal. The latter violates Sherman, section 2, but only in those instances where market power exists, so that monopolization can be shown. The rule of reason applies. Both are worth study—but not together.

The allocation of costs in the presence of a counterclaim is another source of ambiguity. Antitrust counterclaims were to be recorded as separate suits. Yet cost data, either from the dockets or from the litigant survey, were not segregated between the case in chief and the counterclaim.

Another example is settlement information. The victor in a settlement is inherently difficult to ascertain. Reliance on the motion that accompanied a settlement is not valid, since victories for either side will often be manifest in a stipulated motion to dismiss with prejudice. One suggestion is to consult the trial judge or magistrate familiar with the progress of discovery and preliminary motions in an antitrust case. Such a source might provide an objective view of whether the settlement, when it came, represented a victory for plaintiff or defendant. At the least one ought not to depend on information from only one side. My previous comments about the danger of relying on survey data from only one side are equally applicable when dealing with who won a settlement.

Conclusion

In the foregoing, I have raised some criticisms. My criticisms are pointed only because I see lawyers and economists already succumbing to the temptation to rely on the data beyond their validity. This should not mask my fundamental judgment that the Georgetown project was professionally conducted and constitutes the most meaningful contribution ever to available antitrust data.

Also, since I am hopeful that additional data might be gathered, I offer a few specific suggestions for improving the quality of what is collected and reported. My recommendations are as follows:

1. Rely on no point estimates. Insist on confidence intervals in all uses of these data.

2. Collect more data. Doubling the size of this data base would likely eliminate the problems stemming from small cell sizes.

3. Reject any survey data derived from litigants unless answers are obtained from both sides of the same case.

4. Eliminate ambiguous multiple element categories in the recording of all data. If a category presently reads, "*A* or *B*," replace it with two categories, "*A*" and "*B*." The researcher can later combine the two if that is deemed desirable.

5. In the collection of any additional data, invest more time in acquainting paralegals with the common practices of antitrust litigation.

6. Explore the possibility of running a control on the reported settlement information by comparing the litigants' views of who prevailed with that of the presiding judge or magistrate.

Detrebling versus Decoupling Antitrust Damages: Lessons from the Theory of Enforcement

A. Mitchell Polinsky

One of the most talked about ideas in antitrust policy during the past several years is the notion of "detrebling" private antitrust damages.[1] This concept has several variations. Sometimes it refers to a mandatory reduction of treble damages to single damages for certain types of private antitrust actions (e.g., suits against joint research ventures), and other times it refers to a discretionary reduction of the damage multiplier on a case by case basis. For purposes of this comment the critical feature of all of the detrebling proposals is that the plaintiff receives what the defendant pays.[2]

In sharp contrast to the attention given to detrebling is the almost complete absence of consideration given to the concept of "decoupling" antitrust damages. Decoupling refers to a system of liability in which the plaintiff receives something different than what the defendant pays. For example, the defendant might pay treble damages, with the plaintiff's receiving only single damages (the difference being collected by the government). To my knowledge, the concept of decoupling antitrust damages was first proposed by Warren Schwartz in an article in the *Georgetown Law Journal* in 1980,[3] and then was completely ignored until it received brief mention in the paper by Salop and White, chapter 1 in this volume.

The principal message of this comment is that the emphasis in antitrust policy discussions on detrebling—to the virtual exclusion of decoupling—is misplaced. I will argue, using the principles of the economic theory of enforcement, that there is a stronger case in favor of decoupling. I will also show, contrary to the presumption of Schwartz and of Salop and White, that the optimal system of decoupling may require that the plaintiff receive more, rather than less, than what the defendant pays.[4]

In the first part of the comment, the economic theory of enforcement is briefly reviewed. Then, in the second part, the lessons of the theory for choosing between detrebling and decoupling, and for the optimal design of the decoupling system, are discussed. In the final part of the comment, some remaining questions that need to be addressed before decoupling can be recommended in practice are mentioned.

The Economic Theory of Enforcement

The modern theory of enforcement began with a seminal paper by Gary Becker on crime and punishment.[5] Becker's theory, which assumes that the government does the enforcing, is easily explained. (In summarizing Becker's reasoning, I will refer to firms, although the same logic can be applied to individuals). Suppose firms obtain some gain from engaging in an activity that imposes costs on others. Examples of such activities include polluting the air, evading taxes, and attempting to monopolize an industry. If it were costless for the public enforcement authority to catch or observe firms when they engage in a harm-creating activity, presumably every firm would be caught and fined an amount equal to the external cost of the activity. Firms then would engage in the activity only if their private benefits exceed the external cost. And, from society's perspective, such behavior would be efficient.

However, in most situations it is difficult or costly for the enforcement authority to catch firms that impose external costs. If as a result firms are not always caught, they would engage in the harm-creating activity too often unless they were made to pay more than the harm caused when they *are* caught. Then, according to Becker's theory, the fine could be raised to a level such that, as before, firms would engage in the activity only if their private gains exceed the external cost. Since this outcome can be achieved for any given probability of catching firms and since it is costlier to catch a larger fraction of those engaging in the activity, Becker argued that the enforcement authority should set the probability very low and the fine correspondingly high.[6] This low probability/high fine combination characterizes the optimal system of public enforcement.

In a subsequent paper Becker and George Stigler suggested that a system of competitive private enforcement—in which the first individual or firm to discover and report the violation would receive the fine—could duplicate the outcome under optimal public enforcement.[7] This suggestion was quickly challenged by William Landes and Richard Posner.[8] Landes and Posner claimed that private enforcement would lead to too much enforcement relative to optimal public enforcement.[9] Their intuitive explanation was based on the following observations. Under public enforcement, if detection were certain, the fine should be set equal to the external damage caused by the activity. By raising the fine and lowering the probability of detection, the same level of deterrence can be achieved at less cost. Under private enforcement, however, they pointed out that raising the fine would lead to a *higher* probability of detection because self-interested private enforcers would be induced to invest more in enforcement. From this observation they concluded that a private system of enforcement would lead to "overenforcement."[10]

In a paper following this exchange, I showed that Becker and Stigler's hypothesis (that private enforcement could duplicate the public enforcement outcome) might be wrong for a different reason than that identified by Landes and Posner.[11] The main point of my paper was that private enforcement would lead in a wide range of circumstances to *too little* enforcement relative to optimal public enforcement.[12] This result, which tends to occur when the external damage from the violation is large, can be explained as follows.

Under private enforcement, individuals or firms are willing to invest in enforcement only if they at least break even—that is, only if their fine revenue is at least as great as their enforcement costs. Under public enforcement, however, the optimal probability/fine combination may result in fine revenue that is less than enforcement costs. This is particularly likely to occur when the damage from the violation is large since it is then optimal to deter most, if not all, potential violators. Because the fine that can be imposed is limited (by the net worth of the potential violators), optimal public enforcement may require a high probability of detection and correspondingly large enforcement costs. But if most potential violators are deterred and the fine that can be obtained from those who are not is limited, the fine revenue collected by the public enforcement authority may well be less than the cost of enforcement. If so, private enforcers would not be willing to invest enough in enforcement to achieve the same level of deterrence as under public enforcement since they would not be able to break even. In other words, a private system of enforcement could lead to "underenforcement."

This summarizes the principal results in the economic theory of enforcement that are relevant to the present discussion.

Lessons from the Theory

There are two lessons that I wish to draw from the theory of enforcement, one concerning the choice between detrebling and decoupling, and the other relating to the optimal design of a decoupling system.

Detrebling versus Decoupling

One of the principal conclusions of the theory was that if private enforcers receive the fine paid by the injurer, it is generally impossible to achieve the optimal combination of the probability of detection and the fine. If the same fine is used as under optimal public enforcement, the resulting probability of detection (generated by the self-interested choices of private enforcers) may be too high or too low. In other words, if the enforcing is done privately, there may be too much or too little enforcement. The same conclusion applies to private damage actions in antitrust law since, under the current system, the plaintiff generally receives what the defendant pays.[13]

Advocates of detrebling presumably believe that awarding successful plaintiffs three times their damages induces them and their lawyers to invest too much in the detection and prosecution of antitrust violations. The only way to reduce enforcement under the present system is to reduce the damage multiplier.[14] However, as the discussion of the theory of enforcement makes clear, this response may not be the cheapest way to attain the desired level of deterrence. It may be socially preferable to raise, not lower, the amount paid by the defendant while reducing the incentives for plaintiffs and their lawyers to invest in enforcement. If antitrust damages are decoupled, the lower level of deterrence that is desired can be achieved more cheaply by awarding the plaintiff less than what the defendant pays.

It should be stressed, however, that the advantage of decoupling over detrebling does not depend on whether it is desirable to reduce the level of deterrence from that currently generated by treble damages. The reasoning behind this conclusion is essentially the same as that used in the previous paragraphs, specifically, that the decoupling approach can attain the same level of deterrence as any damage multiplier, but wish a lower probability of detection and therefore with lower enforcement costs. The details of the argument follow.

First, select the best possible damage multiplier in a system in which the plaintiff receives what the defendant pays. This multiplier could be less than or greater than three. Whatever the multiplier is, it will generate some probability of detection as a result of the investment incentives of private enforcers.

Now consider a system of decoupled damages. Under this system, raise the amount paid by the defendant from the level determined by the best damage multiplier.[15] If the plaintiff still were to receive the same amount as under the damage multiplier approach, the level of deterrence would be higher in the decoupled system because the probability of detection would be the same but the defendant would be paying more. Therefore, without changing what the defendant pays (from the now higher level), reduce the amount awarded to the plaintiff until the resulting probability of detection falls to a level such that the defendant is deterred to the same degree under both systems.

It is now easy to see why the decoupling approach is superior to the damage multiplier approach. Each approach can achieve the desired level of deterrence of antitrust violations. But the decoupling approach can attain this level of deterrence with a lower probability of detection, and therefore with lower enforcement costs. Thus, *regardless of whether it is desirable to lower, raise, or leave unchanged the present damage multiplier of three, the decoupling approach is preferable to the damage multiplier approach.*

Optimal Decoupling

Because of the focus on *reducing* private antitrust enforcement by detrebling antitrust damages, it is not surprising that the few individuals who have considered decoupling have taken for granted that the optimal system of decoupling would award the plaintiff *less* than what the defendant pays. This presumption would be correct if private enforcement is excessive under the damage multiplier approach, since it would then be desirable to discourage plaintiffs and their lawyers from investing too much in detection and prosecution.[16]

However, as noted earlier, private enforcement may lead to under-enforcement rather than overenforcement. If private enforcement is inadequate, then the optimal system of decoupling would require that the plaintiff receive *more* than what the defendant pays (with the subsidy presumably coming from the government). For reasons explained earlier, this outcome is most likely to occur when the damage from the violation is large. Thus *the optimal system of decoupling could award the plaintiff more or less than what the defendant pays.*

The implications of this conclusion for antitrust policy are straightforward. In those areas of antitrust law in which it is thought that overenforcement currently is a problem—for example, with respect to joint research ventures—the plaintiff could be given less than what the defendant pays. In areas in which underenforcement might otherwise occur—for example, with respect to horizontal price fixing—the plaintiff could be awarded more than what the defendant pays.

It should be pointed out, in passing, that the conclusion that the optimal system of decoupling could award the plaintiff more than what the defendant pays is not inconsistent with argument used to show that decoupling is superior to detrebling. The earlier argument demonstrated that there always exists some system of decoupling (in the example used, the plaintiff receives less than what the defendant pays) that is preferable to the best damage multiplier. It did not purport to derive the best system of decoupling, as is done here.

Concluding Remarks

The concept of decoupling is not an abstract curiosity derived from the economic theory of enforcement. There are several instances in which damages already are decoupled, although not always for the reasons suggested in this comment. For example, given current tax laws, antitrust damages are in effect decoupled in all private antitrust actions that follow successful criminal prosecutions by the government. In these cases all of the plaintiff's award may be treated as taxable income, while only one-third of the defendant's payment can be deducted.[17] Thus, with the tax consequences taken into account, the plaintiff receives less than what the defendant pays (and the difference goes to government). Although the tax treatment of antitrust damages is not designed to promote optimal deterrence, this example shows that an explicit policy of decoupling antitrust damages would not be as radical a departure from current practice as might be thought.

Before decoupling can be recommended to policymakers, several additional issues need to be considered. Since these issues have not yet been analyzed in a systematic way, I will only list some of the questions that remain to be answered:[18]

• How should a system of decoupling deal with out-of-court settlements? For example, if at trial the plaintiff would receive less than what the defendant pays, should the settlement be "taxed" by the same amount? By the same percentage? What if the court is unable to monitor the settlement? Will out-of-court settlements tend to subvert or enhance the desirable effects on deterrence of the decoupling approach?

• If at trial the plaintiff would receive more than what the defendant pays, why won't the parties "fabricate" an offense in order to obtain the implicit governmental subsidy? How should a system of decoupling respond to this possibility? Can fabricated offenses be adequately deterred simply by the threat of penalties for such behavior?

• What will be the impact of a system of decoupling on the price of the product sold by the defendant? For example, if the plaintiffs are purchasers of the defendant's product and if they would receive less at trial than what the defendant pays, won't their demand for the product—and consequently the price—be lower than what it would be if they were to receive exactly what the defendant pays? How will the price be affected if the plaintiffs are competitors of the defendant? Suppliers to the defendant? Dealers of the defendant? Are the price changes induced by a system of decoupling desirable?

• If a system of decoupling can deal satisfactorily with the issues raised by these questions, decoupling may be superior to detrebling not only in theory, but also in practice.

Notes

The preparation of this comment was supported by a grant from the Center for Economic Policy Research at Stanford. I wish to thank Daniel Rubinfeld and Steven Shavell for helpful suggestions in response to an earlier draft.

1. *See, e.g.,* House Comm. on the Judiciary, 98th Cong., 2d Sess., Study of the Antitrust Treble Damage Remedy (Comm. Print 1984) (prepared by G. Garvey); Easterbrook, Detrebling Antitrust Damages, 28 J. L. & Econ. 445 (1985).

2. Of course this is also a feature of the present system of treble damages, as well as of proposals to increase the damage multiplier. As will be seen, the principal points of this comment apply regardless of the level of the damage multiplier. My focus is on detrebling because most recent proposals have been to reduce the multiplier.

3. Schwartz, An Overview of the Economics of Antitrust Enforcement, 68 Geo. L. J. 1075, 1092–96 (1980). *See also* Warren Schwartz, Private Enforcement of the Antitrust Laws: An Economic Critique, 10–15 (1981); Landes & Posner, The Private Enforcement of Law, 4 J. Legal Stud. 1 (1975). Landes and Posner in turn built upon a foundation laid by Gary Becker and George Stigler. Becker & Stigler, Law Enforcement, Malfeasance, and Compensation of Enforcers, 3 J. Legal Stud. 1, 13–16 (1974).

4. My intellectual debt to Warren Schwartz will be obvious to anyone who has read his earlier statements, *supra* note 3, on the topic of this comment. My contribution here is to state the case for decoupling more systematically and to correct the misimpression that the optimal system of decoupling necessarily awards the plaintiff less than what the defendant pays. (In the original version of the Salop and White paper, it was presumed that the plaintiff would receive less than the defendant pays. However, in the published version the possibility, that the plaintiff should receive more than the defendant pays was considered.—*Editor*)

5. Becker, Crime and Punishment: An Economic Approach, 76 J. Pol. Econ. 169 (1968).

6. *Id.* at 191–193. The logical implication of this argument is that the fine should equal a firm's net worth. This extreme implication of Becker's theory is not essential to my analysis of detrebling and decoupling.

7. Becker & Stigler, *supra* note 3, at 13–16. They did, however, raise the possibility at the end of their discussion that private enforcement might not be optimal and that a tax on private enforcers might be desirable.

8. Landes & Posner, *supra* note 3.

9. *Id.* at 14–15.

10. *Id.* at 15.

11. Polinsky, Private versus Public Enforcement of Fines, 9 J. Legal Stud. 105 (1980).

12. *Id.* at 107, 113–14.

13. The analogy between competitive private enforcement and private damage actions in antitrust law is not perfect. In the former context, anyone can become an enforcer, whereas in the latter context, only the antitrust victim can, at least nominally, do the enforcing. Moreover, in the antitrust context, the victim must share the award with his lawyer. However, these differences do not seem essential, especially when one considers the entrepreneurial role played by plaintiff antitrust lawyers.

14. I am of course ignoring other means by which enforcement could be reduced, such as changing the allocation of legal costs or changing other procedural or substantive rules. These considerations are beyond the scope of this comment.

15. If the damage multiplier is so high that it is not possible to raise the amount paid by the defendant, then a slightly different argument would have to be used. However, the conclusion would be the same.

16. A more precise version of this point is as follows. If, under the damage multiplier approach, private enforcers would overenforce when the damage multiplier is such that the defendant is paying as much as possible, then it is desirable under the decoupling approach for the plaintiff to receive less than what the defendant pays. (An analogous statement could be made with respect to the next paragraph.)

17. *See* A.B.A. Antitrust Section, Antitrust Law Developments 484–86 (2d ed. 1984). The tax treatment of the plaintiff is determined by the nature of his underlying claim; if it is a claim for the recovery of lost profits or other ordinary income, his recovery is taxable as ordinary income. *Id.* at 484–85.

18. Many of the questions have been answered either in the context of general discussions of private versus public enforcement or in the context of specific discussions of private antitrust enforcement (in which the plaintiff receives what the defendant pays). Whether, or to what extent, the answers apply to a system of decoupling is unclear.

Comment on the Salop-White and Teplitz Papers

F. M. Scherer

One of the many fascinating questions raised by the Salop-White and Teplitz papers and the rich Georgetown data compendium they describe is whether antitrust case outcomes yield in any meaningful sense "truth." I put the key word "truth" in quotes because the antitrust laws have a complex history of legislative intent and can be interpreted to serve multiple and sometimes conflicting goals, so that more than one outcome might be "true" to facets of the law.

Salop and White (chapter 1) adopt a simpler standard when they observe that "only for the cases in which the plaintiffs receive a final favorable judgment—about 3 percent of all private antitrust cases, or about 35 cases per year—do we know that violations have occurred." In other words, the proof of truth is winning a final court judgment. Although simpler, the standard is questionable. My own experience in reading cases and the analytic commentaries on them is that final judgments are distressingly error prone, garbling or misrepresenting the facts, doing violence to accepted standards of economic analysis, or (more debatably) reaching outcomes inconsistent with (my view of) the spirit of the antitrust laws. One confirmation of trouble is that among the cases analyzed by Kauper and Snyder (chapter 7) in which the government as pathbreaker was successful in proving violation, 53 percent of the follow-on cases were dismissed, which implies a clear loss for the plaintiffs.

A standard on which many of us might agree is to ask whether the alleged practices actually had anticompetitive effects in the sense of raising prices and/or profit margins. Testable hypotheses along this line would ask whether, in lines in which plaintiffs achieved one or another form of treble damages litigation victory, there were significant differences in profits relative to control groups not subjected to suits or adverse judgments, or whether price or profitability patterns differed significantly during time periods covered by complaints, as contrasted to other (pre- or post-complaint) periods. Such tests would seldom be possible if the behavior challenged occurred in local markets too small to be identifiable. However, 44 percent of the cases involved respondents active in manufacturing, for which particularly rich data exist, and (an overlapping) 44 percent of the cases pertained to markets for which the bounds were national or international. Thus in our quest to determine whether private antitrust litigation reaches "truth" from the perspective of economic performance, it might be useful to link the Georgetown data set to other data sets such as the Producer Price Index four-digit industry disaggregations, Census of Manufactures physical product unit value and industry price-cost margin data, and (for only the four years, 1974–1977) the Federal Trade Commission's Line of Business data.

An example will illustrate what we might learn from such linkages. I served as economic advisor to Judges Edwin Robson and Hubert Will in the *Folding Carton* case (MDL 250). At the time damages claims were under consideration, we sought systematic evidence on how the cartel's breakup in 1974 affected industry profitability. But except for some materials prepared and submitted in the heat of advocacy, none was available. Since then, however, FTC Line of Business data for the relevant time periods have been published. For FTC industry category 26.10, "paperboard containers and boxes" (including also corrugated containers, covered by a parallel multidistrict litigation), operating income as a percentage of assets, and the decile in which the paperboard container industry's returns fell, were as follows:

	Operating income as percent of assets	All-industry decile
1974	17.4	Third
1975	11.7	Sixth
1976	9.3	Eight
1977	5.0	Tenth

The median returns for all 235 to 238 industry categories on which data were published lay in the range of 12.1 percent (1974 and 1975) to 13.7 percent (1977). The sharp fall in returns with the transition from conspiracy to competition in paperboard containers is unmistakable. Although containers may be an extreme example, judging inter alia from the large damage settlements, it would certainly be interesting to know whether similar patterns accompany (with appropriate lags) the initiation of other treble damages actions.

A sidelight of the folding carton case warrants mention. Opt-out plaintiff Pillsbury showed persuasively that it had been hit especially hard by the conspiracy, and it received unusually high damages. What is interesting is *why* the prices it paid were so high. In soliciting bids from folding carton manufacturers, it insisted that if a vendor wanted to bid on any carton, it had to bid on (and be prepared to supply) *all* of the 40 to 60 cartons Pillsbury used. Small suppliers had neither the clerical nor the manufacturing resources to enter such a game, and so the set of bidders was limited to firms participating actively in the conspiracy. Pillsbury therefore lacked quotations from smaller "off the phone" suppliers who might have shown the possibilities for lower prices. Despite what amounted to contributory negligence in its choice of a bidding system, Phillsbury was compensated generously. Plainly, changes in the treble damages law are needed to do justice in such cases.

I return now to my main "truth" theme. Salop and White argue repeatedly that a higher damages multiplier leads to more effort by the contending parties, which in turn means that "the parties gather more evidence and provide the court with more analysis, [so] the court will be better equipped to decide the case correctly." I accept the first of their premises but am most skeptical about the sequitur. From experience as an economic consultant in large cases (e.g., *U.S.* v. *IBM* and the FTC's breakfast cereal case) as well as small, I am persuaded that beyond some moderate litigation cost level, the probability of a "true" decision falls, not rises, with additional litigation expenditure and trial length. I would go so far as to argue that the downturn in the probability of "truth" begins with trial durations in excess of 10 to 15 days. This is so because the prospect of a brief, tightly managed trial focuses the parties on the central issues, just as the prospect of hanging in a fortnight concentrates the mind. In contrast, when "big" cases are permitted by clients and the courts, many peripheral issues tend to be explored; yet attorneys are loath to admit that they are running up the client's bill and consuming the court's time on matters less important than those they would emphasize in a "tight" case. Thus, in the effort to maintain a "balanced" offense or defense, perspective is lost. Also, when complex economic interrelationships are at issue, it is easy to overlook the pattern in the cloth while examining each thread separately, as is the tendency in generously funded and leisurely scheduled depositions and trials. And when these "big case" propensities operate, all but the most able judges are apt to be swamped in detail, lose sight of the central issues, and make bad decisions.

This pessimistic view is not only my own. It is shared in Derek Bok's penetrating analysis of merger enforcement problems:[1]

... there are reasons for suspecting that a consideration of all relevant factors may actually detract from the accuracy of decisions made under section 7. This danger consists in part of the possibility that errors in logic and inference will increase when large amounts of complex data must be considered in a conceptual framework that is but partially understood.

Bok in turn endorses the 1951 Report of the Committee of the Judicial Conference of the United States on "Procedure in Antitrust and Other Protracted Cases," which warned, inter alia, that in complicated multi-faceted inquires:[2]

... the principal vice is that such conditions create confusion, magnify uncertainty, multiply the possibilities of error, and otherwise make less certain and less accurate the judicial determination of disputed issues.

If Bok, the committee, and I are correct in this view, Salop and White are misguided in their argument that to support the proper level of legal effort, trebling of damages is better suited to complex rule of reason cases than for simpler per se cases. Theirs is a sharp departure from the widely held view that if gradation is to be introduced into antitrust damage awards, the hard-core per se violations warrant a higher multiplier (on deterrent grounds) than soft-core or even ambiguously detrimental rule of reason "violations." To resolve the issue, we shall have to develop a more sharply honed understanding of what procedural and substantive conditions lead most confidently to "truth" in antitrust litigation.

Notes

1. Derek Bok, "Section 7 of the Clayton Act and the Merging of Law and Economics," *Harvard Law Review* 74 (December 1960): 271, 295.

2. F.R.D. 62, 64 (1951).

Comment: The Counterfactual and Legal Reform

Warren F. Schwartz

In a policy-oriented empirical study one's ultimate concern should be a normative comparision of the relevant consequences under different governing rules, including those that currently apply. A comparison that has received much attention recently is between a regime awarding treble damages and one awarding single damages. But many other possibilities—such as making an unsuccessful plaintiff responsible for the attorneys' fees of the successful defendant, replacing *per se* rules with rules of reason, or having each defendant's liability in a conspiracy case be limited to the same proportion of the damages as its share of the market—similarly raise the basic counterfactual question: How would the world look if such changes were introduced, as compared to how it looks now?

My difficulty with the design of the empirical studies presented at this conference is that they do not focus on the problem of the counterfactual and specify how data with respect to the present system may be used to predict what would happen if the system were changed in various ways. To illustrate the limitations in the usefulness of the data that result from the failure to deal with this question, I will consider the possibility of changing from treble to single damages.

The present studies offer a number of observations with respect to the functioning of the current treble damage system. Economic theory identifies the likely direction of change with respect to these magnitudes if single damages were to replace treble damages. Thus, although a reduction in the damage multiplier, with the associated lessening of incentives to suit, means that a smaller proportion of those violations that do occur will be prosecuted, the reduction in the expected value of the sanction will lead to more violations. It is therefore possible that there will be more or fewer suits in a single damage regime as compared to a treble damage regime.

One could go on to specify a number of additional relevant consequences and identify the expectations predicted by economic theory. The basic point, however, is a simple one. To choose between the two alternatives, these magnitudes need to be determined.

What, however, do the present empirical studies tell us about the counterfactual world in which single damages would be granted? To begin with, it is clear that no effort was made to collect data with respect to another system in which single damages are allowed and compare the results with those obtained for the present treble damage system. Thus, if insights into the functioning of a single damage system are to be gained, they must be derived from relationships among the observations under the treble damage system that on theoretical grounds correspond to the relationships that would obtain with respect to a particular variable between the magnitude of that variable under a treble damage system and under a single damage system. But no theoretical basis for establishing such relationships is offered.

Let me illustrate this difficulty concretely. The present study, in principle, could provide data from which a supply curve for violations in which damages of a particular amount—say, $100,000—could be derived. In simplified terms the price offered for such a violation is $300,000, or three times the damage. One could see how much was spent on each case in this class, plot the data, and derive a supply curve of cases involving $100,000 in damages under a treble damage regime.

The next, tempting, thing to do, if one wanted to know the number of such cases that would be brought under a single damage regime in which $100,000 rather than $300,000 would be recovered, is simply find the $100,000 point on the supply curve that has been derived and conclude that these cases are the ones that would be brought because the recovery would equal the cost.

But it is clear that this not correct. The amount that is expended on a case involving $100,000 in actual damages in a treble damage regime is not a good indication of what would be spent on a case involving $100,000 in actual damages in a single damage regime. The principal point simply is that the expenditures are in part a function of the stakes, which are crucially influenced by the presence or absence of trebling. But there may also be other more subtle differences, as I suggested earlier. For example, costs of detection may be lower in a single damage system characterized by a great number of violations.

Another tempting possibility is to derive a supply curve, based on observations under the existing treble damage regime, not of cases where actual damages are $100,000 but where recovery is $100,000. One could then infer that all cases of this kind where costs were less than $100,000 would be brought in a single damage regime. But this too is an incorrect conclusion. For in these cases only $33,333.33 in damages had to be proved in a treble damage regime, whereas in a single damage regime $100,000 in damages must be proved to recover $100,000. If, as appears plausible, costs rise as the amount of damages at issue increases, a supply curve based on cases of recovering $100,000 in a treble damage regime will systematically understate the costs of recovering $100,000 in a single damage regime.

As far as I can determine, no supply curve of cases derived from observations under a treble damage regime provides significant guidance as to the supply curve that would exist under a single damage regime. Conceivably, economic theory might provide some basis for making the necessary extrapolation. But no solution to this problem was apparently achieved and utilized in designing the present study.

I have dwelled on the single point of the counterfactual because I believe that confronting it is essential to sound policy analysis. It is also a piece of "bad news" that economists must get lawyers to understand and overcome if good decisions with respect to antitrust enforcement are to be made. There is something wonderfully nonthreatening about empirical work when it is characterized as simply "laying out the facts." But when it is viewed, as it must be, as only preliminary to predicting (with nontrivial inaccuracy) what the facts would be under some alternative state of the world, it is both more valuable and more unsettling. I believe that a greater focus on the counterfactual here would have yielded less descriptive data about the present system but more insights into the complex interactions that determine what happens when the law is changed.

Comment

Joe Sims

Assessments of private antitrust ligitation and the treble damages remedy are certainly not new. The 1955 Report of the Attorney General's committee to study the antitrust laws recommended that the trial judge have discretion to award double or triple damages. But the Electrical Conspiracy Cases ended any possibility of that idea's gaining acceptance.

Recently Congress has shown a decided tendency to carve out exceptions to mandatory treble damages:

The Export Trading Company Act of 1982.

The Local Government Antitrust Act of 1984.

The National Cooperative Research Act of 1984.

The attorney general, current and former heads of the Antitrust Division, and the secretary of commerce have called for a reexamination of the treble damage remedy. The ABA has had at least three programs on this subject in the last few years. The House Judiciary Committee has held hearings and even produced a report entitled "Study of Antitrust Damage Remedies." The Reagan administration has already floated one specific proposal for change, and a current interagency task force seems likely to produce another. The Association of the Bar of the City of New York, hardly a bastion of conservatism, has recently issued a report recommending judicial discretion.

All of this sound and fury has to date been notably unencumbered with facts. Everyone has an opinion about mandatory treble damages; until now no one has had very many facts. This project is an attempt to bring the scales into better balance.

This project began out of discussions about the Reagan administration's first proposal to change the treble damage remedy, which was to allow judicial discretion. In attempting to figure out how to react to that proposal, it became clear that the factual record was nonexistent. Several hundred thousand dollars, lots of volunteered time, and enormous effort by many people later, this conference is the culmination of the initial frustrations created by that lack of data.

The message to be drawn from these statistics may not be clear. Indeed, I suspect this data base—undoubtedly the best of its kind ever assembled—

will lead different people to very different conclusions. Nevertheless, some interesting points are clear:

1. Very few consumers use this consumer welfare statute; most antitrust cases are brought by competitors and distributors.

2. The big case is rare; most antitrust cases arc small.

3. There has been a dramatic change in the number and kind of cases in recent years; *Sylvania* did make a difference.

4. Finally, few plaintiffs win litigated cases.

There is of course much more to be learned from this study. I urge close attention.

II

THE OPERATION OF THE LITIGATION SYSTEM

3

The Costs of the Legal System in Private Antitrust Enforcement

Kenneth G. Elzinga and William C. Wood

3.1 Introduction

Sir John Romilly described the judicial system as "a technical system invented for the creation of costs." If this is so, the costs are very difficult to measure and assess. Notwithstanding the difficulties of the task, attempts are made to assess the costs of the judicial system. This paper is in that grain. We attempt to assess some of the costs associated with the American system of private, treble damages-induced, antitrust enforcement.

A primary objective of our study was to understand what kinds of private antitrust cases used the most resources. Cases were classified as to number of plaintiffs, jury versus nonjury, the business practice involved, the antitrust statute allegedly violated, and the type of relief requested. A second objective was to learn the size of legal fees and settlements associated with private antitrust enforcement. From this, the efficiency of transferring funds from defendants to plaintiffs could be studied. A third objective was to understand how legal fees vary across types of cases. Information developed in this part of the study could then be used to predict legal fees in cases for which a few key characteristics were known.

A fourth objective was to classify private actions according to the business relationship between plaintiffs and defendants and from this taxonomy to interpret (in broad brush fashion) the prospects of private antitrust enforcement for reducing market power.

Our endeavors were not entirely inductive. Economic theory suggests certain inefficiencies associated with private antitrust enforcement as compared with a regime of public enforcement. A further objective was to find whatever evidence might be available on the size of these inefficiencies.

The analysis of the data proceeded in three stages. In the first round we examined public data from the court records for the full sample of 1,946 cases. Then a version of the confidential data set constructed from responses to the lawyers' questionnaire (with 285 valid observations) was analyzed. Because docket numbers, dates, and other identifying information had been removed from these cases, it was not possible to link the confidential data with data from court records. Finally, several equations were formulated that permitted linking both the public and private data sets.

3.2 Analysis of the Public Data Set

Nature of the Data

The information obtainable from the large public data set is important because it includes various measures of resources devoted to private antitrust cases. These proxies range from "thickness of case files" to the number of requests for production of documents (see table 3.1). These measures are important to study since they reflect resource costs to society of private antitrust enforcement that embrace more than the legal fees paid by plaintiffs and defendants. Such measures of court resources, however, defy aggregation into pecuniary amounts that would represent total legal resources per case.

We therefore conducted a detailed analysis of six separate measures of resources per case: total docket entries, total number of depositions, duration of case in months, number of trial days, number of judges' rulings, and number of magistrates' rulings.[1] These variables serve as useful proxies of overall legal resource costs. Our confidence in them as cost proxies is heightened by their being highly correlated with each other (see table 3.2). The only variable that showed weak and insignificant correlations with other measures of resources proved to be "total interventions," the sum of

Table 3.1   Descriptive statistics on measures of legal resources per case

Variable	Mean	Standard deviation
Total docket entries	68.16	100.54
Thickness of case file (inches)	7.77	15.58
Number of amendments	0.36	0.63
Number of interventions	0.04	0.35
Number of depositions	4.97	12.59
Number of sets of interrogatories	1.90	3.35
Requests for production of documents	1.74	2.76
Length of case (months)	25.62	23.35
Number of days of trial	0.47	2.67
Number of judges' rulings[a]	2.95	3.56
Number of magistrates' rulings[a]	0.45	2.73

Note: Cases were excluded from these calculations if duration in months was missing, if no illegal practice was coded in the survey data, or if the case was listed as "still pending" or "file missing." This left 1,190 cases.
a. Excluding scheduling and mechanics.

Table 3.2 Correlations among measures of legal resources per case

	Docket entries	File thickness (inches)	Amendments to complaint	Interventions	Depositions	Inter-rogatories	Requests for production of documents	Months[a]	Trial days[b]	Judges' ruling[c]	Magistrates' ruling[d]
Docket entries	1.0000	0.5778**	0.2815**	0.0824**	0.6994**	0.6053**	0.6294**	0.3814**	0.4243**	0.5556**	0.4755**
File thickness (inches)		1.0000	0.2082**	0.0534*	0.3944**	0.3332**	0.3612**	0.2589**	0.4773**	0.3665**	0.3951**
Amendments to complaint			1.0000	0.0911**	0.1853**	0.1776**	0.2393**	0.1594**	0.0605*	0.2778**	0.1150**
Interventions				1.0000	0.0462	0.1917**	0.1013**	0.0722**	0.0389	0.1114**	−0.0022
Depositions					1.0000	0.5358**	0.5673**	0.2806**	0.3004**	0.3695**	0.2794**
Interrogatories						1.0000	0.6680**	0.2756**	0.1415**	0.3770**	0.2129**
Requests for production of documents							1.0000	0.2558**	0.1856**	0.3887**	0.2386**
Months[a]								1.0000	0.2056**	0.2762**	0.1174**
Trial days[b]									1.0000	0.1306**	0.3272**
Judges' ruling[c]										1.0000	0.3024**
Magistrates' ruling[d]											1.0000

Note: Cases were excluded from calculation of correlations if duration in months was missing, if no illegal practice was coded in the survey data, or if the case was listed as "still pending" or "file missing"; this left 1,190 cases. The **indicates correlation is statistically different from zero at the 1 percent significance level; the * indicates 5 percent significance level.
a. Length of case from time of filing to last docket entry.
b. Number of days of trial.
c. Number of judges' rulings other than scheduling or mechanics.
d. Number of magistrates' rulings other than scheduling or mechanics.

interventions on the plaintiffs' side and the defendants' side plus other interventions such as amicus actions.

One of our principal objects was to determine which kinds of cases have large and small resource costs. "Kind of case" was defined in a variety of ways. For example, we looked separately at groups of cases depending on the business relationship between the parties, the illegal practice alleged, and the statute allegedly violated. The results are presented in a series of statistical tables (tables 3.3 through 3.9).[2]

Each table also reports the results of statistical tests on the differences between subsamples. For example, table 3.5 shows that the mean number of docket entries was 76.66 in cases involving competitors producing the same product. The mean number of docket entries was considerably smaller in cases involving all other kinds of relationships between plaintiff and defendant. The difference in number of docket entries was large enough that it could not reasonably be attributed to sampling error.[3]

Separate tests were performed for each classification of cases. The categories were not mutually exclusive. Some were subsets of other included categories, such as "terminated dealerships," a subset of the larger "dealer-agent" category. Tests depending on a mutually exclusive breakdown of cases were therefore not performed.

The difference-of-means tests shown in tables 3.3 through 3.9 have limitations. Performing such tests is a valuable exercise only to the extent that the mean provides a good measure of the central tendency of a set of numbers. The tests' accuracy will necessarily be smaller, the less closely the relevant distribution approximates a normal one. The necessary restrictions on samples brought sample sizes down to uncomfortably low levels for some tests. Out of the 1,946 cases, only 25 with complete records ended in a trial and the granting of relief. The desirable statistical properties of large samples that could be assumed with almost two thousand cases are less likely to hold when only 25 constitutes the sample size. A final caveat concerns the number of individual tests that we performed in the generation of the tables. The number of tests is so large that even if there were no systematic relationships in the data, there would be a number of seemingly "significant" test statistics.

Even a casual reading of table 3.1 casts doubt on the mean as a good measure of central tendency for the numbers involved and on the symmetry of the distributions. The standard deviations, measuring dispersion, are very high relative to the mean. This indicates, for example, that although the average price-fixing case generates 5.23 depositions, any particular price-fixing case could easily generate zero depositions or well over a

Table 3.3   Average legal resources used in class-action and in non-class action cases

Resource measure	Class actions (40 cases)	Non-class actions (1,150 cases)	All cases (1,190)
Docket entries	115.37**	66.52	68.16
Depositions	6.45	4.91	4.97
Duration in months	46.07**[tt]	24.90	25.62
Trial length in days	4.00	8.06	7.94
Judges' rulings[a]	6.22**	2.84	2.95
Magistrates' rulings[a]	0.55	0.45	0.45

Note: Cases were excluded from these calculations if duration in months was missing, if no illegal practice was coded in the survey data, or if the case was listed as "still pending" or "file missing." The ** indicates statistical significance at the 1 percent level of a difference-of-means test; the * indicates a 5 percent significance level; the [tt] indicates a statistically significant Lee-Desu test at 1 percent.
a. Excluding scheduling and mechanics.

Table 3.4   Average legal resources used in jury and nonjury trials

Resource measure	Jury trials (21 cases)	Nonjury trials (50 cases)	All tried cases (71)
Docket entries	212.33	188.98	195.89
Depositions	18.05	16.60	17.03
Duration in months	54.62	50.34	51.61
Trial length in days	10.90*	6.70	7.94
Judges' rulings[a]	4.71	5.36	5.17
Magistrates' rulings[a]	1.86	2.70	2.45

Note: Cases were excluded from these calculations if they did not go to trial. In addition, cases were excluded if duration in months was missing, if no illegal practice was coded in the survey data, or if the case was listed as "still pending" or "file missing." The * indicates statistical significance at the 5 percent level of a difference-of-means test.
a. Excluding scheduling and mechanics.

Table 3.5 Average measures of legal resources per case classified by business relationship of plaintiff to defendant

Relationship	Number of cases	Docket entries	Depositions	Duration of case (months)	Judges' rulings	Magistrates' rulings	Number of trial days	Number of cases to trial
Competitors								
Same Product	382	76.66*	6.89**	24.52	3.02	0.51	8.21	14
Similar Product	106	62.43	5.93	22.00	2.54	0.41	6.09	11
Other	27	86.89	5.67	32.22	2.81	0.11	13.00	2
Supplier	60	57.75	4.85	19.57	3.05	0.18	22.50*	2
Dealer-Agent	430	67.68	4.92	25.16	2.87	0.36	7.72	32
Terminated dealership	176	64.47	5.90	25.62	2.95	0.39	8.75	16
Input purchaser	170	59.55	4.27	23.05	3.01	0.38	2.86	7
Final customer	138	70.33	3.12	28.41†	3.32	0.49	3.00	1
Employee	43	62.21	5.67	24.42	2.81	0.12	9.00	2
State or local government	14	50.00	1.64	26.43	2.57	0.07	0	0
Other	70	67.54	4.57	25.71	2.84	0.23	8.00	5
Licensee	10	91.00	2.40	28.10	2.40	0.20	9.00	3
Franchisee	22	37.59	2.55	18.67	1.86	.05	0	0
Stockholder	11	113.27	5.27	43.35**†	4.09	.91	40.00**	1
For entire sample	1,405	67.34	5.05	24.80	2.89	0.39	8.13	78

a. Cases were excluded from these calculations if duration in months was missing, if no primary business relationship was coded in the survey data, or if the case was listed as "still pending" or "file missing." Because of multiple entries for some cases, subsamples add to more than 1,405. The **indicates a mean statistically different from the mean of all other cases at a 1 percent significance level; the *indicates a significance level of 5 percent; the †indicates a significant Lee-Desu statistic at 5 percent.

Table 3.6 Average measures of legal resources per case classified by alleged illegal practice

Practice	Number of cases	Docket entries	Depositions	Duration of case (months)	Judges' rulings	Magistrates' rulings	Number of trial days	Number of cases to trial
Price fixing	264	81.00*	5.23	32.37**††	3.25	0.43	12.25*	12
Naked cartel	12	88.83	4.17	42.08*	2.58	0.08	28.00**	1
Merger-joint venture	53	66.77	4.68	24.79	2.68	0.28	5.50	2
Asset accumulation	55	76.05	6.84	24.36	3.93*	0.87	11.00	3
Price discrimination	132	63.45	4.12	21.94	2.83	0.33	5.20	5
Predatory pricing	74	87.81	8.01*	27.96	3.57	0.93	6.33	3
Exclusive dealing	192	74.24	4.97	26.98	3.24	0.52	8.47	15
Refusal to deal	253	57.90	4.03	22.49*†	2.89	0.63	8.63	19
Vertical price discrimination	47	81.45	6.94	28.60	2.68	0.89	5.33	3
Vertical price fixing	91	72.99	5.08	29.01	2.88	0.34	8.75	8
Dealer termination	93	67.09	5.41	23.60	3.24	0.71	6.87	8
Inducing government action	7	54.57	1.57	37.71	2.43	0	0	0
Other practice	55	47.40	3.76	20.13†	2.85	0.07	7.67	3
Restraint of trade	37	58.59	2.27	17.16*†	1.78*	0	4.00	2
Monopolization	26	60.88	4.81	28.42*	2.12	0.08	0	0
Conspiracy	12	76.75	3.08	28.75	2.75	0	2.50	2
For entire sample	1,190	68.16	4.97	25.62	2.95	0.45	7.94	71

Note: Cases were excluded from these calculations if duration in months was missing, if no illegal practice was coded in the survey data, or if the case was listed as "still pending," or "file missing." Because of multiple entries for some cases, subsamples add to more than 1,190. The ** indicates a mean statistically different from the mean of all other cases at a 1 percent significance level; the * indicates a significance level of 5 percent; the †† indicates a significant Lee-Desu statistic at 1 percent; the † indicates a significant Lee-Desu statistic at 5 percent.

Table 3.7 Average measures of legal resources per case classified by statute allegedly violated

Statute	Number of cases	Docket entries	Depositions	Duration of case (months)	Judges' rulings	Magistrates' rulings	Number of trial days	Number of cases to trial
Sherman, section 1	983	71.65**	5.37*	26.85**††	3.10**	0.49	7.71	65
Sherman, section 2	609	76.11**	6.22**	27.44**	3.24**	0.56	9.24	45
Sherman, unspecified	54	61.83	4.85	26.26	2.74	0.37	10.00	2
Clayton, section 2	256	72.32	5.44	25.46	2.96	0.55	8.36	11
Clayton, section 3	162	67.85	4.87	26.85	2.83	0.30	6.09	11
Clayton, section 7	76	70.82	5.79	27.29	3.45	0.74	15.33	3
Clayton, section 8	8	120.25	12.62	24.62	3.25	2.87*	2.50	2
Clayton, other	353	64.06	5.16	25.66	2.96	0.33	8.00	19
Clayton, unspecified	53	70.36	3.36	24.77	3.21	1.30*	15.33	3
Other antitrust	175	104.20**	10.00**	32.67**††	3.55*	0.75	10.93	14
Antitrust not a significant issue	274	56.81*	5.11	24.18†	2.62	0.32	6.12	16
For entire sample	1,190	68.16	4.97	25.62	2.95	0.45	7.94	71

Note: Cases were excluded from these calculations if duration in months was missing, if no illegal practice was coded in the survey data, or if the case was listed as "still pending" or "file missing." Multiple claims of violations were made for most cases, bringing the total of subsamples to well over 1,190. The ** therefore indicates, at a significance level of 1 percent, that cases mentioning the indicated section of the law had a statistically different mean from cases that did not mention the indicated section of the law; the * indicates a significance level of 5 percent; the †† indicates a significant Lee-Desu statistic at 1 percent; the † indicates a significant Lee-Desu statistic at 5 percent.

Table 3.8 Average measures of legal resources per case classified by relief granted

Relief granted	Number of cases	Docket entries	Depositions	Duration of case (months)	Judges' rulings	Magistrates' rulings	Number of trial days	Number of cases to trial
Court award	56	143.75	9.36	45.04	4.52	1.57	9.57	23
Dealer reinstatement	1	427.00	68.00**	118.00**	11.00	0	29.00**	1
Changes in pricing	2	53.00	1.50	36.00	3.00	0	7.00	1
Cease and desist	2	352.50	19.50	59.00	10.00	2.00	5.00	1
Injunctive relief	18	142.33	7.94	41.67	3.78	2.17	5.86	7
For entire sample	62	142.97	9.08	44.14	4.66	1.48	9.12	25

Note: Only cases in which relief was granted were included in this calculation. In addition, cases were excluded if duration in months was missing, if no illegal practice was coded in the survey data, or if the case was listed as "still pending" or "file missing." Because of multiple relief granted in some cases, subsamples add to more than 62. The ** indicates a mean statistically different from the mean of all other cases at a 1 percent significance level; the * indicates a significance level of 5 percent. The Lee-Desu tests did not reveal any statistically significant differences.

Table 3.9 Average measures of legal resources per case classified by relief requested

Relief requested	Number of cases	Docket entries	Depositions	Duration of case (months)	Judges' rulings	Magistrates' rulings	Number of trial days	Number of cases to trial
Divestiture-exit	41	65.76	8.78	34.29**†	3.41	1.17*	0	0
Dealer reinstatement	40	87.65	7.20	20.60	4.55**	0.62	3.40	5
Dealer elimination	5	32.80	.60	14.40	1.60	0	0	0
Changes in pricing	85	87.07	6.54	29.29††	3.08	0.31	12.33	3
Changed dealer restrictions	90	67.40	4.47	22.10	2.74	0.02	9.80	5
Patent-trademark access	28	82.39	4.36	27.39	4.04	0.64	3.33	3
Cease joint action	546	74.81*	5.38	26.47†	3.29**	0.51	10.23*	31
Employment	11	98.63	3.73	21.91	2.18	1.27	0	0
Requirement of purchase	12	107.17	5.67	23.00	3.92	3.08**	34.00**	1
Requirement of dealing	96	72.72	5.43	22.66	2.96	0.54	11.00	8
Other	55	58.27	4.67	20.85	2.69	0.42	6.00	1
Injunctive relief	241	56.38	3.74	20.28**††	2.30**	0.15	7.13	15
Costs	79	52.58	4.32	22.08	1.78**	0.09	9.00	5
Attorneys' fees	96	55.27	4.66	24.06	1.70**	0.04	14.60	5
Temporary restraining order	10	51.90	1.90	12.90	4.00	0	0	0
Treble damages	89	84.58	6.04	24.09	2.39	0.54	17.25*	4
Punitive-exemplary damages	13	98.31	7.31	29.62	3.85	2.00**	0	0
Decree of violation	13	27.77	1.00	15.77	0.46*	0.15	0	0
Declaratory judgment	10	55.10	1.10	29.50	2.40	0.10	4.00	1
Void contract	15	83.40	7.33	24.07	4.27	2.40	5.00	2
Other relief deemed by court	16	31.25	2.44	16.87	1.87	0.69	0	0
For entire sample	1,291	67.60	5.06	27.72	2.90	0.39	7.84	73

Note: Cases were included in these calculations only if some specific request for relief was coded in the survey data. Cases were excluded if duration in months was missing or if the case was listed as "still pending" or "file missing." Because of multiple entries for some cases, subsamples add to more than 1291. The ** indicates a mean statistically different from the mean of all other cases at a 1 percent significance level; the * indicates a significance level of 5 percent; the † indicates a significant Lee-Desu statistic at 1 percent; the †† indicates a significant Lee-Desu statistic at 5 percent.

dozen. The dispersion is simply too high to label 1 as a very low number of depositions or 12 as a very high number of depositions.[4]

The overall picture shown by table 3.1 indicates that what is called an "antitrust case" in this data set is quite different from, say, a bushel of #2 soft red wheat on a commodity exchange. Antitrust cases are very heterogeneous occurrences. Many of the observed court records show that a complaint was filed but not pursued. They were not "cases" at all in the sense of disputes resolved by the direct action of the judicial system; as a result their burden upon the judicial system was nominal. In other instances cases stretched out for years and were resolved only after multiple appeals. The reported averages of the six measures we studied therefore may seem suspiciously low to antitrust practitioners who think of a case as something more involved.

As noted earlier, for most of the tests we excluded cases that were still pending or missing at the conclusion of the survey period. But in tables involving the duration of cases in months, we report the results not only of difference-of-means tests but also results of an additional test especially suited to the statistical problem of duration of cases.

A more efficient technique to extract information from a sample with still-pending cases was developed by E. Lee and M. Desu (1972) to characterize the survival times of medical patients under various treatment regimes. The Lee-Desu test compares the survival curves of patients given different treatment to see whether one treatment regime's survival rate is significantly different, and not just due to sampling error. Just as some patients survive an exceptionally long time after contracting a disease, so some court cases drag on "forever" before being resolved. The Lee-Desu test permits treating a court case as having a well-defined life from filing to completion.[5] For court cases the Lee-Desu test is used to compare the duration of a case (the time between filing and resolution) across types of cases. An especially attractive feature of the test is that it enables the use of some information from cases that had not been resolved at the end of the survey period. The technique is analogous to the information obtainable from patients' survival until the end of a medical survey period. Such information had to be excluded in a difference-of-means test because cases not yet resolved were themselves excluded from the sample. The Lee-Desu test is also less likely to be unduly influenced by extraordinarily long survival times for individual cases, taking into account as it does the characteristics of an aggregate survival curve. As the tables reporting duration of cases indicate, the Lee-Desu test indicates statistically significant differences in a few instances where the difference-of-means test could not discern a difference.

Findings from the Data

Statistical tests reported in table 3.3 make it clear that class action cases are more costly than the other cases. They generate significantly more docket entries and judges' rulings; in addition the difference-of-means test and Lee-Desu test show that class action cases take so much longer that the difference in duration is not likely due to sampling error. Class action cases generate more depositions and more magistrates' rulings than do other cases, but the differences are not large enough to be statistically significant. Table 3.3 appears to show that class actions involve *shorter* rather than longer trials. However, there were only two class action trials out of a sample of 71, and few general inferences can be made.

The picture is slightly less clear for jury trials, as compared with trials before a judge only. Among the 71 cases that went to trial, the jury trials lasted an average of 10.90 days (table 3.4); the other trials lasted an average of only 6.70 days. This difference was statistically significant at the 5 percent level. Jury trials also generated slightly more docket entries (212.33 vs. 188.98), slightly more depositions (18.05 vs. 16.60), and they lasted longer (54.62 months vs. 50.34 months); these three differences, however, were not statistically significant. The only suggestion that jury trials might be less costly was in the lesser number of magistrates' rulings (1.86 vs. 2.70) and judges' rulings (4.71 vs. 5.36). Again, however, these differences were not statistically significant. Further a smaller number of judges' rulings during a jury trial could hardly be considered to economize much on judicial resources, since the judge would be present anyway. In summary, the only statistically significant evidence from the comparison is that jury trials take longer.[6]

As a classification variable the business relationship between plaintiff and defendant had comparatively little ability to explain differences in legal resources devoted to cases (table 3.5). There were many seemingly large differences across types of cases, but small numbers and large standard deviations in many categories made it impossible to rule out that the differences were due to chance.

Some findings concerning the relationship between the litigants did pass conventional statistical tests and are worth noting. First, when competitors sue direct competitors producing the same product, considerably more docket entries and depositions are likely to result than in other cases. Second, the 11 cases involving stockholders as plaintiffs generated more docket entries, more depositions, and more rulings by judges and magistrates than other cases. The greater duration of stockholder cases was striking—an average of 43.45 months compared with an overall average of 24.80 months. The one stockholder case that went to trial lasted 40 days, against an average for the sample of 8.13 trial days. Although the findings concerning duration and trial days are statistically significant, they must be set against small sample size.

Many proposed antitrust reforms are aimed at changing the legal rules regarding specific practices, such as forms of price discrimination or types of mergers. Consequently, knowledge of the resource costs upon the legal system of trying cases involving these and other business practices would be useful. However, the data set's classification of cases by business practice is so refined that some categories contain only one case. A coarser breakdown, by statute and section allegedly violated, was developed to overcome the small-numbers problem; this of course occurs at the expense of a loss of precision.

Breakdowns of legal resources by alleged illegal practice are contained in table 3.6. Price-fixing cases, far from being short and simple as might be presumed given the per se character of the offense, generated more docket entries and longer trials, with the differences statistically significant at 5 percent. Even that subset of price-fixing cases characterized as "naked cartel" generated longer cases and longer trials than did other types of cases, although there were few allegations of a naked cartel (12) and only one trial (that one lasting for 28 trial days). Predatory pricing cases took up moderately more resources than other cases.

Compared to most civil litigation, private antitrust cases are known to have long lives.[7] But until now no data existed to allow a disaggregated examination of their length. The evidence indicates that the biggest differences in antitrust cases classified by illegal practices appeared to be in their duration. The Lee-Desu test confirmed that price-fixing cases are longer than the others but also indicated that three specific types of cases are significantly shorter: refusal to deal (253 cases), restraint of trade (37 cases), and interference (6 cases).

An alternative to dividing cases by illegal practice is to group them by the antitrust statutes mentioned in the case files (table 3.7). This classification was not very precise because plaintiffs' complaints regularly embrace every provision of law that might possibly apply to their cases. The breakdown had a small number of categories with a large number of cases in each, however, so it overcame small-numbers problems. The main finding from this classification was that cases involving section 1 or section 2 of the Sherman Act consumed more resources than did other cases. They involved more docket entries, more depositions, and more judges' rulings, with the differences statistically significant. In addition these cases had a longer duration than other cases, although the Lee-Desu test and the difference-of-means test were not in agreement on section 2 cases. Two additional findings from these tables are interesting. First, cases that listed the category "other antitrust statute" involved a significantly greater number of docket entries, depositions, and judges' rulings, as well as longer durations.[8] Second, cases that the field workers coded as "antitrust not a significant issue" were resolved more quickly and with fewer docket entries than other cases.

We had hoped to determine if there were differences in the amount of legal resources used in antitrust cases, depending on the type of relief obtained. Once again, small numbers proved to be a problem, in that only 62 complete cases resulted in fully reported relief in the case files (table 3.8). The breakdowns of legal resources by relief granted appear to show that dealer reinstatement cases are relatively costly, but the more tenable conclusion is that there was one very long and costly dealer reinstatement case in the sample.

We therefore analyzed relief according to the types of relief requested, recognizing that some complaints might ask for much more generous and varied relief than was ever expected. These patterns emerged (though small numbers present a continuing caveat). Cases in which a cessation of joint action was requested had more docket entries but were shorter than other cases according to the Lee-Desu test (table 3.9). The Lee-Desu test also indicated that cases asking for changes in pricing, or for divestiture or exit, lasted longer than other cases. As would be expected, cases seeking injunctive relief were shorter than others on average.

One cost variable that can be examined directly in monetary terms is the awarding of costs and attorneys' fees. Such awards were not very common in the sample. There were only 196 awards, 71 to plaintiffs and 125 to defendants. The awards were modest, with the average for plaintiffs being $8,510.12 and the average for defendants being $6,795.76 (table 3.10). Attorneys' fees were not awarded very frequently, either. There were 49 awards to plaintiffs, averaging $341,238.18, and 9 awards to defendants, averaging $15,553.94. The private treble damages bar clearly receives most of its remuneration from direct billings and contingency fees, not from court-mandated costs and attorney's fees.

Table 3.10   Awards of costs and attorneys' fees

Status of award	Number of cases	Average award
Costs awarded to plaintiff	71	$8,510.12
Costs awarded to defendant	125	6,795.76
Total costs awards	196	7,416.77
Attorneys' fees awarded to plaintiff	49	$341,238.18
Attorneys' fees awarded to defendant	9	15,553.94
Total fees awards	58	290,700.94

Note: Average awards are in 1984 dollars. An additional nine cases, with legal fee awards averaging $14,077,57, were not included because the data set did not indicate which party received the fees.

3.3 The Confidential Data Set

Nature of the Data

In the economic analysis of law, where litigation is construed as an investment of resources to attain a future goal, legal fees constitute an important component of the resources to be invested.[9] Legal fees are not the only cost associated with the investment. Plaintiff's time also may be extensively required and therefore be an expensive component in the decision calculus. The virtue of legal fees for researchers is that they already are monetized.

Yet past analysts have been unsuccessful in saying much about the size and determinants of legal fees and settlements, simply because the information is so sensitive and confidential. To overcome this problem, survey research made available to the authors of papers in this volume included an unprecedented effort at gathering information on attorneys' fees charged and settlements reached in private antitrust cases. The confidential character of the survey produced 285 valid responses specifying such information as the total billings to the client and the size of settlements.[10]

Before examining the results of the confidential survey, it is important to establish whether the cases on which confidential data are available are representative of the rest of the sample. The researchers were issued a list of docket numbers that identified cases for which the attorneys had submitted valid responses. Although the list did not permit identifying individual responses by docket numbers, it did provide a way of testing the representativeness of responses. As table 3.11 indicates, cases for which confidential data are available were in general more complex than other cases. The confidential cases involved significantly more docket entries, deposi-

Table 3.11   Legal resources for cases with and without confidential data available

Variable	Mean, nonconfidential	Mean, confidential	p-value
Total docket entries	69.95	114.39	0.0000
Number of depositions	5.23	9.67	0.0002
Length of case (months)	23.30	31.92	0.0000
Number of days of trial	9.09	14.80	0.1058
Judges' rulings[a]	2.72	3.82	0.0000
Magistrates' rulings[a]	0.33	0.96	0.0003

Note: The p-value reported is from an F-test of the equality of means between the two subpopulations—cases for which confidential data were available and all other cases. Intuitively, this p-value is "the chance that it is correct to assume the cases with confidential data available are representative of the other cases." This test was run for the entire sample of 1,946 cases except for "number of trial days," which included only those 105 cases in the sample that went to trial.
a. Excluding scheduling and mechanics.

tions, and rulings by judges and magistrates. They also had a significantly longer duration.

Further examination of the confidential sample indicates that although the cases were bigger than average, the sample did not include information from the megacases. The highest legal billing reported was $1.78 million—an amount well below billings in the most costly cases. Therefore the sample overrepresents the medium-size cases, with important gaps at the top and the bottom. This bias in the sample is a disadvantage if inferences about the overall private enforcement regime are to be made. However, it is an advantage in studying cases of great policy interest—the "middle range" of cases that go well beyond the filing of a complaint.[11]

Several other limitations to the data should be noted. First, some selection bias seems inevitable. Those lawyers who took the time and trouble to fill out the questionnaire may be different from those who failed to respond. Second, there appeared to be a problem for some respondents in attributing resources and billings to a particular case. Law firms often are performing a variety of assignments for their clients, with some joint costs that cannot meaningfully be broken out. Third, multiple firms worked on some cases, but only one law firm's billings were reported. Fourth, reported cash settlements may be only a fraction of a plaintiff's gains from bringing an action. Other provisions, such as the requirement to deal, often were involved in settlements. It would be difficult to estimate and assign the monetary value of such a settlement. Finally, the confidential data included very few examples of responses from both sides of a given case. Such questions as the relationships between plaintiffs' and defendants' fees for the typical case therefore had to be inferred indirectly.

Table 3.12   Plaintiffs' unadjusted gains in confidential cases

Case number	Attorneys' fees	Cash settlement[a]	Unadjusted gain	Ratio of fees to settlement
1	150,000	50,000,000	49,850,000	0.003
2	13,000	−15,000	−28,000	0.87
3	235,000	650,000	415,000	0.36
4	200,000	250,000	50,000	0.80
5	200,000	1,550,000	1,350,000	0.13
6	22,010	45,000	22,990	0.49
7	200,000	1,260,000	1,060,000	0.16
8	220,000	450,000	230,000	0.49
9	30,000	25,000	−5,000	1.20
Simple mean	141,112	6,023,889	5,882,777	0.50
Mean attorneys' fees/mean cash settlement				0.023
Mean attorneys' fees/mean absolute cash settlement[b]				0.023
Mean attorneys' fee/mean cash settlement, excluding cases with negative cash settlement				0.023

Note: These figures apply only to those cases in which there was a cash settlement and attorneys' fees were reported. The absence of dates in this confidential data made adjustment for inflation impossible.
a. A negative number indicates a payment to a defendant.
b. This calculation shows the ratio of mean attorneys' fees to mean cash settlements when negative settlements are taken as positive for the purposes of the calculation; that is, the mean *absolute* value of cash settlements is used.

Results from the Confidential Data

Using the confidential data set (without identifying information), we examined how the size of settlements compared with attorneys' fees. We first wanted to analyze the gains and losses of the parties, which depend significantly on the size of legal fees.[12] We then wanted to discover what could be determined about the efficiency of private antitrust as a distributional system, construing legal fees as a transactions cost of distributing wealth to the presumed victims of market power.

Table 3.12 presents plaintiffs' net recovery in the nine cases for which settlement size and attorneys' fees were both present. Subject to the limitations of net recovery defined as settlement minus attorneys' fees, it is clear that seven of the plaintiffs did quite well, with settlements well beyond fees. It is of course possible that these plaintiffs did not do nearly as well when costs of other resources they expended were considered. Abstracting from all costs except legal fees, net recovery was negative for two of the plaintiffs. In one case the net recovery was negative because the $30,000 attorneys' fee exceeded the $25,000 cash settlement. In another the settlement involved a $15,000 payment to the defendant in addition to the $13,000 in attorneys' fees. In the other seven cases the litigation as investment appeared to pay off: the recovery exceeded legal fees.

However, table 3.12 dramatically demonstrates how sensitive the summary statistics are to only slight changes in their calculation. If fees are calculated as a fraction of settlement for each case, and then the fractions are averaged, the result is 0.50. This would appear to show that for each dollar of cash settlement to a plaintiff, 50 cents is taken up by attorneys' fees. With only a slight change in procedure, however, it could be shown that the correct figure is only two cents. Mean attorneys' fees for the sample of nine cases were $141,112, as against mean settlements of $6,023,889. Dividing those two figures yields $0.02, suggesting that lawyers only "get in their two cents worth." A more realistic assessment is simply that most of the settlements and fees are modest, but one big case with very small attorneys' fees and a large $50 million settlement, under alternative procedures, produces a very different mean.

As table 3.12 indicates, alternative calculations of the ratio of fees to settlements are not very sensitive to one additional problem—the presence of negative settlements (indicating the plaintiff actually paid the defendant). The alternative calculations, excluding the negative settlements or taking their absolute value, still yield a ratio of 0.023, identical to three decimal places.

Even more difficult problems exist in interpreting the defendants' apparent losses (table 3.13). In individual cases, especially small ones, fees could show a very high proportion to settlements—as high as 62.77 to 1. This does not mean that the defendants "lost" by paying attorneys so much. Good defense work could have lowered the potential settlement amount substantially. It is clear, though, that in some cases a very small redistribution took a great deal of resources to accomplish. The simple mean of the ratio of defendants' fees to settlements was 5.19. This should not be construed as a finding that a typical private antitrust case involves $5.19 in defendant legal fees to redistribute $1 in settlement because the simple mean exaggerates the contribution of small cases with a high ratio of legal fees to settlements. Such cases were common in this sample (see table 3.13).

Alternative calculations of the ratio of fees to settlements yield more realistic results. Overall, the defendants paid attorneys about the same (mean fee of $176,402) as they gave up in the settlement (mean settlement of $173,596), making the overall ratio of fees to settlements 1.016. This

Table 3.13   Defendants' unadjusted losses in confidential cases

Case number	Attorneys' fees	Cash settlement[a]	Unadjusted loss[b]	Ratio of fees to settlement[c]
10	225,000	200,000	425,000	1.13
11	55,758	20,000	75,758	2.79
12	10,312	9,542	19,854	1.08
13	12,984	5,000	17,984	2.60
14	301,453	371,000	672,453	0.81
15	3,250	142,900	146,150	0.02
16	20,000	2,000	22,000	10.00
17	2,380	−30,000	−27,620	0.08
18	13,007	17,000	30,007	0.77
19	112,200	40,000	152,200	2.80
20	15,702	20,000	35,702	0.79
21	38,276	28,500	66,776	1.34
22	110,000	100,000	210,000	1.10
23	95,000	75,000	170,000	1.27
24	347,000	−500,000	−153,000	0.69
25	41,084	100,000	141,084	0.41
26	85,000	113,000	198,000	0.75
27	70,000	5,500	75,500	12.73
28	170,000	150,000	320,000	1.13
29	37,687	50,000	87,687	0.75
30	1,522,000	750,000	2,272,000	2.03
31	186,651	350,000	536,651	0.53
32	150,000	300,000	450,000	0.50
33	120,753	15,000	135,753	8.05
34	60,000	100,000	160,000	0.60
35	130,000	7,500	137,500	17.33
36	75,000	30,000	105,000	2.50
37	10,000	−5,000	5,000	2.00
38	99,632	12,000	111,632	8.30
39	85,022	10,000	95,022	8.50
40	27,500	100,000	127,500	0.27
41	1,784,356	750,000	2,534,356	2.38
42	90,000	2,000	92,000	45.00
43	15,000	−2,000,000	−1,985,000	0.001
44	19,520	311	19,831	62.77
45	11,000	5,600	16,600	1.96
46	3,500	12,000	15,500	0.29
47	5,500	5,000	10,500	1.10
48	19,569	80,000	99,569	0.24
49	875,000	5,500,000	6,375,000	0.16

Table 3.13 (continued)

Case number	Attorneys' fees	Cash settlement[a]	Unadjusted loss[b]	Ratio of fees to settlement[c]
Simple Mean	176,402	173,596	349,999	5.19
Mean attorneys' fees/mean cash settlement				1.016
Mean attorneys' fees/mean absolute cash settlement[d]				0.587
Mean attorneys' fees/mean cash settlement, excluding cases with negative cash settlement				0.670

Note: These figures apply only to those cases in which there was a cash settlement and attorneys' fees were reported. The absence of dates in this confidential data made adjustment for inflation impossible.
a. A negative number indicates a payment to a defendant.
b. A negative number indicates that the defendant had a gain rather than a loss.
c. This column reflects absolute values of the ratio and therefore includes no negative numbers.
d. This calculation shows the ratio of mean attorneys' fees to mean cash settlements when negative settlements are taken as positive for the purposes of the calculation; that is, the mean *absolute* value of cash settlements is used.

simple mean would tend to indicate that it took a little more than a dollar's worth of defense fees alone in the redistributing of a dollar worth of relief. In table 3.13, however, the presence of negative settlements (indicating that the defendants received money) complicates the calculation considerably. If the mean *absolute* settlement is divided into mean attorneys' fees, the result is 0.587, indicating that defendants spent on their attorneys a little over 58 cents per dollar of settlement paid. Finally, if mean attorneys' fees are divided by the mean cash settlement excluding cases with negative settlements, the resulting ratio is 0.670. Thus, under different methods of figuring the mean, the amount of defendant legal fees involved in a redistribution of $1 worth of settlement lies between 58 cents and $1.02.

Using some of the 200-plus questionnaires that contained partial information on fees and settlements, one could construct further estimates of plaintiffs' and defendants' losses and gains. It is unlikely, however, that any one figure characterizing the distributional efficiency of private antitrust could emerge unchallenged since the calculations are sensitive to the method of computation. We would only note that the smallest of the estimates would put combined plaintiffs' and defendants' legal fees in the neighborhood of 60 cents per dollar's worth of settlement. Since compensation to the victims of market power is the most distinctive feature of private enforcement, it is worth considering the efficiency of private action as a redistribution device. At 60 cents of transaction cost per dollar transferred, private antitrust cannot be considered a highly efficient redis-

Table 3.14   Estimation of legal fees from linked public and private data

Variable	Regression coefficient	Standard error	t-statistic
Docket entries	−200.71	52.75	−3.80**
Thickness of files	683.94	171.57	3.99**
Production of documents, plaintiff	3,123.53	3,463.96	0.90
Production of documents, defendant	13,932.8	5,225.04	2.66**
Naked cartel	51,034.2	26,597.1	1.92*
Asset-patent accumulation	112,536	30,162.9	3.73**
Duration of law firm's involvement	31.26	8.99	3.48**
Number of consultants	55,984.6	5,286.81	10.59**
Executives' time	35.83	16.80	2.13*
Amendments to complaint	10,641.0	7,412.82	1.44
Interventions, plaintiff	110,040	38,439.5	2.86**
Interrogatories by defendant	−4,052.37	2,656.59	−1.58

Dependent variable: reported billings
Constant term = −10,971
R-squared = 0.75
F-statistic = 23.46**
n = 109 cases

Note: Estimation of reported billings was conducted using linear regression with a constant term and the indicated variables. The ** indicates statistical significance at the 1 percent level; the * indicates a 5 percent significance level.

tributive mechanism.[13] In the traditional view of private actions, treble damages are designed to compensate those financially injured by restraints of trade. The data from the confidential survey indicate that private antitrust is not laudable as an efficient institution for redistribution.

Inferences from the Linked Confidential and Public Data
Potentially the most powerful inferences from the data would come from the linked data set combining information from court records with confidential questionnaires. The two questions addressed through combining these data were: (1) What are the characteristics of cases likely to have unusually high, or unusually low, legal fees? and (2) What legal fees are likely to be charged in cases of various types? We specified equations aimed at shedding light on these questions.[14]

Of the infinite variety of regressions that could be used to characterize the size of legal fees, a very simple linear specification involving a small subset of the variables provided a high degree of explanatory power. Table 3.14 reports the results of this simple linear specification, with all dollar figures indexed to 1984 levels. In keeping with Donald N. McCloskey's

(1985) admonition for full disclosure, we report that this equation was not the first one we tested. The equation was developed by testing all the variables in the confidential data set and selected plausible variables from the hundreds in the public data set for their explanatory power. Because of limitations on the computational power of the software used to analyze the confidential data, variables were analyzed by blocks instead of in a full stepwise implementation. In short, our confession is that we engaged in modest data mining.[15]

The equation is capable of explaining 75 percent of the variation of legal fees across cases, with eight reported variables exceeding conventional significance levels and four other variables of interest noted. Some of the variables are just alternative measures of the magnitude of the case, variously defined and have the expected positive signs.[16] The variables measuring thickness of case files and duration of law firms' involvement indicate that thicker case files and longer involvements are associated with higher billings. Two other variables indicate that large numbers of defense requests for documents and defense interrogatories are associated with high legal fees. In addition large numbers of interventions on the plaintiff's side are associated with high fees.

Of the alleged illegal practices, one is strongly associated with higher legal fees: anticompetitive accumulation of assets or patents. Also associated with higher fees, but less strongly, is price fixing by alleged "naked cartels" (marginally significant at 5 percent). Other variables specifying alleged illegal practices had very little explanatory power.

A finding of special interest emerges when the variable measuring consultants' involvement is examined. In cases with larger numbers of consultants, legal fees are markedly higher. The statistical effect is due to two sources: the payment to consultants, which directly increases billings, and the greater complexity of cases in which consultants are employed.

The time of executives involved in antitrust cases is strongly and positively associated with legal fees; that is, cases in which executives spend considerable time working with the attorneys are cases in which legal fees are likely to be high. Executive involvement therefore has a twofold cost for client companies: the cost of the executives' time, and the associated cost for the law firm that results in the higher billings.

The number of docket entries is by itself positively correlated with legal fees. However, the number of docket entries has a negative coefficient when the other explanatory variables are included. Our interpretation is that cases are not especially expensive if they generate more docket entries than would be expected given the levels of other legal resources; in fact, they are less expensive. For example, a case that involved many single pieces of correspondence submitted separately would have a large number of docket entries but would not be an expensive case by other measures.

The number of amendments to the complaint and number of requests for production of documents by the plaintiffs were positively but not strongly associated with legal fees. Defense interrogatories were weakly and negatively associated with legal fees, indicating that large numbers of interrogatories by defense counsel do not necessarily indicate a case is complex by other measures. This may reflect the use of interrogatories strictly as a strategic defense tactic even in relatively uncomplicated cases.

In interpreting all of these coefficients, it is worthwhile to remember that measures of legal resources are highly intercorrelated (table 3.2). Therefore it is risky to attribute the explanatory power of any given coefficient strictly to the variable measured. The number of depositions proved to have less explanatory power and so was excluded from the equation, meaning that some of this variable's explanatory power was assumed by the other variables correlated with it.[17]

Most of the explanatory power of the regression equation was present in the confidential variables. An additional version of the equation, omitting all confidential explanatory variables, was estimated to see how much of the variation in attorneys' fees could be explained by publicly known data. The results were surprisingly good, with 35 to 43 percent of the variation explainable with nonconfidential information. Table 3.15 reports the

Table 3.15   Estimation of legal fees from public data alone

Variable	Regression coefficient	Standard error	t-statistic
Docket entries	−210.83	69.00	−3.05**
Thickness of files	574.70	242.25	2.37*
Production of documents, defendant	12,713.8	4,301.3	2.96**
Duration of case	28.84	10.63	2.71**
New York cases	35,073.4	17,664.1	1.98*
Naked cartel	61,140.7	35,436.6	1.72
Asset-patent accumulation	151,832	34,737.4	4.37**

Dependent variable: reported billings
Constant term = 2,118.79
R-squared = 0.35
F-statistic = 11.49**
n = 156 cases

Note: Estimation of reported billings was conducted using linear regression with a constant term and the indicated variables. The ** indicates statistical significance at the 1 percent level; the * indicates a 5 percent significance level.

estimation of legal fees as a function of only the publicly available characteristics of the cases.[18]

The variables measuring thickness of case files, number of requests for production of documents by defendants, and duration of the case were strongly associated with higher legal fees. In addition legal fees were higher in the New York district filings. Two alleged illegal practices, "naked cartel" price fixing and accumulation of assets and patents, were again associated with higher legal fees, although in this version of the equation the "naked cartel" variable did not pass conventional tests of statistical significance.

By stretching the data analysis to the limit and making heroic assumptions, legal fees can be estimated for all the alleged illegal practices in tables 3.6. Using the coefficients from table 3.15, we obtained for each case a predicted value of total legal billings for the case. We then averaged the predicted values across each alleged illegal practice. The results are presented in table 3.16.

Table 3.16 Estimated mean legal fees per case (plaintiffs' plus defendants') classified by alleged illegal practices

Practice	Estimated mean legal fees	Number of cases
Price fixing	$284,829	264
Naked cartel	792,075	12
Merger-joint venture	350,215	53
Asset accumulation	1,220,319	55
Price discrimination	220,684	132
Predatory pricing	275,065	74
Exclusive dealing	272,181	192
Refusal to deal	291,286	253
Vertical price discrimination	232,000	47
Vertical price fixing	263,370	91
Dealer termination	277,396	93
Inducing government action	311,982	7
Other practice	238,712	55
Restraint of trade	120,209	37
Monopolization	222,581	26
Conspiracy	99,437	12
Entire sample	282,439	1,190

Note: Cases were excluded from these calculations if duration in months was missing, if no illegal practice was coded in the survey data, or if the case was listed as "still pending" or "file missing." Because of multiple entries for some cases, subsamples add to more than 1,190. All figures are in the 1984 dollars.

These estimates are more valid for the middle range of cases than for extensions up to the "megacases" or for downward extensions to the unpursued filings. They are valid only to the extent that the same linear relationship holds in the subsample for which confidential data were available and for the overall sample. Such an assumption is to a large degree untestable. Conventional significance figures are not applicable to our estimates, since the estimates were derived from a difficult-to-characterize mix of regression and mean-substitution procedures. However, the estimates are the best evidence available on the relative legal costs of different types of antitrust fees. The coefficients underlying the estimates explained more than one-third of the variation within the sample, which is very respectable for cross-sectional statistics but is far from overwhelming.

Private Cases: Procompetitive or Strategic?
After these efforts with inferential statistics, we now engage in a less sophisticated exercise in descriptive statistics. Table 3.17 describes the primary relationship of the plaintiff with the defendant in the sample of

Table 3.17   Relationship of plaintiffs to defendants in private antitrust litigation

Relationship	Number of cases	Percentage of total	Percentage of total depositions
Competitors			
Same product	433	22.3	37.1
Similar product	124	6.4	8.9
Other	29	1.5	2.2
Supplier	68	3.5	4.1
Dealer-agent	487	25.1	29.8
Terminated dealership	195	10.1	14.6
Input purchaser	203	10.5	10.2
Final customer	157	8.1	6.1
Employee	48	2.5	3.4
State or local government	21	1.1	0.3
Other	78	4.0	4.5
Licensee	15	0.8	0.3
Franchisee	23	1.2	0.8
Stockholder	14	0.7	0.8
Entire sample	1,946		

Note: Subsamples do not sum to exactly 1,946 because of multiple entries for some cases, missing coding of the business relationship for some cases, and the presence of 22 cases in which there was an uncoded verbal description of business relationship.

cases surveyed in the data set. Similar numbers from a restricted sample appeared earlier in table 3.5. The middle column of table 3.17 portrays the numbers from the entire sample by themselves for singular scrutiny.

Of the 14 possible listed relationships between the litigants, the table reveals that the most common was that of the plaintiff's being a dealer, agent, or distributor of the defendant. Just over 25 percent of the cases fall in this category. This statistic by itself suggests that the costs of private enforcement exceed the social benefits for one fourth of all private enforcement.

One need not hold the Chicago School position—that all loose-knit vertical relationships should be per se legal—to imagine that many of these vertical antitrust cases have nothing to do with the alleviation of market power or the restoration of consumer surplus. Anyone who has witnessed a sample of terminated dealership cases can testify that most of these cases, if not all, are contract disputes that have escalated into antitrust claims by dint of plaintiffs' hopes of extracting larger monetary settlements or awards than contract law might enable. As contract disputes, the cases may well involve legitimate grievances. But as antitrust suits having any connection with maintaining competition, some—if not many—of them are unfounded.

After *Illinois Brick* in 1977, it became more likely that plaintiffs who are dealer-agents might be suing cartelists, in that final consumers of a cartel's products could no longer secure standing (except in unusual circumstances). This means that some of the dealer-agent cases listed in table 3.17 might have efficiency merits even to a Chicagoan who would otherwise take a skeptical view of dealers as plaintiffs. However, data in chapter 1 by Salop and White (table 1.8) reveal that instances of dealers' alleging price fixing are rather modest: most dealer suits are for refusal to deal, tying, exclusive dealing, dealer termination, and price discrimination. Fewer than 10 percent pertained to horizontal price fixing. If the data set's catchall categories of conspiracy, restraint of trade, and monopolization are included with dealers' suits alleging horizontal price fixing, the percentage of dealers' suing as potential aggrieved customers rises to 18.9 percent of the dealer cases.

In recent years antitrust authorities have begun to view with skepticism a plea for antitrust action against a firm by that firm's competitor. Under this interpretation of antitrust, for example, if Chrysler objects to a merger between rival auto companies, this is perceived to signal not a concern by Chrysler of impending market power by the merging parties but rather of impending efficiencies resulting from the merger.[19] Put differently, the "new antitrust strategy" (as defined and discussed later) is seen as protectionism. Suspicious of this ulterior motive, federal antitrust authorities have become reluctant to pursue litigative proposals brought to them by private parties seeking government antitrust action against their competitors.

Private attorneys, however, may be willing to file lawsuits of this character. Of the 142 challenges to mergers and joint ventures in the data set, 82 (59.4 percent) were by competitors. Table 3.17's breakdown confirms that private antitrust suits brought by firms against their competitors are common, not rare. The second most common relationship between the litigants was that of competitors—firms producing the same product. Over 22 percent of the cases covered in table 3.17 were of this category. The next most common category is very similar to this: firms producing a similar product. Over 6 percent of the plaintiffs and defendants produced similar or substitute products.

One need not adopt the interpretation that *every* antitrust complaint filed by a firm against a rival is on its face protectionist in order to be sobered by the statistical makeup of the plaintiff-defendant relationship. To the extent that private antitrust enforcement enables plaintiffs to raise their rivals' costs or lessen the latter's ardor for hard competition, the data reveal that there have been many opportunities for such behavior.

Other plaintiff litigation categories that probably would not improve competition significantly include stockholder, franchisee, employee or former employee, supplier, and other competitor. All of these involved minor percentages of the litigation sample. For practical purposes they can be ignored.

If one is considering the costs to the legal system of private antitrust enforcement, our interpretation is that the procompetitive benefits of much of private antitrust activity are modest if not nil. Too many of the wrong kinds of suits are being brought. If we assume such suits consume, directly and indirectly, nontrivial amounts of society's scarce resources, the case for treble damages in their present form is a weak one.

Putting aside lawsuits where the plaintiff is or was a rival of the defendant, litigation where the plaintiff has or had a loose-knit vertical agreement with the defendant, and the miscellaneous categories of lawsuits portrayed in the table, one is left to consider lawsuits brought by final customers (or end users), companies to whom the defendant is supplier, and state or local governments. That is, one has winnowed the data set down to where traditional economic theory might expect plaintiffs to have been losers as a result of the exercise of market power. Given the potential for economic benefits from litigation by these plaintiffs, society may want to bear the costs of the litigation system. But such cases encompass only a fraction of private antitrust enforcement.

Table 3.17 reveals that of all the litigation surveyed in the data set, less than one-fourth (21.5 percent) involved plaintiffs whose economic relationship with the defendant was of the character where there was likely to have been a genuine welfare loss to be remedied or alleviated by the litigation. To put the matter more starkly, over three-fourths of the treble damage litigation was of an economic character where economists potentially would not expect efficiency-enhancing consequences if the plaintiffs prevailed. In the numerical majority of the cases, society is unlikely to be the beneficiary, in terms of capturing consumer surplus gains. This assessment is strengthened when the percentage of costs per type of case, proxied by the number of depositions, is considered (rightmost column of table 3.17).[20] Of the depositions observed in the sample, more than 37 percent occurred in cases of competitors suing their direct rivals, and almost 30 percent occurred in the dealer-agent cases.

Moreover, of the approximately 400 lawsuits where the plaintiff's relationship with the defendant was that of a customer (where losses in consumer surplus because of defendant's market power may have been possible), one presumes that in some fraction of these instances, plaintiffs' cases were groundless (i.e., without merit in reducing market power). For example, in a case where a plaintiff alleges price fixing by defendant suppliers, the plaintiff may have been mistaken (or filed a nuisance suit). A plaintiff will not always correctly identify or show defendants to be restraining trade.

Our assessment is that only a minority of the cases in the data set, and presumably in private antitrust generally, have any connection with improving or maintaining competition. The costs that many private actions impose on the legal system constitute a net loss to society in securing the economic goals of antitrust. The litigation is unrelated to the goals of deterring the exercise of market power. If a standing rule were adopted that eliminated as plaintiffs those bringing suits where there is unlikely to be any allocative harm, many of these suits would be denied standing at the outset, thus conserving on judicial resources and maintaining an economizing purpose to the antitrust laws.[21]

3.4 Costs Not Directly Measured in the Data

The Infrastructure of Antitrust

Data collection for this project necessarily focused on the readily measurable characteristics of antitrust cases, such as types of cases filed, damages claimed, and the disposition of cases. Partly as a result, our paper has focused to this point on the open and explicit costs of the litigation system. It is important, however, also to focus on the more subtle costs generated by the very existence of a private antitrust system and the strategic responses of firms to that system.

The data set only hinted at a costly infrastructure that has grown up to support the institution of private enforcement. For example, in the midst of the numerous IBM cases, a specialized reporting service emerged whose only purpose was to disseminate information about the cases.[22] More generally, the institution of private enforcement requires a greater allocation of public resources in the form of courts, clerks, judges, and other government-consumed resources that are not part of the expenditures of the litigants.

Consequences of Strategic Behavior

To understand the costs of antitrust brought on by strategic behavior, we must briefly consider the decision-making process of potential plaintiffs.[23] Initiating an antitrust action, at one level of abstraction, is much like any other investment decision a firm makes. Just as the firm must attempt to judge the uncertain revenues that flow from costly investment in a new plant, so must the firm attempt to judge the uncertain benefits that may come from incurring the costs of an antitrust action.[24]

For the would-be plaintiff, the dollar benefit of an antitrust action depends on two terms: the probability of a favorable resolution and the monetary-equivalent value of a favorable resolution. Cash awards and settlements are only the most visible of the gains to be had; we will discuss other gains shortly. In addition to the potential benefit a prospective plaintiff will also weigh the variance, or dispersion, of potential outcomes. It will favor actions that more predictably lead to favorable outcomes.

A major part of the firm's incentives arise from the system of multiple damages liability imposed solely on the alleged holder of market power. Under such a regime plaintiffs will be induced to behave strategically, overinvesting in antitrust cases in a way that contracts the wealth of the economy.

The first of the economic costs is that of perverse incentives. Because of the prospect of multiple damages, a customer of a monopolist or cartel has less incentive to seek out substitutes. In fact, the customer may shop opportunistically, preferring to suffer damages now in order to benefit from the treble damages awarded later. Part of the customer's investment in the antitrust action is the current suffering of damages. Trebled damages, considered together with a high enough probability of winning, may make such a course of action attractive in comparison with the firm's other investments.

The data we surveyed, dealing with what actually happened in antitrust cases rather than the opportunities potentially open to firms, can say little about the size of these costs. The sketchy evidence of table 3.12 is that plaintiffs did relatively well in their cases, but there is no evidence at all on unexploited opportunities to mitigate damages. The case for the existence of perverse incentive effects remains one supported by anecdotal evidence and founded on the economic theory of human behavior—that individuals' behavior is affected by economic incentives. The potential social costs from the exercise of perverse incentives, however, may be smaller than has been previously believed. The data indicate that there have been relatively few private actions involving horizontal price fixing and overcharges. In the typical private action there is no customer buying at supracompetitive prices and therefore no monopoly damages to run up by overbuying.

The data set is more informative on a second inefficiency induced by private treble damages actions, the misinformation effect. This occurs when private litigants fabricate antitrust cases when no anticompetitive harm to the economy exists.[25] There is clear evidence that the number of such cases is substantial. More than a fifth of the cases in table 3.7 (concerning the alleged violation involved) were coded by the field workers as "antitrust not a significant issue." The confidential questionnaires filled out by the attorneys were even more revealing of misinformation effects. One attorney wrote in a space left for comments, "Essentially a collections case; antitrust suit a litigation tactic to induce settlement at a lower figure." Another attorney, in explaining the absence of full billing figures, wrote, "Case was part of a general takeover defense & was not separately billed to client." Other questionnaires contained similar comments: "Essentially a breach of contract action"; "This case was primarily a contract dispute"; "Theft of trade secrets case rather than anti-trust"; "Distributor, terminated for inadequate sales, brought suit & then filed for bankruptcy, cmplt. was dismissed voluntarily."

At several stages in the development of the public and private data sets, the field workers and the analysts at Cambridge Research were confronted with the difficulty of what to do with such cases, when informed by attorneys or others that the cases were "not really antitrust." In one sense these are not cases dealing with genuine trade restraints, in that they have nothing to do with maintaining a competitive economy. In another sense these cases certainly are antitrust cases, in that they are made possible by the antitrust statutes and made into more attractive investments for plaintiffs by the potential for treble damages.

In a world without judicial error, the misinformation effect would never result in treble damages being paid; the courts and juries would recognize the flawed nature of lawsuits and rule against them. But even in such a world the misinformation effect would be an economic drag upon judicial resources. Resources would be spent as the system discovered the flawed nature of the plaintiff's case. Misinformation suits might be filed in the hope that defendants would offer some settlement rather than engage in the cost of litigation. In a world of judicial uncertainty the incentive to settle is heightened by the extensive use of juries in private antitrust actions. In class actions, where the trebling feature of antitrust can generate damage claims that are enormous, management's decision may be to settle, not so much to remove a nuisance action against it, but as an in terrorem response to the repercussions of even a slim chance of losing. Economic theory informs us that multiple damages will induce the misinformation effect by making an investment in antitrust cases more attractive.

Economic theory also teaches that the magnitude of the misinformation effect, and its consequent drag upon the judicial system, will be a function of the risk aversion of corporate managers and the uncertainty associated with antitrust litigation, especially in the face of changing legal, evidentiary, and class certification standards. The more risk averse is management, the more defendants will succumb to financial settlement though innocent (or in circumstances when their antitrust counsel puts a high probability on a judicial finding of innocence).

The scope for the misinformation effect became more pronounced in the era of what Arthur D. Austin (1978) calls the "new antitrust strategy." In this era private plaintiffs seek not only the up-front payment of treble damages but also the long-term benefit of a defendant's softening of its rivalry toward them. This may come in the form of less price competition, more favorable supply contracts, and other of what Austin calls the "noncompensatory goals" of private antitrust litigation: seeking the modification of defendants' behavior in a way favorable to the plaintiff. A softening of rivalry can be even more valuable than cash settlements to some plaintiffs, although assigning a dollar value to such implicit concessions is speculative at best (and was not attempted in our calculations of the net recovery by plaintiffs).

There is a third inefficiency associated with private antitrust enforcement: reparations costs. These are the costs of resources used in determining and allocating damages (in contrast to public enforcement, where no reparations are made). The compensation element of private enforcement extends the negotiation process in settled suits, requires greater judicial, legal and clerical resources associated with the compensation task, and because of the magnitude of some awards, induces more rent-seeking behavior on the part of plaintiffs (and their counsel). All of this is a cost to society.

As one illustration of this cost, in class action antitrust cases (where attorneys' fees of millions of dollars can be at stake) much of the courts' time in the reparations process must be spent on disputes about the intralawyer allocation of these fees. In guarding against the conflict of interest between class members and their counsel, judges must become regulators. Indeed, the procedure in such cases bears a resemblance to public utility regulation.

In the case of public utilities a regulator must ascertain what should go in and what should stay out of the firm's rate base and then determine the proper rate of return that owners should be allowed to make, given the riskiness of the industry. From this calculation a price (or rate structure) is set.

In the same way that utilities have had incentives to build up their capital input base (Averch and Johnson 1962), the plaintiffs' attorneys in class action suits face incentives to build up the labor input base. Lawyers also have an incentive to exaggerate the complexity of the case in order to enlarge the multiplier to be applied to the base of hours expended, just as utilities have incentives to overstate the riskiness of their endeavors in seeking higher returns.

A commonly advanced remedy for the ills of utility regulation today is deregulation, and it may be time to consider the deregulation of attorneys' fees—paradoxically, through turning to public enforcement. Under public enforcement deregulation of attorneys' fees is accomplished because attorneys (as employees of the antitrust agencies) are hired at market wages to provide the litigative input. This eliminates the need for judicial input in certifying classes, in determining the classes' legal representation, and in deciding the compensation of plaintiffs' attorneys.

3.5 Interpretations and Implications

Juries in Antitrust Trials

The statistical tests reported in table 3.4 lend weight to proposals to abolish the use of juries in antitrust enforcement. The tests indicate that jury proceedings consume more legal resources. The tests are concerned directly with private enforcement, but there is a sound argument for abolishing the use of juries in public actions as well. In either type of case the question of liability can be prolonged and technical. In one complex antitrust trial that had led to a deadlocked jury, the foreman was asked by the judge whether such cases should be tried by juries. The man responded, "If you can find a jury that's both a computer technician, a lawyer, an economist, knows all about that stuff, yes, I think you could have a qualified jury, but we don't know anything about that." [26] Other jurors in the same trial were polled, some arguing as well that complex antitrust cases might better be tried by the judge rather than a jury.

The conventional reason to remove jurors from antitrust is the complexity of the issue.[27] That is, a reduction in enforcement error is thought to be the benefit from such an action. The results of our study provide a different reason, one falling on the cost side of the equation: jury trials are a greater drag on the judicial system. Table 3.4 shows that jury trials last over 60 percent longer than do cases decided by judges. The average length of a case tried by jury is somewhat longer than nonjury litigation.[28]

Of the 1,946 cases in the data set, jury trials were requested in 1,193 of the cases. Of the 1,193 the overwhelming proportion of the requests were by plaintiffs (only 43 were by defendants; 3 were by both). One interpretation of this lopsided pattern is straightforward: the 43/1,193 ratio may reflect the extent to which plaintiffs hope to cast antitrust as a "good guys versus bad guys" dispute.

The relatively higher cost of jury trials is consistent with the results found by Dennis Weller and Michael K. Block (1979) in their analysis of the costs of judicial services. In studying the California superior court system, they found that jury trials cost more than nonjury trials. The recommendation to abolish jury trials is consistent with the proposal of Richard A. Posner in his book (1985) on the federal courts. He writes:

Among the politically infeasible proposals that deserve serious attention is the abolition of the jury trial in civil cases—a course that the rest of the civilized world took long ago.... Abolition would have a substantial effect on the workload of the federal district courts. The average federal civil jury trial in 1983 lasted 4.48 days, compared to 2.21 days for the average nonjury trial. If the difference is multiplied by the number of jury trials, and then divided by the number of district judges, this yields a saving (if all jury trials were converted into nonjury trials) of 22 days per judge per year.[29]

For the sample of cases we studied, the average case that went to trial consumed eight trial days. But the jury trials consumed an average of 11. Every antitrust case tried by a judge holds out the prospect of not only improving on the result but reducing immediate court costs by three days per case, not to mention the other economies that would accrue in pretrial resources saved.

The High Costs of Price Fixing Cases

The high resource costs associated with price-fixing cases (table 3.6) may at first glance seem surprising, given the per se character of the price-fixing offense. What raises the resource ante in these cases, in our judgment, is not the legal precision associated with the offense but the imprecision associated with its proof.

A per se rule does not entail judicial economies if there is ambiguity and a lack of predictability in the standards of proof. If the offense is construed only as taking the form of an explicit agreement, then resource costs might be moderate. Even then, the search for the explicit agreement—the costs of uncovering the hot document—can be high, reflecting the extreme labor intensity of the task. If, however, the offense of price fixing is construed broadly as something that more accurately might be called "tortious excessive contacts," [30] then the resource costs of litigating price fixing cases can be high indeed. Further augmenting the costs of private price-fixing litigation is the expenditure of resources to measure the amount and incidence of damages, a cost not normally associated with price-fixing cases brought by the government.

To express this in a more precise way, the expected recovery for a plaintiff can be represented as

$$E(R) = pkMD,$$

where p is the probability of showing to the judge's satisfaction that the alleged practices took place, k is the probability that the judge will find those practices illegal, M is the damage multiple (under current law, 3), and D is the amount of damages. Changes in antitrust policy and the case law affect these parameters. Changes in standards of evidence, for example, can affect p. Declaring a violation to be per se illegal changes k from a probability to a certainty, making $k = 1$. The damage multiple, M, can be changed upward or downward, as a number of reform proposals have suggested. Finally, the amount of damages, D, is subject to various definitions, expansions, and limitations.

Notice that it may not be possible to change one parameter in the expression without inducing changes in other parameters. For example, raising the damage multiple—and thereby making the financial penalty heavier for convicted defendants larger—might induce judges to demand more rigorous proof of an offense, lowering p or k.[31]

The costliness of price-fixing cases also can be interpreted through this expression. With the damage multiple (M) set at 3 and a per se rule ($k = 1$), the expected return from filing price-fixing cases would be high, other things equal. But other things are not equal. The attractiveness of price-fixing cases causes some complaints to be filed even if the probability of proving price fixing is low (i.e., even if p is small). In these cases the attempt to construct the inference of price fixing may take a great deal of effort and evidence. Recognizing the per se character of the offense, judges may insist on higher standards of proof than they otherwise would. Finally, the attractiveness of increasing D, or measured damages, invites the plaintiff to devote resources to getting a high estimate of D and the defendant to hire its own consultants and experts to counter with a lower estimate of D.

The Megacases and the Great "Middle Range"

Statistical outliers can influence the opinions of even those who have prolonged experience working with numbers. In studying private antitrust litigation one's attention repeatedly goes to the *IBM* and *AT&T* cases with regard to the complexity and duration of antitrust litigation. When considering awards and settlements, it is the $50 million in the *Fine Paper* litigation, the $173 million settlement in the *Plywood* litigation, the $350 million paid by manufacturers of corrugated containers—and other settlements and awards of this stature—that come to mind. The uncommon cases become the common examples.

One of the virtues of the data set used in our study is that it illuminates the extent to which the megacases are outliers that may distort our understanding of private antitrust enforcement as a whole. Public policy should consider the economic consequences of the large antitrust case. Its size alone may dictate special institutional arrangements. But public policy informed only by the megacase may be unfitting for the modal private action.

One virtue of the judicial cost study by Trubek et al. (1983, 80–81) is its focus on what they called "ordinary litigation." They were concerned with civil litigation in the "middle range," and their sample excluded disputes in which the initial claim was below $1,000 and also excluded megacases. Their inquiry focused on whether ordinary litigation entailed the problems commonly associated with the court system: long delays, exorbitant legal fees that eat up recoveries, and complex judicial maneuvering. They found the "typical" case in federal courts and state courts of general jurisdiction to be the following:

1. Unusual if litigated, since only one in nine disputes even reaches the filing state.

2. Modest in its financial stakes, with the amount in dispute usually being less than $10,000.

3. Procedurally simple, so much so that the typical case will be settled without a judicial verdict or judgment (there will be pretrial activity, but rarely a trial).

4. Modest in its legal input, with less than 30 hours spent by the lawyers on each side.

5. A paying proposition for both sides, in that the plaintiff typically recovers more than half its legal fees and the defendant pays legal fees less than the amount by which the initial claim was reduced by the judicial process (White et al. 1983, 83–84).

Trubek and his colleagues found the real world of ordinary litigation often "at odds with the image held by many in the public and some in the legal profession" (1983, 122).

It would be instructive to understand as well the costs of the "typical" private action. Two estimates recently were offered of the cost of litigating an ordinary predation case. One was $3 million; the other, $30 million.[32] The tenfold character of the discrepancy is disturbing. As it stands, the data set provides only limited assistance in settling the difference in estimates. But consider a "typical" antitrust case as being the sort of case defined by the measures of central tendency in table 3.1. Such a case would involve 68 docket entries, and five depositions would be taken. The case would most likely not go to trial, and the whole process from the filing of the complaint to the final docket entry would take just over two years. We estimate that the combined legal fees of plaintiffs and defendants would be just over $280,000. This picture of ordinary litigation in antitrust suggests something far different from cases that become the subject of legend.[33]

3.6 Conclusions

Not long ago the only significant dissenter on the topic of treble damages was Thurman Arnold. Today criticism of this form of antitrust enforcement is to be found in many quarters. Moreover an openness to reform exists to an unparalleled extent.

Even in this atmosphere of restraint and examination, private antitrust enforcement remains a durable institution. Chapter 1 by Salop-White records the number of private antitrust cases commenced during the period 1941 to 1984 (see table 1.1). In every year from 1971 through 1984, more than 1,000 cases have been filed in the federal courts alone. This figure is less than that in the heyday period engendered by the electrical equipment cases. And the trend has been slightly downward during the last decade (1,216 cases per year for 1980 to 1984 compared to 1,432 for 1975 to 1979). Private antitrust may be a declining industry, but it is hardly comparable in its shrinkage to domestic shoe manufacturing or sugar growing.

This paper peers inside this industry to reveal the various forms that private antitrust actions take and the relative costs of each. Much of the paper is an exercise in taxonomy and measurement. The opportunity of interpreting the statistical measures is one that is shared with the reader.

Our analysis of the data indicates that it is easy to exaggerate the costs of private enforcement upon the litigation system. Newsworthy cases are not the norm, and although the typical private antitrust suit partakes of more resources than the typical civil action, it does not absorb litigation resources of a major proportion. Our analysis also indicates that in those instances where the prevailing case law is relatively straightforward, such as price fixing, the litigation costs of private enforcement still do not come cheap.

The types of cases brought in the private enforcement arena, as judged by the relationship between plaintiff and defendant, are disturbing, suggesting that much of private enforcement has little to do with improving resource allocation and deterring market power. This assessment is consistent with earlier research in the field of law and economics that concluded that private enforcement has economic inefficiencies that public enforcement of the antitrust laws does not share.

If private treble damages actions constitute a declining industry, does this form of antitrust enforcement merit continued attention? To an economist the focus of interest is not so much on whether an industry is large or small, but instead on the benefits to society of the resources used by the industry—and whether these benefits could be secured with a smaller expenditure of resources. If the benefit society seeks is enhanced economic efficiency from a reduction of market power, then the payoffs of private antitrust seem modest. It is hard to say whether the costs of private enforcement are "small" or "large" in any absolute sense. Still, the costs do seem larger than would be required to operate a nonreparations based system of public enforcement, one that imposed larger penalties upon violators than is now the norm.

Notes

The authors would like to thank William Breit, Saul X. Levmore, Steven C. Salop, David Scheffman, Richard Schmalensee, and Lawrence J. White for helpful comments on an earlier draft. James R. Pagano provided valuable research assistance.

1. The number of rulings was defined to exclude routine decisions by judges and magistrates on scheduling and mechanics.

2. Although there was at least some information for 1,946 separate cases, the survey data were incomplete for many of the cases, making restrictions on the sample necessary. Each table indicates how the sample was restricted for the calculations. Cases that were marked as "file missing" or "still pending" were routinely excluded. In addition cases were excluded from the calculations if no primary illegal practice was noted in the survey data. For the tables describing the business relationship between plaintiff and defendant, cases in the data set were excluded where the business relationship had not been noted.

3. The interpretation of the significance test is worth emphasizing. A high test statistic does not indicate substantive significance, nor does a low figure indicate a relationship is absent. Rather, the interpretation in this instance is that there is a difference large enough that it is not likely due to sampling error. For competitors producing the same product, the chance is only 5 percent that the observed difference in the number of docket entries could be attributed to sampling error rather than an actual difference.

4. These latter instances are the "megacases," in the terminology of Trubek et al. (1983).

5. The test was implemented by Grossman et al. (1981) in their survey of civil litigation.

6. It should be noted that table 3.4 compares jury and nonjury cases only if they went to trial. Another exercise would compare trials ending in jury verdicts with *all other* possible resolutions of a case—some of them, such as settlement or summary judgment, being much shorter and less complex. Such a comparison is appropriate if the assumption is that in the absence of juries, those cases that otherwise would be tried before juries would be resolved with the same mix of solutions present in the sample. In this comparison cases ending in a jury verdict generated significantly more docket entries, depositions, judges' rulings, and magistrates' rulings. The jury cases also had significantly longer mean durations and survival times. It is clear, however, that most of the effect is from the different amounts of resources going to fully litigated cases as opposed to cases resolved without trial. To summarize, jury verdicts clearly take more trial days than do verdicts from a judge and take more legal resources than the average from all other possible resolutions of a case.

7. The durability of antitrust cases is not a new phenomenon attributable to the sophistication of the specialized antitrust bar. Delay tactics have existed from the outset of the Sherman Act. In the initial attempts to undo the Standard Oil trust, the attorneys for the trust invoked a state statute that compelled all testimony to be taken in longhand. After much wrangling, Standard

Oil's counsel finally permitted a typewriter to be used but never agreed to the use of shorthand. See Bruce Bringhurst (1979, 92–93).

8. This category could embrace state antitrust statutes or other statutes with antitrust features.

9. For an example of this approach, see Gould (1973).

10. See chapter 2 by Teplitz.

11. In this respect, the sample is similar to the sample studied by the Civil Litigation Research Project and reported in Trubek et al. (1983).

12. For a detailed consideration of plaintiffs' and defendants' incentives, see chapter 1 by Salop and White.

13. If a program required exactly 60 cents in redistributional costs to transfer $1, this would translate to a "leakage" of 37.5 percent, to use the terminology of Okun (1975). That is, $1.60 of income would have to be taken from a plaintiff to confer $1 worth of relief to a defendant after paying the lawyers their 60 cents, and 60 cents divided by $1.60 is 37.5 percent. Such a leakage would place a program well beyond the limit of 15 percent leakage that Okun (1975, 94–95) judged marginally acceptable for redistributions not clearly targeted as being from the very richest to the very poorest. For some estimates of redistributional leakages, and a general discussion, see Browning and Johnson (1984).

14. The analysis was performed at the Cambridge Research Institute. We are indebted to Marshall Tracht at CRI for his diligence in overcoming the difficulties of running regressions by "remote control."

15. We recognize that this process prevents a classical statistical interpretation of our significance tests, and we therefore offer the customary R-squared, F-, and t-statistics for two purposes: first, to indicate the numerical degree of the associations, and second, to facilitate comparison with other papers in the literature that engage in undisclosed data mining. For those who would judge an equation simply by the unadjusted R-squared, we report that in a subset of 53 cases with especially complete information, an unadjusted R-squared of 0.93 can be achieved. The equation reported in table 3.14 was estimated for 109 cases with slightly less complete files; we judged the increased sample size to be worth the loss of numerical explanatory power.

16. Note that there are two main obstacles to interpreting this equation as a production function, a relationship showing how "inputs" (e.g., docket entries and interrogatories) are combined to produce an "output" (the dependent variable, legal fees). First, legal fees are not a good measure of legal output; they are more likely to measure the legal inputs, such as lawyer time, devoted to the case. Second, the equation includes two variables for "type of case" in addition to the variables measuring physical characteristics of cases. A pure production function approach would exclude such variables, including only the physical characteristics. An implication is that our equation allows certain types of cases (naked cartel and asset-patent accumulation) to show higher legal fees than would be expected just from the numbers of docket entries, interrogatories, and other characteristics of the cases.

17. We thought that our equation might fit more poorly for the bigger cases in our sample, a circumstance that would call for correction of the estimates by a weighting procedure. However, a standard test indicated that the problem was absent. Extensive testing was not possible, since we did not have full access to the linked public and private data. A Glejser test employing the absolute value of awards as the variable associated with potential heteroskedasticity proved to be insignificant at conventional levels. See Maddala (1977, 262). There still is little assurance that the equation would fit the megacases well, and the negative test

result may indicate only the relative uniformity among cases for which questionnaires were returned.

18. This was not the first equation that we tried using only nonconfidential data. A restricted subset of 69 cases produced an R-squared of 0.43, using the variables concerning thickness of case files, production of documents, and damages claimed. We found that the number of cases could be more than doubled—to 156—if we dropped the variable measuring damages claimed, since that variable was missing for a number of cases in which confidential data were available. In preparing to project results onto a set of more than a thousand cases, we felt that the larger sample size warranted settling for a lower R-squared.

19. Chrysler should welcome higher prices as a result of market power; it should not welcome lower costs on the part of its rivals.

20. We are indebted to Richard Schmalensee for suggesting calculations of this sort to us.

21. For a discussion of the importance of the standing issue in reforming private antitrust action, see the discussion in Breit and Elzinga (1986).

22. Reporting Service Follows Antitrust War against IBM, *The Washington Post*, October 6, 1974, p. H3. Some subscribers of this periodical undoubtedly were law firms engaged in the cases and whose legal fees had the cost of this newsletter embedded in them. But legal fees would not pick up the full costs. Also subscribing were investors, financial analysts, and suppliers of IBM, as well as rivals and customers. Such expenditures, and others of this character, are part of the total cost of the private enforcement enterprise.

23. The costs examined here were first set forth in Breit and Elzinga (1974).

24. See Gould (1973) on this general approach.

25. The misinformation effect is a different inefficiency from the perverse incentives effect. In the latter, an actual trade restraint exists—which provokes the inefficient behavior on the part of a plaintiff.

26. See IBM Is Granted Directed Verdict in Memorex Case, *The Wall Street Journal*, August 14, 1978, p. 3.

27. To remove such litigation from the realm of juries is not to belittle their intelligence but rather to recognize the economic-technological-accounting-statistical complexity of antitrust.

28. One of the leading members of the private antitrust bar has suggested this reason for the greater costliness of jury trials: it takes much more time to explain matters to a jury than to a judge. "You certainly have to make it a good deal fancier and it costs a good deal more if you are going to have to spend months before a jury explaining something that you could explain to a judge in a week or ten days," observed Harold E. Kohn (1968, 11).

29. Posner notes that not all of this time would be saved in that the Federal Rules of Civil Procedure require judges to prepare written findings of fact and conclusions of law in cases not tried before a jury. But he concludes that with the abolition of juries in civil cases there "would undoubtedly be a considerable time saving." See Posner (1985, 130).

30. The term was suggested by James F. Kirkham, and one of the coauthors is indebted to him for discussions on this point.

31. See chapter 5 by Calkins.

32. See Easterbrook (1981, 335) and sources cited therein.

33. Typical cases therefore involve few of the startling hourly figures that get the attention of the more modestly paid general public. When a prominent member of the antitrust bar expected over $600 per hour for his labor, and another charged $15 per hour for his son's time

moving boxes of trial documents, the press noticed. See Paul Taylor, A Lawyers' Fee-for-All: $610 an Hour? in *The Washington Post*, April 10, 1983, p. Cl.

References

Austin, Arthur D. 1978. Negative Effects of Treble Damage Actions: Reflections on the New Antitrust Strategy. Duke Law Journal (January): 1353–1374.

Averch, Harvey, and Johnson, Leland L. 1962. Behavior of the Firm under Regulatory Constraint. *American Economic Review* 52 (December): 1052–1069.

Breit, William, and Elzinga, Kenneth G. 1974. Antitrust Enforcement and Economic Efficiency: The Uneasy Case for Treble Damages. *Journal of Law & Economics* 17 (October): 329–356.

Breit, William, and Elzinga, Kenneth G. 1985. Private Antitrust Enforcement: The New Learning. *Journal of Law & Economics* 28 (May): 405–443.

Breit, William, and Elzinga, Kenneth G. 1986. *Antitrust Penalty Reform: An Economic Survey*. Washington, D.C.: American Enterprise Institute.

Bringhurst, Bruce. 1979. *Antitrust and the Oil Monopoly: The Standard Oil Cases, 1890–1911*. Westport, Conn.: Greenwood Press.

Browning, Edgar K., and Johnson, William R. 1984. The Trade-Off between Equality and Efficiency. *Journal of Political Economy* 92 (April): 175–203.

Easterbrook, Frank. 1981. Predatory Strategies and Counterstrategies. *University of Chicago Law Review* 48 (Spring): 263–337.

Gould, John P. 1973. The Economics of Legal Conflicts. *Journal of Legal Studies* 2 (June): 279–300.

Grossman, Joel B., Kritzer, Herbert M., Bumiller, Kristin, and McDougal, Stephen. 1981. Measuring the Pace of Civil Litigation in Federal and State Trial Courts. *Judicature* 65 (August): 86–113.

Kohn, Harold E. 1968. Evaluation of an Antitrust Claim, Prospective Cost of Litigation, Standing to Sue and Preparation of Suit. *Antitrust Law Journal* 38: 7–15.

Lee, E., and Desu, M. 1972. A Computer Program for Comparing K Samples with Right-Censored Data. *Computer Programs in Biomedicine* 2: 315–321.

Maddala, G. S. 1977. *Econometrics*. New York: McGraw-Hill.

McCloskey, Donald N. 1985. The Loss Function Has Been Mislaid: The Rhetoric of Significance Tests. *American Economic Review Papers and Proceedings* 75 (May): 201–205.

Okun, Arthur M. 1975. *Equality and Efficiency: The Big Tradeoff*. Washington, D.C.: Brookings Institution.

Posner, Richard A. 1985. *The Federal Courts: Crisis and Reform*. Cambridge: Harvard University Press.

Stelzer, Irwin M. 1985. The Treble Damage Remedy: Should It Be Eliminated? Unpublished paper.

Trubek, David M., Sarat, Austin, Felstiner, William L. F., Kritzer, Herbert M., and Grossman, Joel B. 1983. The Costs of Ordinary Litigation. *UCLA Law Review* 31 (October): 72–127.

The Wall Street Journal. IBM Is Granted Directed Verdict in Memorex Case. August 14, 1978, p. 3.

The Washington Post. Reporting Service Follows Antitrust War against IBM. October 6, 1974, p. H3.

The Washington Post. A Lawyers' Fee-for-All: $610 an Hour? April 10, 1983, p. C1.

Weller, Dennis, and Block, Michael K. 1979. Estimating the Cost of Judicial Services. Technical report CERDCR-1-79. Center for Econometric Studies of the Judicial System. Hoover Institution, Stanford University, May.

4

Settlements in Private Antitrust Litigation

Jeffrey M. Perloff and Daniel L. Rubinfeld

4.1 Introduction

In this chapter a simple theory of settlement behavior is used to analyze the data from the Georgetown project on private antitrust litigation. The empirical version of the model is used to simulate the effect on settlements of a reduction in the damage multiplier from its current level of three. The simulations indicate that reducing the damages multiplier in antitrust cases could dramatically lower the settlement rate as well as affect the propensity of plaintiffs to bring suits and to win suits that go to trial.

In recent years there has been substantial attention paid by lawyers, politicians, and academics to the volume and form of private antitrust litigation.[1] Treble damages has been a focal point because there has been serious concern as to whether the benefits of discouraging inappropriate business behavior outweigh the costs of the litigation process.[2] Public discussion about the costs of litigation often focuses on the cost of trial even though a substantial portion of cases end without a court trial.[3] Most of the academic literature on antitrust deterrence and litigation has also generally ignored settlement as well—at least as far as questions of optimal damages and choice of damage multiplier are concerned. Rather, the literature has focused primarily on the deterrence associated with the payment of compensatory damages by a defendant when a case is lost.[4]

By building on recent theoretical work on the economics of the litigation process and on data from the Georgetown project, this chapter expands current knowledge about antitrust settlements.[5] Section 4.2 provides a nontechnical description of a framework for describing and evaluating the antitrust litigation process. Litigation consists of three interdependent strands: first, the decision by the plaintiff whether to file suit; second, the decisions by plaintiff and defendant whether to settle; and third, the decisions by both parties as to what type of effort to put forth during the trial.

The process is inherently interdependent because the decision to sue depends on one's expectations as to the likelihood of settlement and trial and on the gains or losses associated with each. Likewise, expectations concerning the effort to be put forth at trial affect the probability of litigation and settlement. Thus, while the second strand of the litigation process (settlement) is emphasized, it is essential that the analysis take into account the relationship between settlements and the decision to bring suit and to expend effort at trial. In appendix A the three strands of the litigation process are examined in more detail.

In section 4.3 the empirical analysis is presented. Settlement rates are shown to vary systematically with the nature of the case and the stakes involved. For some policy purposes it is important to look at conditional settlement rates—how settlement rates vary when one variable of interest changes while other variables are held fixed. Therefore we examine conditional settlement rates, using a statistical model to evaluate the probability that cases settle. We also simulate the effects of a change in the damage multiplier on the settlement rate. In appendix B the process of simulation is described in greater detail. Section 4.4 contains some brief concluding remarks.

4.2 The Economics of the Litigation Process

The decisions by firms to engage in harmful anticompetitive activities, as well as their decisions to behave defensively to avoid antitrust suits, are economic in character. Antitrust rules can alter this behavior by changing the incentives that the firms are likely to face. One example of such an incentive, the one that will be a primary focus of this paper, is the treble damages remedy. The larger the damage multiplier, the greater the likelihood that injured parties will file antitrust suits. The threat of such suits gives potential defendants an incentive to cut back or eliminate both illegal and merely questionable conduct.

Another example of the incentive created by trebling damages is the possibility that a plaintiff will bring a "nuisance suit": a suit with a low probability of winning that is filed with the prospect of inducing a defendant to settle a potentially winning case solely to avoid trial costs and the prospect of an adverse (albeit unlikely) court ruling.[6] Extortion is not limited to plaintiffs; defendants can act in a similar manner either by filing inappropriate countersuits or by complicating the plaintiff's case in such a manner as to increase substantially the plaintiff's costs relative to the defendant's.

Similarly the damage multiplier will generate incentives for potential plaintiffs to bring suit, for the parties to evaluate whether to settle or go to trial, and for the parties to expend effort during trial. In this section we briefly examine the decision to bring suit and to choose a level of effort at trial, but again concentrate on the settlement decision.

To give some focus to the analysis, we consider the hypothetical policy experiment in which the current treble damages rule is replaced by a double damages rule—that is, the damages multiplier is reduced from three to two. The choice of a multiplier of two is arbitrary and does not imply any views on our part about the advantages or disadvantages of such a policy change.[7]

The implications of changes in settlement rates that result when damage penalties are altered are quite complex to evaluate because of the interdependent nature of all of the strands of the litigation process. However, the importance of these changes can be illustrated by an example. We assume that the average litigation cost of a settled case is $100,000 and the average cost of a tried case is $300,000.[8] Therefore, if the change from treble to double damages were to increase the percentage of cases going to trial by 10 percent, while leaving the number of cases filed unchanged (approximately 1,200 cases are filed each year), then the additional attorney's fees plus court costs alone would be $24 million per year.[9] Of course this number substantially underestimates the total social cost of litigation since court costs and nontrial costs of the parties (time spent by executives, etc.) are not taken into account. Clearly the additional costs of operating the legal system could be substantial.

The Incentive to Bring Suit
In assessing the decision to bring a suit, the prospective plaintiff must balance the costs of bringing suit against the potential gains. These gains include, in addition to any monetary rewards received at trial or through settlement, the benefit of changes in the defendant's behavior that might arise out of the settlement negotiations or the trial. (For simplicity, these nonmonetary effects are ignored in the following discussion.) If the plaintiff were able to look into a crystal ball and determine the exact nature of the reward to be received, if any, then the plaintiff would bring suit if the value of those gains outweighed the cost of litigation (the cost of bringing the suit to the point of trial and the cost of the trial). However, uncertainties concerning the activities of the defendant, the availability of evidence, the legal standard to be applied, the actions of the jury or judge, and the attitudes and perceptions of the defendant make the decision to litigate a more complex one.

It is important to realize that not all harmful behavior will be detected and that not all detected violations will be litigated. In addition not all suits that are brought will involve harmful or inappropriate behavior. Since both the plaintiffs' and the defendants' attitudes toward risk and uncertainty can affect the decision to bring suit, it is useful to distinguish decision making by "risk-neutral" parties from that by "risk-averse" parties. Risk-neutral individuals or firms make decisions solely on the basis of the expected return associated with their actions, as calculated by multiplying the probability of each possible outcome with the value gained if that outcome occurs. They are willing to take a "fair" bet: one in which the expected return to winning equals the expected cost of losing. Risk-averse individuals or firms discount the expected return by the negative value or cost that they associate with any uncertainties involved (they are unwilling to take a fair bet). We will assume that both plaintiffs and defendants are risk-neutral throughout most of the analysis that follows; however, we will comment occasionally on the effect of risk-aversion on our settlement discussion.

Assume that the plaintiff believes that bringing suits has the outcomes shown in table 4.1. If the suit is brought, the cost of the suit prior to

Table 4.1   Plaintiff's decision to bring a suit

	Treble damages	Double damages
Cost of suit (dollars)		
Cost of suit settled	100,000	100,000
Cost of suit tried	300,000	300,000
Possible rewards for plaintiff (dollars)		
Damage award	100,000	100,000
Multiple damage award (trebel or double)	300,000	200,000
Settlement amount (assumed equal to the expected trial reward)	150,000	100,000
Probabilities		
Case being settled	0.8	0.8
Case being tried	0.2	0.2
Plaintiff winning case that is tried	0.5	0.5
Expected cost and rewards (dollars)		
Expected litigation costs ($0.2 \times \$300,000 + 0.8 \times \$150,000$)	140,000	140,000
Expected reward ($0.2 \times 0.5 \times \$300,000 + 0.8 \times \$150,000$) ($0.2 \times 0.5 \times \$200,000 + 0.8 \times \$100,000$)	150,000	100,000
Net return to plaintiff (dollars, expected reward minus expected cost)	10,000	$-40,000$

settlement is $100,000. If the suit is brought to trial, an additional cost of $200,000 is involved. The plaintiff has a 50 percent probability of winning the trial. If the plaintiff does win, he receives a compensatory damage award of $100,000 that, when trebled, will be $300,000.

To simplify the calculations and the analysis, we assume also that the probability that the case will go to trial is 20 percent and the probability that the case will be settled is 80 percent.[10] The assumption that the settlement probability does not change as the damage multiple is adjusted will be relaxed later.

Further we assume that under treble damages, if the case is settled, the plaintiff will receive a settlement award of $150,000—an amount exactly equal to the expected or average award from trial to be received by plaintiff at the time of settlement. (Recall that the plaintiff wins only half the time.) A risk-neutral plaintiff will compare the expected cost of litigation, $140,000, with the expected reward from bringing suit, $150,000. Clearly it will be in the economic interest of the plaintiff to bring suit. If the plaintiff is sufficiently risk averse, however, the net return of $10,000 may not be sufficient for the plaintiff to incur the uncertain outcomes associated with bringing suit.

Consider how the switch from treble to double damages alters the decision calculus of the plaintiff. The expected cost of litigation remains $140,000. However, if the settlement remains equal to the expected reward from trial and the probability of settlement remains unchanged, the expected reward from bringing suit will be reduced from $150,000 to $100,000. Now the suit is not desirable even from the point of view of a risk-neutral plaintiff.

This example illustrates an important point: if we take the extent to which there is harmful behavior by prospective defendants as given and hold the probability of settlement and the cost of suits constant, the reduction of the damage penalty from treble damages to double damages will lower the number of suits brought by plaintiffs.

This example indicates that the natural consequence of lowering the damage multiplier is to increase prospective defendants' incentives to engage in inappropriate behavior since both the probability of being sued and the expected losses from suit will fall. Similarly prospective plaintiffs are discouraged from bringing nuisance suits. Thus the reduced deterrence of "bad behavior" must be balanced against the gain to society from fewer nuisance suits that might inhibit business practices.[11]

Our numerical example in table 4.1 must be modified, however, if a change in the damage multiplier affects the settlement probability. Assume for the moment (as we will argue below is correct) that the switch from treble damages to double damages increases the probability of trial, say, from 0.2 to 0.3, without changing the trial outcome. Then the expected return from bringing suit under double damages remains at $100,000, on the assumption that the settlement amount equals the expected return at trial.[12] However, the expected cost of litigation increases from $140,000 to $160,000.[13] This example suggests that failure to take into account the effect of changes in antitrust damages on settlement behavior can cause an analysis such as the one in table 4.1 either to overstate or to understate the loss of deterrence associated with the removal of treble damages. The loss of deterrence will be understated if expected costs increase more than does the expected reward from bringing suit. The loss will be overstated, however, if the expected costs increase less than the expected reward. Information on the costs of litigation and the effect of damages on settlement probability is necessary if the direction of such a change in incentives is to be determined for the magnitude of the effect to be calculated.

The Incentive to Settle
Since a substantial proportion of all antitrust cases are settled, and settlements avoid the cost of trial, it is important to evaluate the effect of changing damage rules on the likelihood and the nature of settlements. While discussing this issue, we take as given that a suit has been brought and ask how a change in the damage rule from treble damages to double damages might alter the probability that a suit is settled.

A useful place to begin the analysis is with the assumption that both the plaintiff and the defendant are neutral toward risk and place the same value on the outcome of the lawsuit. In other words, both the plaintiff and the defendant perceive that the plaintiff has the same probability of winning the cases if it goes to trial, and both agree on what the damages will be if the court rules in favor of the plaintiff. In this simple world, there is room for settlement since settlement avoids trial costs for both plaintiffs and defendants. Presumably the settlement will be for an amount that falls within the range from a low of expected damages less the plaintiff's litigation costs to a high of expected damages plus the defendant's litigation costs, with the actual settlement amount a function of the relative bargaining abilities of the two parties. When the parties are risk averse, both parties tend to gain even more from settlement, but the settled amount will depend upon the relative aversion to risk of the parties as well as their bargaining skills.

There are two factors that tend to prevent settlements. First, the bargaining effort itself may lead to breakdowns as the parties make strategic decisions geared toward finding out more information about the prospect of winning at trial and the possibility of getting a bigger share of the "bargaining surplus." The exact nature of the bargaining process and the likelihood of trial is a complex issue that involves assumptions about the information available to both parties and the nature of the process by which each party updates its information.[14]

For example, if the bargaining involves sequential offers by the parties, with the party lacking information making an initial offer and the knowledgeable party responding, strategic behavior by the uninformed party would be unlikely. However, if the informed party makes the initial offer, strategy can become important since the informed party could make its offer with some knowledge about the likely behavioral response of the uninformed party. Given the current state of the economic analysis of strategic situations of this type, it is not possible to predict accurately the effect of a change in the damage rule on the likelihood of settlement due to strategic behavior. For this reason we will ignore the effects of strategic bargaining by parties with differential information in the analysis that follows.

A second source of settlement breakdown comes about when the parties have differential expectations about the likelihood of winning at trial or the size of trial damages. Assume for the moment that both the plaintiff and the defendant are risk neutral and that both face trial costs of $30,000 (pretrial costs are sunk costs and do not affect the settlement decision). Assume also that the plaintiff expects the court to determine at trial that damages are $200,000 while the defendant expects to pay only $100,000. The plaintiff will be willing to settle for any amount greater than $170,000 ($200,000 − $30,000) while the defendant's maximum offer will be $130,000 ($100,000 + $30,000).[15] Thus there will be no settlement, and trial will occur. If however, the plaintiff expects damages to be $100,000 and the defendant, $200,000, there will be a settlement in the range between $70,000 and $230,000. We refer to this range of settlement ($40,000 = $170,000 − $130,000 in the first example and $160,000 in the second example) as the settlement "gap," with a positive gap associated with cases in which settlement is likely and a negative gap associated with cases that we would expect not to settle.

This example can be generalized. For a given lawsuit a settlement is likely to occur if the defendant expects to lose more at trial (including trial costs) than the plaintiff expects to gain (net of trial costs). That is, settlement is likely if the difference or gap between the defendant's expected loss and the plaintiff's expected gain is positive. A formal analysis is provided in appendix A.

There are a number of important corollaries that follow from this basic principle. First, other things equal, the higher is the defendant's expected loss from trial and the lower is the plaintiff's expected gain, the more likely that the case will settle.

One instance in which the plaintiff and the defendant are likely to differ in the relative values they place on the outcome of a trial occurs when the defendant expects to be involved in future litigation of the same type. In this case the loss to the defendant can be substantially magnified because of the reputation or precedent that will be created by a trial loss rather than a settlement. Reputation, as we use the term, describes the "character" of the defendant (or plaintiff) in terms of his willingness to go to trial or settle and his willingness to expend effort if and when the case goes to trial. When defendants are concerned about reputation, we would expect a higher proportion of cases to settle, and as a consequence those cases that go to trial would be ones in which the defendant is relatively confident of victory. Therefore we would expect a higher proportion of tried cases to be won by the defendants.[16] We realize of course that the value that the defendant places on reputation may be directly related to the size of the multiplier since a higher multiplier implies greater expected damages.

Prior to looking at the data, we predicted that because of the reputation effect, antitrust cases would involve a very high settlement rate and that defendants would win a large percentage of cases that go to trial. Our expectations were born out since 86 percent of all cases are settled and over two-thirds of all cases going to trial are won by defendants.

A second corollary is that the greater are the costs of trial to either party, the more likely will the case settle, simply because the returns to avoiding trial are higher for both parties. To the extent that a switch from treble damages to double damages leads parties to spend less at trial (since less will be at stake), the switch will make it more likely than before that trials will occur. Such an analysis cannot be complete, however, without taking into account the effect of the change in damage rule on the expectations of the two parties.

Assume that the costs of going to trial are fixed and known by both parties.[17] If the defendant's expected return from going to trial net of trial costs is greater than the plaintiff's, there will be a positive settlement gap. If costs are zero, then, as the damage multiplier increases, the settlement gap will increase by an equal percentage. Similarly, if costs are nonzero and increase in proportion to the damage multiplier, the gap will change by an equal percentage. If, however, costs increase to a lesser degree than does the damage multiplier, a more reasonable assumption in our view, then the gap will change by less than does the multiplier.

In our model a positive settlement gap does not ensure a settlement, nor does a negative settlement gap ensure a trial. There are two reasons for uncertainty about outcomes that need not have a symmetric effect on the settlement-trial decision. First, each party's perception of the expected return from trial and litigation costs cannot be known or predicted with certainty. Therefore, it is important to distinguish the settlement gap that can be measured from the true unknown settlement gap. We might expect that a plaintiff in a price-fixing case that is a follow-on to a government case places a high probability on his chance of winning a suit, but we cannot know that probability with certainty. As a result our determination that the measured settlement gap is positive might occur when the true settlement gap is negative. Likewise a negative measured settlement gap might occur when the true settlement gap is positive.

A second source of uncertainty arises because bargaining about settlement can break down. Even when the true settlement gap is positive, the parties might disagree about the division of the "gains from trade" or "bargaining surplus," and the case might go to trial. While the first source of uncertainty is likely to be symmetric, the second is not. The possibility of settlements' not occurring when the true settlement gap is positive due to strategic behavior strikes us as more likely than the prospect that a negative settlement gap will lead to settlement. Nevertheless, this latter possibility cannot be ruled out since one party might make an otherwise unreasonable settlement demand, expecting it to be declined, in the hope that the demand will affect future settlement negotiations with the same party. Alternatively, one of the parties may estimate incorrectly the value of a non-monetary concession, or the lawyers representing each side may expect to face each other repeatedly and may want to appear cooperative.

The removal of treble damages will generally reduce the size of a settlement gap that is positive and therefore will lower the probability that a settlement will be reached.[18] (See appendix A for a more complete discussion.) Correspondingly a negative settlement gap will decrease in absolute magnitude, thereby increasing the probability of settlement. Since most cases settle and therefore are associated with positive settlement gaps, we concentrate on the former possibility.

As a result of a reduction in the damage multiple, a random disturbance or change in either party's expected return from trial may change the settlement gap from positive to negative, thus making the plaintiff's expected gain higher than the defendant's and therefore making a trial more likely. Suppose, for example, that the cost of meeting and negotiating a settlement is $5,000. Unless the gap is thought to be at least $5,000, it will not pay for the parties to meet to discuss settlement. Had the gap been $10,000, a settlement would be more likely to occur.

As another example, suppose that one party considers himself a shrewd bargainer. He expects to capture nearly the entire gap by taking a firm stand. He announces that he will not settle unless he gets the entire gap, and he plans to stick to this position until the night before the trail is scheduled to start. However, it may be too late, at that time, for a less extreme settlement to be struck. Presumably, the smaller is the gap, the less costly will such an extreme bargaining stance appear. Thus the larger is the gap, the less likely is the occurrence of such a problem.

In all of these examples, a "perverse" result occurs only because the gap is small (either positive or negative). If the gap becomes large, settlements or trials occur with much greater certainty. Even in the case of a small positive gap, however, we still expect a settlement more often than not. Similarly we expect a trial more often than not if the gap is negative (even if only slightly negative).

If a reduction in the damage multiplier increases the gap, we would expect the probability of settlement to rise, whereas, if a reduction in the gap occurs, we would expect the probability of settlement of fall. Clearly a change in the damage multiplier will lower the gap in some cases and raise it in others.

To illustrate the possible effects of a change in the damage multiplier, we consider three examples described in table 4.2.[19] In all the examples we assume that initially each party expects to spend $10,000 at trial under treble damages as shown in the first column of the table.

In the first example each party is relatively pessimistic about his own prospects. The plaintiff expects the court to award $20,000 in damages, which, after trebling, yields the plaintiff $50,000 net of trial costs (assumed, for simplicity, not to be paid by the losing defendant). Since the defendant expects to lose $30,000, which, when trebled, yields the plaintiff $100,000 (= 3 × $30,000 + $10,000), the settlement gap is $50,000; and settlement is likely.

In the second and third examples each party is relatively optimistic about his own prospects. In the second example the gap is − $7,000, so a trial is likely. In the third example, even though each party is relatively optimistic, the court costs are relatively high (compared to the expected damage award), and the gap is $5,000; the probability of a settlement is greater than one-half.

Table 4.2   The effect of a change in the damage multiplier on the gap (dollars)

	Treble damages	Double damages	
Each party's expected trial costs	$10,000	$10,000	$7,000
Relative pessimism (positive gap)			
Plaintiff's expected net gain (expects damages = $20,000)	$50,000	$30,000	$33,000
Defendant's expected total loss (expects damages = $30,000)	100,000	70,000	67,000
Gap	50,000	40,000	34,000
Relative optimism (negative gap)			
Plaintiff's expected net gain (expects damages = $30,000)	80,000	50,000	53,000
Defendant's expected total loss (expects damages = $21,000)	73,000	52,000	49,000
Gap	−7,000	2,000	−4,000
Relative optimism (positive gap)			
Plaintiff's expected net gain (expects damages − $20,000)	50,000	30,000	33,000
Defendant's expected total loss (expects damages = $15,000)	55,000	40,000	37,000
Gap	5,000	10,000	4,000

If the damage multiplier falls from three to two and expected trial costs remain unchanged, then the probability of a settlement falls in the first example but rises in the other two examples as shown in the second column. Indeed, in the second example, where a trial was likely under treble damages, a settlement becomes more likely under double damages.

It is quite possible, however, that if the damage multiplier is reduced, the parties will spend less at trial. This result is shown in the third column where each party's court costs fall from $10,000 to $7,000. Here the probability of settlement falls in the first and third cases and rises in the second.[20]

We conclude from these examples that a reduction in the damage multiplier will lower the probability of settlement in most cases if either of the following are true: first, if the losses expected by defendants are greater than the gains expected by plaintiffs, for reputational or other reasons, or second, if a reduction in the damage multiplier leads to a corresponding fall in court costs.

Most of our analysis has focused on the case in which the parties are risk neutral. If we were to account explicitly for risk-averse plaintiffs and defendants, the analysis would be altered slightly. For example, risk-averse parties are more likely to settle a given case than are risk-neutral parties. If risk aversion increases with the magnitude of the losses involved, a reduction in the damages multiplier will reduce the amount of risk and therefore, other things equal, increase the likelihood that the case will go to trial. Accordingly, failure to take risk aversion into account is likely to generate a conservative estimate of the effect of a reduced-damage multiplier on the probability that cases will go to trial. A more careful accounting of the effects of risk aversion, however, would need to distinguish between the component of the settlement gap that is due to potential savings in litigation costs and the component that represents the difference in the parties' expected valuations of the case.

The Trial Expenditure of Both Parties

A decrease in the treble damages multiplier could have a substantial effect on the expenditures that both plaintiffs and defendants make at trial and indirectly alter the decision to go to trial in the first place. In this subsection we consider each of these arguments in turn. For any given multiple each party involved in a trial will increase its effort or expenditures to the point where further increases would be unproductive (i.e., a further marginal increase in costs would not raise expected marginal gains by as much).[21] We believe that, under reasonably general circumstances (for comparable antitrust issues), the expenditures of the parties will be directly related to the stakes involved in the case.[22]

Assume that a plaintiff was spending $20,000 on a case in which the probability of winning was one-half and the multiplied-damage award, if won, was $54,000, so the expected return is $27,000. The plaintiff chose not to spend more because he assumed (for a given effort by the defendant) that an additional expenditure on the case would not increase the expected return sufficiently to be worthwhile. If damages were changed from treble to double damages, the $20,000 effort may no longer be worthwhile since, if victorious, the multiplied damages fall from $54,000 to $36,000, and the expected return falls to $18,000.

A similar argument holds for the defendant. As a result we expect that the expenditures at trial for at least one, if not both, parties will fall when the damage multiple is reduced. Of course, with both parties' adjusting their efforts during the trial, the net effect of the change in effort on the likely outcome of the trial is unclear and may not change at all.[23] In addition, in an uncertain world, the possibility of strategic behavior on the part of either party makes it difficult to predict how behavior would change. For example, when damages were detrebled, the plaintiff might choose to expend greater effort on the theory that the defendant would expend less effort (for the reasons given previously) and that that extra effort would substantially increase the probability of winning the lawsuit. The argument could go the other way, however, with the defendant's choosing to expend greater effort and the plaintiff's expending less effort.

The possibility of strategic, game-theoretic behavior becomes more important from our perspective, however, when we take into account the relationship between effort made at trial and the possibility of settlement. One possible outcome of a reduction in the damage multiplier is that the plaintiff will increase expenditures and the defendant will reduce expenditures or, simply, that the plaintiff will decrease expenditures by less than will the defendant. If both parties have similar perceptions about this prospect prior to going to trial, the settlement decision can itself be altered. In this particular example the removal of treble damages is seen by both parties to increase the likelihood that the plaintiff will make a greater relative effort than the defendant if the case goes to trial. This greater effort will increase the plaintiff's expected return from trial but will decrease the defendant's. If the case had previously been one that was on the borderline between settlement and trial, it would now be more likely to go to trial.

Of course this particular example is not the only possibility. If the defendant increased his effort or reduced his effort by less than the plaintiff, the settlement probability would rise rather than fall. We believe, however, that the first example is more likely. In complex antitrust cases it is the trebling of damages that makes an extensive and expensive defense (and offense) worthwhile. If damages were detrebled and defendants were expected to reduce substantially their efforts, the ratio of plaintiff to defendant effort would increase—as would the probability of a case going to trial. Unfortunately, the Georgetown data set provides little if any evidence that can help to settle this important, but difficult, empirical question.

4.3 An Empirical Study of Settlements

In order to predict the effect on settlement of changing the damage multiplier, we need to know the factors that "cause" settlements. In this section we develop a model of settlement behavior based on characteristics of cases and then use that model to simulate the effects of a change in the damage multiplier on the probability that settlements will occur.

First we describe the nature of the Georgetown data set briefly, highlighting some issues concerning the measurement of settlements and do fining some additional variables that we added to the data set. Then we present an analysis of the relationship between settlement rates and case and litigant characteristics that is "unconditional" in the sense that it does not control for changes in other characteristics. Finally, we describe the statistical model of settlement behavior and the simulation experiments.

The Data Set
We analyzed only those cases that were ended or closed prior to a trial or that were tried with a known outcome. In particular, we dropped from our sample all cases that had unknown outcomes (e.g., the file was missing), that were statistically closed, that were transferred or remanded to state courts, that were dismissed by the court or dismissed for other reasons, or that were consolidated.[24]

An outcome is defined to be a settlement if a settlement was known to occur, or if there was a pretrial stipulation and order, or a pretrial withdrawal. This definition leaves open the possibility that some of the cases we have classified as settlements were dismissed rather than settled. However, we have found that most of our conclusions were not altered by modifications in the settlement definition.

To determine the size of the litigants, we obtained measures of sales revenues (and other factors not reported here) for many of the larger parties.[25] We further classified companies as being small firms (less than $1 million in sales and/or not one of the 100,000 largest firms), large firms (more than $1 million in sales but not in the Fortune 500), Fortune 500 firms, government agencies, associations, individuals, and other. Categorical dummy variables (1 if in the category, 0 if not) were used to describe individuals, small firms, large firms, Fortune 500 firms, organizations, and governmental agencies; and actual sales data were used for both large and Fortune 500 firms. Because we dropped several observations in which sales data were missing for large and Fortune 500 firms, our results may differ slightly from those reported in other studies of the Georgetown data.

The analysis used two data sets, the first involving cases in which class action certification was requested ($N = 145$) and the second involving no request for class action status ($N = 1,002$). The overall settlement rate in the class action request sample was 78.6 percent, which is less than the 86.5 percent rate for the no-request sample.

Case and Litigant Characteristics of Settled Cases and Trial Outcomes
Table 4.3 illustrates the relationship between settlement rates and the nature of the plaintiffs and defendants involved. Looking first at the

Table 4.3 Number of cases and percent settled, by size of firm

Plaintiffs	Defendants						
	Indi-viduals	Small firms	Large firms	Fortune 500 firms	Organi-zations	Govern-ment agency	Total[a]
Individuals	3	15	16	19	12	b	75
	33.33	86.67	75.00	73.68	91.67		78.67
Small firms	12	231	362	144	24	2	820
	91.67	85.71	87.57	80.56	87.50	50.00	85.73
Large firms	7	50	100	31	4		197
	85.71	92.00	91.00	90.32	75.00		90.86
Fortune 500 firms	2	2	7	8		1	21
	100.00	100.00	100.00	75.00		0.00	80.95
Organizations		3	1		6	1	11
		33.33	0.00		66.67	100.00	54.55
Government agency		2	11	7	2		25
		100.00	63.64	57.14	100.00		72.00
Total[a]	27	331	510	210	80	10	1,169
	85.19	86.41	87.45	80.48	85.00	80.00	85.29

Note: Figures in the first row of each category are number of cases, and figures in the second row indicate percent settled.
a. Row and column totals may exceed the sum of the cells because the type of firm of both parties may not be known.
b. Blanks indicate no data available.

settlement behavior of plaintiffs, we note (from the summary column) that when the plaintiff is a large firm, 90.9 percent of the cases are settled, and that when the plaintiff is an organization, only 54.5 percent of the cases are settled. In calculating these rates, we did not control for other differences between the cases and therefore describe these as unconditional probabilities. In general, we find that, when the plaintiff is an organization (e.g., a union or a governmental agency), the plaintiff settles fewer cases than if the plaintiff is a firm.[26]

We expected to find that settlement rates among defendants were higher for firms than for other defendants and higher, the larger the firm involved. A brief examination of the summary row in table 4.3 suggests, however, that there is little overall variation by type of defendant. In our sample small firms are more likely to settle, the larger the firm that is suing them. The same pattern applies for large firms and for Fortune 500 firms, with the exception that the settlement rate is low when one Fortune 500 firm sues another. However, in both cases the sample size is sufficiently small that it would be dangerous to generalize.

Consistent with the preceding discussion, we expected to find that defendants for larger firms won a higher percentage of cases than did defendants for smaller firms. This pattern was borne out to some extent since small and large firms won 67 percent of their tried cases while Fortune 500 firms won 80 percent. Indeed, the "David versus Goliath" story may be oversold. Size appears to overpower the plaintiff-defendant distinction since Fortune 500 plaintiffs won three of four of their tried cases and small firms were more successful as plaintiffs than were individuals. The relationship between firm size (measured in terms of sales) and settlement rates, however, is not a clear-cut one.

Table 4.4 describes the settlement rates classified by the relationship of the plaintiff to the defendant, the size of the market, the alleged violation, the remedies requested, and whether a jury trial was demanded. Settlement rates are highest when the plaintiff is a competitor, supplier, or buyer (usually involving a continuing relationship) and lowest when the plaintiff is a licensee, employee, or dealer (often involving termination of dealerships). In addition predation and merger cases have high settlement rates while price-fixing cases and refusals to deal have relatively low rates.

The fact that settlements are so dominant in cases involving firms of all sizes has important implications for any analysis of the settlement-trial decision. The data are consistent with the view that defendants have relatively more at stake or are more pessimistic than plaintiffs. As a result, defendants settle cases that might be viewed as close (in terms of chances of winning) at the time the settlement decision is made. If the treble damages remedy is reduced to double damages, some of these close cases will involve lower stakes for the defendant and will be tried rather than settled.

The Statistical Model of Settlement
Based on the theoretical discussion in section 4.2, we expect the decision to settle to be a function of the settlement gap—the difference between the defendants' expected losses in a trial and the plaintiffs' expected gains from that trial. If we had data describing each side's pretrial beliefs, it would be relatively easy to test this theory. Since the data set contains virtually no direct information on the parties' beliefs, we are forced to take an indirect approach.

We hypothesize that the settlement gap is a function of the characteristics of the case and the litigants as well as differences in the courts (which may vary by jurisdiction and over time). For example, one might expect that the size of the market (international, national, regional, or local), firm size, industry or other litigant characteristics, and the relationship between

Table 4.4   Number of cases and percent settled, by case characteristics

	Number of cases[a]	Percent settled
Plaintiff's relationship to the defendant		
Competitor	433	89.39%
Supplier	58	93.10
Dealer	361	82.83
Buyer	173	90.17
Customer	107	83.18
Employee	44	81.82
Licensee	40	80.00
Size of market		
United States	499	87.38
Region	189	79.37
World	54	81.48
Local	241	84.65
Alleged violation		
Price fixing	277	81.23
Merger	76	92.11
Patent	76	86.84
Price discrimination	219	85.39
Predation	133	90.98
Tying	277	84.48
Refusal to deal	336	82.14
Vertical restraints	185	85.41
Boycott	112	90.18
Dealer termination	132	83.33
Breach of contract	38	81.58
Monopolization	73	87.67
Fraud	31	80.65
Nonantitrust	212	87.26
Not pertinent	253	84.59
Remedies		
Divestiture	32	93.75
Reinstatement	145	84.14
Change in pricing	64	81.25
Access	22	42.89
Other categories		
Jury demanded by plaintiff	684	85.53
Jury demanded by defendant	26	84.62
Countersuit	24	83.33
Diversity of citizenship	106	88.68

a. The total number of cases includes some that did not end in a pretrial settlement or a trial (e.g., a postjudgment settlement or a judgment for the defendant or a counterclaim).

the parties (competitor, supplier, customer, etc.) would be important indicators of the propensity to settle. One reason is that these variables indicate the presence or absence of "deep pockets," or they indicate the likelihood of repeat litigation in which reputation may be an important consideration. Similarly, a countersuit or the type of complaint (price fixing, dealer termination, or primarily not antitrust) may influence settlement rates by affecting the probability of an ultimate victory in a case. Comparable arguments can be made about the request for a jury trial and the jurisdiction in which the trial is heard.

The statistical model allows us to estimate the probability of settlement (the "dependent" variable) conditional on the characteristics of the cases and the parties involved (the "independent" variables). The estimated model can then be used to test which of these factors have a statistically significant effect upon the settlement rate and to calculate how much the settlement rate would change as we change one of these characteristics while holding all the other factors constant. For example, we might want to know the effect of a change in damages on the settlement probability for cases involving particular types of plaintiffs in which competitors are suing each other.

Cases in Which Class Action Was Requested

We begin by discussing the subsample of 145 observations for which class action status was requested and in which 78.6 percent of the cases settled. In a little over a quarter of these cases, classes were certified. There was surprisingly little difference in the percent certified of those cases that settled (26.0 percent) and those that did not (29.0 percent).

The details of the estimated equations appear in appendix B. Those factors or variables that had a statistically significant effect on settlement probability were the year of filing, variables reflecting the size of the market (international or local), the number of plaintiffs and the number of defendants, whether predation or tying was alleged, whether the defendant was an organization, and whether the parties were competitors or the plaintiffs bought from the defendants.

We found in addition that some, but not all, groups of variables had a collective effect that was statistically significant. Specifically, the variables that describe the relationship of the plaintiffs and defendants, the types of alleged offenses, the jurisdiction, and the industry did not have collectively significant effects. However, the market-size variables, type-of-parties variables, and the group of remaining variables (countersuits, certification of a class, number of plaintiffs and defendants, and the year) were statistically significant as groups.

To get a sense of how substantially these factors affect the probability of settlement, consider a hypothetical case in which the case characteristics are taken to be the characteristics of the entire sample of class action cases filed. If the number of defendants increased from the sample average of nine to ten, the probability of settlement would rise 4.4 percentage points (from 78.6 percent to 83.4 percent). If the number of plaintiffs increased from the sample mean of three to four, the settlement probability would increase 1.4 percentage points (to 80.0 percent). If the year were 1977 (instead of the average of 1976), the probability of settlement would increase by 4.4 percentage points.

Other case and litigant variables have more substantial effects. For example, if the case involved a worldwide market, the probability of settlement would fall to virtually zero. Similar large decreases in settlement probability occur if the market is local (-78.5 percentage points), or if predation is alleged (-65.7 percentage points). If the plaintiff and defendant are competitors, on the other hand, the probability of settlement rises 21.3 percentage points so that settlement is a near certainty. Similarly, if the defendant is an organization, the percentage falls by 20.3 points.

The estimated model has reasonable predictive power within the sample being studied: 86.9 percent of the cases can be correctly classified as settling or going to trial (64.6 percent of the cases that went to trial were correctly predicted while 93.0 percent of the settled cases were correctly predicted). Various other measures of the explanatory power of the model are also relatively high for a cross-sectional model of this type.

The No-Request Sample
We estimated the general model using the entire sample of 1,002 observations that did not have requests for class action status (86.5 percent of which involved settlements). Those factors that did have a statistically significant effect include one market-size variable, whether the defendant was a Fortune 500 firm, whether the plaintiff was a supplier, and the type of offense alleged (price fixing, predation, fraud, and refusal to deal). Of the groups of variables, the alleged offense and the plaintiff's relationship to defendants had a collectively significant effect while the others did not.

We obtained similar qualitative results for the sample of no-request cases as with the class action request cases. The predictive power was also quite similar. The model correctly classifies 86.7 percent of the cases. While the model correctly predicts 99.9 percent of the cases that settled, it does poorly with respect to cases that go to trial, predicting only 2.3 percent correctly. Similarly other measures of the predictive power of this model are relatively low.

Because this model has limited predictive power, we are hesitant to put much weight on its estimates of the amount by which the probability of settlement changes as we change one factor while holding other factors constant. With this caveat, we note that an allegation of price fixing, an allegation of refusal to deal, or an allegation of fraud decreased the probability of settlement (by 9.2, 10.7, or 16.3 percentage points, respectively). An allegation of predation raises the probability by 7.1 percentage points. If the plaintiff was a supplier of the defendant, however, the probability of settlement increased by 8.6 percentage points.

We performed one additional experiment. We added a variable measuring the damages demanded by the plaintiff to the model. This factor was not statistically significant, we believe, because of the unrealistically high demands that are made in many cases (so that demands and actual damages are largely uncorrelated). If the damage demand had been related to the settlement rate, it would have permitted us to simulate the effect of a reduction in damages directly using its estimated coefficient. Instead, we take a different approach.

Simulations

Our analysis predicts that the effect of a reduction in the multiplier on the probability of settlement depends on the extent to which the settlement gap is due to joint trial costs and to the divergence in expectations between the parties. For cases in which the gap is large and positive (in part because plaintiff's perceived probability of the plaintiff winning is higher than defendant's), the probability of the settlement will fall as the damage multiplier falls. For cases in which the gap is negative, the probability of settlement will increase as the multiplier falls. If costs were zero or, more generally, if costs change in proportion to the multiplier, the decline in the damage multiplier will cause the settlement gap to move toward zero at a proportional rate. On balance, cases that settled before the change in the multiplier become more likely to settle, while cases that did not settle become even less likely to settle.

If, however, costs vary to a lesser degree than does the damage multiplier, then the settlement gap will change by less than does the multiplier. Indeed, in cases in which costs are relatively large and unchanging and each party is relatively optimistic about his own prospects, it is possible that the settlement gap could move farther from zero as the damage multiplier falls.

Clearly, further information about costs and expectations would be needed before one could predict the effects of a change in the multiplier with any great accuracy. To obtain a sense of the likely direction and magnitudes of the settlement effects, we have performed a number of simulation experiments that account for some of the more plausible possibilities.

To the extent that the statistical model measures the settlement gap, we can simulate the effect of a decline in the damage multiplier. We evaluate the effect of a one-third reduction of the settlement gap. Since the cost of litigating will probably not fall as much as does the damage multiplier, a one-third reduction in the gap corresponds to a more than one-third reduction in the damage multiplier (so that the multiplier falls from three to less than two).[27]

Using the model based on the no-request sample, if we reduce the gap by one-third, the average probability of settlement falls by 8.5 percent (from 86.5 percent to 78.0 percent).[28] In the class action request sample, however, the average probability of settlement falls by only 2.3 percent (from 78.6 percent to 76.2 percent). Figure 4.1 illustrates graphically the simulation experiment for the entire sample. The light solid line describes the initial distribution of the probability of settlement and is obtained from the statistical model. The vertical axis measures the fraction of cases with gaps of each size. When the damage multiplier is reduced, the probability of settlement distribution is shifted as shown by the dark solid line. The mean

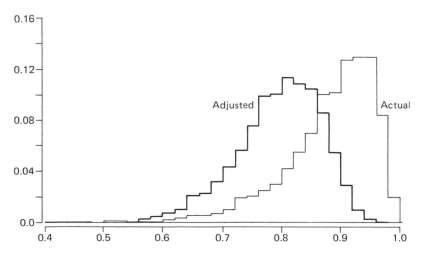

Figure 4.1 Probability of settlement

of the distribution of the probability of settlement shifts toward the zero point and becomes more concentrated.

The simulation results differ depending on how sensitive costs are to the reduction in the multiplier. In general, we find that when the cost function is relatively linear and costs are not a large component of the gap, then the probability of trial increases by somewhat less than 8.5 percent in the no-request sample. When costs are large and substantially nonlinear, the fraction of cases that go to trial may increase by much less than 8.5 percent and could (although we think it unlikely) decrease.

Thus we conclude that there is a distinct possibility that the fraction of cases settled will fall substantially. Because of incomplete information on costs, however, we believe that these simulations provide an upper bound estimate of the effect of lowering the damage multiplier on the fraction of cases that settle.

It is possible that we have not adequately controlled for the increased probability of settlement for cases that nearly settled (and the decreased probability for cases that barely did not settle) in our experiments so that the simulation results may be over- or understated. Even if we overstate the fall in the probability of settlement by one-half, however, there would still be a substantial increase in the additional litigation costs from the additional share of cases that would be litigated when the damage multiplier is reduced.

4.4 Conclusion

We have developed a model of the litigation process in which settlements play an important role. In the process we have argued that a change in the damage multiplier will have a direct effect on the probability that an antitrust case will go to trial by influencing the number of violations and the likelihood that a given violation will lead to a suit being brought.

Based on our empirical and simulation analyses, a reduction in the damage multiple from three could increase substantially the fraction of litigated cases that go to trial. Similarly, a reduction in the multiplier would alter the effort that parties make during trial with at least one and possibly both parties' reducing their effort. Moreover we expect that defendants (especially large defendants concerned with their reputations) would win a smaller share of cases brought to trial.

4.5 Appendix A: Theory

In this appendix we present a simple static model of the litigation process. Litigation involves three interdependent strands:

1. The decision by the plaintiff whether to file suit.

2. The decisions by plaintiff and defendant whether to settle.

3. The decision by both parties as to the amount of effort to put forth during the trial.

These decisions may be viewed as a sequential process, starting with the third strand and working backward. By estimating how much effort each side will expend at the trial, one can describe the parties' expectations about the likely outcome of the trial. Based on the parties' estimates about the trial outcome, including an allowance for their trial costs, the two sides may decide to settle. Settlement allows the parties to avoid the costs and uncertainties associated with a trial. The expected return to initiating a lawsuit then depends on the expected value if the case settles and the expected value if it goes to trial weighted by the respective likelihoods of a settlement and a trial. Thus the decision to bring suit depends on the probability of settlement and the size of the settlement as well as the expected trial outcome.

Effort at Trial

The decision as to how much effort each party will expend at trial may be modeled as a game. For simplicity in the following analysis, we abstract from the dynamics of settlement and information transfer, assume all parties are risk neutral, and assume that each party must pay its own litigation costs.

Consider cases that will go to trial. The plaintiff's (p) expected return just prior to trial is the expected damage award (the probability of winning in court times the damage award) times the damage multiplier, m, minus the costs, c_p, incurred at the trial stage:

$$m V^p(c_p, c_d) - c_p,$$

where $V^p(c_p, c_d)$, the expected damage award, is a function of the trial costs of the plaintiff and the trial costs of the defendant, c_d, which reflect their effort or preparation. We assume that $V_1^p \ (\equiv \partial V^p / \partial c_p)$ is positive and V_2^p is negative: more effort by either party increases that party's probability of winning and/or size of judgment.

Similarly the defendant's (d) expected loss at a trial is

$$-mV^{\mathrm{d}}(c_{\mathrm{p}}, c_{\mathrm{d}}) - c_{\mathrm{d}},$$

where $V^{\mathrm{d}}(c_{\mathrm{p}}, c_{\mathrm{d}})$ reflects the expected losses in this case and in future cases through damage to the defendant's reputation (adverse precedent in future cases).

By choosing the appropriate c_{p}, the plaintiff attempts to maximize the expected return to trial:

$$\max_{c_p} mV^{\mathrm{p}}(c_{\mathrm{p}}, c_{\mathrm{d}}) - c_{\mathrm{p}}. \tag{1}$$

The first-order condition for a maximum is

$$mV_1^{\mathrm{p}}(c_{\mathrm{p}}, c_{\mathrm{d}}) + mV_2^{\mathrm{p}}(c_{\mathrm{p}}, c_{\mathrm{d}})\theta_{\mathrm{p}} = 1, \tag{2}$$

where θ_{p} is the plaintiff's "conjectural variation" about how the defendant's effort or costs will change as the plaintiff's effort or costs increase ($\theta_{\mathrm{p}} \equiv dc_{\mathrm{d}}/dc_{\mathrm{p}}$). Equation (2) says that the plaintiff will set the marginal benefit from more effort equal to the marginal costs of one more unit of effort or cost, $1 \ (= dc_{\mathrm{p}}/dc_{\mathrm{p}})$.

Correspondingly, the defendant attempts to minimize the expected loss at trial:

$$\min_{c_d}[-mV^{\mathrm{d}}(c_{\mathrm{p}}, c_{\mathrm{d}}) - c_{\mathrm{d}}]. \tag{3}$$

The first-order condition is

$$-mV_2^{\mathrm{d}}(c_{\mathrm{p}}, c_{\mathrm{d}}) - mV_1^{\mathrm{d}}(c_{\mathrm{p}}, c_{\mathrm{d}})\theta_{\mathrm{d}} = 1. \tag{4}$$

If the plaintiff has Nash expectations that the defendant's costs will not vary as c_{p} varies, then equation (2) may be written as $c_{\mathrm{p}} = f(1/m)$, where $f(\cdot)$ is the inverse of V_1^{p} (holding c_{d} constant). Thus, as m increases, c_{p} will increase (since V_1^{p} is positive). That is, when more is at stake, the plaintiff will invest more effort at trial. The same argument could be made for the defendant. As Salop and White (chapter 1) show, where the V functions are identical and homogeneous of degree one, both c_{p} and c_{d} will change by the same amount. Indeed, even in the more general case ($\theta_{\mathrm{p}} \neq 0, \theta_{\mathrm{d}} \neq 0$), we would usually expect both c_{p} and c_{d} to move in the same direction as m. If, however, a party expected its opponent to "overreact," we might find a perverse relationship between costs and m.

Suppose, for example, that initially the plaintiff chose the high level of effort and the defense chose the low level. When m increases, the defense chooses the high level. The plaintiff anticipating this move realizes that when the defense chooses the high level of effort, the plaintiff cannot win.

The plaintiff now chooses the low level. We believe, however, that in most simple examples costs will move in the same direction as m, although we suggest that the relationship is a nonlinear one, with costs changing less than proportionately to changes in the multiplier.

Settlement

Our model of settlement presumes that the likelihood of settlement depends on the extent to which there is an opportunity for mutually beneficial agreement. The plaintiff's gain, net of litigation cost, is assumed to consist of two components, a systematic component, V^p (which is a function of measurable characteristics of the parties and the lawsuit) and an unmeasurable component, e_p (which is a randomly distributed variable). Likewise the defendant's loss from trial, including litigation costs, can be decomposed into two components—a systematic component, V^d, and a random variable, e_d. In addition the parties' estimates of the combined cost of going to trial may also be measured with error, e_c.

The mutual gains from settlement—the settlement gap (GAP)—is defined as the difference in expectations between the defendant and the plaintiff:

$$\text{GAP} = [m(V^d + e_d) + c_d] - [m(V^p + e_p) - c_p] + e_c$$
$$= mD + C + e = G + e, \tag{5}$$

where $D = (V^d - V^p)$, $C = c_p + c_d$, and $e = m(e_d - e_p) + e_c$.

As we discussed in the text, a few cases in which the settlement gap is positive may go to trial and a few with a negative gap may settle because of strategic behavior.[29] As a result of the two distinct sources of error—measurement of the settlement gap and strategic behavior—there is a complex relationship between the systematic portion of the settlement gap, G, and the possibility that a case will settle.

Cases that settle can fall into one of several different categories, the first three of which involve a positive settlement gap:

1. Cases in which D is positive: each party is relatively pessimistic about his own prospects, and e is positive or negative but small.

2. Cases in which D is negative, but the gap is positive: each party is relatively optimistic about his own prospects, but C (plus e) is sufficiently large so that the settlement gap remains positive.

3. Cases in which D is negative and larger than C, but e is large and positive: the systematic component of the settlement gap is negative, but the parties choose to settle anyway.

4. Cases in which the gap is negative, but settlement occurs due to strategic behavior.

We expect case 3 to be the least important empirically and suspect that case 1 is the most important. The relative importance of these cases has great importance for the simulation experiments that are described in detail in appendix B.

To summarize the effects of all sources of randomness on the likelihood of settlement, we suppose that the probability of settlement can be summarized as an increasing function of the systematic component of the settlement gap: $P(S) = F(G)$, where $P(S)$ is the probability of settlement and $F(\cdot)$ represents a cumulative probability distribution. If G is very negative (e.g., the sides differ greatly in their expectations about the outcome of the trial and both are optimistic), the case will go to trial with near certainty. Similarly, if G is very positive (e.g., when the defendant is worried about its reputation), the case will settle with near certainty. When G is near zero, however, there may be substantial uncertainty as to whether the parties will settle because of bargaining strategies.

Since $F(G)$ is an increasing function of G, the probability of settlement will move in the same direction that G moves when the damage multiplier changes: $dP(S)/dm = f(G)\,dG/dm$, where $f(G)$ is the density function associated with $F(\cdot)$. Thus for the rest of this discussion we concentrate on how G changes as m changes.

The change in the probability that a case settles depends on the change in the systematic component of the gap, G: $dGAP/dm = dG/dm = d(mD)/dm + dC/dm$. Thus the change in the gap will depend on the change in expected valuations and the change in costs.

We start by assuming that trial costs are not affected by a change in m. If the courts do not change the way they assess damages as m changes (so that the V functions remain unaffected), then $dG/dm = D$. Therefore, as m increases, the likelihood of a settlement will rise if D is greater than zero and will fall otherwise. Put differently, a lowering of the damages multiple will increase the probability of trial for those cases currently likely to settle and will decrease the probability of trial for those cases now likely to go to trial.

If costs change as m goes up, the analysis can become substantially more complicated, in part because the expectations of the parties matters. As an example, we assume that both parties have Nash expectations and that their V functions are identical and are homogeneous of degree zero [$V^p = V^d = V(c_p/c_d)$] so that their costs will increase by an equal amount in equilibrium: $dC/dm = dc_p/dm = dc_d/dm > 0$. Then the expected change in

G as m changes is $dG/dm = D + dC/dm$. If D is initially positive, both terms are positive so $dG/dm > 0$. If D is negative, then the sign of dG/dm depends on the relative size of D and dC/dm.

Thus a fall in m can either raise or lower the probability of settlement in individual cases. If D was initially positive, then $G (= mD + C)$ was positive, and this case was very likely to settle. As m falls, G falls since both the mD and C terms fall; that is, cases that were very likely to settle become less likely to settle.

If D was initially negative, however, then a reduction in m may either increase or decrease the gap, depending on whether the increase in the mD term or the fall in the C term dominates. Thus cases that were likely to go to trial initially $(G < 0, C < -mD)$ may become more or less likely to settle. Also some cases that were somewhat likely to settle $(D < 0$ but $C > -mD$, so $G > 0)$ may become either more or less likely to settle as m falls.

As a result on theoretical grounds alone we cannot predict the net effect of a change in m. The question can only be answered using empirical evidence. For example, if it were known (as we have contended in the text) that most cases are currently very likely to settle, then it is highly likely that D is positive in most cases (e.g., defendants put great weight on reputation) so that a fall in m will lead to a reduction in the probability of settlement. Unfortunately, in cases that are at the borderline between settling and not, the effect is ambiguous without additional information about the relative sizes of D and dC/dm.

The Decision to Sue and to Take Care

Whether the plaintiff will file suit depends on his expectations about the possibility of settlement and the likely outcome of a trial. If a violation of the antitrust law is detected by a risk-neutral plaintiff, the plaintiff will bring suit when the expected return from the suit is greater than the expected cost:

$$r[mV^p(c_p, c_d) - c_p] + (1 - r)M > b, \tag{6}$$

where r is the probability that the case will go to trial, $(1 - r)$ is the probability the case will settle, M is the expected settlement amount if the case settles, and b is the plaintiff's costs up to a settlement or the beginning of a trial. As discussed earlier, M lies between $V^p - c_p$ and $V^d + c_d$.

It follows from (6) that the more optimistic is the plaintiff (the larger is V^p), the more likely that a suit will be brought. If an increase in m did not affect the probability of settlement or costs (an unrealistic assumption), then it would cause an increase in the number of suits. Since the plaintiff will only settle if M is greater than the expected return to a trial, an increase in the probability of settlement, other things equal, will increase the probability that a suit will be brought.

4.6 Appendix B: Empirical Results and Simulation Model

Statistical Model

In this part of this appendix we report two probit equations describing the probability of settlement, one probit equation of plaintiffs' probability of winning at trial, and a variety of statistical tests based on these equations. The probit equation on settlement may be written as

$$P(S) = F(\mathbf{X}\boldsymbol{\beta}),$$

where $\mathbf{X}$ is a vector of characteristics of the litigation and the parties, $\boldsymbol{\beta}$ is a vector of coefficients, and $F(\cdot)$ is the cumulative normal density function that accounts implicitly for omitted variables and the possibility that the settlement negotiation process is stochastic and that parties may not settle cases where it collectively pays for them to do so.

This equation was estimated for just the cases in which class action status was requested and for the no-request sample as shown in appendix table B4.1. The sample sizes are 145 and 1,002, respectively. Based on a likelihood ratio test, the coefficients are collectively significantly different from zero at the 0.05 level in both equations. By any of the R^2 measures, the fit of the class action request equation is many times better than the fit of the no-request sample equation.

Based on likelihood ratio tests of whether various groups of variables in the class action request equation (table B4.1) are collectively significant at the 0.05 level, the type of party $[\chi^2(14) = 29.73]$ and the other variables $[\chi^2(7) = 15.86]$ are collectively significant at the 0.05 level. In the no-request sample, the alleged offense $[\chi^2(14) = 24.32]$ and plaintiffs' relationship to defendants $[\chi^2(7) = 13.12]$ are collectively significant at the 0.05 level.

The Simulation Model

The effect of a change in the damage multiplier on the probability of settlement will, in general, depend on the following factors:

1. The relative magnitudes of the two components of the systematic portion of the settlement gap (the difference in expected losses at trial) and joint trial costs.

Table B4.1 Probit estimate of settlement

Variable	Class action request sample		No-request sample	
	Coefficient	Asymptotic standard error	Coefficient	Asymptotic standard error
Jurisdiction (J)				
Atlanta	4.775	0.11	−0.055	−0.22
New York	0.629	0.98	0.100	0.66
Chicago	1.014	1.26	−0.031	−0.19
Kansas City	−2.101	−1.54	0.167	0.60
Market size (M)				
U.S.	−1.582	−1.67	−0.072	−0.40
Region	−0.450	−0.56	−0.388	−2.02**
World	−3.643	−2.14**	0.061	0.19
Local	−2.290	−2.13**	−0.089	−0.46
Type of party (P)				
Plaintiffs				
Individual	0.035	0.02	0.184	0.45
Small firm	−1.427	−0.85	0.368	1.07
Large firm	4.151	0.09	0.499	1.34
Sales (large firm)	−0.004	−0.04	−0.00005	−0.71
Fortune 500 firm			−0.293	−0.50
Sales (Fortune 500 firm)			0.00002	0.59
Organization	−5.388	−1.96**	−0.254	−0.40
Governmental agency	−1.567	−0.82	−0.298	−0.66
Defendants				
Individual	−5.142	−0.04	0.509	1.15
Small firm	−1.542	−1.26	0.304	1.18
Large firm	0.080	0.06	0.310	1.17
Sales (large firm)	−0.00008	−1.88*	−0.00001	−0.84
Fortune 500 firm	−1.771	−1.37	0.316	1.07
Sales (Fortune 500 firm)	0.00002	0.23	−0.00001	−2.06**
Organization	−0.582	−0.38	0.371	1.33
Governmental agency	−4.876	−0.03	−0.302	−0.54
Plaintiff's relationship to defendant (R)				
Competitor	3.213	2.20**	0.163	1.23
Supplier	−0.133	−0.08	0.610	1.96**
Dealer	0.900	1.16	−0.063	−0.42
Buyer	1.474	1.73*	0.290	1.63
Customer	0.633	0.90	0.483	1.74
Employee	−0.593	−0.50	−0.250	−0.90
Licensee	−0.970	−0.76	−0.241	−0.81

Table B4.1 (continued)

Variable	Class action request sample		No-request sample	
	Coefficient	Asymptotic standard error	Coefficient	Asymptotic standard error
Alleged offense (C)				
Price fixing	−0.484	−0.88	−0.302	−2.27**
Merger	1.467	0.66	0.382	1.47
Patent	−1.071	−0.82	−0.094	−0.40
Price discrimination	0.690	1.03	−0.156	−1.06
Predatory	−1.916	−1.83*	0.474	2.33**
Tying	1.591	2.02**	−0.035	−0.27
Refusal to deal	0.036	0.06	−0.353	−2.83**
Vertical restraints	−0.421	−0.58	0.069	0.43
Dealer termination	7.065	0.14	−0.046	−0.26
Boycott	4.567	0.07	0.177	0.91
Breach of contract			−0.282	−1.02
Monopolization	4.703	0.06	−0.117	−0.51
Fraud			−0.517	−1.84*
Not antitrust	−0.177	−0.27	0.040	0.29
Other variables (O)				
Year	0.132	1.85*	0.020	0.98
Number of plaintiffs	0.133	1.80*	−0.029	−1.93
Number of defendants	0.046	1.89*	−0.001	−0.14
Class action certified	−0.449	−0.76		
Counter suit	−2.805	−1.18	−0.161	−0.44
Plaintiff demands jury	−0.361	−0.74	0.036	0.31
Constant	−11.117	−1.49	−0.845	−0.51
Log-Likelihood function	−37.749		−359.74	
Likelihood ratio test	74.9941 (47 d.f.)		72.6648 (50 d.f.)	
Maddala R-square	0.40		0.07	
Cragg-Uhler R-square	0.63		0.13	
McFadden R-square	0.50		0.09	
Chow R-square	0.69		0.25	

Prediction success table			**Prediction success table**		
	Actual			Actual	
	0	1		0	1
Predicted 0	20	8	Predicted 0	3	1
1	11	106	1	132	867
Percentage of right predictions		0.869			0.867

2. The effect of the change in the multiplier on each party's expectation as to the trial outcome.

3. The effect of the change in the multiplier on the joint trial costs.

4. The error distribution, including its variance and its skewness, if any.

5. The effect of a change in the multiplier on the error distribution, if any.

Because we do not have sufficient information to analyze and to distinguish among each of these factors, we cannot predict the effects of a change in the damage multiplier on settlement behavior with much reliability. Rather, we view the following simulation exercise as an example of a counterfactual experiment.

We proceed by making a series of assumptions that simplifies the simulation analysis while making it likely that our simulations provide upper bound estimates of the effect of a reduction in the damage multiplier on the probability that cases go to trial. Suppose that the error distribution is symmetric and that its variance remains unchanged by a change in the damage multiplier. The variance obtained from the estimated probit model is used as the basis for the simulation experiments, although alternative distributional assumptions alter the results slightly.

Recall that the systematic component of the settlement gap, G, is given by

$$G = mD + C.$$

If the multiplier is changed by a factor b (e.g., $b = 2/3$), then the new settlement gap is given by

$$G' = bmD + C',$$

where C' represents the new joint costs (presumably, costs are a monotonic but nonlinear function of the multiplier).

To see how our simulation experiments are carried out, consider the special case in which costs change proportionally to the multiplier; that is, $C' = bC$. Here $G' = bG$, so the calculations involved in the simulation experiment are easy to follow. First, we calculate the mean probability of settlement, $EP(S)$, using the estimated probit model: $EP(S) = \text{Mean}[F(\mathbf{X}\hat{\boldsymbol{\beta}})]$. Next, we multiply each estimated gap by the change in the multiplier, b. Then, assuming that F is unchanged, we calculate the mean probability of settlement after the multiplier is changed:

$$EP(S') = \text{Mean}[F(\mathbf{X}\hat{\boldsymbol{\beta}})].$$

Finally, the change in the settlement rate is given by the difference between the two calculated means:

Change in settlement rate $= EP(S') - EP(S)$.

The primary simulation reported in the text of this article involves a reduction in the settlement gap of two-thirds. This reduction is equivalent to a two-thirds reduction in the multiplier if all of the explanatory variables in the probit equation determine the settlement gap and if costs fall proportionately to the decline in the multiplier. More generally, however, the two-thirds gap reduction could be consistent with a host of possible assumptions about the relative size of mD and C and the relationship between C and m. For example, if C represents one-half of the gap and C remains unchanged as the multiplier falls, then a two-thirds reduction in the gap is consistent with a reduction in the multiplier from three to one. In general, the smaller the fraction of the gap represented by joint costs, C, and the more linear the relationship between joint costs and the multiplier, the closer that the experiment of a reduction in the gap will approximate a reduction in the multiplier.

If costs do fall less than proportionally to a change in the multiplier and if costs are relatively large, then our simulation experiment could overstate the magnitude, and possibly the sign, of the effect of the reduction in the multiplier on the probability that cases were settled. In order to evaluate the sensitivity of our simulation experiment to the underlying assumptions, we note that, in the special case in which the distribution of D is symmetric and centered about 0, the simulation experiment is easy to analyze. In this case $G - C = mD$ is centered about 0 and represents the portion of the settlement gap due solely to differences in expectations between the parties. Then $b(G - C)$ represents the difference in expectations associated with a multiplier of bm, and $b(G - C) + C'$ represents the distribution of the gap after the multiplier has been changed. Thus, by subtracting C, multiplying by b, and then adding C' [or, equivalently, by initially adding a quantity $a = (C' - bC)$ after multiplying the gap by b], we can evaluate the change in the gap whatever the assumption that one is willing to make about the relationship between the multiplier and the costs of trial. Note, when the relationship between costs and the multiplier is linear, $a = 0$, and no further adjustment need be made. If, for example, $C = \log m$, then the adjustment factor a equals 0.04.

Our simulation experiments showed that, for values of a associated with essentially linear functions, the effect of a reduction in the multiplier from three to two causes the fraction of cases that go to trial to increase substantially. However, for values of a associated with a nonlinear function, the probability of trial can fall substantially and can, for sufficiently large a, change sign.

In the nonclass-action sample the increase in the fraction of cases that go to trial when the multiplier is reduced by two-thirds is 8.5 percent for $a = 0$, 5.8 percent for $a = 0.1$, and 3.3 percent for $a = 0.2$. When $a = 0.4$, however, the fraction of cases that goes to trial falls by 1.1 percent.[30] (The mean of the initial gap is equal to 1.21 with a standard deviation of 0.45.) Thus, though we believe (as an empirical matter) that a decrease in the multiplier will substantially increase the fraction of cases that go to trial, we cannot rule out the theoretical possibility that the fraction will decrease.

Notes

The authors wish to thank George Frisvold, Nadeem Ilahi, and Jaithara Suckprasert for their capable research assistance. William Baxter, Steven Bundy, Thomas Campbell, Robert Cooter, Paul Joskow, Roger Noll, Mitchell Polinsky, Steven Salop, Richard Schmalensee, Lawrence White, and Donald Wittman made helpful comments. Daniel Rubinfeld's research was supported in part by the Law and Social Sciences program and the National Science Foundation.

1. The volume of antitrust litigation is described in chapter 1 by Salop and White.

2. A recent discussion of treble damages that describes some of these trade-offs is given in Easterbrook (1985).

3. In the sample that we studied, 85.5 percent of all closed cases were settled or dismissed—the latter presumably because some type of agreement had been reached between the parties.

4. Among the articles that have treated the settlement question from a theoretial perspective are Bebchuck (1984), Gould (1973), Landes (1971), P'ng (1983), Posner (1973), Reinganum and Wilde (1985), Salant (1984), and Shavell (1982). Danzon and Lillard (1983) provided an empirical analysis.

5. Our analysis has been heavily influenced by the earlier literature on settlement and trial (especially Posner 1973; Shavell 1982; Priest and Klein 1984; and Polinsky and Rubinfeld 1986).

6. For further discussion see Breit and Elizinga (1974, 1985) and Garvey (1984).

7. The optimal damage multiplier could be higher or lower than three, and if different from three, the necessary change in multiplier need not be of this magnitude.

8. In the Georgetown data the average attorneys' fees plus costs of litigation per case was in the neighborhood of $200,000. Since settled cases are generally (although not always) less complex and costly than tried cases, we have arbitrarily divided the costs of settlement and trial as given in the text. A brief analysis of the lawyer's follow-up survey in the Georgetown study supports this view. The median duration of settled cases was 677 days, whereas the median duration for cases reaching judgment was 1,115 days. Settled cases have a median of 50 docket entries, and cases reaching judgment had a median of 108 entries. Finally, the median lawyers' fees (on a per party basis) were $36,500 for settled cases and $62,500 for cases that reached a judgment.

9. $24,000,000 = (1,200 \text{ cases}) \times (10 \text{ percent}) \times (\$300,000 - \$100,000)$.

10. We estimate that 85.5 percent of all cases in the Georgetown sample were settled. The exact number depends on how a settlement is defined as well as the scope of the sample.

11. A more sophisticated analysis would take account of the possible "errors" that the court might make. If the social cost of wrongly dismissing or discouraging a valid suit is high, then it may be socially worthwhile to manage a legal system in which there are substantial numbers of nuisance suits. Of course, with a different assumption about social costs, the argument could go the other way.

12. The expected return $= (0.3)(0.5)(\$200,000) + (0.7)(\$100,000) = \$100,000$.

13. The expected cost $= (0.3)(\$300,000) + (0.7)(\$100,000) = \$160,000$.

14. This more general Bayesian approach to bargaining, which allows for endogenous settlement offers and the updating of information, is beyond the scope of our discussion here. Several papers that do model the bargaining process in this manner are P'ng (1983), Salant (1984), and Reinganum and Wilde (1985). See also Cooter and Marks (1982) for an excellent discussion of the possibilities for strategic behavior.

15. $\$170,000 =$ expected losses ($200,000) less trial costs ($30,000).

16. This reputation argument and its implications appears in Tollison (1980), Rubinfeld (1984), and Priest and Klein (1984), among others. Of course the reputation argument could apply to plaintiffs as well.

17. This assumption is not absolutely necessary, but it is important that trial costs either fall or not rise sufficiently to increase the settlement gap when the multiplier falls.

18. An important assumption is that the random component is unaffected when the damage multiple is changed. The conclusions of the analysis will hold, however, so long as any change in the stochastic component is less than the change in expected gains and losses.

19. Cooter and Marks (1982, 238) stress an alternative possibility. According to them an improvement in a litigant's prospects can make a trial less risky and therefore increase the demand made in the negotiations process. Because of the possibility of strategic behavior, settlement will become less likely.

20. Notice, however, that in the third example, if the defendant expects damages of $13,500, the gap would rise from $500 to $1,000. This rise in the gap only occurs if the defendant expects damages of less than $14,000.

21. In general, the productivity of one party's effort will depend on the other party's effort.

22. This and related arguments are developed in Rubinfeld and Sappington (1985). Salop and White (chapter 1) note a positive relationship between costs and damage demands.

23. It is certainly possible that increased effort by one party, when countered by increased efforts by the other party, will have no effect on trial outcomes. See chapter 1 by Salop and White and appendix B.

24. In particular, we dropped cases "dismissed pretrial on motion." We also dropped cases in which there was a judgment for the defendant on a counterclaim (since we did not know which party was the "plaintiff" and which was the "defendant") and those cases in which there was a settlement after the judgment.

25. The three primary sources were The National Register Publishing Co., *Directory of Corporate Affiliation "Who Owns Who"*, 1984; Standard & Poor's, *Register of Corporations, Directors and Executives*, Vol. 1, 1984; and Ward's *Directory of the Top 100,000 Private & Public Firms*, Vols. 1 and 2, various years.

26. It should be noted, however, that the standard errors on these probabilities are large (between 0.3 and 0.4 in most cases) so that these differences are not statistically significantly different.

27. Salop and White (chapter 1) note that in a small subset of the cases in the sample, both costs and damages demanded data are available. They estimate that for every 1 percent increase in damages demanded, costs increase by 0.17 percent. Since damage demands are often unrealistically high, however, the effect on costs of changing the damage multiplier may be more substantial. Nevertheless, it is probably reasonable to assume that lowering the damage multiplier will lower costs to a lesser degree. As a result the corresponding damage multiplier will lie between two and one (and we believe will be closer to two).

28. This calculation could be performed for the sample average without actually using the probit estimates simply by using the sample mean and assuming that it is normally distributed. Thus the estimate for the entire sample may not be very sensitive to the lack of fit of the corresponding probit model. Note also that the class action sample generates a smaller simulated change in settlement probability, in part because its distribution has a substantially lower mean and in part because its distribution has a somewhat different shape than the distribution of the entire sample.

29. In general, random components need not be symmetrically distributed. In fact it seems reasonable to us that the distribution of e will be skewed toward positive values. This is consistent with the view that cases in which the systematic component of the gap is positive can lead to trial because of strategic behavior, whereas cases in which the systematic component is negative are unlikely to settle.

30. For class action cases the corresponding numbers are a 2.3 percent increase, a 4.8 percent increase, a 1.3 percent decrease, and a 4.6 percent decrease.

References

Bebchuk, Lucien A. 1984. Litigation and Settlement under Imperfect Information. *Rand Journal of Economics* 15 (Autumn): 404–415.

Breit, William, and Kenneth G. Elzinga. 1974. Antitrust Enforcement and Economic Efficiency: The Uneasy Case for Treble Damages. *Journal of Law & Economics* 17 (October): 329–356.

Breit, William, and Kenneth G. Elzinga. 1985. Private Antitrust Enforcement: The New Learning. *Journal of Law and Economics* 28 (May): 405–445.

Cooter, Robert, and Stephen Marks with Robert Mnookin. 1982. Bargaining in the Shadow of the Law: A Testable Model of Strategic Behavior. *Journal of Legal Studies* 2 (June): 225–251.

Danzon, Patricia M., and Lee A. Lillard. 1983. Settlement Out of Court: The Disposition of Medical Malpractice Claims. *Journal of Legal Studies* 12 (June): 345–377.

Easterbrook, Frank H. 1985. Detrebling Antitrust Damages. *Journal of Law & Economics* 28 (May): 445–468.

Gould, John P. 1973. The Economics of Legal Conflicts. *Journal of Legal Studies* 2 (June): 279–300.

Landes, William M. 1971. An Economic Analysis of the Courts. *Journal of Law & Economics* 14 (April): 279–300.

Landes, William, and Richard A. Posner. 1975. The Private Enforcement of Law. *Journal of Legal Studies* 4 (January): 1–46.

P'ng, Ivan P. L. 1983. Strategic Behavior in Suit, Settlement, and Trial. *Bell Journal of Economics* 14: 539–550.

Polinsky, A. Mitchell, and Daniel L. Rubinfeld. 1986. The Welfare Implications of Costly Litigation in the Theory of Liability. Unpublished manuscript.

Posner, Richard A. 1973. An Economic Approach to Legal Procedure and Judicial Administration. *Journal of Legal Studies* 2 (June): 399–458.

Priest, George L., and Benjamin Klein. 1984. The Selection of Disputes for Litigation. *Journal of Legal Studies* 13 (January): 1–55.

Reinganum, Jennifer P., and Louis L. Wilde. 1985. Settlement, Litigation, and the Allocation of Litigation Costs. Working paper no. 564. California Institute of Technology.

Rubinfeld, Daniel L. 1984. On Determining the Optimal Magnitude and Length of Liability in Torts. *Journal of Legal Studies* 13 (August): 551–563.

Rubinfeld, Daniel L., and David E. M. Sappington. 1985. Efficient Awards and Standards of Proof in Judicial Proceedings. Unpublished manuscript.

Salant, Steven W. 1984. Litigation of Settlement Demands Questioned by Bayesian Defendants. Working paper no. 516. California Institute of Technology. (March, 1984).

Shavell, Steven. 1982. Suit, Settlement and Trial: A Theoretical Analysis under Alternative Methods for the Allocation of Legal Costs. *Journal of Legal Studies* 11 (January): 55–82.

Tollison, Robert, ed. 1980. *The Political Economy of Antitrust/Principal Paper by William Baxter*. Lexington, Mass.: Lexington Books.

Wittman, Donald. 1985. Is the Selection of Cases for Trial Biased? *Journal of Legal Studies* 14 (January): 185–214.

5

Equilibrating Tendencies in the Antitrust System, with Special Attention to Summary Judgment and to Motions to Dismiss

Stephen Calkins

To every action there is always opposed an equal reaction: or, the mutual actions of two bodies upon each other are always equal, and directed to contrary parts.[1]

Treble damages have had an effect on substantive antitrust law, but not a unidirectional one; at times trebling has expanded the law's coverage, at times narrowed it. On procedural aspects of antitrust law, however, trebling's effect has been pronounced and more consistently limiting. In this chapter I explore the extent to which the antitrust treble damage remedy has shaped substantive and procedural antitrust law.[2] Then I report and discuss information from the Georgetown data set concerning the use of summary judgment and motions to dismiss summary judgment in antitrust cases.

To exploit more fully the Georgetown data, I also discuss the kinds of cases in which grants of these summary motions are likely. Examination of the Georgetown data set and review of recent authorities makes clear that pretrial motions by antitrust defendants are frequently successful and play an important role in antitrust litigation. The suggestion in *Poller* v. *Columbia Broadcasting System* that "summary procedures should be used sparingly in complex antitrust litigation,"[3] or at least a broad reading of that suggestion, neither is nor should be the law. One of the ways in which courts may have compensated for treble damages is by being more willing to dispose of cases prior to trial. Summary disposition may be more common in antitrust cases than it would be were there no treble damages, and thus these motions too represent means of equilibration.

5.1 Equilibrating Tendencies in Antitrust Law

Suits challenging violations of the federal antitrust laws may be filed by several categories of plaintiffs: the Department of Justice, the Federal Trade Commission, state attorneys general, and private parties and other purchasers of goods and services (including, in their capacity as purchasers, the federal government, state governments, and even foreign governments). To oversimplify slightly, the Justice Department may seek criminal penalties and actual damages; foreign governments may seek actual damages; state governments may seek treble damages for injuries suffered by the state government (or, in a *parens patriae* action, by natural persons residing in the state); private parties may seek treble damages; and each of these classes of plaintiffs, and the FTC, also may seek civil injunctions.[4] Although there have been minor changes, the basic structure of enforcement—by two federal enforcement agencies supplemented by treble damage actions—has remained constant. What has changed has been the number of treble damage actions. Such suits were relatively unimportant until about 1950. They later became increasingly common, and currently represent the overwhelming majority of antitrust suits.[5]

Since at least as early as the end of the 1950s, commentators have speculated about whether the treble damage remedy may disadvantage antitrust plaintiffs by making it more difficult for them to prevail. More recently, Areeda and Turner have been identified with the position that the treble damage remedy has limited the reach of antitrust law.[6] In particular, they suggest that the specter of large damage awards may have dissuaded courts from extending monopolization law to cover relatively unblameworthy situations.

When a statute has both criminal and civil remedies, it might seem somewhat anomalous to ask whether the civil remedy has inhibited an expansive interpretation. Early Supreme Court cases featured verbal sparring about the interpretation of language that served a dual civil-criminal function.[7] That sparring soon ended, however; as the Supreme Court recognized in *United States* v. *United States Gypsum Co.*, "the [Sherman] Act has not been interpreted as if it were primarily a criminal statute.[8]

In *Gypsum* the Court explicity adopted different standards for criminal and civil antitrust liability. As justification, Chief Justice Warren Burger used reasoning that might seem equally applicable to distinguishing among standards for conduct subject to other punishments of differing severity, as follows:

With certain exceptions for conduct regarded as *per se* illegal ..., the behavior proscribed by the [Sherman] Act is often difficult to distinguish from the gray zone of socially acceptable and economically justifiable business conduct.... The imposition of criminal liability on a corporate official, or for that matter on a corporation directly, for engaging in such conduct which only after the fact is determined to violate the statute because of anticompetitive effects, without inquiring into the intent with which it was undertaken, holds out the distinct possibility of overdeterrence; salutary and procompetitive conduct lying close to the border line of impermissible conduct might be shunned by businessmen who chose to be excessively cautious in the face of uncertainty regarding possible exposure to criminal punishment for even a good-faith error of judgment.[9]

Areeda relies on *Gypsum* to argue that "punitive treble damages are sufficiently analogous to criminal sanctions to call for the same limitations" but acknowledges that this view has not been generally adopted.[10]

A number of commentators, including Areeda and Turner, have suggested the converse: that fear of overdeterrence has limited the reach of antitrust law, making lawful conduct that otherwise would be unlawful and causing plaintiffs to lose suits they otherwise would win. Antitrust law also could have been limited, at least recently, as a reaction to the sheer volume of litigation. Without the lure of trebling, numerous lawsuits would not have been filed—or would have been filed in different forums or for different causes of action. Moreover, because the complexity and burden of litigation presumably increase as a function of the stakes, with higher stakes' justifying greater effort and thus leading to greater complexity and burden,[11] trebling may have exacerbated courts' impatience with antitrust suits. For several reasons related to trebling, therefore, courts may have limited antitrust law.

The logic of this suggestion is seductive but open to question on several grounds. First, courts may feel obligated to discern and follow legislative wishes with considerable faithfulness. *Gypsum's* line between civil and criminal enforcement is relatively sharp, so the adoption of separate liability standards followed easily. The difference between single and treble damages is less pronounced. Perhaps that difference is not sufficiently great to make outcomes under a treble damage regime much different from what they would have been with only single damages. Second, much of Supreme Court antitrust jurisprudence involves government suits, and the threat of treble damages may have been of less concern during the period when fewer private suits were filed and many of those that were filed apparently followed government litigation. Third, and most important, the same incentive provided by trebling for burdensome litigation has given plaintiffs an incentive to seek to expand the coverage of antitrust laws.[12] Only with trebling would some suits be filed, or at least filed as federal antitrust claims. Trebling can make worthwhile the pursuit of novel theories. Thus private enforcement through treble damages may have broadened the antitrust laws, rather than limited them.

In fact trebling probably has both limited and expanded coverage, at different times and for different parts of the law. This is suggested by a brief review of major substantive and procedural antitrust standards.

Substantive Law

Before reviewing particular substantive antitrust standards, I will compare standards under the antitrust laws to standards under the Federal Trade Commission Act, the closest approximation to a controlled experiment comparing the antitrust laws with and without treble damages. Section 5 of that act declares unlawful "unfair methods of competition," and conduct may be condemned under section 5 without fear of treble damage recovery since there is no private right of action.[13] Under this statute the FTC may challenge conduct prohibited by the antitrust laws, and although the vitality of this authorization is mooted, the Superme Court has written that the FTC also may attack other unfair and anticompetitive practices. Section 5 is an imperfect proxy for detrebled antitrust laws, however, for four reasons: (1) section 5's language and legislative history color judicial interpretation of it; (2) the FTC's zealousness and its interest in expanding the reach section 5 varies from time to time, and the institutional incentives affecting FTC enforcement policy differ significantly from those affecting private enforcement; (3) the latitude given the FTC in interpreting section 5 may depend substantially on the stature of that agency at any given time; and (4) rather than eliminating trebling (and allowing recovery of actual damages), section 5 offers no private right of action at all. Nevertheless, comparison of FTC and antitrust law jurisprudence is useful to an understanding of the impact of treble damages.

Comparison of Federal Trade Commission and Antitrust Law   The extent of the difference between section 5 and the antitrust laws used to be clear. Section 5 could be used to prohibit countless activities immune from antitrust challenge, or at least language in Supreme Court decisions said as much. In *FTC* v. *Motion Picture Advertising Service Co.* the Court wrote that the FTC Act was designed to fill the gaps in the Sherman and Clayton Acts and "to stop in their incipiency acts and practices which, when full blown, would violate those Acts."[14] The reach of section 5 was then extended to prohibit conduct that violated the "spirit" of the antitrust laws. In *Atlantic Refining Co.* v. *FTC* the FTC condemned as a section 5 violation an agreement between Goodyear and Atlantic Refining, and the Supreme Court affirmed, even though the agreement was not a tying agreement and thus did not violate the antitrust laws, because the arrangement nevertheless had the "central competitive characteristic" of a tying agreement—namely, "the utilization of economic power in one market to curtail competition in another."[15] This use of section 5 to reach the "spirit" of the antitrust laws was further refined in *FTC* v. *Brown Shoe*,[16] in which the Court upheld the FTC's banning of Brown's franchise program because the program reduced buyer freedom and thus was in conflict with the "central policy" of the antitrust laws.

The most capacious interpretation of section 5 is *FTC* v. *Sperry & Hutchinson Co.*, in which the Court declared that section 5 empowered the FTC to reach conduct that threatens competition even though it does not "infringe either the letter or the spirit of the antitrust laws." [17] This armed the FTC with the power, as one commentator stated, to "formulate and enforce competition policy on its own initiative." [18]

The breadth of this mandate has been called into question by several recent decisions. In *E. I. Du Pont de Nemours & Co.* v. *FTC*, the Second Circuit restrained the FTC in its attempts to expand the scope of section 5. [19] The FTC had held that while it is difficult to establish when consciously parallel activities violate section 1 of the Sherman Act, it is a "more manageable task" to proscribe such practices under section 5. [20] The Court of Appeals, however, held that the FTC did not have the power to prohibit conduct without some indication of oppressiveness—that is, anticompetitive intent or an absence of an independent legitimate business purpose.

In *Official Airline Guides, Inc.* v. *FTC*, the Second Circuit reversed the FTC's order requiring a monopolist airline guide publisher (the Reuben H. Donnelley Co.) to change its publication practices. [21] The court stated that Donnelley had the right to decide with whom it would deal. The court was unwilling to allow the FTC to "delve into . . . . 'social, political, or personal reasons' for a monopolist's refusal to deal," and "to substitute its own business judgment for that of the monopolist in any decision that arguably affects competition." [22] Thus, even though a section 5 action may be appropriate where a Sherman or Clayton Act violation is not, the Second Circuit requires the FTC to use the same analytical process that is used in applying the Sherman and Clayton Acts. Recent FTC decisions follow this teaching and show a new hesitancy to read section 5 as extending beyond the antitrust laws. [23]

On balance, then, are FTC standards more encompassing than antitrust standards? The answer is a cautious "yes." The Supreme Court has not endorsed the more rigorous scrutiny now being given to FTC orders. The continued vitality of the traditional principles was evidenced recently in *United Air Lines, Inc.* v. *CAB*, [24] an opinion upholding a CAB finding that the biased computerized reservations systems provided by airlines constituted unfair methods of competition. (The decision was based on section 411 of the Federal Aviation Act, which is "essentially a copy of section 5" of the FTC Act. [25] The Court reasoned that this form of conduct by a monopolist probably would be illegal ("whether rightly or wrongly") under traditional monopoly law and thus could be prohibited by the CAB prior to an airline's achieving monopoly power. *United Airlines* is a traditional "incipiency" opinion, and nothing would prevent another court from writing another one in a well-chosen FTC case.

Moreover, for purposes of this paper's inquiry, it matters less whether today the FTC enjoys different standards than whether it has enjoyed them from time to time. In fact section 5 has been somewhat less constraining than the antitrust laws. Though litigated orders demonstrate this additional freedom, it is illustrated most sharply by the FTC's initiatives. Examples include the FTC's *Lockheed* consent order banning certain foreign payments, its "shared monopoly" cereal lawsuit, and its suit against the big oil companies.[26] More recently, Commissioner Terry Calvani has succumbed to the siren call of section 5 and is suggesting its use against lawyers who assist firms engaged in otherwise unilateral predatory conduct.[27] Section 5 thus seems to include within its reach violations of the antitrust laws and a little more.

To what extent, however, does that "little more" stem from the absence of a private right of action? Certainly this feature did not play a prominent role in the development of the expansive view of FTC jurisprudence. One searches the Supreme Court cases in vain for a thoughtful explanation of why certain conduct should be prohibited only when private parties may not sue. Rather, the focus was on the peculiar legislative history of the FTC Act.[28] It was to this tradition and to the words themselves that the Court pointed in writing expansively about section 5.[29]

Only recently have commentators and the FTC itself regularly focused on the absence of a private right of action. Areeda and Turner point to this as the only colorable justification for divergent standards (and would prefer that the distinction between evaluating conduct for damages and for injunctive relief be imported into the antitrust laws).[30] Other commentators calling for activist FTC approaches rely in part on this unique feature.[31] In its *Ethyl* decision the FTC expressly relied on this distinction, advocating its approach as having "the advantage of not extending liability to private causes of action, resulting in treble damage liability, or creating a prima facie case in a private treble damages action."[32]

One remains with the common dilemma of what weight to give words. Does the early absence of such language mean the point was unimportant? Was such language used in *Ethyl* to justify a decision that would have been made regardless? I think the absence of a private right of action made a difference. Consider the *Reuben H. Donnelly* case. It seems unlikely that such a limitless concept (a duty not to be arbitrary) would have been espoused in a Sherman Act case. The *United Airlines* decision would have been far more difficult were treble damages at stake. Moreover the risk of creating excessive recoveries has dissuaded the Antitrust Division from filing certain lawsuits.[33] On balance, the FTC's freedom from private follow-on litigation has made a modest difference, for better or worse.

Would an effect also have been felt from the presence of only a single damage private right of action, as opposed to a right to treble damages? Given the modest difference between FTC and antitrust standards, and that only a portion of that difference can be attributed to the absence of a private right of action, it seems unlikely that such a difference in remedy would have caused much variance in substantive standards.

Comparison of FTC law and antitrust law thus provides only very modest support for the argument that trebling has limited the reach of the antitrust laws. However, because of section 5's peculiar language, history, and enforcement mechanism, that comparison does not disprove the argument, either.

Antitrust Standards Arguably Affected by Treble Damages Which substantive antitrust law standards would be different were there no treble damage "bonanzas"? Court opinions and commentators suggest the following candidates:

1. Monopolization. Areeda and Turner express concern that the treble damage remedy has made courts hesitant to expand monopolization law.[34] The suggestion has merit. Certainly it seems hard to imagine the sweeping language of the key cases—*Alcoa, Griffith, Loraine Journal,* and *Grinnell*—in cases where only money was sought.[35] To critics, the recent narrowing of the monopolization offense is typified by two private suits, *Berkey Photo* and *Telex.*[36] Moreover it is in the monopolization area that the FTC, unrestrained by the risk of setting antitrust law precedent, has been at its most adventuresome.[37] It also was in a monopolization case that a federal court first accepted the Areeda-Turner invitation to tailor liability to relief, by granting JNOV (a judgment notwithstanding the jury verdict) for a defendant on all damage claims but reserving judgment on injunctive relief.[38] Finally, the principal virtue of the cost-based approach to predatory pricing claims is clarity, and those courts adopting these tests have done so in response to a perception that private litigation was threatening to *lessen* competition.[39] Thus there is considerable support for the Areeda-Turner suggestion.

It would be a mistake, however, to overemphasize the role of treble damages in limiting monopolization law. A collection of early expansive monopolization cases should include *Eastman Kodak Co. v. Southern Photo Materials Co.*, where a private treble damage plaintiff succeeded in an effort not dissimilar from one unsuccessfully assayed by the Federal Trade Commission three years earlier.[40] In *United Shoe Machinery Corp.*, one of the expansive monopolization opinions, Judge Charles Wyzanski indicated his awareness of the possibility of treble damage recoveries, and indeed that case was followed by a private action.[41] Perhaps the most controversial case limiting monopolization law—*United States v. Empire Gas Corp.*[42]—was a government case seeking equitable relief, whereas the most controversial case expanding monopolization law—*Lessig v. Tidewater Oil Co.*[43]—was a private treble damage action. Moreover the retreat from *Alcoa* is shown most sharply by an FTC decision (*du Pont*),[44] cost-based pricing rules are enshrined at the FTC,[45] and the FTC's attempt to use section 5 to expand monopolization law was rebuffed by the Second Circuit.[46] Finally, *Aspen Highlands*[47] reminds us that wronged private parties continue to seek, and occasionally find, treble damage relief.

How then would monopolization law differ were there no trebling? Not as much as others have suggested. Single damages still would be available, so this would not be a world with Areeda-Turner's and the *SCM* district court's damageless violations. Actual damages in a monopolization case can be substantial. Moreover equitable relief can be far more harsh than damage awards. For example, the FTC's aborted efforts featured such drastic remedies as mandatory licensing of a treasured trademark and divestiture of brand names.[48] Decrees such as those could cost a defendant far more than even very substantial damages. Finally, *Official Airline Guides* demonstrates the reluctance of modern courts to sanction economic engineering in the name of antitrust. "No-fault" monopolization is unlikely even were there no treble damages. Rather, trebling has affected monopolization law primarily by stimulating the filing of such a large number of suits that observers began to believe that nonmeritorious suits were being filed for strategic, anticompetitive purposes. Courts responded by beginning to terminate such cases comparatively early.[49] In the process monopolization law may have become slightly less amorphous and protean, but it is still capable of being adapted to new circumstances where conduct cries out for redress.

2. Horizontal restraints.   The classic expansive Supreme Court language condemning agreements whose purpose or effect is to influence price is found in criminal antitrust cases,[50] so it seems unlikely that trebling inhibited the development of antitrust law's treatment of horizontal restraints. Moreover the Supreme Court's recent qualifying of the per se ban of price fixing occurred in civil actions not involving treble damage claims,[51] which could suggest that the existence of that remedy played little part in the decisions. This cannot be proved, of course. In recent years the Court has become very aware of treble damages, and the fear of overdeterrence or windfall losses may silently underlie decisions. Nevertheless, the current reconsideration probably would have occurred even in a single damage world. (If anything, trebling may have expanded price-fixing coverage by providing an incentive for the entrenchment of the ban against maximum prices.[52]) Nor does the treble damage remedy appear to have limited the reach of the prohibition of horizontal market division or customer allocation. Although the essential Supreme Court cases, *Sealy* and *Topco*,[53] are government injunctive cases, *Topco* was decided the same year as *Hawaii* v. *Standard Oil Co. of California*,[54] where the Court demonstrated concern about excessive use of treble damages. Given the contemporaneous focus on that issue, it seems unlikely that a treble damage suit would have been decided differently.

Four categories of horizontal restraints are more likely candidates for finding an impact of trebling. First, the Supreme Court's recent partial rejection of the intraenterprise conspiracy doctrine probably resulted in part from the Court's dismay at the excessive seeking of treble damages. Chief Justice Warren Burger explained that the Court's decision "will simply eliminate treble damages from private state tort suits masquerading as antitrust actions." [55] Crediting or blaming treble damages for this result is unfair, however, since it was in private treble damage cases that the doctrine was established.[56] If treble damages deserve partial responsibility for the doctrine's death, they also deserve partial responsibility for its birth and life.

The *Pick-Barth* doctrine—that a conspiracy to eliminate a competitor by unfair means violates the Sherman Act[57]—is the second category of horizontal restraints where treble damages probably played an important role. As the Fifth Circuit stated in the leading case rejecting the doctrine, "only if the defendant can gain an increment of monopoly through his unfair competition would the additional sanctions of the Sherman Act, including treble damages and criminal sanctions, be appropriately used to deter him. Single damages or equivalent injunctive relief is thought sufficient to compensate a firm for unfair competition." [58] However, were it not for the lure of treble damages, these cases might not have been brought under the antitrust laws in the first place; all of the *Pick-Barth* cases are private. Again treble damages may deserve credit for both expansion and retreat.

The third part of horizontal restraint law likely to have been affected by treble damages is the confused law of group boycotts. The lower courts apparently reacted to the incessant stream of suits by limiting the kinds of concerted refusals to deal that will be found per se illegal. The Supreme Court has now tentatively endorsed these limitations.[59] Moreover *Fashion Originators' Guild*,[60] one of the early Supreme Court cases with expansive language, featured a challenge under the FTC Act. Since other important expansive Supreme Court boycott cases—namely, *Klor's*, *Radiant Burners*, and *Silver*[61]—featured suits for treble damages, again it seems doubtful that trebling chilled the initial expansion of the law; instead, it may have served as tonic. Perhaps the recent retrenchment would have been prevented or delayed had trebling not stimulated so many suits, but again the evidence of the remedy's net effect is uncertain.

Finally, the treble damage remedy may have had a significant effect on the development of conscious parallelism and data dissemination law. The delivered pricing cases were first brought under the Federal Trade Commission Act, and most of the other important expansive Supreme Court cases featured government injunctive suits.[62] The cold water of *Theatre Enterprises*,[63] a private treble damage case, stands in sharp contrast. Although courts have rebuffed the FTC's efforts to exploit section 5 to expand this part of the law, its continued exploration of the bounds of illegality[64] suggests that antitrust law may have been limited by concerns about trebling. It thus seems likely that treble damages has limited the expansion of the law concerning horizontal coordination short of actual agreements.

3. Vertical restraints.   The treble damage remedy currently seems to be limiting the breadth of antitrust law's condemnation of certain vertical restraints. *Monsanto*'s attempt to draw sharp lines appears to be a response to a concern about trebling, as suggested by the following:

[I]t is of considerable importance that independent action by the manufacturer, and concerted action on nonprice restrictions, be distinguished from price-fixing agreements, since under present law the latter are subject to per se treatment and treble damages. . . . If an inference of [a price-fixing] agreement may be drawn from highly ambiguous evidence, there is a considerable danger that the doctrines enunciated in *Sylvania* and *Colgate* will be seriously eroded. . . . In sum, "[t]o permit the inference of concerted action on the basis of receiving complaints alone and thus to expose the defendant to treble damage liability would both inhibit management's exercise of independent business judgment and emasculate the terms of the statute." Thus, something more than evidence of complaints [about price-cutting distributors] is needed. There must be evidence that tends to exclude the possibility that the manufacturer and nonterminated distributors were acting independently.[65]

In earlier years, too, the probable effect of trebling was seen in the vertical restraints area. The doctrine of "patent misuse" condemned a number of largely vertical restrictions, but only for purposes of making patents unenforceable, not for purposes of finding antitrust illegality.[66] The current Justice Department, appalled by the path taken by this rogue doctrine, unrestrained by trebling's sobering companionship, is seeking to limit misuse to antitrust violations.[67] Indeed, most of the expansive Supreme Court language in the vertical restraints area was written in cases that did not involve treble damages.[68] The Supreme Court reversed the direction of these cases in *GTE Sylvania*, a private treble damage case (albeit not one in which this factor was highlighted) that itself had been anticipated by the scores of lower court decisions crafting exceptions to *Schwinn* in part to deny treble damages.[69]

Again, however, the possible limiting effect of treble damages should not be overstated. That remedy probably deserves credit for two of the more extreme applications of vertical restraint law, *Albrecht* and *Fortner*.[70] Responsibility for current Supreme Court views also must be shared with the dramatic changes in accepted economic learning that occurred in the decade prior to *GTE Sylvania*. But trebling probably has contributed to the current limiting of vertical restraint law.

4. Jurisdictional reach of the antitrust laws.   A number of courts have ruled that antitrust's extraterritorial reach should be decided in part by considerations of international comity.[71] Some courts regard such considerations as proper elements of the determination of subject matter jurisdiction; others regard review of these considerations as appropriate only in deciding whether to exercise jurisdiction. Whatever the context, several factors to be weighed in evaluating comity considerations are likely to be affected by the size of the antitrust sanction, including the "[d]egree of conflict with foreign law or policy" and the "[p]ossible effect upon foreign relations if the court exercises jurisdiction and grants relief."[72] Since foreign abhorrence of treble damages is legend, any balancing process weighing such factors could conceivably come out differently were only single damages available. Given the paucity of cases engaging in such a balancing process, however, and doubts as to the frequency with which that process has affected outcomes, it seems unlikely that many cases would be decided differently were there no treble damages.

The effect of trebling on the domestic jurisdictional reach of the antitrust laws is also ambiguous. In a series of private treble damage cases decided during the past decade, the Supreme Court substantially relaxed jurisdictional limits, leading commentators to wonder whether the requirement of interstate effects continues to serve as a meaningful restriction.[73] It seems doubtful that government lawyers or plaintiffs entitled only to single damages would have pushed the outer bounds of antitrust coverage so far.

The relaxation of the commerce requirement caused the courts to be "deluged with complaints" alleging that denial of medical staff privileges restrained trade.[74] This wave may have crested; some courts are becoming more reluctant to find jurisdiction.[75] Although this may be simply a retreat from an overexuberant reading of the Supreme Court cases, it may be reinforced by concern about the availability of treble damages. For instance, the Seventh Circuit recently adverted to an antitrust damage request of $13.5 million, before trebling, when it required the pleading of specific facts from which the requisite effect on commerce could be inferred.[76] Moreover, although many of these private suits seek injunctive relief, there may have been less of an unseemly "deluge" had treble damages not enticed plaintiffs.

Even if the possible current retrenchment finds support in concern about trebling, that would not demonstrate that trebling has limited the domestic jurisdictional reach of the antitrust laws. If the cases relaxing jurisdictional requirements would not have been brought or pursued vigorously without the lure of treble damages, then that remedy may have served to broaden the reach of the antitrust laws, not to limit it. The net effect is difficult to gauge.

5. *Antitrust exemptions.* Trebling has increased the number of antitrust exemptions and probably broadened them. If nothing else, horror stories about gargantuan penalties imposed (or threatened to be imposed) on constituents attract notice on Capitol Hill, and the greater the damages threatened, the more cost-effective the hiring of high-priced lobbyists becomes. Without treble damages, there might well be no Local Government Antitrust Act of 1984, National Cooperative Research Act of 1984, Shipping Act of 1984, Export Trading Company Act of 1982, or, perhaps, Soft Drink Interbrand Competition Act,[77] to mention only recently enacted exemptions.

Congressional concern about treble damages also may have buttressed judicial concern and led to broader interpretations of existing antitrust exemptions. This suggestion is easiest to support for the state action exemption.[78] The dissenting justices in *Cantor* and *Lafayette* expressed dismay at the liability with which municipalities were being threatened, and the Court in *Lafayette* reserved on the questions of remedy.[79] Some of the recent generous readings of the state action exemption surprised commentators looking only at the logic of the Court's previous interpretations,[80] and the perceived treble damage problem undoubtedly played a role. It also may have played, or will play, a role in broadening other exemptions.

Procedural and Remedial Law, Other Than Summary Motions.
Several nonsubstantive parts of antitrust law may have developed differently were there no trebling.

In Pari Delicto   In *Perma Life Mufflers, Inc.* v. *International Parts Corp.*, the leading case rejecting the in pari delicto defense in private antitrust actions, five justices endorsed this defense where a plaintiff equally and voluntarily participates in the challenged conduct.[81] Trebling was featured prominently in the opinions preserving this much of the defense. To Justice John Harlan it seemed "bizarre . . . to pay violators three times their losses in doing what public policy seeks to deter them from doing."[82] Justice Thurgood Marshall could not "agree that the public interest requires that a plaintiff who has actively sought to bring about illegal restraints on competition for his own benefit be permitted to demand redress—in the form of treble damages—from a partner who is no more responsible for the existence of the illegality."[83] Moreover, one court has written that the interest in preventing windfall gains "justifies application of the complete involvement defense to an action for treble damages," but not to an action seeking injunctive and declaratory relief.[84] Thus, the treble damage remedy may have played a role in the development of this doctrine and may play a role in the future.

Class Actions   Fewer class action damage requests would "shock the conscience" and be rejected for sheer oppressiveness[85] were there no treble damages. Thus class actions probably would be more easily certified were there no trebling. The legal standards would not necessarily be different, but those standards, as applied, probably would lead to some different outcomes.

Proof of Damages Ever since *Bigelow* v. *RKO Radio Pictures, Inc.*[86] antitrust courts have been forgiving of imperfections in plaintiffs' proofs of damage. In recent years, however, *Bigelow* has been qualified by the regular insistence on a "fair degree of certainty" as to the *fact* of injury,[87] as opposed to the amount. Some courts may be limiting *Bigelow* even more directly by requiring a fairly careful "segregation" between injuries caused by lawful conduct and those resulting from unlawful conduct or, sometimes, even among injuries caused by different illegal activities.[88] More generally, courts are scrutinizing damage claims more rigorously than they once did.[89] Although proof again is in short supply, it seems probable that trebling is a factor in this change.[90]

Standing Plaintiffs would find standing rules more hospitable in a single damage world. It is here that we see most unequivocally a limiting consequence of the treble damage remedy.[91] The role of the treble damage remedy in limiting standing is clear not just from plausible references to it in decisions limiting standing—although such decisions have attached significance to trebling with unusual consistency over time—but from comparison of antitrust standing principles with related legal concepts and from the focus on trebling in current antitrust standing principles themselves. Although "narrow" standing rules currently may be gaining support from the focus on consumer welfare as the principal or sole antitrust concern,[92] such rules also owe their existence in part to trebling.

From the beginning, treble damages have been featured in standing decisions. The first "direct injury" case, *Ames* v. *American Telephone & Telegraph Co.*, warned that "a construction of the act which makes the defendant liable to sextuple damages is certainly to be avoided."[93] Similarly, perhaps the leading "target area" opinion, *Calderone Enterprise Corp.* v. *United Artists Theatre Circuit*, cautioned that "if the flood-gates were opened to permit treble damage suits by every creditor, stockholder, employee, subcontractor, or supplier of goods and services that might be affected, the lure of a treble damage recovery, implemented by the availability of the class suit . . . would result in an over-kill."[94] Numerous other decisions reflect similar worries about treble damages, with the concern sometimes cast in terms of "potentially ruinous liabilities,"[95] sometimes unfair "windfalls,"[96] and sometimes an inundation of plaintiffs lured by treble damages.[97] Judge Ralph Guy said that his decision to deny standing in a case before him was

predicated on that line of authority that holds in general that the Anti-Trust Laws are being over-used today, and that they are used in many instances in which traditional common law or other statutory forms of action would suffice, and that the principal reason they are being used in that regard is because of the triple-damage remedies that they afford. They afford plaintiffs not only an additional bite at an apple, but a much larger bite at an apple. And they provide considerable leverage because of that factor.[98]

By its terms the Court's current approach to standing makes trebling important. *Associated General Contractors* requires consideration of (among other things) the "risk of duplicate recoveries," which is exacerbated when damages are trebled; avoidance of unnecessary complexity of litigation, a problem that would be eased were the stakes less high; and the speculativeness of the claimed damages, which would be less of a concern were damages not trebled.[99] Trebling also played a central role in the decisions to limit standing, in effect, in *Illinois Brick* and *Hawaii* v. *Standard Oil*.[100] These decisions turned on the risks of duplicate recoveries and of burdening the legal system with complex litigation, both of which would be reduced were there no trebling.

That all of this judicial language represents reality, and trebling is important, also is suggested by the cases adopting more expansive views of standing where only injunctive relief is sought. Both *Illinois Brick* and *Hawaii* v. *Standard Oil* are limited to where damages are sought. Recent decisions have held that competitors may seek to enjoin mergers for which they could not recover damages[101] and that associations may seek injunctive relief for members who would have to sue individually for damages.[102] Since equilibrating tendencies suggest that standing will be broader for injunctive relief than even for single damages, the marked difference in approach to standing to seek injunctive relief as opposed to treble damages does not prove that standards in a single damage world would be more relaxed that at present, but the difference is suggestive.

The final reason to believe that trebling is limiting standing is the very strictness of antitrust standing. In *Associated General* the Court explained that standing was rooted in common law causation,[103] but the difference between the two concepts is breathtaking. In antitrust suits, licensors, franchisors, and lessors who are foreseeably injured by illegal conduct regularly are denied standing;[104] in torts, on the other hand, "there are quite remarkable events which have been taken in stride by various courts as within the boundaries of the jury's permission to find foreseeability" (and thus causation).[105] In torts, courts cheerfully find that numerous defendants have "proximately caused" an accident and that numerous plaintiffs should be allowed to recover for a single wrong;[106] in antitrust cases we find courts searching for "*the* appropriate antitrust enforcer," a member of "this select class of plaintiffs that can impose the deterrent sting of treble damages at the smallest cost of enforcement."[107] Finally, and very important, in torts "proximate cause . . . is ordinarily a question of fact for the jury, to be solved by the exercise of good common sense in the consideration of the evidence in each particular case";[108] in antitrust, standing is to be decided as a matter of law by the court.[109] It is inconceivable that trebling was not a key factor in the evolution of such dissimilar approaches.

5.2   Summary Judgment and Motions to Dismiss

The treble damage remedy appears to have caused courts to view defense motions for summary judgment and motions to dismiss for failure to state a claim ("motions to dismiss") more favorably, The effect of trebling can be seen in judicial language, legal standards, and comparative results.

Because the Georgetown project's data base provides a unique opportunity to explore the use of these motions in antitrust cases, the discussion that follows is not limited to the impact of trebling on their use. The data show that motions for summary judgment and motions to dismiss are sought in antitrust cases with a high degree of success and play an important role in antitrust litigation—contrary to the suggestion of *Poller*, the "lessons" of which continue to be recited regularly. Moreover a consistent if sometimes unspoken recent theme is that disposal of antitrust cases prior to trial is to be encouraged.

The discussion will proceed as follows. First, to put the data in context, I will review the conventional wisdom about the use of summary judgment and motions to dismiss. Findings from the data will then be presented and appraised.

Conventional Wisdom on Motions to Dismiss

In General   The motion to dismiss is viewed with scorn by the leading procedure authorities. The following discussion by Wright and Miller is typical:

The motion to dismiss for failure to state a claim is viewed with disfavor and is rarely granted. Rule 8 indicates that a complaint need only set out a generalized statement of facts from which defendant will be able to frame a responsive pleading. Few complaints fail to meet this liberal standard and become subject to dismissal.[110]

Charles Wright cites a 1962 sampling for the Advisory Committee on Civil Rules that "suggests that [rule 12(b)] motions [which include motions to dismiss for failure to state a claim, and on other grounds] are made in only about 5% of all cases, and that in fewer than 2% of all cases do such motions lead to a final termination of action."[111] The leading Supreme Court discussion of the standard for dismissing complaints continues to be *Conley* v. *Gibson*, where the Court wrote that "a complaint should not be dismissed for failure to state a claim unless it appears beyond doubt that the plaintiff can prove no set of facts in support of his claim which would entitle him to relief."[112]

However, past experience may not forecast the future. Concern about litigation excesses has been widely noted. The effects of this concern can be seen in the recent amendments to the Federal Rules, particularly rule 11, and in the emergence of rule 68 as a more potent force.[113] Inevitably this concern is changing ways of thinking about motions to dismiss.

In Antitrust Suits   At one time antitrust complaints were held to a higher standard than other complaints, and motions to dismiss antitrust complaints enjoyed a warm reception by the courts. In part this was a response to the perceived greater complexity and burdensomeness of antitrust cases,[114] which is related to trebling; in part this was a response directly to trebling. As a 1939 student note explained:

Whether triple damages are punitive in nature has been disputed, but pleading requirements at any rate have assumed the same protective character that is typical of criminal prosecutions. Not only must the complaint allege violation, injury and proximate cause, but it must do so with enough specification to warn the defendant of the particular offense and convince the court that a cause of action has been stated, since the remedy is drastic and must be strictly construed. The degree of particularity is intermediate between the requirements of a criminal indictment and equitable bill.[115]

As antitrust litigators know, that special, rigorous approach to antitrust complaints gradually died, or at least courts said it did. The same pleading standards are said to apply in antitrust as in other cases.[116] Indeed, one can find support for the proposition that more relaxed standards apply in antitrust cases, because of the difficulty of proof.[117] As the Supreme Court wrote in *Rex Hospital*, "in antitrust cases, where 'the proof is largely in the hands of the alleged conspirators,' dismissals prior to giving the plaintiff ample opportunity for discovery should be granted very sparingly." This was a "concededly rigorous standard."[118]

Little empirical work has explored the effect of this standard. In 1961

Fred Freund relied on a handful of cases to conclude that "it is a signal feat for a party permanently to enjoy the fruits of a dismissal for failure to state a claim." [119] This continues to be the accepted wisdom. Indeed, one noted plaintiffs' lawyer has claimed that until the Supreme Court's decisions in *McCready* and *Associated General Contractors*, "Often, lawyers who counsel potential plaintiffs [would] tell them, 'Don't worry. I can draft a complaint that will get you into court and will allow you to engage in sufficient discovery so we can determine whether the defendant has done anything wrong.'" [120]

Benjamin DuVal's review of antitrust treble damage actions filed in the Northern District of Illinois, July 1, 1966, through June 30, 1973, is inconsistent with this generally accepted wisdom. He found that 10.8 percent of all terminated nonclass action suits and 17.3 percent of all terminated class action suits were "involuntarily dismissed." (However, "involuntary dismissal" included more than failure to state a claim. Only four of the nine class suits involuntarily dismissed were dismissed for failure to state a claim.) [121]

Dicta in two recent Supreme Court cases suggest that the Court may be interested in easing the standard for dismissing cases. In a footnote wholly unnecessary to the result in *Associated General Contractors*, the Court wrote that the lawfulness of defendant's conduct might have been "evident" had the trial court required plaintiff to describe the antitrust violation "with particularity." It added that "certainly in a case of this magnitude, a district court must retain the power to insist upon some specificity in pleading before allowing a potentially massive factual controversy to proceed." [122] In *Reiter* v. *Sonotone Corp.* the Court wrote that its decision (that consumers may recover for overcharges) "need not result in administrative chaos, class action harassment, or 'windfall' settlements if the district courts exercise sound discretion and use the tools available." The Court cautioned that "courts must be especially alert to identify frivolous claims brought to extort nuisance settlements." [123] These are invitations for the lower courts to require some specificity in antitrust complaints—specificity that might be unnecessary were the stakes less high and the controversy commensurately smaller.

As shown later, this invitation apparently is being accepted and indeed was being accepted even before issued. In *Havoco of America, Ltd.* v. *Shell Oil Co.*, Judge Pell, affirming the dismissal of an antitrust complaint, observed that "if the allegations of the complaint fail to establish the requisite elements of the cause of action, our requiring costly and time consuming discovery and trial work would represent an abdication of our judicial responsibility." [124] Similarly, in *Sutliff, Inc.* v. *Donovan Cos.*, Judge Posner cited *Associated General* and wrote, "The heavy costs of modern federal litigation, especially antitrust litigation, and the mounting caseload pressures on the federal courts, counsel against launching the parties into pretrial discovery if there is no reasonable prospect that the plaintiff can make out a cause of action from the events narrated in the complaint. [125]

Conventional Wisdom on Summary Judgment

In General   Rule 56, which authorizes summary judgment, is deceptively simple. Any party may move for partial or complete summary judgment, and "the judgment sought shall be rendered forthwith if the pleadings, depositions, answers to interrogatories, and admissions on file, together with the affidavits, if any, show that there is *no genuine issue as to any material fact* and that the moving party is *entitled to a judgment as a matter of law*." A motion may be granted in part or in full. When a motion is properly supported, "an adverse party may not rest upon the mere allegations or denials of his pleading, but his response, by affidavits or as otherwise provided in this rule [i.e., by depositions or answers to interrogatories], must set forth specific facts showing that there is a genuine issue for trial. If he does not so respond, summary judgment, if appropriate, shall be entered against him." When the affidavit(s) of the nonmoving party show why he cannot present essential facts by affidavit, the court "may refuse the application for judgment or may order a continuance to permit affidavits to be obtained or depositions to be taken or discovery to be had." [126]

Buried within the unpretentious words of the first part of this rule lie some of the law's most troublesome issues:

1. What is a question of "fact," as opposed to "law"? It is routinely said that a court hearing a motion for summary judgment should not resolve disputed fact issues but may (and perhaps should) resolve disputed issues of law. [127] But which issues are fact, which are law? Particularly troubling are "mixed questions of fact and law," or, as they are also described, questions requiring the application of legal standards to facts. The customary illustration is taken from negligence law: how fast the defendant was traveling is a question of fact; whether traveling at that speed was negligent is a mixed question of fact and law. [128] Although most commentators agree that both determining speed and deciding whether that speed is negligent should be considered fact questions (and thus answered by the jury in a jury case), [129] there is less agreement on other issues of mixed fact and law. [130]

2. What facts are material? Facts are material if they make a difference.[131] Yet, if the law is unclear, it takes great courage to say that any fact could not make a difference.

3. What is a "genuine issue" of material fact, or, perhaps more important, how convincingly must a movant prove the absence of a "genuine issue"? Several courts have added to the confusion by embellishing the words of the rule by adding, for instance, that summary judgment must be denied if the "slightest doubt" remains.[132] This kind of rule-supplementing has fallen from favor.[133] The seriously difficult problem is how to resolve cases where nonmovants have not shown a genuine issue as of the date of decision, but might be able to create one through discovery or at trial. The civil rights case *Adickes* v. *S. H. Kress and Co.* suggested that the movant had to show the impossibility of evidence creating a genuine issue of fact, but that case has been limited.[134] Difficulty nevertheless arises whenever plaintiffs plan to develop evidence not yet available to them.[135]

These troublesome issues obviously are more challenging in some kinds of cases than in others. Much ink has been spilled discussing the appropriate (or likely, which may not be the same thing) situations for summary judgment. Look for its use, one is told, in (1) small cases, where little is at stake,[136] (2) cases with simple facts,[137] (3) cases turning on documents, rather than witnesses,[138] and (4) bench trials, where the traditional and Constitutionally required deference to a jury is not a factor.[139] On the other hand, summary judgment is said to be unlikely in the converse situations, and where (1) credibility is central[140] (2) the nonmovant has unequal access to facts, or for some other reason requires discovery,[141] (3) the legal issues are complicated,[142] (4) courts' dockets are uncrowded, so trial time need not be conserved,[143] and (5) the court is in the Second Circuit.[144] Litigators are warned that unsuccessful motions cause delay, expose facts and strategy to the opposition, and may create bad law;[145] judges are warned that summary judgment orders suffer an uncommonly high rate of reversal, [146] although some dissent from this conventional wisdom has been voiced.[147]

As for actual frequency of use, commentators tell us that the summary judgment motion "is put to little use except in cases that depend on documentary evidence or on determination of a question of law in a case involving undisputed facts," [148] but some observers detect a trend toward increased usage.[149] The few empirical studies of summary judgment generally confirm that it is used only in a small percentage of cases but find that movants enjoy healthy success rates.[150]

The most important study is probably the one by William McLauchlan.

McLauchlan examined all cases filed in the Eastern Division of the Northern District of Illinois during the 1970 fiscal year. Summary judgment was sought in 4.0 percent of all cases and was granted in 2.3 percent. Motions were granted 51.6 percent of the time, or in 58.7 percent of the cases in which a motion was filed. Defendants fared much better than plaintiffs; 24.0 percent of plaintiff's motions were granted, whereas 62.1 percent of defense motions were.[151]

McLauchlan also sampled reported federal cases from 1938 to 1968. Motions were granted in 58.3 percent of the cases in which they were made and were granted or partly granted in 73.4 percent. McLauchlan speculates, probably correctly, that these figures are biased upward because his sample included appellate decisions, and more grants than denials are appealed. Defendants were more likely to move than plaintiffs; only 21.7 percent of the sample involved motions only by plaintiffs. Plaintiffs also were less successful. They won 54.3 percent of their motions (62.9 percent including partials), whereas defendants won 70.0 percent (73.9 percent including partials). Appelate courts affirmed 51.4 percent of the cases.[152]

In Antitrust Cases   The conventional wisdom about summary judgments in antitrust cases comes in three flavors. Some say summary judgment is uniquely inappropriate in antitrust cases, some say antitrust cases are no different than others, and a few are starting to say summary judgment is unusually desirable in antitrust cases.

The confusion is in part grammatical. In a much quoted passage in *Poller*, the Supreme Court wrote that "summary procedures should be used sparingly in complex antitrust litigation where motive and intent play leading roles, the proof is largely in the hands of the alleged conspirators, and hostile witnesses thicken the plot." [153] Does this mean that summary judgment should not be used frequently in antitrust cases because "motive and intent play leading roles" in such cases, or does it mean that summary procedures have little use in those antitrust (and other) cases in which motive and intent happen to play leading roles? Logic would indicate the latter, and the Court reinforced logic six year later, in *First National Bank* v. *Cities Service Co.*, where the Court declined to read normal summary judgment principles out of antitrust cases.[154] Nevertheless, the felicitous words of *Poller* are ambiguous, and they have acquired a charmed life of their own.

Poller's words regularly are featured in the writings of commentators and courts, some of which continue to view summary judgment as inappropriate to antitrust. Wright, Miller, and Kane say that antitrust cases "are by their very nature poorly suited for disposition by summary judgment."[155] The Trade Regulation Reporter states that summary judgment "is used in antitrust cases, but not to the same extent as in other lawsuits."[156] Von Kalinowski writes that "the Supreme Court has indicated that summary judgment should be granted sparingly in complicated cases, particularly antitrust cases."[157] Thus *Poller*'s words are given prescriptive, as well as descriptive, effect.

Both uses of *Poller* are under assault. At various times during the past 15 years commentators have discerned a trend toward increased use of rule 56 in antitrust cases.[158] Some of these, and others,[159] have advocated such a trend. The force of this assault has shifted the conventional view concerning the appropriateness of antitrust summary judgments toward equality with nonantitrust cases.

For some, the pendulum has swung past the point of equality. These authorities point to the treble damage remedy (and the related complexity of litigation) as reasons why summary judgment has an especially important role in antitrust cases. This view has its genesis in Justice Harlan's dissent to *Poller*. He argued that "having regard for the special temptations that the statutory private antitrust remedy affords for the institution of vexatious litigation, and the inordinate amount of time that such cases sometimes demand of the trial courts, there is good reason for giving the summary judgment rule its full sweep in this field."[160] This dissent has been cited with increasing frequency in the past decade.[111] The most prominent current judicial endorsement of summary judgment's favored status in antitrust cases is *Lupia* v. *Stella D'Oro Biscuit Co.*, but there are other examples.[162] As in Justice Harlan's *Poller* dissent, the focus in these opinions is on trebling and complexity/burden.

For all the discussion of summary judgment in antitrust cases, however, there has been little empirical exploration. McLauchlan's sampling of reported federal cases, 1938 to 1968, found that summary judgment was granted outright in 54.2 percent of the antitrust cases where sought and was granted or partially granted in 68.5 percent. (Comparable figures for all cases were 58.3 and 73.4 percent.) Antitrust's "win ratio" for outright grants (50.4 percent) was higher than the comparable figure for all statutory actions. McLauchlan attributed this to the supposed amenability of per se violations to summary treatment.[163] In DuVal's Chicago study summary judgment was granted in only 7 of the 191 terminated cases (3.7 percent), once for a plaintiff and six times for defendants. Summary judgment was granted only in nonclass actions.[164]

Finally, a study by National Economic Research Associates reviewed all private antitrust suits pending in the Southern District of New York during part or all of 1973 to 1978. This study reported that "summary judgment and other motions" by defendant—apparently including involuntary motions to dismiss, since they are not otherwise taken into account—represented 13 percent of all terminated cases, compared to the 81 percent of all terminations accounted for by settlement and voluntary dismissals. (Only 2.5 percent of all cases were tried.) Only defendants won summary judgment. It occurred most frequently in cases whose primary violation was boycotting (5 of 31 cases), exclusive dealing (3/24), predatory pricing (1/8) horizontal mergers (1/8), price discrimination (2/17), patent/technology abuses (1/9), and dealer termination (2/24).[165]

This modest amount of empirical work suggests that *Poller* never entirely succeeded in discouraging parties from seeking or trial courts from granting summary judgment. The importance of summary judgment in antitrust litigation also is supported by the surprisingly large number of Supreme Court decisions upholding or ordering summary judgment.[166] Those cases overwhelmingly reflect plaintiff (typically government) victories, however, which is very different from the pattern revealed by the Geogetown data set.

Findings from the Georgetown Data Set

The Georgetown data set provided a rich, although flawed, collection of information on summary motions in private antitrust cases. To make available the findings of the data set, what follows and is recorded on the accompanying tables is a detailed presentation of information on the use of these motions in various kinds of antitrust cases.

Findings from the data set support this chapter's principal theme in several ways: (1) by showing that summary dispositions are unexpectedly common in antitrust cases, including jury cases, (2) by suggesting that some recent changes in antitrust law that may have resulted, in part, from a reaction to the specter of trebling have made courts more hospitable to summary motions, and (3) by showing that defendants have unexpectedly good success in particular kinds of antitrust cases where stakes are high (i.e., in class actions and where requested damages are large).

Two econometric models were formulated to help explain the circumstances under which motions to dismiss and motions for summary judgment are granted.[167] In model I (table 5.1) the dependent variable (involving cases in which one or more defense motions to dismiss were granted) was regressed on 21 independent variables. In model II (table 5.2) the dependent variable (involving cases in which one or more defense motions

Table 5.1 Model I: defense pretrial motions for failure to state a claim

Independent variable	Parameter coefficient	Standard error	Chi-square	P-test
Jury demand[a]	0.1068	0.1939	0.30	0.5817
Number of defendants named in suit	0.0129	0.0096	1.82	0.1776
Crossclaim or counterclaim	0.7641	0.4561	2.81	0.0939
Plaintiff's business relation to defendant				
Competitor, same product	0.2987	0.2210	1.83	0.1765
Terminated dealership	−0.2266	0.3502	0.42	0.5175
Final customer or end user	−0.3207	0.3982	0.65	0.4206
Employee or former employee	0.5910	0.4604	1.65	0.1993
Lessee	1.2779	0.8187	2.44	0.1186
Franchisee	0.8562	0.6653	1.66	0.1981
Stockholder	1.2856	0.7188	3.20	0.0737
Alleged violation				
Sherman Act, section 2	−0.2273	0.1913	1.41	0.2347
Clayton Act, section 2	0.0641	0.2355	0.07	0.7854
Horizontal price fixing	−0.1076	0.2720	0.16	0.6924
Predatory pricing	−0.4230	0.5386	0.62	0.4323
Exclusive dealing or tying	−0.0633	0.2961	0.05	0.8305
Refusal to deal	0.0574	0.2590	0.05	0.8246
Vertical price fixing	−0.6306	0.5297	1.42	0.2339
Inducing government action	0.5681	1.1118	0.26	0.6093
Damages claimed in complaint	−0.0007	0.0012	0.33	0.5652
Date of last docket entry	0.0737	0.0310	5.63	0.0176
Class action requested	0.2420	0.2824	0.73	0.3915

Dependent variable = 1 if case had one or more defense motions to dismiss for failure to state a claim granted

Intercept coefficient = −3.1422

Model chi-square = 28.25 with 21 d.f. with P-value = 0.1333

Number of independent variables − 21

Number of cases[b] = 1,737

a. Defined as a dummy variable with 1 = jury demand by plaintiff, defendant, or both; 0 = no jury demand.
b. Excluding those cases with missing files, missing values, or unknown outcomes, and cases pending or on appeal.

Table 5.2 Model II: defense pretrial motions for summary judgment

Independent variables	Parameter coefficient	Standard error	Chi-square	P-test
Jury demand[a]	0.1623	0.2708	0.36	0.5490
Plantiff's business relation to defendant				
Competitor, same product	−0.1096	0.3059	0.13	0.7201
Terminated dealership	0.5648	0.3403	2.75	0.0970
Final customer or end user	−1.3478	0.7573	3.17	0.0751
Employee or former employee	−0.0347	0.7763	0.00	0.9643
Stockholder	1.9766	0.7150	7.64	0.0057
Alleged violation				
Sherman Act, section 2	0.2457	0.2528	0.94	0.3311
Clayton Act, section 2	0.3229	0.2885	1.25	0.2631
Horizontal price fixing	0.3386	0.3274	1.07	0.3010
Predatory pricing	−0.2791	0.6341	0.19	0.6597
Exclusive dealing or tying	−0.0497	0.3913	0.02	0.8989
Refusal to deal	0.0267	0.3369	0.01	0.9368
Vertical price fixing	−0.3800	0.6163	0.38	0.5374
Damages claimed in complaint	0.0006	0.0004	2.14	0.1434
Date of last docket entry	0.1377	0.0444	9.61	0.0019
Number of depositions noticed by plaintiff	−0.0039	0.0083	0.22	0.6384
Number of depositions noticed by defendant	−0.0077	0.0126	0.38	0.5380
Number of interventions noticed by plaintiff	0.1108	0.0609	3.31	0.0689
Number of interventions noticed by defendant	−0.0512	0.0689	0.55	0.4572
Number of requests for production of documents by plaintiff	0.0500	0.0702	0.51	0.4764
Number of requests for production of documents by defendant	0.1746	0.0790	4.88	0.0271
Class action certified[b]	0.5771	0.6039	0.91	0.3393

Dependent variable = 1 if case had one or more defense motions for summary judgment granted; 0 otherwise

Intercept coefficient = −4.8187

Model chi-square = 59.24 with 22 d.f. with P-value = 0.0000

Number of independent variables = 22

Number of cases[c] = 1,737

a. Defined as a dummy variable with 1 = jury demand by plaintiff, defendant, or both; 0 = no jury demand.
b. Defined as a dummy variable with 1 = class certified and either not appealed or affirmed; 0 = other cases.
c. Excluded those cases with missing files, missing values, or unknown outcomes, and cases pending or on appeal.

for summary judgment were granted) was regressed on 22 independent variables. Both regression models were estimated using logit analysis; cases that were pending or an appeal, whose file was lost or whose outcome was unknown, were excluded from the estimation.

Descriptive statistics on the use of summary judgment and motions to dismiss also were developed. The data set shows that the most important motions are defendants' motions for summary judgment and motions to dismiss, and these are the data presented in the tables that follow. Two important caveats should be noted. First, perhaps because many sample sizes are limited, many difference (as compared with sample means) are not statistically significant. For most data, confidence levels have been determined, and where differences are statistically significant this is noted.[168] (For descriptive purposes some differences that are not statistically significant also are noted.) Second, except for the two econometric models and unless otherwise specified, all figures are based on total cases in the data set, some of which are still pending. This does not materially affect success rates by motion, but it may mean that the importance of these motions in disposing of cases is somewhat understated, particularly for recent years.[169]

Frequency   Prospects for a plaintiff seeking summary relief are bleak. Plaintiffs' motions for summary judgment, partial summary judgment, or something called "no substantive issue of fact in dispute" were filed in only 95 of 1,946 cases (4.9 percent) and were granted or partially granted in only 16 (0.8 percent), for a success rate (by case) of 16.8 percent.[170] No longer is there merit—if there ever was—in the suggestion that per se rules account for the unexpectedly high use of summary procedures in antitrust cases.

For defendants, the picture was much brighter. Pretrial motions for summary judgment and motions to dismiss (here, not just for failure to state a claim) were granted or partially granted in 900 cases.[171] This would be 46.2 percent of the data set's 1,946 cases, but obviously it involves double counting.

Motions to dismiss for failure to state a claim were granted in 142 cases (7.3 percent),[179] and granted or partially granted in 179 cases (9.2 percent). If one adds grants and partial grants of defense motions for lack of standing, "plaintiffs'" motions to dismiss counterclaims, and "plaintiffs'" motions to dismiss for failure to state a claim (the last two of which probably are actually defense motions), motions to dismiss for failure to state a claim were granted, as a practical matter, in 170 cases (8.7 percent) and were granted or partially granted in 216 cases (11.1 percent). By comparison, fewer than 6 percent of all cases were tried. Success rates for motions to dismiss for failure to state a claim also were quite high. Motions were granted in 44.0 percent of cases in which they were filed and were granted or partially granted in 55.4 percent.

Summary judgment was only a little less important. What the questionnaire calls "summary judgment" was granted for defendants in 4.2 percent of all cases.[173] and was granted or partially granted in 5.3 percent. Motions were successful in 53.6 percent of the cases in which made and successful or partially successful in 68.0 percent. If one adds to defense "summary judgment" motions those defense motions labeled "no issue" and "no substantive issue," which appear to be summary judgment motions, and defense motions for partial summary judgment, one finds motions being granted for defendants in 6.9 percent of all cases and granted or partially granted in 9.1 percent.

Both sets of results are somewhat surprising, given the traditionally expressed hostility toward summary relief in antitrust cases. Especially remarkable is the importance of motions to dismiss. The frequency with which motions were filed and granted is much higher than the figures suggested for all cases by Charles Wright.[174] Also surprising were the summary judgment figures. Summary judgment was granted in a higher percentage of cases (4.2 percent) than McLauchlan found was average (2.3 percent). Success rates were only just below McLauchlan's averages. Since high quality information about current use of summary procedure outside of antitrust is lacking, one cannot be certain that these procedures are used more commonly in antitrust cases. But it seems unlikely that they are used less commonly.

Over Time   Defendants have been markedly more successful in winning summary relief in recent years. In both regressions the parameter coefficients for date of last docket entry (the nearest approximation for decision date) were positive and statistically significant.

Dismissals were ordered at less than average rates before 1980 (although the differences are not significant), except for cases with last docket entries in 1977 (the year of *Illinois Brick*) (table 5.3). From 1980 to 1983 motions were filed in increasing numbers (in 25 percent of all cases ending in 1982–83) and, although success rates were somewhat inconsistent, motions were granted in increasing percentages of cases, rising to 11.2 percent of all cases ending in 1982 (significant at a 5 percent confidence level) and 15.6 percent of all cases ending in 1983, the year of *Associated General Contractors* (significant at a 1 percent confidence level). There is a sharp drop in all percentages for cases with last docket entries in 1984. This appears to be

Table 5.3 Defendant's motions to dismiss for failure to state a claim, by date of last docket entry

	Total cases	Cases with one or more motions filed	Cases with one or more motions filed (% of total)	Cases with one or more motions granted	Cases with one or more motions granted (% of total)	Cases with one or more motions granted (% of cases with 1+ motions filed)	Motions filed	Motions granted	Motions granted (% of motions filed)
All cases	1,946[a]	323	16.6%	142	7.3%	44.0%	489	232	47.4%
1973	28	2	7.1	1	3.6	50.0	2	1	50.0
1974	97	9	9.3*	6	6.2	66.7	16	11	68.8
1975	137	15	10.9**	7	5.1	46.7	22	8	36.4
1976	151	25	16.6	10	6.6	40.0	33	12	36.4
1977	160	24	15.0	13	8.1	54.2	36	19	52.8
1978	179	28	15.6	9	5.0	32.1	33	12	36.4
1979	215	24	11.2**	13	6.0	54.2	32	20	62.5*
1980	172	26	15.1	12	7.0	46.2	36	17	47.2
1981	201	34	16.9	15	7.5	44.1	62	35	56.5
1982	152	38	25.0***	17	11.2**	44.7	63	37	58.7*
1983	167	41	24.6***	26	15.6***	63.4***	61	37	60.0**
1984	242	45	18.6	10	4.1*	22.2***	73	15	20.5**

Note: * significant at 10 percent confidence level; ** significant at 5 percent confidence level; *** significant at 1 percent confidence level.
a. Includes 7 cases for which the last docket entry was in 1985 and 38 cases not recorded as having a last docket entry dated 1973–1985.

an aberration, but it was only partly caused by inclusion of pending cases.[175]

Table 5.4 shows spurts in success rates and frequency of granting summary judgment in 1976 and in 1978 (the latter may reflect the important 1977 Supreme Court decisions). In the 1980s, except for 1982, defendants enjoyed success rates of 50 percent or more, filed motions in increasingly large percentages of cases, and saw summary judgment being granted in increasingly large percentages of all cases.[176]

By Court   Differences among the five jurisdictions—and particularly between San Francisco and the other four—are striking (tables 5.5 and 5.6). Summary procedures play a more important role in the more active antitrust courts. Plaintiff or defense motions to dismiss, for lack of standing, or for complete or partial summary judgment were granted in 20.2 percent of San Francisco's 485 cases, 12.5 percent of New York's 666, 12.1 percent of Chicago's 571, 10.2 percent of Kansas City's 88, and 7.4 percent of Atlanta's 136.[177]

It is understandable that the more active antitrust courts might be more receptive to summary procedures. Exposure to a subject matter should improve a court's ability to identify unmeritorious claims and disputes of fact that are not genuine or not material. Litigated cases may also lead to greater clarity of legal standards. Experience with numerous antitrust cases also may heighten a court's interest in limiting the burden on judicial resources.

San Francisco stands out as unusually receptive to summary dispositions. This may be a legacy of the IBM litigation, or it may reflect the admonitions of Judge William Schwarzer. Contrary to some suggestions, New York is also quite receptive to summary procedures. Perhaps in response to the perceived Second Circuit hostility to antitrust summary judgment, however, motions to dismiss appear partially to substitute for summary judgment.

By Demand/Damages   The limitations of the data cast doubt on any conclusions concerning use of summary procedures in cases of differing dollar magnitudes. The best information reveals only damages claimed in complaints, and this is available for less than half the sample. As Stephen Susman noted at the conference, sophisticated antitrust lawyers often choose their damage figures later in the proceedings. Moreover the dollar figures reflected in the attached tables have not been adjusted for inflation.

Nevertheless, summary motions apparently are being granted with regu-

Table 5.4 Defendant's motions for summary judgment, by date of last docket entry

	Total cases	Cases with one or more motions filed	Cases with one or more motions filed (% of total)	Cases with one or more motions granted	Cases with one or more motions granted (% of total)	Cases with one or more motions granted (% of cases with 1+ motions filed)	Motions filed	Motions granted	Motions granted (% of motions filed)
All cases	1,946[a]	153	7.9%	82	4.2%	53.6%	225	112	49.8%
1973	28	2	7.1	0	0	—	2	0	—
1974	97	5	5.2	3	3.1	60.0	7	3	42.9
1975	137	3	2.2***	1	0.7***	33.3	3	1	33.3
1976	151	10	6.6	6	4.0	60.0	12	7	58.3
1977	160	8	5.0	3	1.9	37.5	11	3	27.3
1978	179	10	5.6	9	5.0	90.0**	14	11	78.6**
1979	215	13	6.0	6	2.8	46.2	13	6	46.2
1980	172	16	9.3	9	5.2	56.3	20	11	55.0
1981	201	15	7.5	8	4.0	53.3	24	12	50.0
1982	152	14	9.2	6	3.9	42.9	22	7	31.8*
1983	167	15	9.0	10	6.0**	66.7	30	15	50.0
1984	242	37	15.3***	20	8.3***	54.1	61	34	55.7

Note: * significant at 10 percent confidence level; ** significant at 5 percent confidence level; *** significant at 1 percent confidence level.
a. Includes 7 cases for which the last docket entry was in 1985 and 38 cases not recorded as having a last docket entry dated 1973–1985.

Table 5.5 Defendant's motions for failure to state a claim, by district

	Total cases	Cases with one or more motions filed	Cases with one or more motions filed (% of total)	Cases with one or more motions granted	Cases with one or more motions granted (% of total)	Cases with one or more motions granted (% of cases with 1+ motions filed)	Motions filed	Motions granted	Motions granted (% of motions filed)
All cases	1,946	323	16.6%	142	7.3%	44.0%	489	232	47.4%
Atlanta	136	15	11.0**	3	2.2***	20.0*	29	7	24.1**
New York	666	106	15.9	55	8.3	51.8*	140	75	53.6*
Chicago	571	115	20.1**	45	7.9	39.1	170	73	42.9
Kansas City	88	16	18.2	6	6.8	37.5	16	6	37.5
San Francisco	485	71	14.6	33	6.8	46.5	134	71	53.0

Note: * significant at 10 percent confidence level; ** significant at 5 percent confidence level; *** significant at 1 percent confidence level.

Table 5.6 Defendants' motions for summary judgment, by district

	Total cases	Cases with one or more motions filed	Cases with one or more motions filed (% of total)	Cases with one or more motions granted	Cases with one or more motions granted (% of total)	Cases with one or more motions granted (% of cases with 1 + motions filed)	Motions filed	Motions granted	Motions granted (% of motions filed)
All cases	1,946	153	7.9%	82	4.2%	53.6%	225	112	49.8%
Atlanta	136	15	11.0*	6	4.4	40.0	21	11	52.4
New York	666	35	5.3***	18	2.7***	51.4	43	19	44.1
Chicago	571	32	5.6***	18	3.2	56.3	49	28	57.1
Kansas City	88	0	0.0***	0	0.0***	—	0	0	—
San Francisco	485	71	14.6***	40	8.2***	56.3	112	54	48.2

Note: * significant at 10 percent confidence level; ** significant at 5 percent confidence level; *** significant at 1 percent confidence level.

larity at all dollar levels. The conventional wisdom—that is, that summary procedures are used primarily in low dollar cases—received no support. In the summary judgment regression the parameter coefficient for damages claimed was positive but would be significant only at a 15 percent confidence level; in the motion to dismiss regression it was negative but not significant. Tables 5.7 and 5.8 reveal use of summary motions at each of six arbitrarily chosen levels of claimed damages. Summary judgment was ordered *most* frequently at $500,001 to $1,000,000 (at a 10 percent confidence level), whereas dismissal was ordered *least* frequently at the next lowest damage level ($100,001 to $500,000) (at a 5 percent confidence level). Results at the highest dollar level (more than $5 million) differ (with statistical significance) from other cases only in that the success rate (by motion) for motions to dismiss was unusually high. Thus summary procedures are used, if anything, more regularly when the dollars at issue are large.

Plaintiff's Business Relationship to Defendant(s)   Defendants had greatest success winning dismissal of suits brought by stockholders and state or local governments (table 5.9). They had greatest success winning summary judgment against terminated dealers and stockholders and had least success against final customers or end users and against companies to which defendant was a supplier (table 5.10).

In both regressions the parameter coefficients for stockholders were positive and significant. Five of the six motions for summary judgement were granted (significant at a 5 percent confidence level), and all other measures of success were high (although not significantly). Presumably shareholders have an unusually serious standing problem. Also presumably on standing grounds, defendants were quite successful in having suits by employees or former employees dismissed. However, the differences are not significant, and defendants had only average success in obtaining summary judgments. By all measures, defendants did well in suits brought by state or local governments. The success rate for motions to dismiss was significantly high (at a 5 percent confidence level).

Summary judgment was granted in an unusually large number of terminated dealer cases (at a 1 percent confidence level, and the parameter coefficient was positive and significant), which may reflect the maligned character of these suits. However, dismissals were granted in a below average percent of cases, although the difference is not significant. In suits by distributors and dealers, defendants enjoyed above average success in

Table 5.7 Defendants' motions to dismiss for failure to state a claim, by damages claimed (from complaint)

	Total cases	Cases with one or more motions filed	Cases with one or more motions filed (% of total)	Cases with one or more motions granted	Cases with one or more motions granted (% of total)	Cases with one or more motions granted (% of cases with 1 + motions filed)	Motions filed	Motions granted	Motions granted (% of motions filed)
All cases	812[a]	147	18.1%	67	8.3%	45.6%	238	119	50.0%
$1–10,000	36	3	8.3	2	5.6	66.6	7	3	42.9
$10,001–100,000	106	23	21.7	9	8.5	39.1	30	12	40.0
$100,001–500,000	194	22	11.3***	9	4.6**	40.9	32	16	50.0
$500,001–1,000,000	111	17	15.3	9	8.1	52.9	32	22	66.7*
$1,000,001–5,000,000	168	40	23.8**	17	10.1	42.5	66	24	36.4**
More than $5,000,000	197	42	21.3	21	10.7	50.0	71	42	49.2*

Note: * significant at 10 percent confidence level; ** significant at 5 percent confidence level; *** significant at 1 percent confidence level.
a. Only cases with damages claimed on complaint.

Table 5.8 Defendants' motions for summary judgment, by damages claimed (from complaint)

	Total cases	Cases with one or more motions filed	Cases with one or more motions filed (% of total)	Cases with one or more motions granted	Cases with one or more motions granted (% of total)	Cases with one or more motions granted (% of cases with 1+ motions filed)	Motions filed	Motions granted	Motions granted (% of motions filed)
All cases	812ᵃ	65	8.0%	40	4.9%	61.5%	105	52	49.5%
$1–10,000	36	0	0.0***						
$10,001–100,000	106	7	6.6	4	3.8	57.1	9	5	55.5
$100,001–500,000	194	16	8.2	8	4.1	50.0	28	13	46.4
$500,001–1,000,000	111	13	11.7	9	8.1*	69.2	18	11	61.1
$1,000,001–5,000,000	168	12	7.1	8	4.8	66.7	19	10	52.6
More than $5,000,000	197	17	8.6	11	5.6	64.7	31	13	41.9

Note: * significant at 10 percent confidence level; ** significant at 5 percent confidence level; *** significant at 1 percent confidence level.
a. Only cases with damages claimed on complaint.

Table 5.9 Defendants' motions to dismiss for failure to state a claim, by plaintiffs' primary business relationships

	Total cases	Cases with one or more motions filed	Cases with one or more motions filed (% of total)	Cases with one or more motions granted	Cases with one or more motions granted (% of total)	Cases with one or more motions granted (% of cases with 1+ motions filed)	Motions filed	Motions granted	Motions granted (% of motions filed)
All cases	1,946	323	16.6%	142	7.3%	44.0%	489	232	47.4%
Competitor, same product	433	89	20.6**	41	9.5	46.1	124	58	46.8
Competitor, similar or substitute product	124	23	18.5	11	8.9	47.8	31	14	45.2
Supplier	68	10	14.7	4	5.9	40.0	14	6	42.9
Dealer, agent or distributor	487	78	16.0	30	6.2	38.5	117	56	47.9
Terminated dealership	195	31	15.9	11	5.6	35.5	37	13	35.1
Company to whom defendant is a supplier	203	33	16.3	14	6.9	42.4	56	23	41.1
Final customer or end user	157	26	16.6	10	6.4	38.5	52	23	44.2
Employee or former employee	48	11	22.9	6	12.5	54.5	15	7	46.7
State or local government	21	5	23.8	3	14.3	60.6	14	10	71.4**
Other	90	18	20.0	12	13.3**	66.7	28	18	64.3
Licensee	15	5	33.3*	0	0.0	0.0	6	0	0.0**
Lessee	9	3	33.3	2	22.2	66.7	6	4	66.7
Franchisee	23	3	13.0	3	13.0	100.0	6	6	100.0**
Stockholder	14	4	28.6	3	21.4	75.0	11	6	54.5

Note: * significant at 10 percent confidence level; ** significant at 5 percent confidence level; *** significant at 1 percent confidence level.

Table 5.10 Defendants' motions for summary judgment, by plaintiffs' primary business relationship to defendant(s)

	Total cases	Cases with one or more motions filed	Cases with one or more motions filed (% of total)	Cases with one or more motions granted	Cases with one or more motions granted (% of total)	Cases with one or more motions granted (% of cases with 1+ motions filed)	Motions filed	Motions granted	Motions granted (% of motions filed)
All cases	1,946	153	7.9%	82	4.2%	53.6%	225	112	49.8%
Competitor, same product	433	36	8.3	19	4.4	52.6	57	23	40.4*
Competitor, similar or substitute product	124	6	4.8	3	2.4	50.0	7	3	42.9
Supplier	68	5	7.4	3	4.4	60.0	5	3	60.0
Dealer, agent, or distributor	487	42	8.6	26	5.3	61.9	68	37	54.4
Terminated dealership	195	22	11.3*	15	7.7***	68.2*	38	24	63.2*
Company to whom defendant is a supplier	203	11	5.4	6	3.0	54.5	14	7	50.0
Final customer or end user	157	9	5.7	3	1.9	33.3	13	3	23.1*
Employee or former employee	48	3	6.3	2	4.2	66.7	6	3	50.0
State or local government	21	2	9.5	2	9.5	100.0	2	2	100.0
Other	90	9	10.0	4	4.4	44.4	11	4	36.4
Licensee	15	1	6.6	1	6.6	100.0	1	1	100.0
Lessee	9	0	0.0	0	0.0	—	0	0	—
Franchisee	23	0	0.0	0	0.0	—	0	0	—
Stockholder	14	3	21.4	3	21.4	100.0	6	5	83.3**

Note: * significant at 10 percent confidence level; ** significant at 5 percent confidence level; *** significant at 1 percent confidence level.

winning summary judgment but below average success in seeking motions to dismiss. None of the differences are significant. These defense motions were granted much more regularly in the 1980s.[178]

Dismissal also was ordered frequently in suits brought by competitors (particularly competitors making the same product), which might seem to support claims that these tend to be questionable suits, but the difference is not significant. Moreover the relatively high rate at which these cases are dismissed is accounted for only by increased filings of such motions; the success rate (by motion) is low (at a 10 percent confidence level for same product competitor suits). Dismissals played especially important roles in suits ending in 1980 and 1983.[179] Summary judgment was used only at average rates in competitor suits, but the importance of summary judgment in these cases has increased in recent years.[180]

Finally, summary motions have been relatively important in suits brought by (1) final customers or end users, and (2) companies to whom defendants were suppliers. By most measures defendants have done poorly in seeking summary judgment; success rate (by motion) against final customers or end users is significantly low (10 percent confidence level), and use against these persons and against companies to whom defendants are suppliers is somewhat (but not significantly) below average. In the regression the parameter coefficient for the former is negative and significant. Suits by these categories of plaintiffs also are dismissed at below average rates, although the differences are not significant. Perhaps summary motions are relatively unimportant in these suits because courts view the suits as likely to have merit, or as fact dependent. Surprisingly, over time one sees only a modest (and not significant) spurt for cases ending in 1977, the year of *Illinois Brick*.

By Statute and Alleged Illegal Practice   Tables 5.11 through 5.14 report information about defendants' motions to dismiss and motions for summary judgment by primary alleged illegal practice and by the antitrust statutes allegedly violated. Patterns here are hard to detect, and one fears a certain amount of miscategorization or unhelpful categorization.[181]

Countersuits and Cross-Claims   Thirteen percent of all countersuits and cross-claims, which are notoriously frivolous, were dismissed. Although this was not significantly high, in the comparable regression the parameter coefficient for this variable is positive and significant. No summary judgment motions were filed.[182]

Table 5.11 Defendants' motions to dismiss for failure to state a claim, by antitrust statutes allegedly violated

	Total cases	Cases with one or more motions filed	Cases with one or more motions filed (% of total)	Cases with one or more motions granted	Cases with one or more motions granted (% of total)	Cases with one or more motions granted (% of cases with 1 + motions filed)	Motions filed	Motions granted	Motions granted (% of motions filed)
All cases	1,946	323	16.6%	142	7.3%	44.0%	489	232	47.4%
Sherman Act, section 1	1,461	252	17.2	105	7.2	41.7*	385	172	44.7***
Sherman Act, section 2	910	168	18.5*	61	6.7	36.3***	249	95	38.2***
Sherman Act, unspecified	144	28	19.4	15	10.4*	53.6	40	22	55.0
Clayton Act, section 2	352	66	18.8	28	8.0	42.4	107	47	43.9
Clayton Act, section 3	216	41	19.0	10	4.6	24.4***	62	18	29.0***
Clayton Act, section 7	119	17	14.3	10	8.4	58.8	30	15	50.0
Clayton Act, section 8	11	3	27.3	2	18.2	66.7	4	2	50.0
Clayton Act, other section(s)	512	86	16.8	29	5.7**	33.7**	131	55	42.0

Note: * significant at 10 percent confidence level; ** significant at 5 percent confidence level; *** significant at 1 percent confidence level.

Table 5.12 Defendants' motions for summary judgment, by antitrust statutes allegedly violated

	Total cases	Cases with one or more motions filed	Cases with one or more motions filed (% of total)	Cases with one or more motions granted	Cases with one or more motions granted (% of total)	Cases with one or more motions granted (% of cases with 1 + motions filed)	Motions filed	Motions granted	Motions granted (% of motions filed)
All cases	1,946	153	7.9%	82	4.2%	53.6%	225	112	49.8%
Sherman Act, section 1	1,461	119	8.1	64	4.4	53.8	174	86	49.4
Sherman Act, section 2	910	77	8.5	46	5.1**	59.7	119	64	53.8
Sherman Act, unspecified	144	13	9.0	7	4.9	53.8	20	9	45.0
Clayton Act, section 2	352	36	10.2	19	5.4	52.8	48	26	54.2
Clayton Act, section 3	216	15	6.9	8	3.7	53.3	23	12	52.2
Clayton Act, section 7	119	8	6.7	5	4.2	62.5	11	6	54.5
Clayton Act, section 8	11	0	0.0	0	0.0	—	0	0	—
Clayton Act, other section(s)	512	51	10.0*	26	5.1	51.0	77	35	45.5

Note: * significant at 10 percent confidence level; ** significant at 5 percent confidence level; *** significant at 1 percent confidence level.

Table 5.13 Defendants' motions to dismiss for failure to state a claim, by primary alleged illegal practice

	Total cases	Cases with one or more motions filed		Cases with one or more motions granted			Motions filed	Motions granted	
		Number	% of total	Number	% of total	% of cases with 1+ motions filed		Number	% of motions filed
All cases	1,946	323	16.6%	142	7.3%	44.0%	489	232	47.4%
Horizontal price fixing and market allocations	333	51	15.3	22	6.6	43.1	70	28	40.0
"Naked cartel"	12	3	25.0	1	8.3	33.3	3	1	33.3
Merger/joint venture among horizontal competitors	61	4	6.6***	2	3.3	50.0	7	4	57.1
Asset accumulation or patent accumulation	64	16	25.0*	6	9.4	37.5	28	14	50.0
Price discrimination	147	26	17.7	7	4.8	26.9*	42	12	28.6
Predatory pricing	84	12	14.3	5	6.0	41.7	14	6	42.9
Exclusive dealing or tying	225	40	17.8	15	6.7	37.5	58	23	39.7
Refusal to deal	282	47	16.7	20	7.1	42.6	65	24	36.9*
Vertical price discrimination	50	8	16.0	4	8.0	50.0	20	16	80.0***
Vertical price fixing or squeeze	101	9	8.9**	5	5.0	55.6	16	6	37.5
Dealer termination	101	15	14.9	5	5.0	33.3	24	11	45.8
Inducing government action	9	2	22.2	2	22.2	100.0	8	7	87.5***
Other	122	24	19.7	13	10.7	54.2	32	19	59.4
Restraint of trade	41	10	24.4	6	14.6*	60.0	15	11	73.3**
Boycott	11	2	18.2	0	—	—	2	0	—
Monopolization	33	7	21.2	1	3.0	14.3	7	1	14.3

Note: * significant at 10 percent confidence level; ** significant at 5 percent confidence level; *** significant at 1 percent confidence level.

Table 5.14 Defendants' motions for summary judgment, by primary alleged illegal practice

	Total cases	Cases with one or more motions filed		Cases with one or more motions granted			Motions filed	Motions granted	
		Number	% of total	Number	% of total	% of cases with 1 + motions filed		Number	% of motions filed
All cases	1,946	153	7.9%	82	4.2%	53.6%	225	112	49.8%
Horizontal price fixing and market allocation	333	28	8.4	15	4.5	53.6	37	15	40.0
"Naked cartel"	12	2	16.7	0	0.0	0.0	2	0	0.0
Merger/joint venture among horizontal competitors	61	4	6.6	2	3.3	50.0	13	2	15.4**
Asset accumulation or patent accumulation	64	4	6.3	0	0.0	0.0	5	0	0.0*
Price discrimination	147	12	8.2	7	4.8	58.3	17	10	58.8
Predatory pricing	84	7	8.3	5	6.0	71.4	11	6	54.5
Exclusive dealing or tying	225	21	9.3	10	4.4	47.6	28	11	39.3
Refusal to deal	282	19	6.7	13	4.6	68.4	36	16	44.4
Vertical price discrimination	50	3	1.5	2	4.0	66.7	3	2	66.7
Vertical price fixing or squeeze	101	7	6.9	3	3.0	42.9	16	3	18.8**
Dealer termination	101	10	9.9	6	6.0	60.0	14	8	57.1
Inducing government action	9	0	0.0	0	0.0	—	0	0	—
Other	122	9	7.4	6	4.9	66.7	13	9	69.2*
Restraint of trade	41	2	4.9	2	4.9	100.0	3	3	100.0
Boycott	11	0	0.0	0	0.0	—	0	0	—
Monopolization	33	3	9.1	1	3.0	33.3	5	1	20.0

Note: * significant at 10 percent confidence level; ** significant at 5 percent confidence level; *** significant at 1 percent confidence level.

Jury Suits   Although commentators suggest that summary procedures are used less frequently in jury cases, antitrust litigation does not fit this pattern. Instead, summary judgment was ordered more frequently in jury cases than in nonjury cases (at a 10 percent confidence level). Dismissals were ordered more commonly although not significantly so. In both regression models the coefficients for jury demand were positive although not statistically significant.

Class Actions   Defendants had good success in obtaining summary decisions in class actions, but the differences are not significant. Where a class action had been requested, motions to dismiss were filed in 17.7 percent of the cases and granted in 8.5 percent. Where classes were certified and either not appealed or appealed unsuccessfully, defendants filed for summary judgment in 10.7 percent of the cases and were successful in 7.1 percent. In both regressions the parameter coefficients for these variables were positive but not statistically significant. Sixty percent of the motions to dismiss and 46 percent of the motions for summary judgment were granted.

Appeals, Over Time   Most summary dispositions are affirmed if appealed, which is precisely opposite the conventional wisdom. Of 57 appeals of dismissals, only 9 were granted (15.8 percent) and 5 were partly granted (total: 24.6 percent). Of 49 appeals of summary judgment, 10 were granted (20.0 percent) and 5 were partly granted (total: 30.1 percent). This is not a new development. Rather, it is only recently that plaintiffs have started winning.

Discussion

This paper's most important finding is that summary judgments and dismissals for failure to state a claim appear to be ordered as frequently in antitrust cases as in other cases, and they even may be ordered more frequently. Even in jury cases courts regularly granted these defense motions. Summary judgments and dismissals for failure to state a claim each were ordered in more antitrust cases than went to trial. Both kinds of summary dismissals were ordered with significantly greater frequency in recent years. Moreover grants of both kinds of motions usually were affirmed if appealed. The role of these procedures is quite one-sided, however; plaintiffs have had much less success than defendants.

This finding of relatively frequent use of summary orders takes on particular significance when considered in light of the tradition of judicial hostility to summary procedures in antitrust cases. Given the enunciated standards for reviewing these motions, and given the complexity of many antitrust cases, one would expect summary procedures to be used rarely (indeed, many commentators have said they are), but this is not the case.

This unexpected finding can be explained, at least in part, by the treble damage remedy. A number of courts recently have suggested that the in terrorem effect of the treble damage remedy makes summary procedures particularly appropriate in antitrust suits. The finding that these procedures in fact are used with relative frequency suggests that many courts share this thinking. That use of these procedures remains constant or rises with increasing damage requests, and is as great or greater in class action suits as other ones, also supports this conclusion, since conventional wisdom would predict a decline with increasing complexity, and complexity should be associated with high damage requests and class status. Apparently some courts want to prevent finders of fact from deciding high stakes cases.[183]

Courts appear more willing to grant defense motions for summary relief when the costs of erroneous plaintiff verdicts are relatively high. A good example of this is provided by the recent Supreme Court case, *Bose Corp.* v. *Consumers Union of United States, Inc.* The issue was the same distinction between facts and law that is so important in summary judgment, although the context was the scope of review under rule 52 (a). The Court wrote:

A finding of fact in some cases is inseparable from the principles through which it was deduced. At some point the reasoning ... crosses the line between application of those ordinary principles of logic and common experience ... into the realm of a legal rule.... Where the line is drawn varies according to the substantive law at issue. Regarding certain largely factual questions in some areas of the law the stakes—in terms of impact on future cases and future conduct—are too great to entrust them finally to the judgment of the trier of fact.[184]

Bose involved the First Amendment, so the comparison to antitrust is imperfect. But this recognition that the stakes of litigation should affect the latitude courts give juries suggests that trebling increases the use of summary procedures.

Additional support for the proposition that trebling has increased the use of summary procedures is provided by the nature of the cases apparently accounting for the increased use of these procedures in the 1980s. Summary procedures are now being used frequently in predatory pricing cases, where courts have turned to objective tests. Especially very recently, they are being used regularly in price discrimination suits, where *J. Truett Payne*[185] has offered an easy route to the resolution of cases (by showing that disputed issues are not material). Defendants also have enjoyed very recent success in tying/exclusive dealing cases, where the increased clarity following *Jefferson Parish* has enabled courts to decide cases as a matter of law, and in refusal to deal cases, which may reflect *Monsanto*'s limiting of jury discretion. Defendants' recent successes in winning dismissal also can be explained by *Brunswick*, *Illinois Brick*, and *Associated General Contractors*. Thus several changes in antitrust law, some of which may have been affected by the treble damage remedy, have made summary procedures more readily available. It thus seems likely that reduction of the stakes, by detrebling, would tend to reduce the granting of antitrust defense motions to dismiss and motions for summary judgment.

5.4 Conclusion

Where penalties are perceived as inappropriately severe, the legal system will endeavor, subject to institutional constraints, to prevent or reduce the frequency of their imposition. First, the mandatory nature of the treble damage remedy and its perceived severity would suggest that the antitrust system has made adjustments to the penalty by reducing the breadth of the antitrust laws. There is a countervailing tendency, however; that remedy also may have induced private plaintiffs to pursue some theories that otherwise would have been ignored. An admittedly speculative review of trebling's probable effect on substantive antitrust law suggested that the effect has not been unidirectional; were there no trebling, some substantive antitrust standards would be broader and some narrower. It seems clear, however, that without trebling procedural antitrust law would be more hospitable to plaintiffs.

Second, findings from the Georgetown data set concerning motions for summary judgment and motions to dismiss for failure to state a claim in antitrust cases show that summary procedures are used with at least as much regularity in antitrust cases as in other cases and that use of these motions has increased in recent years. The frequency with which these motions are granted is partly a function of trebling. One of the ways in which courts have adjusted to the treble damage remedy is by being relatively more willing to keep cases from going to trial.

What does this tell us about the consequences of any legislation to eliminate the treble damage remedy? Existing legal standards would not instantly change; indeed, Congress might insist in its legislation that legal standards be preserved. However, over time adjustments would come. Suits could be expected to shift to state courts or feature alternative (nonantitrust) grounds of illegality. There would likely be fewer opportunities to expand the law, but also less pressure to limit access to the courts. Gradual easing of procedural barriers to suits, especially standing rules, could be expected, and plaintiffs would have greater success reaching trial. Perhaps, although this is difficult to predict, the enforcement agencies might have more success in advocating novel theories of illegality. What is clear is that changing the penalty almost certainly would give rise to at least partially compensating adjustments in substantive and procedural antitrust standards.

Notes

1. I. Newton, Mathematical Principles of Natural Philosophy, Law of Motion III (A. Motte Trans. 1934).

2. This is not the first paper to suggest such a connection, of course. *See, e.g.*, Study of the Antitrust Treble Damage Remedy, a Report of the House Comm. on the Judiciary, 98th Cong., 2d Sess. 27–33 (Comm. Print Serial No. 8, 1984) (hereinafter *Garvey Study*); II P. Areeda & D. Turner, Antitrust Law § 331b2 (1978); Calkins, Illinois Brick and its Legislative Aftermath, 47 Antitrust L.J. 967, 983 (1978).

A revised and expanded version of this paper discusses three other examples of the legal system's equilibrating tendencies. The examples are drawn from criminal law, the Racketeer Influenced and Corrupt Organizations Act (RICO), and torts. Calkins, Summary Judgment, Motions to Dismiss, and Other Examples of Equilibrating Tendencies in the Antitrust System, 74 Geo. L.J. 1065 (1986).

3. 368 U.S. 464, 473 (1962).

4. *See* ABA Antitrust Section, Antitrust Law Developments *(2d)*, chs. 5–7 (1984 & Supp. 1986) [hereinafter Antitrust Law Developments].

5. *See* M. Handler, H. Blake, R. Pitofsky, & H. Goldschmid, Cases and Materials on Trade Regulation 128–29 (2d ed. 1983); Posner, A Statistical Study of Antitrust Enforcement, 13 J.L. & Econ. 365, 373 (1970).

6. II P. Areeda & D. Turner, *supra* note 2, at 150; *see* Garvey Study, *supra* note 2, at 33; Breit & Elzinga, Private Antitrust Enforcement: The New Learning, 28 J.L. & Econ. 405, 439 (1985) (same). Although the discussion that follows focuses on enunciated standards of liability, trebling's effect also may have been felt in the application of those standards.

7. *See* Northern Sec. Co. v. United States, 193 U.S. 197, 358 (1904); *id.* at 401–02 (Holmes, J., dissenting); United States v. Trans-Missouri Freight Ass'n, 166 U.S. 290, 353 (1897) (White, J., dissenting).

8. 438 U.S. 422, 439 (1978).

9. United States v. United States Gypsum Co., 438 U.S. 422, 440–41 (1978) (footnote and citations omitted).

10. P. Areeda, Antitrust Analysis 59–60 (3d ed. 1981).

11. *See* Trubek, Sarat, Felstiner, Kritzer, & Grossman, The Costs of Ordinary Litigation, 31 UCLA L. Rev. 72, 102–09 (1983).

12. *But cf.* DuVal, The Class Action as an Antitrust Enforcement Device: The Chicago Experience (II), 1976 Am. Bar Found. Research J. 1273, 1275–77.

13. 15 U.S.C. §45 (1982); *see* Antitrust Law Developments, *supra* note 4, at 340–41. Comparison also could be made to the antitrust laws of foreign countries or certain states, but extraneous differences seem even greater. As suggested at the conference, one also could compare antitrust standards before and after the tax treatment of treble damages was changed in 1969.

14. 344 U.S. 392, 394–395 (1953).

15. 381 U.S. 357, 369 (1965).

16. 384 U.S. 316, 321 (1966).

17. 405 U.S. 233, 239, 244 (1972).

18. Averitt, The Meaning of "Unfair Methods of Competition" in Section 5 of the Federal Trade Commission Act, 21 B.C.L. Rev. 227, 275 (1980).

19. 729 F.2d 128 (2d Cir. 1984).

20. *In re* Ethyl Corp., 101 FTC 425, 652 (1983).

21. 630 F.2d 920, 928 (2d Cir. 1980), *cert. denied*, 450 U.S. 917 (1981).

22. 630 F.2d at 927 (quoting United States v. Colgate & Co., 250 U.S. 300 (1919)); *see also* Boise Cascade Corp. v. FTC, 637 F.2d 573 (9th Cir. 1980).

23. *See* General Motors Corp., 3 Trade Reg. Rep. (CCH) ¶ 22,165 (June 21, 1984); General Foods Corp., 3 Trade Reg. Rep. (CCH) ¶ 22,142 (Apr. 6, 1984).

24. 5 Trade Reg. Rep. (CCH) ¶ 66,704 (7th Cir. July 3, 1985).

25. *Id.* at 63,370.

26. Lockheed Corp., 92 F.T.C. 968 (1978) (consent order); Kellogg Co., [1970–73 Transfer Binder] Trade Reg. Rep. (CCH) ¶ 19,898 (FTC complaint filed 1972), *dismissed*, 99 F.T.C. 8 (1982); Exxon Corp., [1973–1976 Transfer Binder] Trade Reg. Rep. (CCH) ¶ 20,388 (complaint announced July 17, 1973), *dismissed*, 98 F.T.C. 453 (1981).

27. T. Calvani, Remarks before the ABA Antitrust Section Annual Meeting (July 9, 1985), *reprinted at* 5 Trade Reg. Rep. (CCH) ¶ 50,475.

28. *See* ABA Antitrust Section, Monograph No. 5, Vol. 1, The FTC as an Antitrust Enforcement Agency 4 (1981).

29. *See, e.g.*, FTC v. Sperry & Hutchinson Co., 405 U.S. 233 239–44 (1972).

30. II P. Areeda & D. Turner, *supra* note 2, at 26.

31. Averitt, *supra* note 18, at 251 n.112; Reich, The Future of Unfair Methods of Competition, 50 Antitrust L.J. 801 (1982).

32. Ethyl Corp. [1979–1983 Transfer Binder] Trade Reg. Rep. (CCH) ¶ 22,003, at 22,560 (FTC 1983), *rev'd sub nom.* E.I. Du Pont de Nemours & Co., 729 F.2d 128 (2d Cir. 1984).

33. Interview with Thomas E. Kauper, former assistant attorney general for the Justice Department's Antitrust Division.

34. II P. Areeda & D. Turner, *supra* note 2, at 150.

35. United States v. Aluminum Co. of America, 148 F.2d 416 (2d Cir. 1945); United States v. Griffith, 334 U.S. 100 (1948); Lorain Journal Co. v. United States, 342 U.S. 143 (1951); United States v. Grinnell Corp., 384 U.S. 563 (1966).

36. Berkey Photo. Inc. v. Eastman Kodak Co., 603 F.2d 263 (2d. Cir. 1979) *cert. denied* 444 U.S. 1093 (1980); Telex Corp. v. IBM, 510 F.2d 894, 927 (10th Cir.), *cert. denied*, 423 U.S. 802 (1975).

37. *See In re* Reuben H. Donnelley Corp., 95 F.T.C. 1 (1980), *rev'd sub nom.* Official Airline Guides, Inc. v. FTC, 630 F.2d 920 (2d Cir. 1980), *cert. denied*, 450 U.S. 917 (1981); Kellogg Co., [1970–1973 Transfer Binder] Trade Reg. Rep. (CCH) ¶ 19,898 (FTC complaint filed 1972), *dismissed*, 99 F.T.C. 8 (1982).

38. SCM v. Xerox Corp., 463 F. Supp. 983, 998 (D. Conn. 1978), *remanded*, 599 F.2d 32 (2d Cir.), *supplemental opinion*, 474 F. Supp. 589 (D. Conn. 1979), *aff'd on other grounds*, 645 F.2d 1195 (2d Cir. 1981), cert. denied, 455 U.S. 1016 (1982).

39. See generally Austin, Negative Effects of Treble Damage Actions: Reflections on the New Antitrust Strategy, 1978 Duke L.J. 1353; Baumol & Ordover, Use of Antitrust to Subvert Competition, 28 J. Law & Econ. 247 (1985).

40. *Compare* Kodak, 273 U.S. 359 (1927) with FTC v. Raymond Bros.-Clark Co., 263 U.S. 565 (1924).

41. United States v. United Shoe Machinery Corp., 110 F. Supp. 295, 345 n.2 (D. Mass. 1953), *aff'd per curiam*, 347 U.S. 521 (1954).

42. 537 F.2d 296 (8th Cir. 1976), *cert. denied*, 429 U.S. 1122 (1977).

43. 327 F.2d 459 (9th Cir.), *cert. denied*, 377 U.S. 993 (1964).

44. E. I. Du Pont de Nemours & Co., 96 F.T.C. 650 (1980).

45. *E.g.*, International Tel. & Tel. Corp., 3 Trade Reg. Rep. (CCH) ¶ 22,188 (FTC July 25, 1984); General Foods Corp., 3 Trade Reg. Rep. (CCH) ¶ 22,142 (FTC April 6, 1984).

46. Official Airline Guides, Inc. v. FTC, 630 F.2d 920 (2d Cir. 1980), *cert. denied*, 450 U.S. 917 (1981).

47. Aspen Skiing Co. v. Aspen Highlands Skiing Corp., 105 S. Ct. 2847 (1985).

48. *See* Borden, Inc., 92 F.T.C. 669 (1978), *aff'd*, 674 F.2d 498 (6th Cir. 1982), *vacated and remanded for entry of consent order*, 103 S. Ct. 2115 (1983); Kellogg Co., [1970–1973 Transfer Binder] Trade Reg. Rep. (CCH) ¶ 19,898 (FTC complaint filed 1972), *dismissed*, 99 F.T.C. 8 (1982).

49. See § II.C., *infra*.

50. United States v. Socony-Vacuum Oil Co., 310 U.S. 150, 224 & n.59 (1940); United States v. Trenton Potteries Co., 273 U.S. 392 (1927).

51. National Collegiate Athletic Ass'n v. Board of Regents of the Univ. of Okla., 104 S. Ct. 2948 (1984); Broadcase Music, Inc. v. CBS, 441 U.S. 1 (1979). *But cf.* Arizona v. Maricopa Country Medical Soc'y, 457 U.S. 332 (1982).

52. *See* Albrecht v. Herald Co., 390 U.S. 145 (1968); Kiefer-Stewart Co. v. Joseph E. Seagram & Sons, Inc., 340 U.S. 211 (1951). *But cf.* Arizona v. Maricopa Country Medical Soc'y, 457 U.S. 332 (1982).

53. United States v. Sealy, Inc., 388 U.S. 350 (1967); United States v. Topco Assocs., Inc., 405 U.S. 596 (1972).

54. 405 U.S. 251, 263 64 (1972).

55. Copperweld Corp. v. Independence Tube Corp., 104 S. Ct. 2731, 2745 (1984).

56. *See* Perma Life Mufflers, Inc. v. International Parts Corp., 392 U.S. 134 (1968); Kiefer-Stewart Co. v. Joseph E. Seagram & Sons, Inc., 340 U.S. 211 (1951). *But cf.* Timken Roller Bearing Co. v. United States, 341 U.S. 593, 598 (1951); United States v. Yellow Cab Co., 332 U.S. 218 (1947).

57. Albert Pick-Barth Co. v. Mitchell Woodbury Corp., 57 F.2d 96,102 (1st Cir.), *cert. denied*, 286 U.S. 552 (1932).

58. Northwest Power Prods., Inc. v. Omark Indus., Inc., 576 F.2d 83, 89 (5th Cir. 1978), *cert. denied*, 439 U.S. 1116 (1979).

59. Northwest Wholesale Stationers, Inc. v. Pacific Stationery and Printing Co., 105 S. Ct. 2613 (1985); *see* Antitrust Law Developments, *supra* note 4, at 43–49.

60. Fashion Originators' Guild of Am. v. FTC, 312 U.S. 457 (1941).

61. Klor's, Inc. v. Broadway-Hale Stores, Inc., 359 U.S. 207 (1959); Radiant Burners, Inc. v. People Gas Light & Coke Co., 364 U.S. 656 (1961); Silver v. New York Stock Exch., 373 U.S. 341 (1963).

62. FTC v. National Lead Co., 352 U.S. 419 (1957); FTC v. Cement Inst., 333 U.S. 683 (1948); Triangle Conduit & Cable Co. v. FTC, 168 F.2d 175 (7th Cir. 1948), *aff'd by an equally divided Court sub nom.* Clayton Mark & Co. v. FTC, 336 U.S. 956 (1949); *see* United States v. Container Corp. Of America, 393 U.S. 333 (1969); Interstate Circuit, Inc. v. United States, 306 U.S. 208 (1939). *But see* American Tobacco Co. v. United States, 328 U.S. 781, 810 (1946) (classic definition of conspiracy written in a criminal case).

63. Theatre Enters. Inc. v. Paramount Film Distrib. Corp., 346 U.S. 537 (1954).

64. *Compare* American Society of Internal Medicine, 3 Trade Re. Rep. (CCH) ¶ 22,242 (FTC advisory opinion April 19, 1985) *with* United States v. American Soc'y of Anesthesiologists, Inc., 473 F. Supp. 147 (S.D.N.Y. 1979).

65. *Monsanto Co.* v. *Spray-Rite Service Corp.*, 104 S. Ct. 1464. 1470–1471 (1984).

66. *See, e.g.*, Duplan Corp. v. Deering Milliken, Inc., 444 F. Supp. 648, 695 (D.S.C. 1977), *aff'd in part, rev'd in part*, 594 F.2d 979 (4th Cir. 1979), *cert. denied*, 444 U.S. 1015 (1980); *Antitrust Law Developments, supra* note 4, at 489.

67. *See* S. 1841, Title IV (98th Cong., 1st Sess.).

68. United States v. Arnold, Schwinn & Co., 388 U.S. 365 (1977); United States v. Loew's Inc., 371 U.S. 38 (1962); United States v. Parke, Davis & Co., 362 U.S. 29 (1960); Northern Pac. Ry. v. United States, 356 U.S. 1 (1958); International Salt Co. v. United States, 332 U.S. 392 (1947); Dr. Miles Medical Co., v. John D. Park & Sons Co., 220 U.S. 373 (1911). *But see* Fortner Enters., Inc. v. U.S. Steel Corp., 394 U.S. 495 (1969); Albrecht v. Herald Co., 390 U.S. 145 (1968); Simpson v. Union Oil Co., 377 U.S. 13 (1964).

69. Continental T.V., Inc. v. GTE Sylvania Inc., 433 U.S. 36 (1977); *see* ABA Antitrust Section, Monograph No. 2 *Vertical Restrictions Limiting Intrabrand Competition* (1977).

70. Albrecht v. Herald Co., 390 U.S. 145 (1968); Fortner Enters., Inc. v. U.S. Steel Corp., 394 U.S. 495 (1969).

71. E.g., Laker Airways Ltd. v. Pan American World Airways, Inc., 604 F. Supp. 280 (D.D.C. 1984).

72. Mannington Mills, Inc. v. Congoleum Corp., 595 F.2d 1287, 1297–98 (3d Cir. 1979).

73. *E.g.*, McLain v. Real Estate Bd., 444 U.S. 232, 235 (1980); Hospital Bldg. Co. v. Trustees of Rex Hosp., 425 U.S. 738 (1980), *reversing* 511 F.2d 678, 680 (4th Cir. 1975); *see* P. Areeda, *supra* note 11, at 133; M. Handler et al., *supra* note 5, at 160.

74. Marrese v. Interqual, Inc., 1984-2 Trade Cas. (CCH) ¶ 66,271, at 67, 179 (7th Cir. 1984), *cert. denied*, 105 S. Ct. 3501 (1985).

75. *See, e.g.*, Seglin v. Esau, 5 Trade Reg. Rep. (CCH) ¶ 66,738 (7th Cir. Aug. 8, 1985); Hayden v. Bracy, 744 F.2d 1338 (8th Cir. 1984); McElhinney v. Medical Protective Co., 1984-1 Trade Cas. (CCH) ¶ 66,054 (6th Cir. 1984) (not for publication); Furlong v. Long Island College Hospital, 710 F.2d 922, 927 (2d Cir. 1983). *But see, e.g.*, El Shahawy v. Harrison, 5 Trade Reg. Rep. (CCH) ¶ 66,888 (11th Cir. Dec. 16, 1985).

76. Seglin v. Esau, 5 Trade Reg. Rep. (CCH) ¶ 66,738, at 63,545 n.6 (7th Cir. Aug. 8, 1985).

77. 15 U.S.C.A. §§ 34–36 (West Supp. 1985); *id.* §§ 4301–4305; 46 U.S.C.A. §§ 1701–1706, 1715 (West Supp. 1985); 15 U.S.C. §§ 4001–4003 (1982); *id.* §§ 3501–3503.

78. *See* S. P. Posner, *The Proper Relationship Between State Regulation and the Federal Antitrust Laws*, 49 N.Y.U.L. Rev. 693, 728 (1974); Note, *Antitrust Treble Damage as Applied to Local Government Entities: Does the Punishment Fit the Defendant?*, 1980 Ariz. St. L.J. 411, 420.

79. Cantor v. Detroit Edison Co., 428 U.S. 579, 615 (1976) (Stewart, J., dissenting). City of Lafayette v. Louisiana Power & Light Co., 435 U.S. 389, 401–02 (1978); *id.* at 440 (Stewart, J., dissenting).

80. *See* Southern Motor Carriers Rate Conference v. U.S. 105 S. Ct. 1721 (1985); Town of Hallie v. City of Eau Claire, 105 S. Ct. 1713 (1985); Hoover v. Ronwin, 104 S. Ct. 1989 (1984). *Compare* J. Briggs & S. Calkins, Antitrust Update, 1984–85, at 28–29 (March 7, 1985) (incorrectly predicting plaintiff would win Southern Motor Carriers) *with* Campbell, Supreme Court Update—State Action Immunity from Antitrust Law, 53 Antitrust L.J. 429, 432 (1984) (incorrectly predicting plaintiff would win *Town of Hallie*).

81. 392 U.S. 134, 46 (1968); (White, J., concurring); *id.* at 147 (Fortas, J., concurring in the result); *id.* at 149 Marshall, J., concurring in the result): *id.* at 154 (Harlan, J., concurring in part and dissenting in part).

82. *Id.* at 154 (Harlan, J., concurring in part and dissenting in part).

83. *Id.* at 151 (Marshall, J., concurring in the result).

84. THI-Hawaii, Inc. v. First Commerce Financial Corp., 627 F.2d 991, 996 (9th Cir. 1980).

85. *E.g.*, Kline v. Coldwell, Banker & Co., 508 F.2d 226 (9th Cir. 1974), *cert. denied*, 421 U.S. 963 (1975); *but see* Chevalier v. Baird Sav. Ass'n, 72 F.R.D. 140, 150 (E.D. Pa. 1976).

86. 327 U.S. 251 (1946); *see also* Story Parchment Co. v. Paterson Parchment Paper Co., 282 U.S. 555 (1931).

87. *See* Antitrust Law Developments, *supra* note 4, at 407–08.

88. *See* MCI Communications Corp. v. American Tel. & Tel. Co., 708 F.2d 1081, 1160–69 (7th Cir.), *cert. denied*, 104 S. Ct. 234 (1983); Berkey Photo, Inc. v. Eastman Kodak Co., 603 F.2d 263, 296–98 (2d Cir. 1979), *cert. denied*, 444 U.S. 1093 (1980).

89. *E.g.*, MCI Communications; Southern Pacific Communications Co. v. American Tel. & Tel. Co., 556 F. Supp. 825 (D.D.C. 1982), *aff'd*, 740 F.2d 980 (D.C. Cir. 1984), *cert. denied*, 105 S. Ct. 1721 (1985); Breit & Elzinga, *supra* note 6, at 420–22.

90. *Cf.* MCI, 708 F.2d at 1162–63.

91. *See* Garvey Study, *supra* note 2, at 29–30; L. Sullivan, Handbook of the Law of Antitrust 773–74 (1977); Breit & Elzinga, *supra* note 7, at 413–22. For purposes of this subsection, "standing" includes the related concepts of "antitrust injury," see Brunswick Corp. v. Pueblo Bowl-O-Mat, Inc., 429 U.S. 477 (1977), "fact of damage," see Antitrust Law Developments, *supra* note 4, at 387–92, and the Illinois Brick limitation, see Illinois Brick Co. v. Illinois, 431 U.S. 720 (1977).

92. *See* Breit & Elzinga, *supra* note 6, at 414–15; Page, Antitrust Damages and Economic Efficiency: An Approach to Antitrust Injury, 47 U. Chi. L. Rev. 467 (1980).

93. 166 F. 820, 824 (C.C.D. Mass. 1909).

94. 454 F.2d 1292, 1295 (2d Cir. 1971) (Mansfield, J.), *cert. denied*, 406 U.S. 930 (1972).

95. *E.g.*, Mid-West Paper Prods. Co. v. Continental Group. Inc., 596 F.2d 573, 586–87 (3d Cir. 1979).

96. *E.g.*, Conference of Studio Unions v. Loew's Inc., 193 F.2d 51, 55 (9th Cir. 1951).

97. *E.g.*, *In re* Industrial Gas Antitrust Litig., 681 F.2d 514, 519–20 (7th Cir. 1982), *cert. denied*, 460 U.S. 1016 (1983).

98. J.F. Reed Co. v. K Mart Corp., 1982-1 Trade Cas. (CCH) ¶ 64,499, at 72,768, 72,770 (E.D. Mich. 1981), *supplemented*, 1982-1 Trade Cas. (CCH) ¶ 64,500 (E.D. Mich. 1981).

99. Associated General Contractors of California, Inc. v. California State Council of Carpenters, 459 U.S. 519, 542–44 (1983).

100. Illinois Brick Co. v. Illinois, 431 U.S. 720 (1977); Hawaii v. Standard Oil Co., 405 U.S. 251 (1972).

101. Monfort, Inc. v. Cargill, Inc., 761 F.2d 570 (10th Cir. 1985), *cert. granted*, 106 S. Ct. 784 (1986); White Consolidated Indus., Inc. v. Whirlpool Corp., 612 F. Supp. 1009 (N.D. Ohio), *vacated on other grounds*, 619 F. Supp. 1022 (N.D. Ohio 1985); Christian Schmidt Brewing Co. v. G. Heileman Brewing Co., 600 F. Supp. 1326 (E.D. Mich.), *aff'd*, 753 F. 2d 1354 (6th Cir.), *cert. dismissed*, 105 S. Ct. 1155 (1985).

102. Mission Hills Condominium Ass'n M-1 v. Corley, 570 F. Supp. 453 (N.D. Ill. 1983).

103. 459 U.S. at 523–33.

104. *See, e.g.*, Antitrust Law Developments, *supra* note 4, at 395–401; II P. Areeda & D. Turner, *supra* note 2, at § 341.

105. W. Prosser & W. P. Keeton, Prosser and Keeton on the Law of Torts 300 (5th ed. 1984).

106. *See id.* at 266–67.

107. *In re* Industrial Gas Antitrust Litig., 681 F.2d 514, 520 (7th Cir. 1982) (Bauer, J.) (emphasis added).

108. Healy v. Hoy, 115 Minn. 321, 132 N.W. 208 (1911), *quoted*, Prosser & Keeton, *supra* note 105, at 321.

109. *E.g.*, Nishimura v. Dolan, 599 F. Supp. 484 (E.D.N.Y. 1984); Zenith Radio Corp. v. Matsushita Elec. Indus. Co., 513 F. Supp. 1100, 1158 n.70 (E.D. Pa. 1981), *aff'd in part, rev'd in part sub nom. In re* Japanese Elec. Prods. Antitrust Litig., *cert. granted*, No. 83-2004 (U.S. Apr. 1, 1985).

110. 5 C. Wright & A. Miller, Federal Practice and Procedure 598 (1969) (footnotes omitted); *see also* 2A J. Moore & J. Lucas, Moore's Federal Practice ¶ 12.07[2. – 5](1985); 27 Fed. Proc., L. Ed. § 62,465, at 575.

111. C. Wright, *The Law of Federal Courts* 432 (4th ed. 1983).

112. 355 U.S. 4, 45–46 (1957).

113. See Fed. R. Civ. P. 11 Advisory Committee Note, *reprinted in* 28 U.S.C.A. Rule 11 (West Supp. 1985); *Marek* v. *Chesny*, 105 S. Ct. 3012 (1985).

114. *See, e.g.*, New Dyckman Theatre Corp. v. Radio-Keith-Orpheum Corp., 16 F.R.D. 203, 205, 206 (S.D.N.Y. 1954).

115. Note, Fifty Years of Sherman Act Enforcement, 49 Yale L.J. 284, 297 (1939) (citations and footnotes omitted).

116. *E.g.*, McElroy, Federal Pre-Trail Procedure in an Antitrust Suit, 31 Sw. L.J. 649, 679 (1977); Nagler v. Admiral Corp., 248 F.2d 319 (2d Cir. 1957); *see also, e.g.*, Note, Antitrust Enforcement by Private Parties: Analysis of Developments in the Treble Damage Suit, 61 Yale L.J. 1010, 1033–34 (1952).

117. *E.g.*, 2A Moore's Federal Practice, *supra* note 110, at ¶ 8.17[3].

118. Hospital Bldg. Co. v. Trustees of Rex Hosp., 425 U.S. 738, 746 (1976).

119. Freund, The Pleading and Pre-Trail of an Antitrust Claim, 18 ABA Antitrust Section Rep. 15, 18 (1961).

120. Susman, *Standing in Private Antitrust Cases: Where is the Supreme Court Going*, 52 Antitrust L.J. 465, 466 (1983); *see also* P. Areeda, *supra* note 10, at 96.

121. DuVal, *supra* note 12, at 1306–07, 1342. The figures cited in the text combine DuVal's numbers for "clustered" and "unclustered" cases. Staff of Senate Comm. on Commerce, 93d Cong., 2d Sess., Class Action Study 8–9 (Comm. Print 1974).

122. 459 U.S. 519, 528 (1983).

123. 442 U.S. 330, 345 (1979).

124. 626 F.2d 549, 553 (7th Cir. 1980) (citation omitted).

125. 727 F.2d 648, 654 (7th Cir. 1984) (citation omitted).

126. Fed. R. Civ. P. 56(c)–56(f).

127. *E.g.*, 10A C. Wright & A. Miller, Federal Practice and Procedure § 2725 (2d ed. 1983).

128. *Id.*

129. *E.g.*, Prosser & Keeton, *supra* note 105, at § 37; Weiner, The Civil Jury Trial and the Law-Fact Distinction, 54 Calif. L. Rev. 1867, 1876–77 (1966).

130. *Cf.* Asbill & Snell, Summary Judgment under the Federal Rules—When an Issue of Fact Is Presented, 51 Mich. L. Rev. 1143 (1953); Schwarzer, Summary Judgment under the Federal Rules: Defining Genuine Issues of Material Fact, 99 F.R.D. 465 (1984); Weiner *supra* note 129. Separating issues of fact from issues of law also implicates the Constitutional right to a jury trial. *See* Jorde, The Seventh Amendment Right to Jury Trial of Antitrust Issues, 69 Calif. L. Rev. 1 (1981).

131. *E.g.*, Note, Summary Judgment under Federal Rule of Civil Procedure 56—A Need for Clarifying Amendment, 48 Iowa L. Rev. 453 (1963); *see also* Schwarzer, *supra* note 130, at 480.

132. *E.g.*, 10A *Federal Practice and Procedure*, *supra* note 127, at 97–98.

133. *E.g.*, Louis, Summary Judgment and the Actual Malice Controversy in Constitutional Defamation Cases, 57 S.C.L. Rev. 707 (1984); Rogers, Summary Judgments in Antitrust Conspiracy Litigation, 10 Loyola U.L.J. 667 (1979).

134. 398 U.S. 144 (1970); *see* Currie, Thoughts on Directed Verdicts and Summary Judgments, 45 U.Chi. L. Rev. 72 (1977); *see also* Sonenshein, State of Mind and Credibility in the Summary Judgment Context: A Better Approach, 78 Nw. U.L. Rev. 774 (1983).

135. *See generally* Louis, Federal Summary Judgment Doctrine: A Criticial Analysis, 83 Yale L.J. 745 (1974).

136. Cohen, Summary Judgment in the Supreme Court of New York: A Factual Study of Rule 113, 32 Colum. L. Rev. 830 (1932); Sandler & Corderman, Winning a Summary Judgment, 10 Litigation No. 3, at 15 (Spring 1984); Factors Affecting the Grant or Denial of Summary Judgment, 48 Colum. L. Rev. 780 (1948).

137. Kennedy, The Federal Summary Judgment Rule—Some Recent Developments, 13 Bklyn. L. Rev. 5 (1947); *Factors Affecting*, *supra* note 136.

138. *E.g.*, Cohen, *supra* note 136, at 854.

139. J. Friedenthal, M. Kane, & A. Miller, Civil Procedure 440 (1985); Gellhorn & Robinson, Summary Judgment in Administrative Adjudication, 84 Harv. L. Rev. 612 (1971); *Factors Affecting*, *supra* note 136.

140. *E.g.*, 10A Federal Practice and Procedure, *supra* note 127, at § 2730.

141. *E.g.*, Louis (1984), *supra* note 133.

142. 10A Federal Practice and Procedure, *supra* note 127, at 85–88.

143. Hays, The Summary Judgment, 28 F.R.D. 126, 133 (1960); Kennedy, *supra* note 137; Note, Use of Summary Judgment by Type of Case, 36 Minn. L. Rev. 515 (1952).

144. C. Wright, The Law of Federal Courts 668–69 (4th ed. 1983).

145. Sandler & Corderman, *supra* note 136; Stamper, Rule 56: Using Summary Judgment Motions, 7 Litigation No. 3, at 36 (Spring 1981).

146. Littlejohn v. Shell Oil Co., 483 F.2d 1140, 1145 (5th Cir.), *cert. denied*, 414 U.S. 1116 (1973); R. Fellmeth & T. Papageorge, A Treatise on State Antitrust Law and Enforcement: With Models and Forms 45 (1981); Pollak, Liberalizing Summary Adjudication: A Proposal, 36 Hastings L.J. 419 (1985).

147. Schwarzer, *supra* note 130, at 467 n.9.

148. F. James & G. Hazard, Jr., *Civil Procedure* 274 (3d ed. 1985); *see also* Hays, The Use of Summary Judgment, 28 F.R.D. 126, 126–27 (1960); A. Miller, The August 1983 Amendments to the Federal Rules of Civil Procedure: Promoting Effective Case Management and Lawyer Responsibility 8 (Federal Judicial Center 1984).

149. Louis (1984), *supra* note 133; Sandler & Corderman, *supra* note 136.

150. Bauman, A Rationale of Summary Judgment, 33 Ind. L.J. 467 (1958); Cohen, *supra* note 136; Guiher, Summary Judgments—Tactical Problems of the Trial Lawyer, 48 U. Va. L. Rev. 1263 (1962); McDonald, The Effective Use of Summary Judgment, 15 S.W.L.J. 365 (1961); McLauchlan, An Empirical Study of the Federal Summary Rule, 6 J. Legal Stud. 427, 436 (1977); Note, Use of Summary Judgment by Type of Case, 36 Minn. L. Rev. 515 (1952). *But see* Hays, *supra* note 143, 126–27 (most motions denied); Staff of Senate Comm. on Commerce, *supra* note 129, at 10 (defendants won motions in 9.2 percent of the unconsolidated, untransferred class actions, and plaintiffs in 10 percent cases).

151. McLauchlan, *supra* note 150, at 449–56.

152. *Id.* at 435–49.

153. 368 U.S. 464, 473 (1962) (footnote omitted).

154. 391 U.S. 253, 289–90 (1968).

155. 10A Federal Practice and Procedure, *supra* note 140, at 313.

156. 2 Trade Reg. Rep. (CCH) ¶ 9196, at 15,455 (1971).

157. 10 J. Von Kalinowski, Antitrust Laws and Trade Regulation 113–5 (1985).

158. *See* Garvey Study, *supra* note 2, at 30 (quoting Robert Pitofsky).

159. *See, e.g.*, Manual for Complex Litigation, Second, ¶ 21.34 (1985); Report to the President and Attorney General of the National Commission for the Review of Antitrust Laws and Procedures 68–70 (Jan. 22, 1979); P. Areeda & D. Turner, supra note 2, at ¶ 316; Rogers, *supra* note 133.

160. Poller, 368 U.S. at 478 (Harlan, J., dissenting).

161. A Westlaw search for citations to Harlan's dissent revealed six appellate decisions dated 1978 or later and only one dated earlier. Seven of the 12 district court cases were dated 1976 or later.

162. 586 F.2d 1163, 1167 (7th Cir. 1978), *cert. denied*, 440 U.S. 982 (1979) ("[T]he very nature of antitrust litigation would encourage summary disposition … when permissible."); *see also, e.g., In re* Municipal Bond Reporting Antitrust Litig., 672 F.2d 436, 440 (5th Cir. 1982); Wilson Indus., Inc. v. Chronicle Broadcasting Co., 598 F. Supp. 694 (N.D. Cal. 1984).

163. McLauchlan, *supra* note 150, at 438–40; *see also* 6-Pt.2, *Moore's Federal Practice*, *supra* note 110, ¶ 56.17[5], at 56-741, 56-742 (2d ed. 1985).

164. DuVal, *supra* note 12, at 1304, 1306.

165. A Statistical Analysis of Private Antitrust Litigation: Final Report, prepared by National Economic Research Associates, Inc. for the American Bar Association Section of Antitrust Law 44, table B23 (Oct. 1979).

166. *See* Arizona v. Maricopa County Medical Soc'y, 457 U.S. 332 (1982); Citizen Publishing Co. v. United States, 394 U.S. 131, 136 (1969); First Nat'l Bank v. Cities Service Co., 391 U.S. 253 (1968); Northern Pac. Ry. v. United States, 356 U.S. 1 (1958); United States v. W.T. Grant Co., 345 U.S. 629 (1953); United States v. United States Gypsum Co., 340 U.S. 76 (1950); International Salt Co. v. United States, 332 U.S. 392 (1947); Associated Press v. United States, 326 U.S. 1 (1945).

167. David Tyler, Jr., and George Spasoff organized the data and helped formulate and prepare the frequency tables and econometric models.

168. Confidence levels were calculated by Alan Penskar.

169. See *infra* notes 172, 173, 175.

170. The data set includes the following plaintiff's "pretrial motions for dismissal": dismissal, dismissal of counterclaim, failure to state a claim, no substantive issue of fact in dispute, summary judgment, partial summary judgment, and other. Plaintiffs filed only 53 motions specifically for summary judgment; seven such motions were granted (13.2 percent) and two were partially granted. The data set also reveals grants or partial grants of plaintiffs' motions for "dismissal" in 11 cases, of plaintiffs' motions for "dismissal of counterclaim" in seven cases, of plaintiffs' motions to dismiss for "failure to state claim" in eight cases, and of "other" pretrial motions for dismissal in 15 cases. The second and third of these probably should be considered defense motions, since plaintiffs facing antitrust counterclaims were to be regarded as defendants.

171. The data set includes the following defendant's "pretrial motions for dismissal": dismissal, failure to obey court, failure to state claim, improper jurisdiction, improper venue, other litigation pending on same issue, lack of jurisdiction, lack of prosecution, lack of standard, no issue, no substantive issue, res judicata, summary judgment, partial summary judgment, statute of limitations, and other.

172. If we exclude cases still pending or on appeal, whose outcome is unknown or whose file is missing, motions to dismiss were filed in 16.8 percent of the cases and granted in 7.9 percent. Success rates were 47.0 percent (by case) and 51.5 percent (by motion).

173. If we exclude cases still pending or on appeal, whose outcome is unknown, or whose file is missing, summary judgment motions were filed in 8.0 percent of all cases and granted in 4.5 percent. Success rates were 55.6 percent (by case) and 50.2 percent (by motion).

174. Conceivably the numbers from the data set are artificially inflated because motions are being granted with leave to amend. My perusal of recent antitrust cases refutes this, however, and preliminary returns from a sampling of reported decisions for cases in the data set confirm that most dismissals seem to terminate lawsuits or major parts of lawsuits. Although complete dismissal and dismissal only of part of an interrelated case are very different things, my review of cases suggests they are being disposed of with considerable finality.

175. Excluding pending cases and cases still on appeal, and cases without files or with unknown outcomes, motions to dismiss were filed in 20.0 percent of the cases with last docket entries in 1984 and granted in 6.2 percent of them. Success rates are 31.0 percent by case (9/29) and 32.6 percent by motion (14/43). Only the last figure is significantly lower than for cases ending earlier.

176. Summary judgment was granted in 6.0 percent of 1983 cases (significantly high at a 5 percent confidence level) and in 8.3 percent of 1984 cases (significant at a 1 percent level). Summary judgment motions were filed in 19.3 percent of the completed cases with known outcomes and located files with last docket entries in 1984, and these motions were granted in 11.7 percent of such cases (significantly high at 1 percent confidence level). Success rates were 60.7 percent (by case) and 60.9 percent (by motion).

177. San Francisco's 20.2 percent is significantly high at a 1 percent confidence level. Each of New York's, Chicago's, and Atlanta's figures are significantly low. The numbers in the text presumably reflect some double counting.

178. In suits by terminated dealers, dismissals, and summary judgments were used significantly more frequently (at a 10 percent confidence level) in 1981 to 1983. In suits by dealers, distributors, and agents, summary judgment was used significantly more frequently in 1983 (at a 10 percent confidence level) and 1984 (at a 5 percent confidence level), and dismissal was used significantly more frequently in 1982 (at a 1 percent confidence level).

179. Seven of ten motions were granted in six of the 30 suits ending in 1980; 17 of 23 motions were granted in 12 of the 44 suits ending in 1983. These success rates are significantly higher than in other years (confidence levels 1 to 10 percent). Use in 1983 also was significantly high (1 percent confidence level).

180. Motions were filed in only two cases ending before 1983, but eight motions were filed in five cases (out of a total of 21) ending in 1983–84. (Four of the eight motions were granted, in three of the five cases.)

181. For further discussion, see Calkins, Summary Judgment, *supra* n.2.

182. Motions to dismiss were filed in 11 (23.9 percent) and granted in 6 (13.0 percent) of the 46 countersuits or cases based on cross-claims, for a success rated (by case) of 54.5 percent. Comparable universe percentages are 16.6, 7.3, and 44.0 percent.

183. Richard Schmalensee suggested testing the "equilibrating tendencies" hypothesis by asking whether summary motions were granted significantly less commonly in horizontal fixing or market division cases, which he presumed would be the cases for which trebling is regarded as most appropriate. If that is the test, it fails; although summary procedures are used somewhat less frequently in these cases, the differences are not significant. The defect in Schmalensee's test is that private plaintiffs' lawyers are aware both of per se rules and of the increasing judicial suspicion of vertical cases; accordingly, many lawsuits are inaccurately described in pleadings as horizontal price fixing or market division cases. Schmalensee's test could be conducted only on more accurately described cases.

184. 104 S.Ct. 1949, 1960 n. 17 (1984).

185. Chrysler Credit Corp. v. J. Truett Payne Co., 103 S.Ct. 212 (1982).

Comment

Ernest Gellhorn

These three studies support a variety of broad conclusions as to how the private antitrust treble damage system operates. One (chapter 3 by Elzinga-Wood) is that private actions, at least for treble damages, should be scrapped as counterproductive and inefficient. Their net effect does not appear to yield a significant increase in consumer welfare. Another (chapter 4 by Perloff-Rubinfeld) is that the damage multiplier should not be reduced if trials are to be avoided and settlements encouraged. But this conclusion assumes that private antitrust actions are beneficial and should be continued. On the other hand, the third study (chapter 5 by Calkins) supports the conclusion that changes in the legal rules are ultimately irrelevant since the system corrects all changes to the center.[1] Whether the courts would substitute a judicially created right of action if the first conclusion (that the system should be scrapped) is accepted is not answered by the study and seems beyond its scope.

Each of these papers also provides intriguing and often counterintuitive insights. Indeed, the Perloff-Rubinfeld settlement study seems counterfactual and will undoubtedly be challenged on theoretical as well as empirical grounds. But the analysis in their paper makes an interesting point about the relationship between the damage multiplier and the pressure to settle and challenges us to review old assumptions that the multiplier increases all litigation incentives. In any case, on the assumption that the data and analysis of these three studies are reliable, they should guide antitrust policy regarding the shape and support given the private damage system.

This is of course a large assumption and, in my view, an unlikely condition. Despite a prodigious effort, the project collected a very limited data set, with as many gaps as meaningful numbers. For example, of the almost 2,000 cases reviewed, only 25 with complete records ended in a trial with relief, only 62 completed actions resulted in fully reported relief in the case files, and only 1 in 7 could be followed up in a questionnaire linking legal fees and the survey data. Of even greater concern is that the studies generally excluded large cases and their results as idiosyncratic. The validity of this decision to focus on the more common and "smaller" cases seems debatable. It depends on what is to be demonstrated by the investigation.

For example, the larger cases are not "outliers" when resource allocations and costs are considered, at least when reviewing overall society costs and benefits. Nor are they irrelevant when focusing on settlement issues.

Even more important in considering these three studies of the operation of the system is the fact that each focuses solely on a particular aspect of the system. There is no effort at an overall assessment, an identification of all the system's costs and benefits, or an estimate of whether it could operate more effectively or efficiently under another regime. The seriousness of this limitation is emphasized also by Calkins's conclusion that no part of the process operates in isolation.

A first conclusion from these studies, then, is the inevitable suggestion of the need for more studies. Future approaches should take a larger view of the data. This may require more data, but that is not my main point. It is that the study design in this instance has focused narrowly on discrete issues in the operation of the private damage system and that larger issues are not addressed as a result.

A related but separate point is that more data are probably needed if positive policy conclusions are to be drawn from any analyses of the operation of the system. Certainly, neither fine tuning nor specific adjustments can be justified by these three studies. Elzinga and Wood, for instance, point out that jury trials and price-fixing cases consume more resources than other private actions. But their measures of resource consumption—primarily the number of docket entries and the inches of file thickness—are extraordinarily crude (and possibly unreliable). Nor did they study either element separately when considering the system's efficiency or overall societal benefit. Without much closer analysis of the relief granted, the other effects of the cases on business conduct, the ability of jurors and judges to understand the issues and make accurate decisions, etc., even these somewhat shaky conclusions seem inconclusive.

These studies illustrate once again the need for a variegated research strategy. Quantitative measures are important and often dispositive, but they also have limitations; where the data cannot be fully collected in this fashion, alternatives must be considered. More specifically, the Georgetown data need to be filled in not only by a more complete inquiry but also by different approaches. Statistical analyses based on file thickness measurements or the counting of docket entries are likely to reveal only rudimentary answers supported as much by intuition as data. Antitrust trials appear to be nonstandard products requiring specific, direct empirical observation from whch judgments can be made as to the efficacy of private treble damage actions.

To me this suggests another approach. It is illustrated by the original and, I think, outstanding research of my colleague, Arthur Austin.[2] He sat through and systematically studied two jury trials between the City of Cleveland and the Cleveland Electric Illuminating Company on a charge of unlawful monopolization. Two juries reviewing the same facts reached contrary results. His study provides a major insight into the operation of the jury system in large complex private antitrust cases. This approach of trial observation, discussions with the attorneys and judge, interviews after the trial with the juries, and a careful review of the entire record provides another picture of the operation of a private antitrust case quite different than that contained in any of these three papers.

The question still open is what, if anything, should be done in the interim. Questions have been raised about the desirability of continuing the current private treble damage system, and a frequent argument for postponing action has been to await the results of the Georgetown study. And now those results are in, yet more studies and data are recommended. There is of course substantial evidence in these papers supporting some reform of the current system. At least the Elzinga-Wood paper strongly suggests that jury trials as well as actions by competitors or suppliers should be curtailed. The Perloff-Rubinfeld study, on the other hand, is focused on the nonsubstantive issue of how to make the system operate more efficiently. And the Calkins study would argue that most changes will have a smaller than anticipated effect. Overall, they hardly make a policy case for change.

But do they militate against change? Some might say yes. To repeat a popular cliche, "If it ain't broke, don't fix it." But where is the evidence that the system is working? The most powerful evidence among these three papers on that question is given by Elzinga-Wood, and they conclude that in 78.5 percent of the cases the plaintiff misused the private action to seek a competitive advantage or obtain contract relief not available under contract law. That is, almost four-fifths of the antitrust cases included in this sample were unlikely to serve consumer welfare.

Within these limits I would urge that the Georgetown study has shifted the burden of proof to those who would maintain the present system, or perhaps any system of private antitrust action. Unless a system can be designed to limit actions to those 21.5 percent of the cases where the action is likely to intensify competition—and no ready statutory characterization seems available—the current system should be abandoned. The presumption of antitrust law is that private markets and private decisions should be favored. Legal intervention is justified only when private economic power is used to impair competition by reducing output and increasing price.

Intervention is costly; it is difficult for courts and agencies to unravel complex economic issues and reach correct results; governmental power to intervene in the economy should be limited to those situations where the net benefit is substantial and likely to be achieved.

Simply stated, the case for private treble damages actions has not been made, and it does not appear that the Georgetown data can support such an argument. History has its rightful claim. But mere longevity is hardly a reason to continue the current private system. Nor is it persuasive to point to the potential for abuse in the creation and use of monopoly power or the establishment of cartels. Both governmental enforcement systems and market incentives to undercut cartels and monopolies are substantial constraints on the misuses of market power. In recent times the advent of foreign competition and the expansion of economic markets through information and transportation advances further limit opportunities for market abuse. Indeed, the latter is another powerful argument for removing the shackles placed by the treble damage system on American producers.

Abandonment of private antitrust actions is likely not only to allow producers to be more competitive, but it will also benefit consumers. The only losers, I suppose, are likely to be the lawyers. We can, I think, make this sacrifice for the common good.

Notes

1. Calkins's point that substantive and procedural rules are interrelated is not a new one, of course. See, e.g., G. Robinson, E. Gellhorn, and H. Bruff, *The Administrative Process*, 3d ed. (St. Paul, Minn.: West Publishing Co., 1986). What is distinctive is his demonstration that the private antitrust system is self-adjusting toward the center.

2. A. Austin, *Complex Litigation Confronts the Jury System: A Case Study* (Frederick, Md.: University Publications of America 1984).

Comment
Walter A. Schlotterbeck

Many of the lawyer participants in this conference undoubtedly will be disappointed to find that our economist colleagues are not able to agree on simple, quantitative, and dispositive answers to the policy issues concerning the treble damage remedy in antitrust cases. Apparently they are no more able than we to conquer the complexity of life, even with the help of equations that look neat and scientific.

Most of us would concede that the effort to bring economic disciplines to bear on legal policy issues has been a very constructive process. Economic analysis has called into question many of our traditional attitudes and responses and helped to promote a more realistic focus on the real effects of particular legal policies.

I would suggest, however, that an eclectic approach might be more fruitful. Most of us do not believe that human beings act as purely economic animals. The idea that all human conduct is economically determined flies in the face of our experience as well as our knowledge. We do not accept the proposition that all thoughts, motivations, and actions originate solely from our economic relationships. Those that do have been singularly unsuccessful in making their case or convincing us to adopt their models.

In a world of scarcity, economic perspectives are of crucial importance. However, I believe the process of bringing an interdisciplinary focus to legal questions cannot stop with purely economic analysis. Political science, organizational practice and theory, and individual and group psychology are among the other disciplines that will have an important role to play. Until we make substantial advances in integrating the perspectives of all of the relevant academic specialities, we have to arrive at our policy decisions in our usual rough and ready way.

The conference seemed to me to confirm the proposition that the private antitrust action, in practice, is not a highly aberrational system. Its basic strengths and weaknesses are well recognized. Moreover Congressman Peter Rodino's address encapsulated the political arguments that will face any attempt to significantly weaken the system.

Nevertheless, in my opinion, we know enough now to make beneficial course corrections in our approach to the treble damage process. The issue of the proper allocation of damages among multiple defendants has long been an issue, and it should be resolved. The current rule of joint and several liability with no contribution and inadequate claim reduction clearly distorts the way the system works. Its continuation can only be based on the theory that nothing you do to a defendant in an antitrust case is too bad.

Currently, trebling of damages is required in all private antitrust actions whether the defendant's activity is clearly heinous, borderline, or inadvertent. The plaintiff's business options to mitigate his alleged losses is largely ignored. If deterrence is the justification for trebling, the courts (or juries) should be given some authority to use discretion in awarding multiple damages. Automatic trebling in all cases, regardless of the circumstances, is an egregiously blunt tool.

Finally, there is the issue of the role of the jury in an antitrust laws. Elzinga and Wood (chapter 3) and Turner (chapter 10) feel that the jury trial is an inadequate mechanism for at least some kinds of cases. In any event, why not have the jury perform its role with full knowledge of the significance of their decisions? The jury should be informed of the treble damage feature inherent in the antitrust case.

The studies show what we all knew, that plaintiffs most often demand jury trials. The private antitrust action frequently has a substantial David versus Goliath aspect. Juries are clearly motivated in all cases by matters such as degree of fault, ability to pay, and concepts of punishment. The precise legal issues before them are frequently not understood, yet they must make a decision. In these circumstances, to withhold from them a key disclosure as to what will automatically be done with their findings makes no sense. It will be argued that with such knowledge the jury might shape its views to try to achieve more "justice" rather than produce a scientifically surgical decision on damages. But isn't that what juries are for?

Comments on the Operation of the Antitrust System

John De Q. Briggs

I begin by suggesting that the findings generated by the presenters in this segment strike a blow for common sense. Many of the major conclusions are unremarkable. Thus Elzinga and Wood (chapter 3) confirm for us that antitrust is indeed a declining industry, that newsworthy cases such as *IBM* and *AT&T* are not the norm, that the jury system imposes excess costs and inefficiencies upon antitrust, and that much of private enforcement has little to do with improving resource allocation or deterrring market power.

Similarly Perloff and Rubinfeld (chapter 4), in analyzing settlements, conclude that the empirical data suggest that a reduction in the damage multiplier might increase greatly the fraction of litigated cases that go to trial and that the increased likelihood of trial associated with a reduced multiplier might alter in some fashion the expense and effort given by the parties to the trial process. They have also given us empirical data tending to confirm that where a plaintiff has a much smaller expectation of his own success than may be perceived by the defendant, then settlement is quite likely, and where the reverse is the case, then settlement is considerably less likely. Though interesting, these observations do not suggest the need for major modifications to competition policy.

Calkins's (chapter 5) contribution, perhaps the most interesting and original, highlights the presence of equilibrating tendencies in the law: the tendency of courts to react to the perception of unfairness in antitrust by creating and imposing rules to mitigate that unfairness. He has provided numerous examples of this tendency at work in antitrust, as well as in other fields.

In short, the data suggest that the need for more study is not great. Rather, now is the time to consider the desirability of change, to debate the wisdom of change, and to implement some changes. Indeed, one of the more important aspects of the project is the relevation that public policy may be formulated intelligently and rationally without the necessity of relying on elaborate or extensive economic and econometric studies.

The recurring theme among those who would alter antitrust in some substantial fashion is that courts and juries are unpredictable and expensive. Changes in the punitive damages multiplier or in the jury system, it is said, would tend to eliminate or mitigate some of this uncertainty. This is true, although it is probably no more true in the world of antitrust than in the world of tort and contract law more generally, with one exception.

In the normal tort case where punitive damages are sought, a plaintiff seeks punitive damages from the jury, and upon a set of written instructions the jury determines whether and how much to award the plaintiff in punitive damages. In antitrust cases, on the other hand, the jury is carefully kept ignorant about the fact that its award of damages will be trebled. This is nonsensical. My own experience in talking with jurors after a judgment has been entered is that they are shocked and astonished to learn that their damage award was trebled. It is often proposed that the jury system be abolished in antitrust cases, and there is much to commend such a change. However, if juries are to continue, then they should be entrusted with all the pertinent information relating to the consequences of their decision, rather than being limited to knowing only one-third of the story.

Another possible approach to the treble damage problem would be to make treble damages discretionary on the part of the court, with certain "hard core" violations being presumptively subject to treble damages but with "soft core" violations, such as vertical nonprice restraints, being presumed to be worthy of only single damages absent egregious circumstances. This would preserve the incentive to search out and prosecute the most socially undesirable conduct, while discouraging somewhat the more routine dealer cases that rarely involve an abuse of market power.

Attorney's fees also play a role in settlements that has probably not been adequately studied. Perloff and Rubinfeld have sought to identify the circumstances under which settlements would be promoted. They hypothesize that if both sides have the same view of the ultimate damages, and where both are risk neutral, there is ground for settlements since trial and its associated costs are avoided. Settlement would be for an amount between the low of expected damages less plaintiff's litigation costs and the high of expected damages plus the defendant's litigation costs. What this theory may not adequately consider is the extent to which the "win/lose" issue might sometimes be more crucial than the "how much" issue in thinking about settlements. This is the case since, whatever the parties may view as the likely damage award, the fact of any damages at all could generate a nontrivial award of attorney's fees, which can in turn affect the likelihood of settlement by changing the nature of the Perloff-Rubinfeld "settlement gap."

Wood and Elzinga have found in the data set certain hints of the existence and size of three particular costs of antitrust litigation. First, they find a reason to believe that the prospect of treble damages induces "perverse incentives" to buy from a monopolist or cartel. Second, they find a "misinformation effect" characterized by litigants, fabricating antitrust cases even in the absence of a restraint of trade. Third, they find indirect evidence of "reparations costs"—the costs of resources used in determining and allocation damages. All these are characterized as inefficiencies associated with private enforcement of antitrust. Yet, even assuming that these costs do exist, they are not costs that differentiate antitrust from other areas of law in any major way.

My point is simply that the data do not suggest a need for major remedial legislation with respect to antitrust, although changes to meet specific problems could greatly improve the operation of the system. The Calkins paper supports this point. The tort/antitrust judicial system has shown itself to be responsive to its own flaws. For example, the judiciary seems to have reacted to the misinformation cost problem by substantially tightening the standard rules, making it more difficult for large classes of plaintiffs to bring suit. The equilibrating tendency of the judiciary has also operated in the other direction. As government or public antitrust enforcement, particularly in the areas of merger and acquisitions, has become nearly nonexistent, some courts have reacted by giving strong support to the efforts of private plaintiffs to obtain injunctive relief against mergers involving competitors. This tendency has brought us decisions such as Monfort of Colorado, Inc. v. Cargill, Inc., 761 F. 2d 570 (10th Cir. 1985), *cert. granted* (Jan. 13, 1985), and Christian Schmidt Brewing Co. v. G. Heileman Brewing Co., 753 F. 2d 1354 (6th Cir.), *cert. dismissed*, 105 S. Ct. 1155 (1985).

Indeed, the main importance of private litigation today may be its impact on executive branch enforcement policy. The current administration is hostile to much of the private litigation (especially in the area of mergers and acquisitions and vertical restraints), primarily because the legal opinions generated by that private litigations are so frequently at odds with the theory of antitrust enforcement that currently dominates enforcement policy both at the Federal Trade Commission and the Department of Justice. (*See* Brief for the United States as amicus curiae in Cargill, Inc. v. Monfort of Colorado, Inc., No. 85-473, *filed* Nov. 4, 1985.) In its *Monfort* amicus brief and elsewhere, the Justice Department has expressed a severe hostility to private actions against mergers by competitors, comparable in some ways to the hostility to private actions involving vertical restraints suggested by the Justice Department's Vertical Guidelines.

To some extent the entire Georgetown study is part of a process that has been evolving for several years, fueled by the belief that antitrust was in need of substantial reform. Serious people within the current administration have proposed the abolition of section 7 of the Clayton Act, and there is pressure within and without the administration to remove the treble damage feature and to "loosen up" antitrust in other ways. [*See* Memorandum for the Domestic Policy Council and the Economic Policy Council from the [Administration] Working Group on Antitrust Reform regarding Proposed Changes in the Antitrust Laws, Nov. 8, 1985; *see also* Global Competition, Report of the President's Commission on Industrial Competitiveness (January 1985).]

In these circumstances it is indeed ironic that antitrust should be the subject of such intense study, debate, and scrutiny at the very time that it may have lost much of its relevance and many of its teeth. Though Secretary Baldridge describes antitrust law as just another obstacle to America's ability to compete effectively (*see* "Making Mergers even Easier," The New York Times, November 10, 1985), there is no evidence of this. To the contrary, governmental intervention has prevented no mergers of any consequence and certainly none in areas beset by foreign competition. In fact the Justice Department has not been particularly successful in the mergers it has challenged [*see, e.g.*, United States v. Calmar, Inc., 612 F. Supp. 1298 (D.N.J. 1985)], and it has challenged few mergers at all even in the face of the recent flood of massive mergers. [*See* "Merger and Acquisition Frenzy," Wall St. Journal at 6B (Jan. 2, 1986).] Meanwhile the Federal Trade Commission has limited itself primarily to mergers or acquisitions involving hospitals, hardly a threat to the foreign export trade of the United States. [*See, e.g.*, Hospital Corp. of America, 3 Trade Reg. Rep (CCH) ¶ 22,301 (FTC Oct. 25, 1985); American Medical Int'l, Inc., 3 Trade Reg. Rep. (CCH) ¶ 22,170 (FTC July 2, 1984).] And where it has brought cases involving (arguably) markets affected by foreign competition, the complaints have typically been dismissed and the criteria for illegality changed significantly [*see* Weyerhaueser Co., 3 Trade Reg. Rep (CCH) ¶ 22,315 (FTC Dec. 12, 1985); Eichlin Mfg. Co., 3 Trade Reg. Rep. (CCH) ¶ 22,268 (FTC June 28, 1985); B.A.T. Indus. Ltd., 3 Trade Reg. Rep. (CCH) ¶ 22,218 (FTC) Dec. 17, 1984)].

At the same time, although with some of the exceptions previously mentioned, the various circuit courts have issued decisions that, as a practical matter, severely restrict the standing of plaintiffs to bring suits. This has been the impact of *Illinois Brick, Brunswick, Associated General Contractors*, and *McReady*. [*See, e.g.*, Bubar v. Ampco Foods, Inc., 1985-1 Trade Cas. (CCH) ¶ 66,387 (9th Cir. 1985); Triple M Roofing Corp. v. Tiemco, Inc., 753 F. 2d 242 (2d Cir. 1985); Nat'l Indep. Theater Exhibitors,

Inc. v. Buena Vista Distribution Co., 748 F. 2d 602 (11th Cir. 1984); Out Front Productions, Inc. v. Magid, 748 F. 2d 166 (3d Cir. 1984); Rie v. Barry & Enright Productions, 731 F. 2d 1394 (9th Cir.), *cert. denied*, 105 S. Ct. 248 (1984).] The Robinson-Patman Act is simply not being enforced, and neither the Justice Department nor the Federal Trade Commission has brought a vertical price-fixing case in several years. Further the Supreme Court's decision in *Copperweld* has, for all practical purposes, virtually eliminated the intraenterprise conspiracy theory, which was for many years a tremendous burden on the system. And in *Monsanto* the Supreme Court gave tremendous backbone to the district courts, motivating them to dismiss at a relatively early stage many types of nonprice vertical restraint cases. [*See, e.g.*, Royal Drug Co., Inc. v. Group Life and Health Ins. Co., 737 F. 2d 1433, 1438 (5th cir. 1984), *cert. denied*, 105 S. Ct. 912 (1985); Tunis Bros. Co. v. Ford Motor Co., 587 F. supp. 267, 272 & n. 15 (E.D. Pa. 1984).]

Given these circumstances, given the fact that the Georgetown data generally suggest the absence of a serious problem attending antitrust as it is now practiced, and given the fact that the Georgetown project studied cases that arose at a time when antitrust enforcement was more vigorous in both the public and private sectors than it is today, the data and the conclusions drawn from the data do not support proposals for major change.

The system does need repair, however, if not overhaul. First, clearly something should be done about the contribution and claim reduction issues, so as to prevent firms with a small share in a discrete market from being subjected to ruinous damages in class actions where the larger firms may have settled, leaving the smaller firms to risk being held jointly and severally liable for the damage amounts attributable to the settled defendants. S. 1300 provides a remedy for this problem, and it should be rapidly implemented.

Second, the role of juries in antitrust cases greatly needs attention. It is doubtful that juries will be abolished in complex antitrust cases, although they should be. Failing that larger reform (which may well be desirable in all complex civil litigation), juries at least ought to be informed as to the consequences of their actions and told that their damage award will be trebled. There is simply no reason to make the punitive treble damage remedy flow from the ignorance of the jury on the subject.

Finally, and perhaps more important, not only should the jury understand that its award may be subject to a multiplier, but the court ought to have the authority and discretion to select the multiplier, thereby permitting treble damages in cases warranting the imposition of severe punitive damages but also permitting the award of only single damages in cases where punitive damages are simply inappropriate. Such an approach would discourage the most socially harmful conduct, while also discouraging the routine dealer litigation that rarely involves the abuse of market power or classic concert of action.

Comment: Critical Factual Assumptions Underlying Public Policy

Joseph F. Brodley

The legal analyst will be keenly interested in whether the Georgetown study of private antitrust litigation sheds light on the critical factual assumptions that underlie public policy. This paper examines four key factual issues central to the policy debate on the merits of private antitrust litigation: (1) whether the damages in antitrust cases are realistically trebled in view of the failure of the statute to award interest from the date of injury, (2) whether the private damage remedy distorts litigation incentives and inflates litigation costs, (3) whether suits by competitors are anticompetitive, and, more generally, (4) whether the costs of antitrust enforcement outweigh the benefits.

Are Damages in Fact Trebled?

The Clayton Act requires a trebling of the damages resulting from an antitrust violation. But the injury is sustained before the damages are paid. Unless therefore the injured plaintiff is able to collect interest on his economic loss, what he receives when the damages are ultimately paid out will be less than three times the injury he suffered when the loss occurred. In fact, the private antitrust remedy fails to give plaintiff prejudgment interest on most of his damage award. The Georgetown study allows us to determine the magnitude of the interest loss and thereby to understand better other facts relating to private antitrust litigation.

The erosion of the treble damage recovery caused by lost interest is a modern development. When the Sherman Act was passed in 1890, the consumer price index had been steady or slowly declining for the previous ten years, so that the return on capital free of investment risk could not have been much above zero.[1] Thus in 1890 and for many years thereafter antitrust plaintiffs did receive full treble damages. But in a world of inflation and high capital costs what was true in 1890 is no longer true today. In recent years the risk-free return on capital has averaged between 8 and 9 percent, and at this writing is about 7 percent, so plaintiff receives considerably less than three times the damages sustained if he is not compensated for lost interest.[2]

In fact the Clayton Act compensates the plaintiff for only a portion of his lost interest. The plaintiff receives no interest whatever between the date of injury and the date of suit, and on two-thirds of the recovery he receives no interest prior to judgment.[3] Inclusion of the lost interest factor results in a striking erosion of the treble damage remedy, particularly in cases involving a collusive or monopolistic overcharge.[4] The Georgetown study shows that the average time lag from the date of injury to final judgment was 6.5 years, 2 years from injury to filing of suit and 4.5 years from suit to judgment. Almost all the class action cases settled, but such cases still consumed fully four years from the filing of suit to settlement, or a total of six years from injury.[5] In present-value terms these delays reduce the average damage recovery in litigated cases from treble to double damages, based on the risk-free return on three-month treasury bills.[6] These results are for litigated cases. In fact most private antitrust cases settle at a significantly earlier date, but the benchmark against which they settle is what can ultimately be recovered in the courtroom.

An understanding of the erosion of treble damages caused by lost interest casts light on other findings and implications of the Georgetown study. First, it may explain, at least in part, why per se cases last longer than other kinds of cases and why the amount recovered varies directly with the length of the case. The withholding of interest on the plaintiff's loss creates a powerful incentive for delay by defendants. The longer the case lasts, the less the defendant pays in present-value terms. Since recoveries were highest in price-fixing cases, this may explain why, despite the availability of the per se rule, naked cartel cases last longer than any other type of case—42 months on average as compared with 25.6 months for the entire sample. Moreover the delay in per se cases was associated with heavy litigation effort, no doubt caused in part by defendants. Thus, naked cartel cases, along with price fixing cases, generated heavy docket entries and resulted in the longest trials.[7] Finally, the amount recovered varied directly with the duration of the case—the longer the case lasted, the more plaintiff recovered.[8] Despite possible alternative explanations suggested by certain of the data, the conclusion that delay in antitrust cases was to some degree interest motivated is highly plausible.[9].

Second, the erosion of treble damages caused by lost interest makes the Elzinga-Wood (chapter 3) perverse incentive hypothesis a less likely story. Under this hypothesis the trebling of damages gives antitrust plaintiffs an incentive to be victimized in order to collect multiple damages. But that incentive is drastically reduced when lost interest is taken into account. If, as I have shown earlier, antitrust damages are not trebled, but only doubled in present-value terms, this reduces the effective return on an investment in victimization over the average 6.5 years case duration to what it would be if the victim had invested the same amount in the Standard and Poor's Stock Index.[10] It would be curious indeed if business managers voluntarily sustained present losses for the right to undertake probabilistic antitrust litigation that would produce a return no greater than what they could earn on an indexed mutual fund—free of litigation risks, legal costs, unreimbursed attorneys fees, expensive diversion of managerial time, and the general hassle of going to court.

Third, the lost interest factor complicates assessment of possible changes in the treble damage multiple. If the antitrust penalty were changed from treble to double damages, as discussed in the Perloff-Rubinfeld paper (chapter 4), that would lead to an effective multiple of only about 1.4 in present-value terms. If antitrust damages were reduced to single damages, plaintiffs would no longer be made whole, and defendants would consequently pay less than the harm they inflict on others. Under interest rates prevailing during the Georgetown study, this would reduce the single damage recovery to either 59 percent or 85 percent, depending on whether award of interest was from the date of injury or the time of suit.

Recent statutes and proposals affecting antitrust damages have recognized the lost interest problem, but in an important group of cases these provisions would fail to make the plaintiff whole due to the neglect of income tax effects. Thus the 1984 National Cooperative Research Act, the 1982 Export Trading Company Act, and the administration's 1986 legislative proposal for changing antitrust penalties provide for interest to be paid from the date of injury. But detrebling provisions have overlooked an income tax factor that will prevent the plaintiff from being fully compensated if any significant part of the injury involves an invasion of plaintiff's investment in capital assets not producing current income. This results from the fact that in the absence of an antitrust violation plaintiff would have paid no tax until such time as he sold the property (at a profit) or the property began producing current income. But the antitrust recovery results in ordinary income to the extent of any gain in the value of the capital asset or interest awarded on the invaded capital.[11]

Strikingly, the administration's proposal would detreble damages in precisely those cases in which tax factors prevent full recovery—that is, where antitrust injuries do not result from overcharge or underpayment but instead constitute invasions of capital.[12] Thus neither the administration's proposal nor any other proposal to detreble damages will make the plaintiff whole unless provision is made to compensate the plaintiff for the taxable nature of damage awards involving the restoration of invaded capital.[13]

Possible Distortion of Litigation Incentives and Inflation of Legal Costs

Elzinga and Wood, reiterating a theme long maintained by Elzinga and Breit, attack the private antitrust remedy because it distorts litigation incentives and inflates enforcement costs. They assert that these effects are caused by the willingness of business firms to become antitrust victims in order to collect antitrust damages (the "perverse incentives" effect), the assertion of fabricated claims (the "misinformation effect"), and the high enforcement costs caused by adjudication of complex damage claims ("high reparations costs"). Examining the Georgetown data, Elzinga and Wood found no data bearing on the first theory—willing victimization—but did find evidence assertedly supporting the other two theories. In fact I think the Georgetown study provides evidence adverse to all three theories.

Willing Victimization

Although Elzinga and Wood found no evidence bearing on the willing victimization theory, there appear to be considerable data in the Georgetown study showing that the return for plaintiffs on antitrust cases is not exceptional. First, even if the plaintiff prevails at trial, what he receives in present-value terms is not treble damages, but something closer to double damages, due to the erosion caused by lost interest.

Second, there is a probability that plaintiff will lose the case and collect nothing at all. In at least 14 percent of the Georgetown cases the plaintiff lost the case either at trial[14] or by preliminary motion.[15] Discounting for this additional adverse factor reduces the expected damage multiple from two to only 1.7 times the damages. Since the average litigated antitrust case lasts 6.5 years, this lowers the annual return on antitrust litigation to no more than 8 percent a year—less than the interest paid in recent years on a money market fund.

Third, several other factors also diminish plaintiffs' expected recovery. These include potential liability to the defendant on nonantitrust counterclaims that would not otherwise have been asserted, nonrecoverable legal costs on such counterclaims and on antitrust claims decided adversely to plaintiffs, the value of managerial time absorbed in litigation effort, and possibly a loss of competitive edge from organizational malaise under a policy of willing victimization.[16]

Fabricated Claims

Elzinga and Wood find evidence of fabricated antitrust claims because in 20 percent of the cases the primary focus of the dispute appeared to be a nonantitrust claim. But to a lawyer that fact is quite unremarkable since at the outset of a case, an attorney drafting the pleadings can have only a partial knowledge of the evidence that can be developed at trial, and yet the pleadings frame the boundaries for discovery. Under these circumstances it is no more than careful legal practice to allege all claims that can be made in good faith, and inevitably some of these will turn out to be secondary.

Thus a 20 percent admixture of secondary claims strikes me as quite within the range that one might expect when allegations must be made in advance of discovery. In addition the assertion of a secondary antitrust claim does not inform as to what, if any, resources were invested in developing it, whether it had tangible effects on settlement or remained secondary throughout the litigation. Indeed, even the appearance as to what is primary and secondary may be deceptive if, as Baxter suggests, there is an incentive for plaintiffs to obscure strong antitrust claims so as not to deter settlement offers from defendants fearful of stimulating similar suits.[17]

Both logic and legal experience also suggest that only a very vulnerable defendant will be seriously frightened by an unsupported antitrust allegation. If an antitrust claim is to have significant value for the plaintiff, he must be prepared to invest substantial resources in developing proof. Given the modest return on antitrust litigation generally, it seems doubtful that plaintiffs would invest significant resources in trying to prove claims devoid of legal merit, or that defendants would turn over substantial sums of money to settle colorless claims. This conclusion is all the more apparent in view of the fact that the typical antitrust defendant is a large corporation, with annual sales of $230 million as compared with $1 million for the average plaintiff, and thus is likely to be sophisticated in antitrust, a repeat player, and entirely capable of sustaining protracted litigation against the plaintiff.[18]

High Enforcement Costs

Finally, Elzinga and Wood criticize private antitrust actions as involving high enforcement costs. They reach that conclusion by evidence drawn from a confidential survey of counsel and litigants, showing that "the smallest of the estimates would put combined plaintiffs' and defendants' fees in the neighborhood of 60 cents per dollar's worth of settlements." But their conclusion is questionable, and it is misleading in its policy implications.

The conclusion can be questioned because it is based on a survey in which the overall response rate was quite low (3.5 percent) and in which the data relating to enforcement costs were even more fragmentary.[19] As a result the conclusion that fees are large in relation to settlements is sensitive to the particular way in which the fragmentary data are combined.[20] Surveying the same evidence, Salop and White (chapter 1) cautioned that response bias might be present since legal fees reported in the confidential survey were higher than average for a larger group of cases within the Georgetown sample, which included litigated cases, and because the survey response was inconsistent with an earlier independent study of fees in antitrust cases.[21] In addition the value of settlements may be understated since no amount was assigned for injunctive or nonmonetary relief obtained by plaintiff.

The conclusion that enforcement costs were excessive in relation to plaintiff recoveries is misleading in its policy implications because it fails to consider deterrence benefits. Thus, even if antitrust litigation were inefficient as a compensatory system, it would not follow that enforcement costs were unacceptably high. Such a conclusion would be justified only if costs were excessive considering both compensation and deterrence objectives, and as we shall see, there is no basis in the Georgetown data for reaching that unfavorable conclusion.

Are Suits by Competitors Anticompetitive?

Some critics of private antitrust enforcement have attacked the motives of competitors who become antitrust plaintiffs. The critics assert that competitors sue other competitors only to foil efficient behavior, which they fear, and never to block cartels and monopolies, which they welcome. It is of interest therefore that two of the papers find some support for this critique in the Georgetown data, but that support is misplaced.

Elzinga and Wood find it a source of serious policy concern that 30 percent of the Georgetown cases, and therefore presumably of all private antitrust cases, were competitor suits. But the fact that competitor suits comprise a significant fraction of private antitrust litigation says nothing about their merit and is cause for concern only if one has already concluded that such suits are anticompetitive.

Calkins (chapter 5) notes that courts granted motions to dismiss in favor of defendants more often in competitor than in noncompetitor cases.[22] But this difference did not hold for summary judgment cases, as one would expect if some inherent deficiency runs through competitor cases generally. Instead, in summary judgment cases competitors fared as well or better, than noncompetitors in resisting such motions.[23] In addition the statistics inform us only that one or more motions to dismiss were granted, not that the case as a whole was dismissed. In fact other evidence in the Georgetown study indicates that in only half of the cases in which motions to dismiss or summary judgments were granted was the case itself dismissed.[24] Thus the Calkins data does not permit the conclusion that competitor suits were subject to a higher *case* dismissal rate than noncompetitor suits, much less that competitor suits were inferior as a group. By contrast, Perloff and Rubinfeld have assembled data showing that the dismissal rate for competitor and noncompetitor cases was substantially the same.[25]

Additional facts developed in the Georgetown study also appear inconsistent with the conclusion that competitor cases are less meritorious than other antitrust cases. The confidential survey data, though admittedly fragmentary, indicate that plaintiffs in competitor cases obtained substantial recoveries, as compared with other antitrust litigants.[26] Moreover the recovery to cost ratio was as high for competitors as for noncompetitors.[27] Neither of these results would be expected if competitors brought antitrust cases primarily to pursue anticompetitive agendas,[28] although the force of these results is limited by the sampling imperfections of the confidential survey.

The conclusion that competitor cases are not systematically anticompetitive also appears plausible. Competitors are the best placed litigant in terms of knowledge of the industry and its economic conditions and are thus likely to be the first to learn of an antitrust violation. Moreover competitors do not face the economic constraints that may inhibit suits by small customers or suppliers against larger firms, who fear being cut off or being discriminated against. Although competitors may have no incentive to stop a purely benign cartel or monopoly, they have understandable reasons to be concerned that a cartel or monopoly may not remain benign, particularly if the plaintiff seeks to undercut the cartel or monopoly price and is only a small firm with limited resources—which the Georgetown study shows is typically the case.[29] In such circumstances a competitor suit may provide an early warning of the presence of cartel conditions.

It is possible of course that a competitor might bring an antitrust action to prevent a more efficient rival from using a cost-lowering practice. But the modern rule of reason permits a defendant to develop fully that fact and to bring to the attention of the court the anticompetitive bias of the plaintiff as a high cost rival. Disclosure, not disqualification, is the preferred approach toward litigants whose private interest may not always accord with the public interest, and the plaintiff's possible bias as a competitor is a transparent fact in antitrust litigation. Moreover since 1977 courts have been able to screen competitor suits under the powerful constraint imposed by the

Brunswick doctrine, which is specifically designed to bar anticompetitive suits. Thus the absence of significant data in the Georgetown study showing that competitor suits are systematically anticompetitive is neither implausible nor surprising.[30]

Do the Costs of Private Enforcement Outweigh the Benefits?

The ultimate policy issue confronting private antitrust litigation is whether the costs of the present enforcement system outweigh the benefits. Although the Georgetown study does not permit a full cost-benefit analysis, by combining the Georgetown data with other available information, it becomes possible to make factually based assessments of several of the primary costs and benefits of private antitrust litigation and enforcement.

Costs
The costs of private antitrust litigation include both the public costs of operating the judicial system and the private costs borne by the parties. The Georgetown study permits an estimate to be made of their magnitude.

Public Costs   The public costs of litigation can be measured in terms of the use of judicial resources. The Georgetown study shows that antitrust litigation consumed a modest amount of resources as measured by the overall number of antitrust cases and the use of trial time.

In terms of number of cases filed private antitrust litigation appears parsimonious in its use of judicial resources as compared with other civil litigation. As shown in table C.1, over the 11-year period spanned by the study, at a time when the number of civil cases increased from 96,000 to 241,000 cases annually, the number of antitrust cases remained essentially constant at approximately, 1,200 cases annually, and indeed since 1980 has been declining. In percentage terms the number of private antitrust cases fell from 1.2 percent of civil cases at the beginning of the period to only 0.5 percent by the end of the period, a relative decline of almost 60 percent.

In terms of use of trial resources the Georgetown study shows that antitrust trials consumed less than 1 percent of available trial time during the 11-year period surveyed. Although antitrust trials were individually long, consuming an average of 11.4 days, the number of trials is small. As a result one would expect that the use of judicial time would be reasonably constrained if the Georgetown sample, comprising one-fifth of all antitrust cases, is representative of the universe of cases. In fact, as shown in table C.2, it appears that five federal judges could have tried all of the antitrust

Table C.1 Private antitrust cases commenced compared with all federal civil cases,
1973–1983

Fiscal Year	Private antitrust cases	All civil cases	Antitrust cases as percentage of all civil cases
1973	1,152	96,056	1.2
1974	1,230	101,345	1.2
1975	1,375	115,098	1.2
1976	1,504	128,362	1.2
1977	1,611	128,889	1.2
1978	1,435	137,707	1.0
1979	1,234	153,552	0.8
1980	1,457	167,871	0.9
1981	1,292	179,803	0.7
1982	1,037	205,505	0.5
1983	1,192	241,159	0.5

Source: Salop and White, table 1.1; R. Posner, *The Federal Courts: Crisis and Reform*
352 (1985).

Table C.2 Use of judicial time in antitrust trials

Average judicial workload in trial days per year (1983)	$\dfrac{\text{Total trial days U.S. district courts}}{\text{Number of district court judges}} = \dfrac{65{,}246}{484} = 135 \text{ days/judge}$
Use of judicial resources in antitrust cases	$\dfrac{\text{Number of trials} \times \text{Average length} \times \text{Sample size adjustment}[a]}{\text{Average judicial workload} \times \text{Number of years surveyed}}$ $= \dfrac{106 \times 11.4 \times 6}{135 \times 11} = 4.9 \text{ judge years}$
Additional time consumed by jury trials[b]	$\dfrac{\genfrac{}{}{0pt}{}{\text{Average additional trial days}}{\text{in jury cases}} \times \genfrac{}{}{0pt}{}{\text{Number of}}{\text{jury cases}} \times \genfrac{}{}{0pt}{}{\text{Sample size}}{\text{adjustment}[a]}}{135 \times 11}$ $= \dfrac{4.2 \times 31 \times 6}{135 \times 11} = 0.5 \text{ judge years}$

Sources: R. Posner, *The Federal Courts: Crisis and Reform* 68, 357 (1985); Teplitz, table 2.6;
Elzinga and Wood, table 3.4.
a. The Georgetown sample comprised one-fifth of all U.S. antitrust cases, but of the 2,874
cases in the sample usable responses were obtained in only 2,348 cases. Hence the
response represents approximately one-sixth of the universe. Telephone interview with
Lawrence J. White.
b. This computation assumed that the percentage of jury cases in the 71 case sample of
trials used by Elzinga and Wood (table 3.4) held true for the entire Georgetown sample,
which included 106 trials.

cases each year, and in view of the decline in antitrust suits, the number of judges would now be less than five. That statistic, which does not exceed the number of federal trade commissioners, scarcely represents a profligate use of judicial resources from a district court bench of 484 judges. Even the much maligned jury trial consumed few trial resources, lengthening the average trial by 4.2 days or about one-half of a judge year annually.

However, these estimates almost surely understate the use of judicial time in antitrust cases because antitrust cases last longer, generate more extensive pretrial activities, and are more likely to settle without trial than civil cases generally. This conclusion is supported by the Georgetown study, which showed that antitrust cases were longer and more complex than civil cases generally,[31] and by a Federal Judicial Center study, which showed that in 1979 federal judges spent 5.4 percent of their time on civil antitrust cases and 0.3 percent of their time on criminal antitrust cases.[32] Adjustments to the 1979 judicial center figure to reflect current conditions of reduced antitrust litigation and public enforcement produce an estimate of judicial time spent on private antitrust cases that does not exceed between 2 and 3 percent.[33] In addition most of this time would be applied to pretrial proceedings, which are less disruptive of the courts' handling of other cases than actual trials. Taking these factors in account and considering that enforcement of the antitrust laws is a vital national policy, the use of judicial time in private antitrust litigation scarcely appears excessive.

Private Costs   The nonpublic or private costs of antitrust litigation include attorneys fees, other legal costs, executive time, and the time spent by outside counsel. The Georgetown study suggests that private costs were relatively modest. Salop and White estimate that attorneys fees for private antitrust litigation totaled $250 million per year. Inclusion of executive time would not increase this figure significantly since according to the confidential survey executives devoted an average of only 30 hours per case.[34]

As pointed out in the Conference deliberations, a total expenditure of $250 million per year for private antitrust enforcement does not appear excessive on its face, even if augmented by the cost of inside counsel. Additional perspective on this figure is gained by comparing it with the cost of government antitrust enforcement. The use of certain assumptions as to the relation between outside fees and government expenditures allows the estimate that the direct cost of government enforcement is no less than $352 million—$88 million by the enforcement agencies and the balance for private counsel.[35] Although the government's antitrust work is not limited to litigation-directed activities, it is striking that private antitrust enforcement supports 90 to 95 percent of all antitrust litigation at a direct cost that appears to be substantially below that attributable to government enforcement.

A Tentative Balancing of Costs and Benefits

The benefits of private enforcement are the deterrence of antitrust violations and the compensation of antitrust victims. The Georgetown study did not attempt to measure the deterrent effects of private antitrust enforcement. But other reliable evidence strongly indicates that private enforcement has a substantial deterrent effect and that such deterrence is needed in view of continued instances of egregious price fixing and other antitrust violations. This conclusion is supported by findings from a recent empirical survey of antitrust attorneys, including almost 400 inside corporate counsel, which indicated a strong need for vigorous antitrust enforcement,[36] and by the views of the enforcement agencies themselves.[37]

In addition private enforcement serves to compensate victims of antitrust violations. The Georgetown study attempted to measure compensation effects in the confidential survey, but the fragmentary response to the survey limited its usefulness. In a more general sense, however, one can conclude that the private enforcement system has produced significant compensation benefits since the bulk of damage recoveries have been paid for price-fixing offenses, including large recoveries in multidistrict litigation, where the losses of antitrust victims are generally thought to be high.

The total benefits of private enforcement, encompassing both compensation and deterrence effects, must surely therefore be assessed as substantial. Since the total costs are moderate, no sufficient basis appears for rejecting the present assumption of antitrust law that the benefits of private enforcement outweigh the costs, and this conclusion has been strengthened rather than diminished by the Georgetown study.

Efficient Deployment of Antitrust Resources

Even if the benefits of private antitrust enforcement exceed the costs, this does not mean that resources are being allocated efficiently within the private enforcement system. Based on the Georgetown data, however, it would appear that the deployment of private enforcement effort and the magnitude of antitrust penalties have been responsive to perceived antitrust injury and changing legal standards. Thus within the last five years private antitrust litigation has concentrated increasingly on price fixing,[38] and damage recoveries have been highest in price-fixing cases.[39] These changes seem quite responsive to shifting legal doctrine, which has placed a stronger emphasis on the price-fixing violation and has developed more exacting standards of proof, particularly for nonprice-fixing offenses.

Finally, the antitrust penalty system itself, when examined in terms of its aftertax and after interest effects, reflects a scaling of penalties that appears responsive to enforcement priorities. As we have already seen, the failure to pay interest from the date of injury significantly reduces the effective damage recovery. But this reduction is balanced by a statutory tax penalty in cases where there has been a prior finding of criminal violation or plea of nolo contendere.[40] In such cases, which almost always involve horizontal price fixing, defendant is barred from deducting two-thirds of the damages from federal income taxes. This statutory provision, which both increases the antitrust penalty and decouples a significant portion of the penalty from the plaintiff's recovery,[41] results in an effective damage multiple of four, assuming a 50 percent tax rate and considering lost interest.[42]

Thus in practical terms the penalty system in private actions is scaled to impose higher than treble damages in cases of hard-core price fixing. On the other side, especially favored transactions, such as R&D joint ventures and export trading companies, are subject to only single damages. This results in an antitrust penalty system that in effect is three tiered: fourfold damages for egregious price fixing, double damages (although called treble) for other antitrust violations in production and sales markets, and single damages for antitrust offenses in R&D and export markets. The conclusion seems warranted therefore that in terms of concentration of private enforcement effort and the recoveries and penalties assessed against the litigants, the deployment of antitrust resources is responsive to current antitrust law, as reflected in the decisions of the courts and the statutes of Congress, and hence within the framework of our constitutional system is socially efficient.

Notes

Helpful comments were received from Ronald Cass, Jane Cohen, Alan Feld, John Leubsdorf, Robert Buchanon, Esq., and from participants in the Boston University legal theory workshop.

1. See *Historical Statistics of the United States*, E.135-36.

2. A recent analysis concludes that the appropriate rate of interest in tort cases should be the defendant's debt rate on a loan for the period from the date of injury to recovery, on the theory that the injury constitutes an involuntary loan from plaintiff to defendant. See Patell, Weil, and Wolfson, *Accumulating Damages in Litigation: The Roles of Uncertainty and Interest Rates*, 11 J. Legal Studies 341 (1982). But the use of defendant's debt rate would not change

the analysis here because whether one uses the interest-free rate or the plaintiff's debt rate, the erosion of the damage award from what it was in 1890 would have been roughly the same.

3. 15 U.S.C. § 15 (a). Interest prior to suit on the untrebled injury is permitted, provided the court finds an award of interest to be just, taking into account such factors as delay and violation of rules. See 1980 U.S. Code Cong. & Adm. Serv., pp. 2716 *et seq.*

4. When the measure of antitrust damages is lost profits, an inflation factor may be implicitly included, especially under the so-called "yardstick approach," which assesses damages based on the profits of comparable firms not affected by the antitrust violation. In that event the stream of earnings that forms the basis of damage award is automatically inflation adjusted. On the other hand, in some nonovercharge cases an adverse income tax effect depressed the effective recovery. See notes 11–13 and related text.

5. This information was furnished to the author by Paul Teplitz, based on computer analysis of the data set. See also Elzinga and Wood, tables 3.5, 3.11. The six-year disposition figure for class action cases assumes an average two-year lag between injury and suit.

6. The precise result will depend on the interest rate used. The average risk-free rate over the 11-year period of the Georgetown study was 8.76 percent, which would produce an effective damage recovery multiple that is very close to two. Using a 7 percent rate, the lowest in recent years, the effective damage multiple would be 2.16, whereas at a 10 percent rate, far from the highest rate in recent years, the multiple would be 1.9.

7. See Elzinga and Wood, table 3.4.

8. See Teplitz (chapter 2). The clear implication is that delay becomes more valuable to defendants as the damages increase so that it becomes profitable to invest resources to protract the case.

Possibly contrary to this conclusion is the finding of a recent study of juries in Cook County, Illinois showing that in personal injury cases juries appeared to award implicit interest based on passage of time. See Carroll, *Jury Awards and Prejudgment Interest in Tort Cases*, Institute for Civil Justice 10–13 (May 1983). But such jury conduct appears less likely in antitrust cases, which involve injuries to broad classes of litigants or to corporate entities, rather than to personalized victims.

9. Kauper and Snyder suggest that follow-on cases, which were predominantly per se cases, last longer than other cases because fewer are dismissed at preliminary stages. See Kauper and Snyder (chapter 7). But they do not present any quantitative data that relate the lower dismissal rate to lengthened disposition time, and thus in the absence of data showing that the delay in antitrust cases was entirely traceable to other factors, the conclusion remains plausible that delay was at least in part caused by the failure of the antitrust remedy to compensate fully for lost interest.

10. See R. Brealey and S. Myers, *Principles of Corporate Finance* 114 (1981) (Standard and Poor's annual return has been about 18 percent in recent years).

11. Internal Revenue Code § 61. See generally, *Antitrust Payments and Recoveries*, 121-4th Tax Management (1984); and von Kalinowski, *Antitrust Laws and Trade Regulation* § 118.02[3] (1985).

Thus, if the plaintiff owned land or a patent that was destroyed in value by an antitrust violation, he would receive the value of the land or patent at the time of injury plus interest to the date of recovery. In the absence of the antitrust violation, however, plaintiff would have been able to hold the land or patent, which would normally be appreciating by at least the inflation-inclusive risk-free interest rate. Until such time as plaintiff might choose to sell the property, that appreciation would result in no taxable income. But due to the antitrust violation on the resulting judgment the gain is realized for tax purposes and is then taxed as ordinary income. Thus the value of plaintiff's original capital would be eroded by the income tax on the interest compensation portion of his award, which he would not have paid had he not been injured and had he continued to hold the capital asset. Indeed, the situation could be even worse for the plaintiff if at the time of loss, the property had a low tax basis. In that event, the plaintiff would also realize a capital gain on the damage award.

12. Treble damages cases are also subject to such a tax diminution, but the issue is more acute under detrebling since the intent of the statute becomes primarily compensatory rather than deterrent.

13. I am indebted to Alan Feld for bringing the tax issue to my attention.

14. See Salop and White, table 1.10 and related text (at least 8 percent of cases lost by plaintiff at trial).

15. See Calkins and Teplitz (motions to dismiss or summary judgments granted against plaintiffs on one or more counts in 11.5 percent of cases, of which 6.2 percent resulted in full dismissals).

16. Perhaps these considerations should be offset by the possibility that a court will assess damages in excess of actual losses, thereby inflating the damage base that is subject to trebling. But this seems less likely in recent years as courts have become increasingly stringent in requiring proof of loss, not hesitating to reverse or reduce excessive jury awards both at trial and appellate levels.

17. See W. Baxter, *The Political Economy of Antitrust* 22 (1979).

18. See Teplitz (chapter 2).

19. Information was available on attorneys' fees in only 50 cases, or 1.7 percent of the total Georgetown sample. Even for this narrow group of cases, information was generally provided for only one side, usually the defendants, so that the total fees and the relation between fees and settlement amount was the result of inference, not a direct data measurement. See Elzinga and Wood.

20. Differing groups of cases within the sample had attorneys fee to settlement ratios that ranged from 2 to 116 percent. *Id.*

21. See Salop and White, table 1.11 and related text.

22. Motions to dismiss by defendants were granted in 9.5 percent of competitor cases involving the same product, and in 8.9 percent of competitor cases involving similar or substitute products, as compared with 7.3 percent of antitrust cases generally. See Calkins.

23. Defense motions for summary judgment were successful in 4.4 percent of cases involving the same product and 2.4 percent of cases involving similar or substitute products, as compared with 4.2 percent of antitrust cases generally. See Calkins.

24. See Calkins and Teplitz.

25. Communication with Jeffrey Perloff on January 17, 1986.

26. This result appears by inference from Salop and White, table 1.8, and Teplitz, who show, respectively, the distribution of competitor cases by type of offense and the recovery per offense (based on linked court survey data). Reading these chapters together, one finds that with the single exception of price-fixing cases, recoveries were generally larger for offenses in which competitor suits were frequent, such as predation and refusals to deal, than for offenses where competitor suits were less frequent, such as dealer terminations.

27. Median recovery to cost ratio for 22 competitor cases was 78 percent, while for 39 noncompetitor cases the ratio was 74 percent. Communication with Paul Teplitz, reporting information obtained from computer analysis of Georgetown data base.

28. If the hypothesis were valid that competitors file antitrust cases in order to pursue anticompetitive agendas, one would expect low recoveries relative to other antitrust cases and high legal fees relative to recoveries. In the absence of such effects it is necessary to posit a theory of systematic judicial error to sustain the thesis that competitor cases lack antitrust merit.

29. See Teplitz (median plaintiff had annual sales of $1 million, as compared with median defendant of $230 million).

30. If there is a reform that might be desirable for competitor suits, it would lie in the area of nonmonetary relief, which the Georgetown study did not attempt to measure. Assertions have been made that nonmonetary settlements may have anticompetitive effects in some competitor cases because it may be cheaper for a defendant to split the anticompetitive pie than to compete. But if this presents a problem, the solution lies not in barring suits by competitors, or limiting damage awards to single damages, but in requiring nonmonetary settlements to be disclosed, perhaps notified to the Antitrust Division and FTC, and made subject to judicial review in appropriate cases.

31. Thus the Georgetown study showed that the median antitrust case lasted 19 months as compared with 10 months for the median civil case, generated 70 docket entries, an eight-inch file, and three judicial orders, all of which presumably exceed the average for civil cases, and resulted in settlements in 88 percent of the cases, as compared with a 72 percent settlement rate for civil cases generally. See Salop and White, table 1.9 and related text.

32. See S. Flanders, *1979 District Court Time Study* (1980), cited in Reich, *The Antitrust Industry*, 68 Georgetown L. J. 1053, 1069 (1980).

33. Three factors necessitate a reduction in the Judicial Center statistic. First, much less time is now being spent on government civil antitrust cases, which in 1979 were being filed at three times the present rate (31 civil cases filed in 1979 as compared with 10 in 1983). Second, as appears in table C.1, the number of private antitrust cases peaked in the years 1976 through 1978, and given the lag in the disposition of antitrust cases, the courts in 1979 would have occupied in adjudicating many of these cases, especially those that were being most heavily litigated. Third, between 1977 and 1983, the number of new antitrust filings declined steeply— 32 percent in absolute terms, and in relative terms from 1.2 percent to only 0.5 percent of all civil filings.

34. See Teplitz. If executive time is valued at $100 per hour, reflecting annual compensation of $150,000 for a 1,500-hour working year, it would add only $3,000 to the cost of the average antitrust case. The study contains no data on time spent by inside counsel.

35. See Budget of the United States, FY 1986 (appendix), pp. I-Y38, II-35 (combined Antitrust Division and FTC antitrust budgets total $88 million). The private costs resulting from government enforcement can be estimated to be approximately $264 million if we assume that each hour of enforcement agency effort evoked one hour of time on the part of nongovernment counsel, an extremely modest estimate, and if we value such time at $125 per hour, as a recent study suggests. See Fisher and Lande, *Efficiencies Considerations in Merger Enforcement*, 71 Calif. L. Rev. 1580, 1673–1674 (1983) (study of attorney time at FTC in 1981 in merger cases). The sum of public and private costs then comes to $352 million.

36. See Beckenstein and Gabel, *Antitrust Compliance: Results of a Survey of Legal Opinion*, 51 ABA Antitrust L. J. 459 (1982).
   Of over 800 antitrust attorneys surveyed 72 percent believed that private antitrust suits had either very great or considerable deterrent value, 72 percent thought that detrebling would inhibit or strongly inhibit antitrust compliance, and no less than 61 percent believed that the enforcement agencies failed to detect most price fixing violations.

37. Thus the recent report of the Working Group on Antitrust Review to the Domestic Policy Council recommended an increase in damages for suits brought by the United States from single to treble damages because it would substantially increase "deterrence of hard core cartel behavior." (BNA Antitrust & Trade Reg. Rep., November 28, 1985, p. 947). Similarly there is strong interest by European enforcement authorities in developing a system of private antitrust damages in order to achieve more effective antitrust deterrence.

38. See Salop and White, table 1.16 (significant increase in number of price fixing cases during recent years, accompanied by drastic decline in vertical cases other than vertical price fixing; price-fixing cases comprised 32 percent of all cases filed in 1983, by far the largest category).

39. See Teplitz (average recovery for plaintiff in horizontal price fixing exceeded $1.1 million, over twice the recovery for the next ranking offense); and Salop and White, table 1.11 and related text (multidistrict awards, which were predominantly horizontal price fixing, averaged $48 million).

40. 26 U.S.C.A § 162g.

41. Decoupling occurs because the effective penalty imposed on the defendant exceeds the plaintiff's recovery. If, as has sometimes been claimed (see the comment in part I by Polinsky), decoupling and an increase in the antitrust penalty have superior enforcement properties, it should be possible to test that effort empirically by measuring the effects before and after the 1970 statutory change that barred defendants convicted of antitrust crimes from deducting two-thirds of damages.

42. From 1981 through at least the end of 1986 many U.S. corporations in capital-intensive industries paid little or no income taxes due to favorable tax provisions effective in 1981. For such corporations the damage multiple would increase to five if the unlawful gain occurred *prior* to 1981 and was taxable at 50 percent and if the recovery occurred *after* 1981. Interestingly, for companies in this category, 1981 would thus provide another empirical measuring point to test the effects of decoupling and increased damages.

III

SPECIAL ISSUES IN ANTITRUST LITIGATION

6

A Comprehensive Analysis of the Determinants of Private Antitrust Litigation, with Particular Emphasis on Class Action Suits and the Rule of Joint and Several Damages

George J. Benston

6.1 Introduction and Overview

Three goals usually are ascribed to the antitrust laws: deterrence of potential violators, retribution against the perpetrators, and compensation to victims. These goals are interrelated: if illegal activities are deterred, victims are not harmed; if violators believe that they will have to give up their gains, they will be deterred; and if victims are harmed, they should be compensated. A fourth goal is common to all law: people should be treated fairly.

Class action suits enter the picture because the expected cost of an individual lawsuit may be greater than the expected return. Consequently, absent a means of reducing these costs by means of a joint action, an antitrust law violator could inflict damages on people and firms with only the fear of government prosecutory action. Furthermore, the costs of discovering antitrust violations and pursuing violators would not be undertaken in many instances absent the rewards that plaintiffs' attorneys can expect from organizing and conducting a class action suit.

The rule of joint and several liability also serves to enhance deterrence by making all jointly charged violators of the antitrust laws liable for the total damages the alleged conspiracy inflicted on the plaintiffs. The rule encourages actions by private plaintiffs by increasing the settlement and judgment amounts that they can expect to obtain.

The trebling of damages and the liability of losing defendants for the legal expenses of plaintiffs (at the court's discretion) additionally increase the expected cost to violators of the antitrust laws. This increase in the amount of damages that the violator would have to pay to its victims and to those who bring private actions may compensate (or overcompensate) them for the expectation that not all antitrust violators will be caught nor all damages accounted for. Concurrently potential violators should be deterred by the prospect of paying more in damages than they received in benefits, should they be caught and found liable.

Were deterring true antitrust violators and compensating true victims and plaintiffs' attorneys the sole goals of the antitrust laws, damages should be multiplied many more times so that potential violators would be more effectively deterred. The statute of limitations might be waived so that all possible damages could be included.

However, it is rarely, if ever, absolutely clear that a charged antitrust law violator actually and intentionally violated the law. Firms that are innocent of violations can be cited by plaintiffs who believe them to be guilty, or who simply see a means of extorting funds from them. Firms that unintentionally violate the law would not be deterred by harsh penalties, because they do not believe that the penalties apply to them. Furthermore the more severe are the penalties and the more likely that firms charged with antitrust law violations will be found liable for damages, the more constrained will firms be in undertaking innovations that could benefit consumers and the economy generally. Thus the enforcement of the antitrust laws entails a trade-off between deterring violators and harming others and the economy.

The trade offs among the goals, and the costs and benefits associated with alternative aspects of private antitrust litigation are analyzed in this chapter with a comprehensive specification of the relevant determinants. The model developed follows the path broken by several writers, including Baxter (1979), Shavell (1982), and Priest and Klein (1984).

Section 6.2 presents the defendants' benefits from antitrust violations. Section 6.3 gives the defendants' costs of actual and alleged antitrust violations. Section 6.4 delineates the private plaintiffs' benefits and costs, through the same stages as given for the defendants. The defendants' and plaintiffs' benefits and costs are brought together in section 6.5, which considers their incentives to settle. Section 6.6 builds on the previous section to analyze the determinants of the settlement amount. The determinants of deterrence are discussed in section 6.7. Section 6.8 specifies the effect on consumer welfare of private antitrust litigation, and section 6.9 considers "fairness." The extent to which the effect of the determinants can be empirically measured and the role of the Geogetown data base for this purpose is the subject of section 6.10. The final section presents the conclusions drawn from the analysis.

6.2 Defendants' Gross Benefit from Antitrust Violations

Three types of defendants can be delineated. One is an intentional violator of the antitrust laws. The second violates the antitrust laws unintentionally, perhaps by adopting a pricing or distribution method that it believes is legal but that is subsequently found to be a violation. The third is an innocent bystander. This firm does not violate the antitrust laws but nevertheless is charged with a violation.

The Intentional Violator's Gross Benefit

On the assumption that the managers of an intentional violator seek only to maximize the monetary wealth of the firm's owners and are risk neutral, they will collude with other suppliers to fix prices (or otherwise violate the antitrust laws) if this action is profitable, that is, if the expected total benefit from price fixing exceeds expected total cost. Furthermore the price fixing will be extended to the point where net total benefit is maximized, where the marginal benefit equals marginal cost. The benefit and cost are aftertax amounts.[1]

The expected benefit from price fixing and collusion is the present value of the sum of the amounts obtained from the victims of the violation (damages inflicted) plus increases in the violator's efficiency (e.g., savings in manufacturing or distribution costs as a result of the joint activities of the colluding producers[2]) and less the cost of establishing and maintaining the collusion (e.g., legal advice and other actions to maintain the cartel, prevent its discovery, and reduce the cost to the corporation should the price fixing or other violation be discovered).[3] The gross benefit may be expressed symbolically as[4]

$$\text{Benefit}_I = \int_{t=0,m} \{D_{It} + EB_{It} - CC_{It}\}e^{-rt}dt, \tag{1}$$

where

D = damages inflicted by I, the intentional violator[5],

EB = efficiency benefits associated with the collusion,

CC = costs of collusion,

t = time from 0 through m,

r = risk-adjusted aftertax nominal discount rate (opportunity cost of funds, including price level adjustment).

The present value of the benefits is calculated for the period during which the price-fixing collusion is expected to remain undiscovered (years 0 through m). Over this period the intentional violator receives the benefit of additional net revenue from the higher collusively determined prices, plus additional efficiency gains less the costs of establishing and maintaining the cartel. It is assumed that the cartel is dissolved at time m because of cheating by fellow colluders, competition from noncartel members, or discovery by the Department of Justice, customers, other firms, or enterprising lawyers.

The Unintentional Violator's Gross Benefit

The unintentional violator differs from the intentional violator in believing that its actions are not against the law. For example, the unintentional violator might jointly sell products because it can offer customers savings in information and other transaction costs, but it might be charged with illegal tying. Similarly exchange of price information as a means of avoiding violating the Robinson-Patman Act may be interpreted as a price-fixing collusion.[6] Numerous other examples could be given.[7]

The unintentional violator also may have reason to believe that its rivals will use the antitrust laws as a means of constraining it. For example, it could be charged with predatory behavior if it cuts prices. As Baumol and Ordover (1985, 254) point out: "obscurity and ambiguity [of the law] are convenient tools for those enterprises on the prowl for opportunities to hobble competition.... Harrassment by lawsuit or even the threat of harassment can be a marvelous stimulus to timidity on the part of competitors." The antitrust laws also can be used to thwart takeovers, as analyzed by Easterbrook and Fischel (1983).[8]

The unintentional violator nevertheless might engage in activities that could result in its being charged with violating the antitrust laws because it believes that the benefit is sufficiently high and/or that the probability that it will be charged with a violation and be forced to pay damages is sufficiently low. To reduce the expected cost, it might expend resources to avoid the appearance of violations, forego engaging in some otherwise beneficial activities, or both.

Therefore the unintentional violator's gross expected benefit is the present value of the gains in efficiency it expects, less the cost of protecting itself against lawsuits:

$$\text{Benefit}_U = \int_{t=0,m} [EB_{Ut} - CP_{Ut}]e^{-rt}\,dt, \tag{2}$$

where

EB = efficiency benefits to U, the unintentional violator, that might be viewed as violations of the antitrust laws,

CP = cost of protecting against lawsuits.

The Innocent Bystander's Gross Benefit

Because plaintiffs almost always benefit from charging all possible antitrust law violators, regardless of the probability of the potential defendants' guilt, it is likely that some innocent bystanders will be swept into their net. The only constraint is the possibility that the court will rule that the charge against a defendant was knowingly frivolous, in which event the costs could (but rarely are) charged against the plaintiffs. Because horizontal collusion conceivably could include all producers of the allegedly price-fixed good, relatively large numbers of defendants tend to be included in price-fixing cases, including innocent bystanders.[9]

Since the innocent bystander does not believe that it is violating the antitrust laws or will be charged with a violation, it does not recognize a benefit related to antitrust. However, it might fear that it will be charged with a violation simply because it is in an industry with a history of past violations or where price increases have occurred. Hence it might have a negative benefit in the form of costs of protection.

6.3 Defendants' Costs of Actual and Alleged Antitrust Violations

Defendants' Costs in General
The expected cost for each of the three types of defendants depends on the probabilities that it will (1) be charged with an antitrust law violation, (2) settle before trial, (3) lose at trial and be liable for damages (be found guilty), (4) settle after trial, (5) appeal and lose, (6) settle after appeal, (7) appeal to the Supreme Court and lose, and (8) settle before the case is decided. These probabilities times the damages amounts (including plaintiff's legal costs) at each stage, plus the defendant's legal and other costs, less any benefit from settling or going to trial (e.g., not having to report a contingent liability or reducing the probability of being sued by other plaintiffs), yield the expected cost to the defendant. The amounts are discounted to the time when the cost is considered by the defendant's managers.

The expected costs at each stage of the process are given by equation (3). All of the costs are contingent on discovery (d) of the antitrust violation. Thus, if $d = 0$, all the amounts are multiplied by zero.

Cost = $\qquad\qquad\qquad\qquad\qquad\qquad\qquad\qquad\qquad\qquad\qquad$ (3)

$$\int_{t=0,w} \{d \cdot st(ST_t + LS_t - BS_t)\}e^{-rt}\, dt, \qquad \text{pretrial settlement,} \qquad (3.1)$$

$$+ \int_{t=0,x} \{d(1 - st)[LT_t + BS_t + gt\, CT_t - (1 - gt)BT_t]\}e^{-rt}\, dt,$$

$$\text{trial cost/benefit,} \qquad (3.2)$$

$$+ \int_{t=0,x} \{d(1 - st)gt(DT_t + LTP_{pt})(1 - sa)(1 - a)\}e^{-rt}\,dt,$$

trial damages,   (3.3)

$$+ \int_{t=0,y} \{d(1 - st)gt\,sa(1 - a)(SA_t + LSA_t)\}e^{-rt}\,dt,$$

post-trial settlement,   (3.4)

$$+ \int_{t=0,z} \{d(1 - st)gt(1 - sa)(a)[LA_t + ga\,CA_t - (1 - ga)BA_t]\}e^{-rt}\,dt,$$

appeal cost/benefit,   (3.5)

$$+ \int_{t=0,z} \{d(1 - st)gt(1 - sa)(a)ga(DA_t + LAP_t)\}e^{-rt}\,dt,$$

appeal damages,   (3.6)

+ settle after appeal or appeal to Supreme Court   (3.7)

where

$t = w =$ the time of pretrial judgment settlement,

$t = x =$ the time of the trial judgment,

$t = y =$ the time of the pre-appeal settlement,

$t = z =$ the time of the appeal decision,

$d =$ probability that the violation will be discovered, $0 \le d \le 1$,

$st =$ probability that a settlement will be reached with the plaintiffs before the trial decision, $0 \le st \le$,

$ST =$ settlement amount paid to the plaintiffs before the trial decision, which includes plaintiffs' legal expenses,

$LS =$ legal and other antitrust-action-related expenses through the time of settlement, aggregated with interest through time w,[10]

$BS =$ benefits related to settling,

$gt =$ the probability that the case will go to trial and the defendant will be found guilty (liable for damages) at trial, $0 \le gt \le 1$,

$LT =$ legal and other related expenses through trial (including the pretrial settlement period), aggregated with interest through time x,

BT = net benefits from going to trial and being found not guilty,

CT = additional costs due to a trial guilty verdict,

DT = damages assessed (including trebling) at trial, limited to the defendant's bankruptcy value,

LTP = legal expenses at trial of plaintiff charged to the defendant,

sa = probability that a settlement before the appeal decision will be reached with the plaintiffs, $0 \leq sa \leq 1$,

a = probability that an appeal will be made and seen through to a decision, $0 \leq a \leq 1$,

SAP = settlement amount paid to the plaintiff before the appeal decision, which includes plaintiff's legal expenses,

LSA = legal and other related expenses incurred from the trial through settlement before appeal decision, aggregated with interest from time x through time y,

LA = legal expenses incurred from trial through the appeal decision, aggregated with interest from time x through time z,

ga = probability that the defendant will be found guilty on appeal, $0 \leq ga \leq 1$,

BA = benefits (similar to BT) of appealing and having trial verdict reversed,

CA = additional costs (similar to CT) of appealing and having trial verdict upheld,

DA = damages assessed against the defendant on appeal, limited to its bankruptcy value,

LAP = legal expenses at appeal of plaintiff charged to the defendant.

In particular, the expected cost of a pretrial decision settlement is the present value of the defendant's expected pretrial decision settlement amount (ST), plus legal and other antitrust-related expenses (LS), such as the cost of plaintiffs' discovery and depositions and the opportunity value of executives' time, less net benefits from settling (BS), which are contingent on the corporation's settling (st) (subequation 3.1). These net benefits include foreclosing additional lawsuits by bringing all potential plaintiffs into the settlement agreement and not having to be contingently liable for damages (particularly where the contingent liability must be disclosed in financial statements). Benefits are reduced by costs, such as increasing the probability (and hence the cost) of additional lawsuits should potential plaintiffs decide that the defendant is an "easy mark." The settlement amount depends on the defendant's expectations of the costs of not settling (shown by the balance of the terms) and on negotiations with the plaintiffs. (The amount for which the plaintiffs might be willing to settle is given by equation 4.) If a settlement is made at this point, $st = 1$, and the balance of the terms (3.2–3.7) are multiplied by zero.

The present value of the defendant's legal costs (including imputed interest) through the trial decision (LT) is given in (3.2). These costs are incurred whether or not the defendant wins at trial. When the case goes to trial, the net benefits from settling (BS) are lost and therefore are a cost. These net benefits include protecting the defendant's reputation and reducing its susceptability to additional lawsuits and are contingent on the defendant's being found not guilty. If the defendant is found guilty (liable for damages) ($gt = 1$), it may incur costs in addition to damages (CT). These costs include loss of reputation and an increased probability and expected cost of additional lawsuits. But if a not guilty verdict is returned ($gt = 0$), it achieves benefits (BT) from repair of its reputation and protection from additional suits. A not guilty verdict also results in the balance of the terms (3.3–3.7) equaling zero.

If the defendant is found liable for damages ($gt = 1$), the expected amount of its cost depends on its not settling prior to an appeal judgment ($1 - sa$) and on its not appealing the decision and judgment ($1 - a$) (subequation 3.3). Should the defendant not settle or appeal ($sa = a = 0$), it will have to pay three times the damages assessed against it (DT), which, with joint and several liability, can be considerably more than the damages (D) it inflicted on its customers, plus the plaintiff's legal expenses through trial (LTP) that are awarded. In this event because there is no post-trial settlement or appeal ($sa = a = 0$), terms (3.4)–(3.7) equal zero.

The present value of the expected cost of a post-trial, preappeal settlement includes the settlement amount (SA) plus the defendant's additional legal expenses (LSA) from the time of trial (x) through time of settlement (y) (subequation 3.4.). If the defendant does not settle, it incurs additional legal expenses through the appeal decision (LA) (subequation 3.5). These expenses are incurred whether or not the defendant wins on appeal. The additional other costs and benefits of losing or winning the appeal (CA and BA) are dependent on the outcome (ga).

The present value of the appeal judgment is contingent on the defendant's not settling and losing at trial and on appeal ($gt = a = 1$) (subequation 3.6). The damage amount (DA) and legal costs awarded to the plaintiffs (LAP) need not be the same as the amounts awarded at trial (DT and LTP).

Finally, the defendant can settle after it has lost the appeal, or appeal to the Supreme Court, which gives rise to the possibilities of settling before the Court grants or denies certiori and having the verdict changed if the Court hears the case and reverses.

The Intentional Violator's Cost

The intentional violator would assess the present value of expected costs at the time it considered violating the antitrust laws. Presumably, it determined that the expected benefits (given by equation 1) exceed the expected costs (given by equation 3). Compared to the other defendants, the intentional violator would appear to have the highest probability of discovery, because it is violating the antitrust laws. However, knowing that it can be discovered, it has an incentive to prevent discovery. It also is better able to assess the probability of being found guilty (liable for damages) at trial, which increases the benefit to it of settling and preventing damaging information about its operations from being revealed at trial. (Being an intentional violator, it has information that should be valuable to the plaintiff, which should reduce the cash settlement demanded by the plaintiffs, as shown in equation 4.) It also is likely to have higher cost of being guilty. Although damages assessed against it would be higher than the amounts assessed against less guilty defendants, with joint and several liability its expected damages need not be higher.

The Unintentional Violator's Cost

The unintentional violator might assess the expected cost of its being charged with violating the antitrust laws at the time it undertook its efficiency creating benefits. It might face a lower probability of discovery and a finding of guilt at trial than the intentional violator. However, given joint and several liability, it might be subject to as great or greater damages and legal expenses. Being innocent of an intentional violation, it might value more than the intentional violator the other benefits from being found innocent and the costs of being found guilty.

The Innocent Bystander's Cost

The innocent bystander would not consider the cost, described in equation (3), of its actions. Nevertheless, when it is charged with violating the antitrust laws, it faces the same cost function as the other types of defendants. Not having been concerned with having to defend itself, it may not have taken steps to purge its files of potentially damaging documents before an action is brought. Thus it is unclear whether the probability of its being found guilty is smaller or greater than the other corporations' probability. However, because it is innocent, it might value being declared not guilty more than the intentional violator.

6.4 The Private Plaintiff's Benefit and Cost

Plaintiff's Benefit and Cost in General

Two types of private plaintiffs may be distinguished: nonclass and class action. Once an alleged antitrust violation is discovered ($d = 1$), each type of private plaintiff's benefit net of cost of pursuing the action by either settling with individual defendants and/or going to trial is the present value of the amounts that may be obtained either through settlement or court-determined award less the plaintiff's costs. Because these amounts are not certain, their expected values are determined by multiplying the amounts by the probabilities that the parties will settle or that the plaintiff will win at trial.

Net benefit to plaintiff = (4)

$$\int_{t=0,w} \{\hat{I}_{D=1,s} st_D (ST_{Dt} - LS_{Dt} + BS_{Dt})\} e^{-rt}\, dt,$$

pretrial settlement, (4.1)

$$+ \int_{t=0,x} \{\hat{I}_{D=1,s}[(1 - st_D)[-BS_{Dt} - LT_{Dt} - (1 - gt_D)CT_{Dt}$$
$$+ gt_D BT_{Dt}]\} e^{-rt}\, dt, \quad \text{trial cost/benefit,} \quad (4.2)$$

$$+ \int_{t=0,x} \{\hat{I}_{D=1,s}(1 - st_D)gt_D(DT_{Dt} + LTD_{Dt})(1 - sa_D)(1 - a_D)\} e^{-rt}\, dt,$$

trial net benefit, (4.3)

$$+ \int_{t=0,y} \{\hat{I}_{D=1,s}[(1 - st_D)gt_D sa_D(1 - a_D)SA_{Dt}] - LSA_{Dt}\} e^{-rt}\, dt,$$

post-trial settlement, (4.4)

$$+ \int_{t=0,z} \{\hat{I}_{D=1,s}[(1 - st_D)gt_D(1 - sa_D)a_D[-LA_{Dt} + ga_DBA_{Pt}$$

$$- (1 - ga_D)CA_{Dt}]\}e^{-rt}\,dt, \qquad \text{appeal cost/benefit,} \qquad (4.5)$$

$$+ \int_{t=0,z} \{\hat{I}_{D=1,s}[(1 - st_D)gt_D(1 - sa_D)a_Dga_D(DA_{Dt} + LAD_{Dt})\}e^{-rt}\,dt,$$

$$\text{appeal,} \qquad (4.6)$$

+ settle after appeal or appeal to Supreme Court, $\qquad (4.7)$

subject to $\sum_{D=1,s} [DT_D] \le TD - ST_O$ and $\sum_{D=1,s} [DA_D] \le TD - SA_O$,

where

D = defendants, $1, 2, \ldots, s$ (used to identify variables that apply to specific defendants),

LTD_D = portion of plaintiff's legal fees at trial paid by defendant,

LAD_D = portion of plaintiff's legal fees at appeal paid by defendant supercedes LTD_D),

TD = total damages that can be proved against all defendants,

ST_O = settlements before trial decision by other defendants $(st_D \ne 0)$,

SA_O = settlements before appeal decision by other defendants $(sa_D \ne 0)$ (supercedes ST_O),

BS_D = net additional benefit of settling,

BT_D, BA_D = benefit of having the defendant found guilty at trial and appeal,

CT_D, CA_D = additional cost of defendant being found not guilty at trial and on appeal.

The other variables are as defined in equation (3).

In particular, the expected net present value of pretrial settlements is calculated at the time when a decision to pursue the defendants is made ($t = 0$) (subequation 4.1). Should the plaintiff settle with only some of the defendants ($0 < st < 1$), a trial will take place if the expected present value of a trial and its aftermath (given by subequations 4.2 through 4.7) is positive. Some plaintiffs obtain special benefits from settling (e.g., a nonclass plaintiff that does not want publicly to disclose information about its operations), and settlements with some defendants rather than others are more beneficial (e.g., when a class plaintiff wants a war chest and gets information that can be used against other defendants). However, a plaintiff might not settle with a particular defendant because of special benefits it obtains from pursuing that defendant, such as constraining the latter from aggressively competing with the plaintiff and establishing the defendant's guilt and the plaintiff's attorney's ability and tenaciousness for other contemplated actions. A trial and appeal may also convey special costs to the plaintiff if it does not win, such as reducing constraints on defendant's practices and the plaintiff's attorney's suffering a public defeat.

For those losing defendants ($gt_D = 1$) that do not appeal ($a_D = 0$), a posttrial settlement could occur, the expected net present benefits of which are shown by subequation (4.4). The expected net present value of an appeal is given by subequations (4.5) and (4.6).

Plaintiffs' Incentives to Discover Antitrust Violations and to Sue

The greater the expected rewards from discovery (given by equation 4), the more plaintiffs will invest in discovery. The expected benefits may be grouped into the probabilities of success and the damage amounts that might be received and costs expended. The greater the settlement or judgment damage amounts, the greater are the benefits from discovery and suit. As equation (4) shows, these amounts are multiplied by a succession of probabilities, as follows: $d \cdot st$; $d \cdot gt$, if $st = sa = a = 0$; or $d \cdot gt \cdot ga$, if $st = sa = 0$. Since the defendant can decide to go to trial and appeal, and since the probability of winning at trial and at appeal are not equal to one, it seems likely that an investment in discovery will not be a positive net present-value project unless the damage award less costs is sufficiently large.

However, the greater the variance of the possible net damage amount, the greater the possibility that suit and/or discovery will be profitable. Higher net damage amounts, and other net benefits as specified in equation (4), can increase the net benefits substantially, whereas lower net damage amounts can reduce the cost of discovery, settlement, and trial only to the amounts invested by the plaintiffs. Thus plaintiffs' expected net benefits are higher when there is a greater variance of outcomes and no cap on the amount of damages that could be collected. This is the situation under the joint and several liability rule.

Nonclass Plaintiffs

Nonclass plaintiffs direct the actions taken by lawyers against the defendant corporations. Should they expend resources to discover the antitrust violation, the net benefit equation (4) would be preceded by the probability that the nonclass plaintiff's discovery efforts would be successful. Although nonclass plaintiffs generally might not search for antitrust violations, they are more likely to spot them as a consequence of their direct dealings with the alleged violator.[11]

Nonclass plaintiffs also might be competitors of the corporation charged with an antitrust violation, which permits them to discover or charge an antitrust violation at relatively low cost. Having discovered the possibility of an antitrust violation, the nonclass plaintiff can ask for a DOJ investigation or file suit immediately.[12] As competitors, nonclass plaintiffs might benefit from suing or from threatening suits because they can achieve such benefits as less effective competition from their rivals.

Class Action Plaintiffs

The plaintiffs' attorneys, rather than the actual plaintiff, are the decision makers in class actions, although they operate under the supervision of the court. As Coffee (1983, 229–230, 234) explains, "four consequences tend to follow from the necessarily weak control that the client can exercise over the attorney in complex class and derivative actions ... (1) risk aversion, (2) the potential for collusion, (3) an inadequate system of property rights, and (4) the disparity of search costs." The third and fourth factors make it unlikely that class action attorneys will discover antitrust violations; because the attorney who discovers a violation cannot prevent other attorneys from joining the action and sharing in the fees, the incentives for discovery are reduced substantially. Furthermore, not having a true client, the class action attorney often does not have access to specific information and documentation about industry practices. Hence Coffee (1983, 220–221), for example, finds that "the available evidence does not provide much support for the thesis that the private attorney general significantly supplements public law enforcement by increasing the probability of detection.... a recurring pattern is evident under which the private attorney general simply piggybacks on the efforts of public agencies ...."[13]

Risk aversion and the potential for collusion make quicker and less advantageous settlements more likely than would be expected in nonclass actions. Risk aversion could characterize class action lawyers because they have to invest their time and money, which is likely to be more limited than the resources available to nonclass plaintiffs. Furthermore the attorneys are not directly compensated for the time value of their investment. Collusion with defendants to settle for amounts that benefit the attorneys more than the class can occur because the class is not in control of the case. These factors do not change the terms in equation (4), though they do affect their values.

In particular, the class action attorneys' benefits from pursuing a case are a fraction of the damages. Prior to the general adoption by the courts of the "lodestar" method of awarded compensation to class action attorneys, their rewards could be expressed as a percentage of the damages paid by the defendants plus expenses awarded by the courts. In this event the damage amounts in equation (4) are reduced by the fraction not obtained by the class plaintiff's attorneys. With the lodestar method the attorneys get the number of hours they devote to the case times their usual billing rates (or a national rate for similar attorneys if the case is a multidistrict action), which depends on their responsibilities in their firms, times a risk and quality multiple. The multiple, which is requested by the attorneys with the acquiescence or adjustment by the court, is supposed to be higher when the risk the attorneys assumed in bringing the action, and their skill and responsibilities in managing it, are greater.[14] Each of these methods of rewarding plaintiffs' attorneys importantly affects their incentives to settle or try an action.

Class action lawsuits also are likely to generate greater total damages. Unlike nonclass suits, damages to each plaintiff by the defendants need not be proved. Rather, the overcharge (in a price-fixing case) times total industry sales to all direct purchasers is the measure of damages. Thus the defendants in a class action suit can number in the dozens and even hundreds. Furthermore the rule of joint and several liability makes each defendant potentially liable for the damages applicable to all defendants— the entire industry. This usually much larger amount increases the class action attorney's expected rewards, which can make a case with a small probability of success worth pursuing.

6.5 Defendants' and Plaintiffs' Incentives to Settle

Settlement in General (without Consideration of Joint and Several Liability and Risk Aversion)[15]

In general, both plaintiffs and defendants have incentives to settle before trial since, by settling, they both save additional legal costs. A particular defendant, D, would be willing to settle if the amount demanded were less than its expected cost of not settling.

On the assumption that the numbers are discounted to present values, the cost of not settling, CNS_D, is derived from equation (3) where $st = 0$ as follows:[16]

$$CNS_D = LT_D + BS_D + gt_D CT_D - (1 - gt_D)BT_D + gt_D(DT_D + LTP_D)$$
$$- ga_D A_D + CA_D, \tag{5}$$

where $ga_D A_D$ is the defendant's expected net benefit from post-trial settlement and appeal (measured as the net expected reduction in cost from post-trial settlements and appeals) and CA_D is the defendant's legal and other costs of the appeal (determined by subequations (3.5–3.7). By not settling, the defendant assumes additional legal expenses, the opportunity loss of the benefit from settling (BS), and the expected indirect cost of losing at trial (CT) less the expected indirect benefit (BT), plus the expected damages and plaintiff's legals costs ($DT + LTP$) less the expected reduction in damages and costs from settling or appealing (A), but plus the cost of the appeal (CA).

The plaintiff, P, would be willing to settle with the defendant if the amount were more than its expected net benefit from not settling. The plaintiff's benefit from not settling with defendant D, BNS_{PD}, is derived from equation (4) as follows:[17]

$$BNS_{PD} = BS_{PD} - LT_{PD} - (1 - gt_{PD})CT_{PD} + gt_{PD}BT_{PD}$$
$$+ gt_{PD}(DT_{PD} + LTP_{PD}) - ga_{PD}A_{PD} - CA_{PD}, \tag{6}$$

where the subscripts denote the benefits and costs to P of dealing with defendant D. The benefit and cost can differ according to the defendant.

By not settling, the plaintiff loses the benefits from settling (BS), such as information that might increase the amounts obtainable from other defendants, its own legal costs (LT), and other expected costs should it lose the case (CT), but gains the expected other benefits from the defendant's being found guilty (BT) plus the damage judgment and legal fees awarded ($DT + LPT$) (as determined by subequations 4.1 and 4.2) less the expected reduction in damages (net of costs) the defendant might achieve in subsequent settlements and appeals ($ga_{PD}A_{PD}$) and less the costs to the plaintiff of the appeal (described by subequations 4.4 through 4.7).

A settlement would be reached when the defendant's cost of not settling exceeds the plaintiff's cost of not settling ($CNS_D > BNS_{PD}$), because the defendant would be better off settling for any amount less than CNS, while the plaintiff would be better off setting for any amount above BNS.

The analysis can be simplified with little loss of meaning by assuming that the parties believe that the probability that the plaintiff will win on appeal is a scalar of the probability that it will win at trial ($ga_D = h \cdot gt_D$, and $ga_{PD} = j \cdot gt_{PD}$). It also seems reasonable to assume that the parties would agree, at least, about the amount of damages (an assumption that need not hold for the rule of joint and several liability) and on plaintiff's legal expenses that would be assessed against a losing defendant. Then the settlement decision can be expressed as dependent on three elements: one is the parties' savings in legal costs and other benefits from settling; this amount is always positive. Second is the defendant's expected other costs and benefits from losing the case at trial; the more the defendant expects to lose, the greater is the net cost to it of not settling. Third is the plaintiff's expected other benefits and costs from winning the case at trial; the less is the sum of these factors, the more the plaintiff gains from settling. Thus, unless the third term is sufficiently positive, the parties will settle, depending on their expectations about which party will win at trial.

Symbolically, the following assumptions about damages and costs are made:

$$DT = DT_D = DT_{PD}, \quad A = A_D = A_{PD}, \quad \text{and} \quad LTP = LTP_D = LTP_{PD}.$$

Total damages are defined as

$$TD = DT - A + LTD.$$

A settlement will be reached if the inequality is satisfied:

$$(LT_D + LT_{PD} + BS_D + BS_{PD}) + [gt_D CT_D - (1 - gt_D)BT_D] + gt_D(TD)$$

$$> [gt_{PD}BT_{PD} - (1 - gt_{PD}CT_{PD})] + gt_{PD}(TD), \tag{7}$$

or

$$gt_{PD} - gt_D < \frac{TBS + TCT_D + TB_{PD}}{TD}, \tag{8a}$$

where

$$EBS = LT_D + LT_{PD} + BS_D + BS_{PD}, \qquad \text{the expense benefit from settling,}$$

$$NCT_D = gt_D CT_D - (1 - gt_D)BT_D, \qquad \text{the defendant's net other cost of trial,}$$

$$NCT_{PD} = gt_{PD}BT_{PD} - (1 - gt_{PD})CT_{PD}, \qquad \text{the plaintiff's net other cost of trial.}$$

The relationship can be simplified further by totaling the benefits of and costs from settling and not going to trial:

$$TBS = EBS + TCT_D + TBT_{PD},$$

yielding

$$gt_{PD} - gt_D < \frac{TBS}{TD}, \qquad\qquad (8b)$$

or

$$TD(gt_{PD} - gt_D) < TBS.$$

Conclusions When the Variables Are Mutually Independent

Though it need not be the situation, each of the variables given in equations (7), (8a), or (8b) are assumed to be mutually independent. In particular, it is assumed that the expected amount of damages does not affect the parties' expenditures on legal and other trial-related costs and the probability that the plaintiff will win. Given this assumption, the following conclusions about settlement can be drawn:

1. A settlement is certain when the defendant has higher or equal expectations of being declared guilty at trial than has the plaintiff ($gt_{PD} \leq gt_D$), unless the defendant's other benefit or plaintiff's cost from the defendant's not being found guilty are very important. These possibilities seem unlikely, because the higher the defendant's expectation of being found guilty, the greater is its costs of not settling; while the lower the plaintiff's expectation of winning, the less is its advantage from not settling.

2. When $gt_{PD} \leq gt_D$, the amounts of the expected damages and the fact that only the defendant might have to pay some of the plaintiff's legal expenses and the other benefits and costs are irrelevant.

3. The more a defendant believes it can demonstrate its innocence (gt_D lower), the less likely is a settlement, ceteris paribus. Conversely, because intentional violators have reason to expect to be found guilty at trial, they are more likely to settle, certeris paribus.

4. If the defendant has lower expectations of being found guilty than has the plaintiff ($gt_{PD} > gt_D$), a settlement is *more* likely to be reached, ceteris paribus, under the following conditions:
• the less are the expected total damages—thus trebling damages or shifting the plaintiff's legal costs to the defendant if the defendant loses de-

creases the probability of settlement because the plaintiff expects to gain more than the defendant expects to lose from going to trial.[18]

• the higher are the plaintiff's and the defendant's legal expenses,[19]

• the higher are the other benefits (e.g., ending of suit and obtaining information) the defendant and plaintiff obtain from settling,

• the less the parties benefit and the more they lose from having the defendant declared to be guilty or not guilty.

5. The greater the difference in perceptions about the plaintiff's winning, the greater the effect of the variables (e.g., a higher TD amount makes settlement less likely the more that gt_{PD} exceeds gt_D).

Conclusions When the Benefit and Cost of Settling Are Functions of Total Damages

Assumptions about the independence of the total benefit from settling (TBS) and the probability that the plaintiff will win at trial are now relaxed. TBS probably is positively related to total damages, particularly with respect to the legal cost portion. The defendant's benefit from removing a contingent liability from its financial statements and freeing its officers from the costs of discovery and concern also are likely to be positively related to total damages (TD). However, a substantial portion of TBS probably are fixed with respect to TD. In particular, a part of the legal fees is fixed, particularly for defendants with relatively small potential liability. The plaintiff's benefit from settling with defendants that have valuable information to trade may even be negatively related to that defendant's potential liability. Higher expenditures on discovery, attorneys, and experts also should be related positively to the probability of winning at trial. Therefore the relationship is unlikely to be completely linear.

Two simplifying assumptions seem reasonable to make. First, the benefit from settling is assumed to be partially linearly related to the total amount of damages. Second, the benefits and costs from settling other than from damages are assumed to cancel each other. The following functional relationships are assumed:

$$TBS_D = ds(TD) = ds_1 + ds_2 TD, \qquad \text{defendant's benefits from settling,}$$

$$TBS_{PD} = ps(TD) = ps_1 + ps_2 TD, \qquad \text{plaintiff's benefits from settling,}$$

$$gt_D = dg(LT_D) = dg_1 + dg_2 LT_D, \qquad \text{defendant's assessed probability that plaintiff will win as a function of defendant's legal and other trial expenses } (LT_D),$$

$$gt_{PD} = pg(LT_{PD}) = pg_1 + dg_2 LT_{PD},$$

plaintiff's assessed probability that it will win as a function of its legal and other trial expenses (LT_{PD}).

(The coefficients before TD and LT are functions, not constants.)

Equation (7) can be rewritten as follows, assuming that the parties' other expected costs and benefits of going to trial (TCT_D and TBT_{PD}) net out to zero:

$$(pg_1 - dg_1)TD + pg_2 LT_{PD} TD + dg_2 LT_D TD$$

$$< ds_1 + ps_1 + ds_2 TD + ps_2 TD. \tag{9}$$

TD can be factored out of the first two terms (pg_1 and dg_1) because they are constants. But the variables with subscripts 2 are positive but unknown functions of LT and TD. If it is assumed that they are simple linear functions of TD, this variable can be factored out to yield:

$$pg_1 - dg_1 + pg_2 LT_{PD} + dg_2 LT_D < \frac{ds_1 + ps_1}{TD} + ds_2 + ps_2. \tag{10}$$

Given these assumption, the conclusions drawn earlier (from equations 7, 8a, or 8b) are modified, ceteris partibus, as follows:

1. Even though the defendant believes more than the plaintiff that it would lose at trial ($pg_1 < dg_1$), it might spend more on its defence to change the outcome, although the plaintiff also has this opportunity. The result with respect to settlement depends on the parties' perception of the consequences of their spending (as shown by $pg_2 LT_{PD}$ and $dg_2 LT_D$), which is unlikely to be continuously linear.

2. Higher spending on legal and other trial related costs ($ds_2 + ps_2$) also increase the right-hand side of the equation. Unless one can specify the effectiveness of this spending for changing the expected outcome of the trial (pg_1 and dg_1), the effect of additional spending on the probability of settlement cannot be determined.

3. Defendants with lower expected total damages are more likely to settle, because as TD gets smaller, $(ds_1 + ps_1)/TD$ gets larger. However, this factor may be of small effect if the fixed legal costs are a relatively small proportion of total costs and other costs and benefits.

Conclusions When the Probability of the Plaintiff's Winning Is Very Small and Damages Are Very Large

The plaintiff would be willing to undertake an action that had a very low probability of success if the total damages that might be awarded are large enough, as shown in equation (4). The damages (TD) could be very great in such actions as class actions suits against a large industry, and/or with damages claimed over a long period, magnified by treble damages, and increased for individual defendants by the rule of joint and several liability. In such instances the plaintiff's self-assessed probability of winning against a particular defendant (gt_{PD}) could be very small, as long as the product ($gt_{PD} \cdot TD$) is greater than its net costs. In this event the defendant's self-assessed probability of the plaintiff's winning (gt_D) could be quite small and yet greater than gt_{PD}. Consequently, as shown by equations (7), (8a), or (8b), the defendant would certainly settle. (Equation 8b shows that the parties settle when $TD(gt_{PD} - gt_D) < TBS$.)

The Effect of the Joint and Several Liability Rule

Pursuant to the rule of joint and several liability, each defendant can be held responsible for the total liability (damages trebled plus plaintiff's legal costs) of all similarly charged defendants less the amount collected in settlements. Consequently defendants can be liable for considerably more than the damages from which they may have benefited. In a price-fixing action, each defendant faces damages equal to the total industrywide sales times the percentage overcharge summed over all years not barred by the statute of limitations, trebled, but less settlements with other defendants ($\sum DT - ST_O$). Thus the plaintiff can approach each defendant and threaten it with this damage possibility. The defendant then is faced with the game of estimating the amounts for which other defendants might settle. Some of these defendants are likely to settle for less than their proportionate share of the damages, for two principal reasons. First, guilty defendants often have information that is valuable to plaintiffs—hence they can sell this information for a lower settlement. Second, plaintiffs benefit from agreeing to lesser amounts than the claimed damages.[20] Therefore each nonsettling defendant's estimate of its possible damage liability would be greater than shown in equation (7). This is shown by the following modification of equation (8b), where the parties settle when the inequality is met:

$$TD_P gt_{PD} - TD_D gt_D < TBS. \tag{11}$$

When $TD_D > TD_{PD}$, the parties could settle even if $gt_{PD} > gt_D$.

The present value to the plaintiff of settling with the first defendant (when there are several defendants and joint and several liability) is given by the difference between the benefit from settling with all defendants less the benefit from settling with all but the first defendant (the negative of equation 6 summed over all defendants less the negative of equation 6 summed over all but the settling defendant). If the defendant has information that could help the plaintiff win its case against the other defendants, the plaintiff might be willing to pay the first defendant to settle. The same calculation is made for each succeeding defendant that offers or is asked to settle. As is discussed further in section 6.6, the amount of damages the plaintiff expects from each defendant (TD_{PD}) tends to increase as defendants settle, ceteris paribus.

Hence, with $TD_D > TD_{PD}$, the expected cost to a defendant of going to trial increase more than the benefit to the plaintiff from going to trial, which makes settlement more likely, ceteris paribus, (see equation 11). In addition, as discussed earlier, defendants with lesser market shares (as a proxy for TD_D) are more likely to settle even if they strongly believe that they would be found not guilty at trial, ceteris paribus, because their expected costs are proportionately greater than they would be were these companies liable only for damages calculated with respect to individual market shares. These conclusions are stronger where the parties are risk averse.

Thus the rule of joint and several liability tends to offset the negative effect of larger total damages, making pretrial settlements more likely.[21] As settlements are made, the damage amount that *could* be assessed against each remaining defendant decreases while the amount for which the plaintiff would be willing to settle increases, which decreases the probability of settlement (as shown by equation 6). But, as the defendants' and plaintiff's expected damage amounts get closer, the probability of settlement increases (as shown by equations 8a and 8b). Which effect dominates depends on the difference between the parties' assessments of the probability that the defendant will be found guilty.

The probability of defendants' settling also depends on the effect of information that is obtained from settlements with other defendants on the parties' assessments of the probability that the plaintiff will win at trial. Settlement will be more likely if the parties' assessments converge; if they do not get closer but gt increases for both, only the settlement amount increases.

In sum, joint and several liability affects both the plaintiff and defendants so as to make pretrial settlement more likely. As the damage amounts expected by the defendants and plaintiff converge, the case will tend to go to trial only if the defendant believes that it is considerably less likely to be found guilty than does the plaintiff and/or if the defendant has significantly large benefits from being declared not guilty at trial or the plaintiff has significantly large benefits from the defendant's being declared guilty, ceteris paribus.

The Effect of Contribution, Claim Reduction, and Individual Responsibility Rules

Contribution   A rule of contribution, if enacted by the Congress, could give defendants found guilty of antitrust violations the legal right to sue coconspirators for contribution of their proportionate share to the damages assessed. A defendant that settled would be subject to a claim of contribution unless the plaintiff's release or covenant not to sue also released the other defendants from liability for the settling defendant's share of the damages. Bills to this effect introduced in the ninety-seventh Congress (first session, 1981) limited the contribution provisions to price-fixing actions and provided for measurement of damages according to the defendants' sales or purchases of goods and services.[22]

If the contribution rule of pretrial settlement agreement did not limit the liability of settling defendants to the amount of their settlement, they clearly would have no incentive to settle. Were the case to go to trial, they would not be present to defend themselves, although they would be subject to a claim by the defendants that lost. If the defendants won, those who settled would not be able to get their funds back. Furthermore they could reduce their legal costs related to contribution claims by not settling and joining with the other defendants in a trial against the plaintiffs.[23]

Claim Reduction (Carve Out)   Under this rule the liability of the class of defendants would be reduced by the amount assessed to the firms that settled. The rule would allow the plaintiff to sue or settle with some or all defendants for the total of damages allegedly inflicted by all defendants. If contribution was also allowed, the defendants that pay the judgment could sue for contribution only those that were not part of the suit or settlements.[24] This rule continues joint and several liability, with the exception that the plaintiff cannot shift damages from the firms with which it settles to other firms. This rule thus reduces the effect of collusion (tacit or explicit) between some defendants and the plaintiff. There still would be an advantage for defendants to settle rather than go to trial and for plaintiffs to bargain for information. However, the incentives would be less than those under the rule of joint and several liability.

Individual Responsibility   Each defendants' liability could be limited to the amount of damages only if imposed on the plaintiffs. This rule would eliminate the rule of joint and several liability. The probability of settlement rather than trial would be less because each defendant's potential liability would be limited to the amount of damages that the plaintiff could show it imposed. (The defendants' and the plaintiff's assessment of the damage amounts would tend to be the same.)

A change from the joint and several liability rule would increase somewhat the plaintiff's cost of settling. With joint and several liability, plaintiffs can be less concerned about settling for too little with some defendants because they can charge the remaining defendants with total industry damages less the settlement amounts. Therefore a contribution, claim reduction, or individual responsibility rule would require them to expend resources to estimate more closely the damages for which each defendant could be liable.

The Effect of Risk Aversion

A risk-averse defendant would prefer a smaller variance of expected damages and other costs, ceteris paribus.[25] For defendants, joint and several liability (compared to contribution, claim reduction, and individual responsibility) increases the variance of outcomes earlier in the action. Hence risk-averse defendants would be more willing to settle, the more so the lower are their market shares, ceteris paribus. Risk-averse plaintiffs also would be more willing to settle. These conclusions also hold for claim reduction and individual responsibility, because, as Polinsky and Shavell (1981, 459) point out, "settlement eliminates the uncertainty inherent in litigation." But there is no uncertainty for contribution, and hence no risk-reduction incentive to settle.

Nonclass and Class Plaintiffs

Nonclass plaintiffs get the entire amount of the damages specified in equation (4). A portion of their legal fees is paid by the defendants if the case goes to trial and the plaintiff wins. The plaintiff's legal expenses reduce the amounts received from the defendants, as agreed between the plaintiff and its attorneys.

However, the class plaintiffs actually are the lawyers. Their rewards equal the legal fees they ask for and are awarded by the court. Thus the benefit to class action plaintiffs that motivate the action are less than the benefit motivating nonclass plaintiffs, ceteris paribus. But the damages that can be awarded generally are greater in a class action suit because the joint and several liability rule does not require proof of damage by specified defendants against individual plaintiffs. Consequently the rewards expected by class action attorneys need not be less than those that a nonclass plaintiff would expect.

Class actions often allow plaintiffs to charge large numbers of defendants with antitrust violations, thereby increasing the amount of damages sought. As noted earlier, a high amount of damages can make an antitrust suit economically desirable for plaintiffs with a small probability of winning against individual defendants. As a consequence the probability of settlement is higher even though both plaintiffs and defendants assume a relatively low probability that the plaintiff will win (gt), because at low levels of gt it is likely that the estimates will be close. Indeed, settlement would be certain if the defendant estimated a higher probability for gt, unless there were offsetting factors as described in equation (7).

Class action attorneys also have incentives to settle rather than go to trial because they must incur their legal and other expenses for certain while getting only an expectation of a fraction of the damages or a multiple of their costs as compensation. Furthermore, should a large proportion of the defendants settle, the plaintiff attorneys can expect only a portion of the remaining potential damages. They can receive only a fraction of the amounts obtained (described by subequations 4.2 through 4.7) or a lodestar-determined amount times a multiple should they win, but they must bear the cost of the action should they lose. Thus settling is likely to be preferable to bringing the remaining defendants to trial.

The model now is applied to the various types of defendants under different assumptions about joint and several liability, contribution, claim reduction, individual responsibility, and risk aversion.

The Intentional Violator

The intentional violator is more likely to settle than the other types of defendants, for several reasons: First, the intentional violator knows it has violated the law; hence its expectation about being found guilty at trial and appeal probably is higher than the probability assessment of the other defendants. (If it is higher than the plaintiff's expectation, it certainly will settle.) Furthermore, if it was indicted (or worse, convicted) as a result of a

DOJ antitrust action, its reputation has already been damaged, and it has less to gain from litigation. This is particularly so because it expects to be found guilty, which reduces the expected value of $(1 - gt)BT$. Also it gains from settling with all possible plaintiffs. Therefore the intentional violator would favor an inclusive class action plaintiff.

Second, the intentional violator has information about the price fixing or other conspiracy to offer the plaintiff. Hence the benefits to the plaintiff (BS) are greater. This information is particularly beneficial to the class action plaintiff, since it rarely has detailed knowledged of industry relationships.[26] This might be the most important determinant of settling early.

Third, the intentional violator is likely to have a relatively large market share (which makes price fixing both practical and profitable). Hence its future legal expenses should be relatively greater.

The rule of joint and several liability does not greatly affect settlement by the intentional violator, because, with its expectation of being found guilty equal to or greater than the plaintiff's expectation, the amount of expected damages is irrelevant. Similarly whether or not its managers are risk averse is irrelevant. However, contribution would act to dissuade the intentional violator from settling.

The Unintentional Violator
It is not clear whether the unintentional violator would consider itself more likely to be found guilty than would the plaintiff, because it had no reason to plan for being charged with an antitrust violation. It has no information to sell to the plaintiff, which reduces the mutual benefits of a settlement. Protection of its reputation and the foreclosure of additional lawsuits increase the benefits from being found not guilty, which reduce its incentive to settle.

However, in considering the costs of further legal action and the expectation that its action will appear to be an antitrust violation, the unintentional violator may find settling worthwhile. Joint and several liability plays a role in this decision, depending on its potential damages. If the unintentional violator has a small market share, joint and several liability increases its potential damages should it lose at trial more than if it has a large market share. Therefore the smaller its market share, the more likely it is to settle. As is the case for defendants generally, risk aversion make settlement more likely and contribution (and, to a lesser extent, the other alternative rules) makes settlement less likely.

The Innocent Bystander

The innocent bystander has no information to sell to the plaintiffs and believes itself to be innocent of violating the antitrust laws, which reduces the benefits from settling. But it faces legal costs and damages in cash and to its reputation and ability to use the capital markets, which increase the benefits from settling. As discussed earlier, the rule of joint and several liability increases the innocent bystander's costs of not settling, particularly when it has a relatively small market share. The contribution, claim reduction, and individual responsibility liability rules would reduce the incentives for the innocent bystander to settle.

6.6 Determinants of the Settlement Amount

Determinants in General

Because the probability of settlement is very high, the determinants of the settlement amounts is of particular importance. Equations (5) and (6) specify the variables that determine the amounts for which defendants and plaintiffs would be willing to settle. The settlement amount would be less than the defendant's cost of not settling and more than the plaintiff's benefit from not settling with that defendant.

Most of the determinants are discussed in the preceding sections; the greater the probability of settling, the greater the amount for which the defendant would be willing to settle and the lesser the amount that would satisfy the plaintiff. Thus settlement amounts are likely to be higher, ceteris paribus, for:

1. unintentional violators and innocent bystanders, because they have no information about antitrust violations in the industry to sell to the plaintiffs,

2. guilty defendants unless they can trade information that could be used to enable the plaintiff to get even larger settlements or damages from other defendants,

3. defendants with more to lose from continuing litigation, such as those that would find capital market transactions more expensive because they must report contingent liabilities and those with relatively small market shares for which fixed legal expenses would be relatively high,

4. class action plaintiffs, because they can claim higher amounts of damages,

5. the applications of the joint and several liability rule, because the amounts of damages for which a defendant could be liable are greater,

6. defendants with relatively small market shares under the joint and several liability rule,

7. the application of the claim reduction and individual responsibility rules as compared with the contribution rule, because the defendants' possible damages would be higher under the latter; indeed, with full contribution, settlements would be unlikely to occur.

The settlement procedure that plaintiffs would be likely to follow under the joint and several liability rule can illustrate some bargaining considerations. For each defendant, the plaintiff estimates the effect of settling on the amounts that could be collected from the other defendants. In making the estimate, the plaintiff would consider that not having some guilty defendants in court would decrease the probability that it would win the case. The plaintiff also would consider the effect of early settlement agreements on bargaining with other defendants, because they are likely to realize that there is a considerable difference between the benefits to the plaintiff from settling and the cost to them of not settling. Additional factors, such as the effect on future defendants and (for nonclass plaintiffs) on competitors of not settling an action, also would be considered.

The defendant similarly would consider the effect of settling on actions taken by future plaintiffs. Defendants contemplating capital market financing would include the costs of having to report a large contingent liability on their balance sheets. Company defendants and plaintiffs also would count as costs demands by the other side for discovery and depositions. Thus without knowledge of these often important costs and benefits, the settlement amount cannot be determined from publicly available data.

Finally, the amount for which the defendant would be willing to settle also depends importantly on the expected costs and benefits from appeals, which is given by subequations (3.5), (3.6), and (3.7).

Data on Settlements

The Corregated Container Antitrust Litigation, one of the few cases where the amounts and order of settlements have been made public, provides some inconsistent evidence.[27] As shown in table 6.1, the first company to settle was St. Regis Paper Co. with 4.0 percent of the market for $0.5 million a point (percent of market sales). The firm was not indicted by the grand jury in the previous DOJ action. The second company to settle was International Paper, a felony-indicted company with 8.3 percent of the market, for $1 million a point. The next three companies to settle were

Table 6.1 Corrugated container litigation

Company	Market share	Settlement date	Settlement amount ($ million)	Amount per market share point ($ million)
Felony indictees				
International Paper	8.3	8/24/78	8.3	1.0
Champion	5.36	12/18/78	24.12	4.5
Weyerhaeuser	7.83	1/06/79	39.15	5.0
Owens-Illinois	5.45	1/12/79	32.70	6.0
Olinkraft	1.22	1/12/79	7.35	6.0
Continental Group	4.22	1/16/79	27.43	6.5
Misdemeanor indictees				
Boise Cascade	2.82	12/18/78	9.89	3.5
Container Corp.	8.56	1/06/79	34.24	4.0
Inland Container	7.29	1/18/79	34.63	4.75
Stone Container	3.05	1/18/79	14.49	4.75
St. Joe Paper Co.	2.62	1/18/79	12.47	4.75
Unindicted companies				
St. Regis Paper Co.	3.97	7/21/78	1.98	.5
Union Camp	3.7	12/13/78	7.40	2.0
Diamond International	.5	12/14/78	1.00	2.0
Dura Container	.37	12/14/78	.75	2.0
Chesapeake Corp.	1.26	12/18/78	3.02	2.4
Longview Fibre	2.58	12/18/78	6.45	2.5
Willamette Industries	4.18	12/18/78	11.29	2.7
Menasha Corp.	1.67	12/18/78	4.59	2.75
MacMillan-Bloedel	2.11	12/18/78	8.44	4.0
U.S. Corrugated	.76	1/25/79	3.07	4.0
Green Bay Packaging	1.71	1/25/79	5.56	3.25

Source: Civiletti (1981–82, 330).

unindicted, with market shares ranging from 0.5 percent to 3.7 percent; they settled for $2 million per point each. They were followed a few days later by five indicted companies and one company that was felony indicted. The unindicted companies settled for from $2.0 million to $4.0 million a point and the indicted company (Champion) for $4.5 million a point. The balance of the settlements show the felony-indicted companies settling for $6.0 million a point, the misdemeanor indictees for from $4.0 to $4.75 million a point, and the remaining unindicted companies for $3.25 and $4.0 million a point. Mead, which was not indicted and had been found innocent in a prior criminal trial, did not settle. It was found guilty in the civil trial and eventually settled for $45 million, or $18 per point (it had a 2.5 percent market share).

To gain some further insights, the settlement amounts and the amounts per point were regressed on the following variables:

1. Market share, in percentage points.

2. Net income in the year of the settlement, in millions of dollars.

3. Stock market return in the year of the settlement as an alternative to net income, in percentages.

4. Order of settlement, coded 1 through 8.

5. Felony indictee (six companies), coded 1 or 0 (if not a felony indictee).

6. Misdemeaner indictee (five companies), coded 1 or 0 (if not a misdemeaner indictee).

7. Intercept.

The regressions were computed for the 16 or 14 companies for which the settlement data were published and for which net income or stock market return data could be found.[28]

Table 6.2 presents the regression coefficients and the probabilities (derived from the absolute t-statistics) that only the settling company's market share and the order of settlement are significant determinants of the amount for which it settled. Interestingly, whether or not it was criminally indicted is not significant. However, the settlement per point regressions indicate that felony indictees tended to settle for about $2 million more per point, a result that may be due to the correlation of 0.38 between market share and felony indictment (significant at the 0.13 level). It also should be noted that the regressions overpredict the settlement amount (and per point) of International Paper, a felony indictee and the second company to settle, by about $2.4 million. Thus, if criminal or misdemeanor indictments are indicators of intentional violations, the Corregated Container Anti-

Table 6.2   Variables associated with settlements in the corrugated container antitrust litigation, partial regression coefficients, and probabilities that absolute coefficients are equal to zero

	Dependent variable: settlement (millions $)			
	Amount		Amount per point	
Market share (percent)	3.52	4.20	−0.10	−0.04
	(0.01)	(<0.01)	(0.48)	(0.66)
Accounting net income (millions)	0.001		0.002	
	(0.97)		(0.66)	
Stock market return on shares		21.02		3.03
		(0.12)		(0.04)
Order of settlement	3.10	3.49	0.53	0.57
	(0.04)	(0.01	(0.01)	(<0.01)
Felony indictee	2.11	−2.09	2.20	1.85
	(0.77)	(0.75)	(0.03)	(0.02)
Misdemeaner indictee	−2.80	−5.97	.61	0.58
	(0.70)	(0.42)	(0.52)	(0.45)
Intercept	−13.17	−36.18	0.97	−2.64
	(0.07)	(0.03)	(0.28)	(0.09)
R^2 (adjusted)	0.68	0.76	0.72	0.87
Number of observations	16	14	16	16
Mean of dependent variable	16.66	16.72	3.85	3.80

trust Litigation indicates that the damages actually paid need not be nearly as great as the amount of benefits from price fixing, on the assumption that the benefits really were attained.

6.7 Determinants of Deterrence of Antitrust Violations

The Intentional Violator's Decision to Break the Law
Equations (1) and (3) specify the determinants of the intentional violator's breaking the antitrust laws (assuming owner's wealth maximization and owners' and managers' risk neutrality). The higher the expected benefits and the lower the expected costs, the more likely the law will be broken. A summary of the expected costs can be seen in equation (5), which gives the cost to a defendant from not settling. This number, stated in present value terms and multiplied by the probability of discovery, is the maximum amount that the intentional violator expects to pay for violating the law. The actual amount depends on the settlement that would satisfy the plaintiff, as specified by equation (6).

It is useful to emphasize the following determinants of the benefits and costs:

1. The greater the elasticity of demand, the less are the expected benefits from price fixing and the higher the costs of maintaining the cartel.

2. The probability that the collusion will be discovered is a positive function of potential plaintiffs' ability to discover and prove violations and their expected benefits from settlements or trial (see equation 4). This is an important reason for the Supreme Court's having decided that only direct purchasers have standing to sue for damages in antitrust cases; they are in the best position to discover violations and stand to obtain greater benefits from initiating cases if the recoveries do not have to be shared with indirect purchasers.[29] However, where private plaintiffs piggyback on a DOJ antitrust action, the expected private benefit from a threatened or completed lawsuit specified in equation (4) is not a determinant of discovery.[30] Rather, the expected benefit is the principal determinant of the amount demanded in settlement.

3. The probability of settlement is a function of the expected damages and legal costs should the issue be decided at trial. As is discussed earlier, joint and several liability and class action suits importantly affect this probability assessment.

4. The expectation of less than certain discovery ($d < 1$) and finding of guilt at trial ($gt < 1$) and on appeal ($ga < 1$) lowers the expected cost to the intentional violator.

5. Receipt of the benefits from price fixing in advance of the costs of defending a lawsuit and paying damages to plaintiffs is likely to reduce the cost of violating the law, particularly when inflation is expected.

Trebling is said to offset the less than certain probabilities of discovery and determination of guilt, the loss of interest, and perhaps the purchasing power value of damages inflicted on others. But it can be shown[31] that a long enough delay between the benefits earned from a violation and the eventual payment of damages to a victorious plaintiff, a high enough inflation rate, and a zero or inadequate interest rate on the award can cause even trebling to fail to deter some violations.[32]

Differences between the Benefits from and Damages Assessed for Antitrust Violations

The preceding analysis assumes that the benefit from antitrust violations (before trebling) is the same as the amount potentially assessed against the violator as damage done to the plaintiffs. However, these amounts are likely to be differ substantially; the benefit can be both higher and lower than the damage amount, with the lower amount predominating.

The damages claimed by plaintiffs can be lower than the violator's benefit for two reasons. First, not all damaged plaintiffs may sue the violator. Some victims may find the costs of bringing suit less than the expected benefits. Second, some direct purchasers may decide not to sue because they benefit more from continuing normal relationships with the violator. This could occur if the direct purchasers share in the violator's price-fixing gains. However, the empirical evidence does not support this possibility.[33]

The claimed damage might be higher than the benefit because of the way damages are measured in antitrust legal actions.[34] In a price-fixing case, the usual method is to multiply the difference between the fixed price and the precollusion price by the defendants' sales during the violation period. The difference in price is determined from reports of conversations or documents that purport to show an intention to raise prices by a given amount, from invoices or price lists showing prices before and after the conspiracy was shown to have been entered into, and/or from indexes of prices before and after the conspiracy. However, many factors are responsible for changes in prices over time. These include changes in the relative prices of labor, materials, and other direct inputs, technology, overhead costs, general price levels, quality and other attributes of the product, distribution costs, and accounting procedures.[35] In dealer termination and predatory-pricing cases the claim often is made that the dealer or firm that was forced out of business would have increased its profits at a constant or even increasing rate were it not for the illegal activity of the defendant. Again, many factors affect an enterprise's net profits, not the least of which is accounting conventions that do not include the recording of opportunity costs.

The reason for believing that the damages in price-fixing cases are more likely to be over- rather than understated is that market pressures and the incentives for producers and consumers to substitute less expensive goods for price-fixed goods tend to erode the initial increase due to a price-fixing conspiracy. It is very difficult for dozens of companies to maintain a conspiracy for many years, particularly when they can compete in ways that cannot be readily policed; the very greed that caused them to conspire is likely to cause them to undercut each other. The gain to the price fixer is also reduced by the costs of maintaining the cartel. In other cases the loss to the dealer and competitor are mitigated by the alternative use to which they could (and most likely did) put their resources. In addition the economic gain to a price fixer and losses to a terminated dealer or competitor driven out of the market by predatory pricing tend to be overstated by accounting conventions, which (among other things) do not record opportunity costs and values and do not completely allocate to products such real price-reducing competitive devices as more favorable credit and delivery allowances and price reductions on simultaneously purchased noncartelized goods. Finally, efficiency benefits that do not result in damage to consumers nevertheless may be counted as damages.

Thus there is reason to believe that much of the benefit from delayed payment of damages and less than unitary probabilities of discovery and having to settle or being found guilty (liable for damages) are mitigated by an overstatement of damages. It also should be noted that companies that intentionally violate the law can pay less in damages than those that are not as guilty, as indicated by the analysis of settlements in the Corregated Container Antitrust Litigation presented in the previous section and by the expectation that the intentional violator can trade information for a lower settlement amount.

Class Action Plaintiffs
Class actions tend to increase the damages to which the intentional violator might be liable relative to the total estimated amount of damages inflicted on victims (some of whom might not find it worthwhile to sue absent a class action). Therefore violation of the law would be deterred.

Allowing class action attorneys to be compensated from the proceeds of settlements and judgments (the American antitrust rule) rather than solely by the class representatives (the "pure" American rule) is very important for the viability of suits where the expected returns to individuals otherwise would exceed their expected costs (nonrecoverable and nonviable cases). Dewees, Prichard, and Trebilcock (1981) show analytically that class action suits would be unlikely to be brought under the pure American rule, a result that would reduce deterrence.

However, class action plaintiffs' lawyers tend not to have information about the market and its workings. Hence the intentional violator has little to fear from an increased probability of discovery. The intentional violator also is in a good position to trade information about the workings of the cartel that can be used by the plaintiffs to build a case against the balance of the industry. These factors reduce the expected cost of settlement faced by the intentional violator. It is not clear therefore whether class actions tend to increase or decrease deterrence.

Joint and Several Liability, Contribution, Claim Reduction, and Individual Responsibility

The rule of joint and several liability affects deterrence primarily by (1) increasing the possible cost to some conspirators from violating the antitrust laws and (2) increasing the probability that the cost will be incurred. As shown in section 6.5, conspirators with relatively smaller expected gross benefit would be subject to relatively greater increases in potential damage assessments. This increases the damage amounts and makes it less likely that the total expected benefit would exceed the total cost. Therefore, unless the conspiracy could find ways to compensate smaller conspirators for the relatively higher risk they face (because they may be liable for more than their share of the total damages—an increase in EB in equation 1), these smaller conspirators would find joining the conspiracy to be unprofitable. But, if the larger conspirators promised the smaller ones additional shares of the benefits from the conspiracy, the result would be a reduction in the benefits that the larger conspirators could expect. Consequently, with total costs increased because the smaller conspirators' costs are higher, but with no increase in total benefits, some conspiracies would be deterred.

The probability that costs would be incurred also would increase, because smaller conspirators would have a greater incentive to inform on the conspiracy should they believe that it will be discovered in any event. Because the smaller conspirators face relatively high costs under the rule of joint and several liability, they can benefit most by purchasing smaller settlements or exemption from prosecution with information about the conspiracy. Furthermore the plaintiff would prefer to settle with a smaller than a larger conspirator; the smaller conspirator should be able to provide the plaintiff with about the same amount of information, while the larger conspirator would be more likely to have the resources to pay the more of the damages ascribed to the conspiracy net of settlements.

But the large conspirators should realize the costs, incentives, and opportunities faced by their smaller brethren. Given the additional costs that smaller conspirators bring and the increase in the probability of discovery and prosecution, it is logical to conclude that conspiracies with smaller conspirators rarely would be profitable ex ante. As smaller conspirators are excluded, some of the remaining companies become the smaller conspirators, and they would be excluded.

If one follows the logic to its end, the conclusion must be that all conspiracies to violate the antitrust laws would be deterred by the rule of joint and several liability except those that are expected to be very profitable. Those conspiracies that are formed should include only a relatively few, roughly equal (in terms of benefits) conspirators. If this reasoning is correct, the explanation for large numbers of firms, including small companies, being charged with price fixing is evidence of nonconspirators' being charged with violations to which they were not parties.

Easterbrook, Landes, and Posner (1980, 344) use similar reasoning to show rigorously that "*any* rule of apportioning damages produces adequate deterrence if the aggregate damages are properly selected." They appear concerned to show that the joint and several liability rule does not allow a firm to profit from a conspiracy, where the expected recoveries and costs inflicted on all intentional violators exceed the total benefits expected by them, by the stratagem of settling early for a fraction of its share of the damages. This result follows only because they assume that all conspirators have perfect (or at least unbiased, if this term were meaningful for such singular events as antitrust conspiracies) foresight as to these amounts and the probabilities that one or more of them will settle for lesser amounts. This assumption leads to the conclusion that the organizing firm cannot cheat its coconspirators because the others will expect it to cheat. As a consequence "whichever firm thinks that it will bear the lion's share of the liability under a no contribution rule will be deterred from participating in the unlawful action; once he drops out, some other firm will face a heavy expected liability, causing him to drop out too; and the process will continue until no firm is left in the ring" (p. 345). Risk averseness further increases deterrence because the range of possible damages is greater under the rule of joint and several liability. Hence they favor continuing the rule, particularly since it encourages settlements.[36]

Polinsky and Shavell (1981) present a similar analysis, except that they emphasize the imposition of costs on corporate decision makers. Contribution may be preferable to joint and several liability, they state, because all conspirators would be liable for damages, and "the certainty of liability will be more of a deterrent to decisionmakers than the magnitude of that liability" (p. 454). Furthermore, though the joint and several liability rule increases deterrence by magnifying liability and increasing uncertainty, "it has socially undesirable consequences ... [because] uncertainty creates disutility for risk averse individuals" (p. 462). They find contribution or claim reduction to be preferrable to joint and several liability for deterrence, but not for settlement—which leads them to conclude: "we recommend the use of claim reduction over contribution or no contribution, and as between the latter two rules, more tentatively, contribution" (pp. 463–464).

Contribution, however, would be likely to reduce deterrence. Under a contribution rule potential coconspirators would not have to be as concerned about one of their members' selling out for a lower settlement. Consequently more firms could be included in a conspiracy. As was noted in section 6.5, contribution also would considerably reduce incentives to settle, which would reduce the ex ante rewards to plaintiffs from discovering and prosecuting antitrust violators. Hence deterrence would be diminished.

Claim reduction and individual responsibility, though, do not have the negative effects of contribution, except as plaintiffs' ex ante rewards are reduced. Overdeterrence also would be reduced, which is a benefit to consumers. When under claim reduction the settling defendants' share of the potential damages are removed from the total that can be obtained from the remaining defendants, the plaintiff would have less incentive to allow an important intentional violator that has information to trade to get off cheaply. Under individual responsibility each defendant is liable only for the damage it inflicted. With the necessity of establishing the amounts of such damages, plaintiffs would have less incentive to bring suit against unintentional violators and innocent bystanders. Thus both rules tend to increase deterrence and decrease overdeterrence. However, if the potential cost to intentional violators still was insufficient to deter intentional violations, consideration should be given to increasing the penalties and/or probability of discovery.

Unintentional Violators and Innocent Bystanders
Deterrence is relevant to the unintentional violator because more stringent antitrust penalties tend to deter it from undertaking efficiency benefits. Higher penalties, and hence higher expected costs, also encourage the unintentional violator to spend more on protection from lawsuits. The result is a tendency toward forgoing proefficiency action that might be viewed as antitrust violations.

Innocent bystanders' decisions are not affected by deterrence. Unfortunately, it often is relatively inexpensive for plaintiffs to include these firms among the defendants, or the plaintiffs may misidentify these firms as intentional violators. Class action suits, in particular, are likely to sweep innocent bystanders into the action as defendants because the plaintiffs do not have to demonstrate that a particular plaintiff was damaged by a particular defendant. The higher and more likely settlements made possible under the rule of joint and several damages increases the rewards to plaintiffs from charging innocent bystanders and unintentional violators with antitrust violations, even when the probability of their winning is small.

Though the unintentional violators and innocent bystanders may be able to demonstrate their innocence in a trial, they face the prospect of legal and other costs and the possibility that they will be adjudged liable for damages (as detailed in equation 3). Under the rule of joint and several liability, the damages can be considerable. The consequence is that firms' owners and consumers will pay the costs of these firms' being charged with antitrust violations.

Conclusions on the Benefits and Costs of Deterrence

Intentional violators of the antitrust laws are likely to benefit considerably from not having to pay inflation-adjusted interest on damages from the time the damages were inflicted on the plaintiffs. For deterrence to be effective, the costs considered by a potential violator should reflect, as closely as feasible, the damages inflicted on its victims and the probability that these costs will have to be paid.

The benefits to the perpetrators from antitrust conspiracies, though, would appear to be overstated (or the damages inflicted on victims overstated), particularly for long-term conspiracies. This conclusion follows from the overestimate of damages for which antitrust law violators are potentially liable and from the expectation that the cost of collusion (including cheating) is likely to be considerable. Short-term conspiracies (e.g., bid rigging), though, are not as subject to this overstatement or to as great a collusion cost. The possibility that the damage to some plaintiffs might be too small to make lawsuits economically worthwhile increases the benefit to potential intentional violators, a benefit that is reduced considerably by the prospect of class action suits.

Intentional violators face lower costs when companies that are not intentional violators are included as defendants by the plaintiff. The intentional violators have information about the violations that can be "sold" to the plaintiff for a lower settlement. This possibility is greatest for class action suits because the plaintiff usually does not have knowledge of the conspiracy from its own experience. This possibility reduces deterrence. However, as noted, class actions tend to increase deterrence by raising the damages beyond those that could be charged by nonclass plaintiffs. At the same time the damages estimated in such cases are likely to be overstated.

The rule of joint and several liability increases deterrence by increasing the damages to which conspirators might be subject and by increasing the incentives for conspirators to settle in exchange for information about the conspiracy. But, considered ex ante, the rule should have the effect of making most conspiracies not worthwhile. Those that are formed should exclude all but a few conspirators who benefit roughly equally. A contribution rule would have the reverse effect; consequently it would appear to be undesirable. Claim reduction and individual responsibility, though, offer the advantage of reducing overdeterrence while not affecting greatly the deterrent effect of potential penalties (considering that intentional violators have greater opportunities than others of settling for smaller amounts).

6.8 Consumer Welfare

Consumer Welfare in General

In considering the effect of antitrust laws and legal rules on consumer welfare, only the real resource cost of antitrust violations on consumers and the economy should be included. The damages inflicted on victims that do not cause them to adopt less efficient alternatives do not represent resource cost. Similarly settlements and judgments are transfers between parties that do not affect the misuse of resources except as they alter behavior. Of course the transfer of resources among persons is very important to them and is a major reason for the enactment and enforcement of the antitrust laws. These transfers are considered in section 6.9 under "considerations of fairness."

The amount of consumer welfare (CW) that might be achieved from deterrence may be estimated from the following equations:

$$CW = \tag{12}$$

$$\int_{t=0,z} \{p_I(ED_{It} + CLC_{It} - EB_{It}), \quad \text{cost of intentional violations,} \tag{12.1}$$

$$- p_U(TLC_{Ut}) - (EBF_{Ut} + CP_{Ut}), \quad \text{cost of mischarging unintentional violators,} \tag{12.2}$$

$$- p_B(TLC_{Bt}), \quad \text{cost of mischarging innocent bystanders,} \tag{12.3}$$

$$- p_P(TLC_P) - p_T(TPC)\}e^{-rt}\, dt, \quad \text{plaintiffs' and public costs,} \tag{12.4}$$

where

t = time,

r = risk-adjusted aftertax nominal discount rate,

p = the probabilities that a company will be charged with an antitrust violation (I = intentional violators, U = unintentional violators, and B = innocent bystanders), that a plaintiff will bring will investigate and pursue the three types of companies ($= P$), or that an antitrust action will be brought to trial,

ED = efficiency damages inflicted by the intentional violators,

CLC = collusion and legal costs incurred by the intentional violators,

EB = efficiency benefits associated with the violation,

EBF = efficiency benefits that the unintentional violators forgo for fear of being charged with antitrust violations, which is a function of the probability that they will be charged with violations, such that the higher the probability, the higher is the cost,

CP = cost of protection against or of avoiding lawsuits, by the unintentional violators, which is a function of the probability that they will be charged with violating the law,

TLC = total legal costs of the unintentional violators, innocent bystanders, or plaintiffs,

TPC = total public costs of Department of Justice investigation and of trial.

Consumer welfare is increased when intentional violators are deterred by legal rules and penalties that increase the expected cost to defendants (e.g., trebled damages, losing defendants' paying plaintiff's legal expenses, joint and several liability, and class action suits that increase damage claims by lowering the cost of suits by people who have been damaged) and increase the probability that defendants will lose at trial (as shown in subequation 12.1). The benefit is the savings of inefficiently allocated resources (ED) and the resources that would have been used by the violators to protect and defend their violations (CLC). But this benefit is reduced by the pro-efficiency benefit (EB) the deterred violator forgoes.

The legal rules and penalties also impose costs on consumers, producers, and the economy. The greater the damages and costs imposed and the greater the probability that a defendant will lose at trial, the greater is the probability that plaintiffs will pursue defendants. Some plaintiffs may not be able to distinguish between defendants that are intentional violators, unintentional violators, or innocent bystanders. Other plaintiffs may not care in which category a potential defendant belongs—their only consideration is the expected net benefit from filing a case against the defendant (as shown by equation 4). In either event the same legal rules and penalties that increase deterrence against intentional violators also increase the probabilities that plaintiffs will bring suit (p_P) and that unintentional violators and innocent bystanders will be named as defendants (p_U and p_B). Thus consumer welfare is reduced because the unintentional violators may forgo efficiency benefits (EBF) and incur costs (CP) to protect themselves from being charged with antitrust violations.[37] The economy suffers from the use of resources for legal actions by the unintentional violators, the innocent bystanders, and the public legal justice system (TLC and TPC).

Joint and Several Liability
The higher and more likely settlements engendered by the rule of joint and several damages lowers the numbers of cases that go to trial, which reduces the burden on the courts. This appears to be the principal reason that Easterbrook, Landes, and Posner (1980) recommend against changing the rule. However, the higher and more likely settlements also encourage plaintiffs to include innocent bystanders among the defendants, which reduces consumer welfare (as specified in subequations 12.1 and 12.2). Considering that less than 20 percent of antitrust actions brought go to trial, it would appear that the consumer welfare cost imposed on innocent parties is greater than the savings in the resources used for trials that are avoided by a higher rate of settlements.

Class Action Suits
Class actions make suits possible that would not otherwise be brought. They also involve the courts as protectors of the rights of the class. Hence class actions tend to increase public costs. The careful studies of class and nonclass suits by DuVal (1976; 1979) and by Bernstein (1978) provide strong evidence that class actions are considerably more burdensome in terms of court time and effort. Bernstein (1978, 365), though, also takes into account the per person recoveries in these cases and concludes that "the class action with 'individually non-recoverable' claims has, at least in the two judicial districts studied, made a net contribution to judicial efficiency despite its effect of increasing case loads"

The court, however, must necessarily monitor and approve the settlement agreements agreed to and fees charged by plaintiffs' attorneys in class actions because the individual plaintiffs cannot meaningfully represent themselves. These costs, however, need not be borne by the public. There seems to be no reason (that a nonlegally trained economist can see) why the court cannot hire expert accountants and economists to audit the agreements, fees, and expense reimbursements submitted, with the costs of the audit paid by the class that, presumably, is the beneficiary thereof.

Conclusions

Increasing the expected cost of antitrust violations does not necessarily increase consumer welfare. In considering the beneficial effect of higher expected damages and more stringent enforcement of laws on deterring resource misuse, policymakers should also include the detrimental effect of greater resources spent on legal and other costs, efficiency benefits lost, and the costs of protection against unjustified lawsuits. Joint and several liability may, on balance, decrease consumer welfare. Class action suits tend to increase consumer welfare; though they impose larger burdens on the courts, the cost could be shifted to the class.

6.9 Considerations of Fairness

Fairness in General

Although economists profess unease in analyzing fairness or equity, it is clear that these considerations play a large role in public policy toward possible antitrust law violators. A legal system is fair, I suggest, if it works against resources' being transferred involuntarily or, as a result of monopoly or monopsony pricing, from one person to another. Use of the legal system to effect involuntary transfers from people who did not violate the law would be unfair.

Exacting damages through the legal system that exceed the amounts necessary to enforce the law also would be unfair, for two reasons. First, it is almost (perhaps entirely) impossible to avoid charging innocent people with legal violations. The higher the penalty, the greater is the unfairness to those innocents. Second, there are no economic crimes so heinous that any punishment would be justified as a means of deterrence or retribution. Antitrust violations clearly are in the category of economic crimes.[38] Hence the damages inflicted should be equated, on the margin, with the benefits to society of deterrence.

An unfairness (*UF*) equation may be specified as follows:

$$UF = \tag{13}$$

$$\int_{t=0,z} \{p_I(DL_{It} + DA_{It} - DO_{It}), \quad \text{net damages inflicted by intentional violators,} \tag{13.1}$$

$$- p_U(DL_{Ut}) - p_B(DL_{IB}), \quad \text{cost of mischarging unintentional violators and innocent bystanders,} \tag{13.2}$$

$$- CW_t\}e^{-rt}\,dt, \quad \text{consumer welfare—equations 12a–12d.} \tag{13.3}$$

where

   p = the probabilities that a company will be charged with an antitrust violation (I = intentional violators, U = unintentional violators, and B = innocent bystanders),

DL = damages as measured by the legal system,

DA = damages additionally inflicted by intentional violators,

DO = damages overmeasured by the legal system.

Unfairness is higher as a result of the damages measured in legal proceedings inflicted by intentional violators (*DL*) plus damages inflicted on people who do not sue (*DA*) (see subequation 12.1). DA may result from victims' not discovering the antitrust violation or not finding it economically worthwhile to bring suit. As was discussed in section 6.7, legally determined damages may be overmeasured (*DO*), which results in resources being transferred from defendants to plaintiffs. This latter effect is considered to be unfair, not only because the punishment does not fit the crime but because resources are transferred to people who did not incur those damages. (This overmeasurement, however, does not include penalties included to compensate victims, ex ante, for the cost of discovering and prosecuting antitrust violations.) The resource misuse inflicted by the intentional violators (*CW*), specified in equation (12), is an additional unfairness that should be charged to the intentional violators.

Fairness is importantly reduced by damages (*DL*) inflicted on unintentional violators and innocent bystanders. An additional measure of unfairness is the costs inflicted on these parties that are included in the consumer welfare equation (*CW*).

Class Action Suits

Class actions increase fairness by making it possible for victims of antitrust violations to sue for damages when the costs of individual lawsuits would exceed the expected benefits. The principal benefit to these victims, however, is deterrence of violations, rather than compensation for wrongs.

Compensation to the class members for antitrust damages borne by them is limited by several factors. One is the difficulty of determining which individuals incurred damages. The small damage amounts that make a class action suit desirable also make it difficult to identify the specific victims.[39] An example of this difficulty is the problems that the court faced in distributing the $6,100,000 settlement arising from the allegation of overcharges by several New York State milk wholesalers.[40] The amount to be distributed averaged $1.50 per household or $0.50 per individual. The cost of distribution was estimated as being at least $2,500,000. Discount coupons on milk cartons were rejected, particularly after objections by other milk producers. The court decided to distribute the settlement "in the Court's discretion to the schools, public, private and parochial, located . . . within the . . . area covered by the complaint, to be used solely for nutrition-related purposes or programs that would not otherwise be funded" (p. 3). Suits *in parens patriae* by state attorneys general have resulted in defendants' penalties' being used to fund further antitrust actions or to bolster state treasuries. Occasionally, though, the damages are returned to the victims. In the *Gypsum* case approximately 70,000 business firms received compensation (King 1977, 68). Perhaps the largest effort to pay damages to consumers was undertaken as a result of the Antibiotics Antitrust Litigation. The settlement fund of over $20,000,000 was distributed to approximately 889,000 claimants in six states. About 17 cents of each dollar of damages claimed was given to consumers.[41]

A second limitation is the incentive of class action attorneys to settle for damages that maximize their welfare rather than the welfare of the class. Rosenfield's (1976, 116–117) study of 104 class action suits revealed that attorneys received 15 percent of the damages obtained in judgments and 21 percent of the damages received in settlements, on the average. Thus he finds that settlement not only yields larger amounts for the attorneys but also saves them the costs of litigating. Latimer (1982, 1571) further points out that:

once a settlement has been reached, the proceeding ceases to be an adversary one. Thus, after a damage figure is agreed upon, attorneys for the defendants have no interest in contesting the size of the settlement fund or how it is distributed; and, if it is a lump sum settlement this lack of interest carries over to the amount of attorneys' fees sought by counsel for plaintiffs.

However, neither Rosenfield's data nor Latimer's observation indicates whether the settlement amount received by the class tends to be less, in present-value terms, than would be amounts received in judgment.

One aspect of class action attorneys' fees that impinge on the amount of the settlements and judgments that redound to the benefit of the class is payment as a multiple of the attorneys' usual fees (the lodestar method) or as a percentage of the damages obtained. As a well-argued debate on the question makes clear (Solovy, Saunders [SS], Block, and Garfield [BG] 1985), there are good arguments for and against both methods. The lodestar method creates incentives as that attorneys will "vigorously prosecute actions in the best interests of the class members, knowing that they will be compensated on an hourly basis so long as their time benefits the class" (BG, pp. 8–9). But it also "necessitates that class counsel delay settlement and engage in excessive discovery and motion practice to ensure the award of a substantial fee" (SS, p. 7). Some attorneys might even be tempted to submit fraudulent claims. The percentage method, on the other hand, "provides an incentive to plaintiffs' attorneys to obtain the best possible result for the class because the better the recovery, the better the fee.... Lawyers are rewarded ... for time saved, rather than time expended" (SS, p. 7). But the percentage method produces "disproportionate results" in the form of "arbitrary and unjustifiable windfalls for class counsel" (BG, p. 8). Furthermore, as Dewees, Prichard, and Tebilcock (1981) demonstrate, the percentage method encourages the filing of lawsuits where the plaintiffs have a small chance of winning, as long as the potential damages are great.

Fairness to the damaged class would appear served well by either method of compensating attorneys as long as a neutral third party, the court, played an active role in monitoring the fees charged. As Solovy, Saunders, Block, and Garfield argue, both methods easily can give rise to overcharges. Considering the potential for unfairness to innocent bystanders and even to unintentional violators, the lodestar method would appear preferable. It rewards plaintiffs' attorneys for pursuing defendants to the point where the marginal additional damages, net of costs, are still positive, while reducing the attorneys' incentives to file against defendants simply because the potential damages are large. Monitoring by the court, though onerous, is necessary, as the questioning of massively excessive attorneys' fees in the Fine Paper Litigation demonstrated.[42] It could be accomplished in much the same way and for the same reason that consumers' claims in the Antibiotics Antitrust Litigation were audited (King 1977).[43] Or, the services of a firm of certified public accountants could be used.

**Joint and Several Liability, Contribution, Claim Reduction, and
Individual Responsibility**

Easterbrook, Landes, and Posner (1980, 340) discuss the issue of fairness
and the liability of defendants and conclude (as do others) that "[a] fairness
argument from the mouth of the intentional wrongdoer is unappealing
because the wrongdoer can avoid his 'predicament' by conforming his
conduct to the law's demands." An additional objection to changing the
joint and several liability rule given in the American Bar Association (1979)
Minority Report (and repeated by many of the plaintiffs' attorneys who
testified at the 1981–1982 House and Senate hearings) is that "each coconspirator is ... indivisibly responsible for all damage caused by all
members of the conspiracy. No plaintiff would have been injured had any
member of the conspiracy insisted on competition or 'blown the whistle' on
the others" (section 2).

These arguments, however, do not speak to the fairness of the larger
damage amounts and incentives to settle that are imposed on unintentional
violators and innocent bystanders. Easterbrook, Landes, and Posner (1980,
342–343) dismiss this concern as follows: "[ex ante] a no-contribution rule
would be unfair only if one group of potential defendants were, for inappropriate reasons, more likely than the other to be selected as the defendant
called on to pay the full damages." The analysis just presented indicates
that intentional violators have the means of shifting damages to unintentional violators and innocent bystanders and plaintiffs have incentives to
file against these firms. Presumably, had Easterbrook, Landes, and Posner
considered this outcome and agreed with it (which seems likely, since the
conclusion that conspiracies should include only a few large firms follows
the logic of their article), they would have concluded that the joint and
several damage rule is "unfair," at least for all except a few defendants in
multidefendant cases.

Contribution appears to be unfair to defendants that have settled because these defendants and the plaintiff reached a deal that both parties
apparently found worthwhile. Consequently there would seem to be no fair
reason to reopen the issue. Similarly there should be no fair reason for the
plaintiff to require the other defendants to pay damages for harms demon-
strably done by defendants with whom the plaintiff has settled.

If we assume that the damages could be equitably assessed against individual defendants, then it would seem that fairness would call for use of the
individual responsibility rule. An objection to this rule, though, is that a
defendant might be financially unable to pay the damages. An individual
responsibility rule might allow a financially strong conspirator to shift the

blame to a bankrupt or financially weak firm, thereby hiding and keeping the fruits of the crime. This then would be a question of fact. Should the court or jury find that other defendants benefited from or were directly responsible for the acts of that defendant, these coconspirators could be held liable for the total damages. But, in the event that some other defendant is not found to be liable for a financially weak defendant's liability, the plaintiff would have to bear the cost. (Of course this is no different from the problem facing many plaintiffs in other types of cases.) In this event one would have to balance the unfairnesses: assessing damages against defendants that might not have imposed costs on the plaintiffs against not imposing damages on defendants that might escape their true liability and not allowing injured plaintiffs to collect fully for their injuries.

The claim reduction rule would obviate the possible problem of stronger defendants' shifting the blame to financially weak defendants. Only the damages attributed to the defendants that settled with the plaintiff would be eliminated from the action. Therefore the plaintiff could tailor its settlement to account for this possibility.

6.10 Empirical Implications of the Analysis

The Probability of Settlement

The model presented in this chapter suggests that predictions about the effect of the antitrust laws and rules on settlement rates would require information concerning the following variables and observations:

1. Knowledge about the defendants' perceptions of their guilt or innocence of violating the antitrust laws is required because intentional violators should be early settlers. However, one cannot simply see which firms settled first to determine relative guilt. Other reasons drive firms to settle. And plaintiffs have incentives to avoid settling with all guilty defendants.

2. The plaintiff's perception of winning at trial is required to determine whether a case was settled because of a difference in the defendant's and the plaintiff's perceptions, or for some other reason.

3. The extent to which the defendant and the plaintiff have other benefits or costs from winning or losing at trial should be estimated. For example, some defendants may choose to settle early, even though they believe themselves to be innocent, because they face high costs from having to report a large contingent liability in their financial statements. Or, plaintiffs that have reputations for toughness to maintain because of other pending cases may choose to litigate or drive a hard settling bargain.

4. The legal cost facing plaintiffs and defendants should be estimated because the extent to which different perceptions about winning affect settling depends importantly on the magnitudes of this cost.

5. Market shares and equities (measured in terms of economic rather than accounting values) of the defendants are necessary, because joint and several liability gives smaller firms incentives to settle early. Plaintiffs also have incentives to settle early with such defendants.

Unfortunately, the Georgetown data do not include information of the type required. While some estimates of the special costs and benefits facing particular defendants and plaintiff might be obtained (though only for a few cases and at considerable cost), the parties' perceptions of their chances of winning at trial would appear to be unobtainable. Indeed, it does not seem possible that any of the required information could be obtained, except the market share and market value of the equity of defendants. These market data are not included in the Georgetown study.

Information on the extent to which cases are settled rather than dismissed or tried is available. Of the 1,579 completed cases analysed by Kauper and Snyder (chapter 7, table 7.6), 12.6 percent were settled, 76.0 percent were dismissed and 11.3 percent were litigated. Salop and White (chapter 1, table 1.10) find that 88.1 percent of the 1,617 cases that were completed were settled, withdrawn, or dismissed. DuVal (1979, table 4) finds that 75 percent of the 151 nonclass Chicago cases and 67 percent of the 27 class cases were terminated by voluntary dismissal. Baxter (1979, table 1-1) reports that 81.7 percent of private antitrust cases during the seven years 1964–70 were "dismissed-action of the parties." Thus settlement or dismissal is by far the most common way of terminating cases. These data are consistent with the expectation that the costs of trial encourage settlement.

The Amount of Settlements
Because the incentives to settle prior to trial are very high, the amounts for which the parties settle are very important for testing the effect of alternative legal rules and practices. It would be desirable to know at least the following:

1. The settlement amounts for defendants identified by market shares and equity amounts.

2. Other information about defendants as listed previously.

3. The order in which settlements were made.

Unfortunately, the Georgetown data provide very little information on even the settlement amounts, and none on the other data. Hence it is not possible to determine the extent to which the rule of joint and several liability resulted in large or small, or innocent or guilty firms' settling for amounts or at times that are consistent with those postulated here. However, even if these data were available, it would not be possible to determine the extent to which an alternative rule, such as contribution, claim reduction, or individual responsibility, would affect the settlement amounts.

Some information about settlements and class action suits is provided by DuVal (1979). From his detailed study he states:

There was little evidence that the inclusion of class allegations in a complaint had an *in terrorem* effect on defendants, leading them to settle irrespective of the merits of the plaintiff's case. The available evidence was too fragmentary to indicate whether certification of the class as distinguished from the inclusion of class allegations in the complaint had a coercive effect. (p. 449)

Judgments

If one could take account of the determinants of settlement just listed, it would be possible to draw inferences from data on the outcomes of cases that were judicially decided. Some indication of the relative merits of the cases, however, can be obtained from pretrial judgments because a defendant that believes itself to be not guilty of an offense has an incentive to press for such judgments rather than settle. The Georgetown study data analyzed by Salop and White (table 1.10) reveal that 28.3 percent of the 192 cases that were litigated resulted in judgment for the plaintiffs. DuVal (1979, tables 3 and 4) finds that 19.5 percent of the 41 cases that were litigated to judgment were decided in favor of the plaintiffs (none of which were class actions). Baxter reports that 15.2 percent of the judgments went to the plaintiffs. If one counts the 76.0 percent that Kauper and Snyder (table 7.6) report were "dismissed" as a victory for the defendants, it appears that the plaintiffs tend to lose. These results are suprising, considering Priest and Klein's (1984) analysis and supporting data. Using a simplified model, they show analytically that plaintiffs should have a 50 percent chance of winning cases that are decided at trial; otherwise it should benefit both parties to settle. If their analysis is correct, it appears that the other factors specified in the model presented here are important determinants of the parties' determination to try the dispute in court.

Deterrence

To measure the extent to which the law and litigation rules affected deterrence, one would have to be able to specify equation (2) (presented in section 6.2). Clearly it is not possible to obtain measurements of the benefit and cost to potential antitrust violators. Nor, as White (1984) points out, can one determine how deterrence is affected by counting the number of cases filed or litigated. If greater damages or an increased probability of detection and a finding of liability is effected, there may simply be fewer violations and hence fewer violators to sue. Or, plaintiffs may have increased incentives to sue even though there are fewer violators, which would give rise to more cases.

The number of cases tried does not provide any insight, because the parties still would have incentives to settle. If the rules favored the defendants, the cost of their not settling (see equation 5) would decrease. If the rules favored the plaintiffs, the benefit from their not settling (see equation 6) would increase. As a consequence the amounts of settlements would change, not the number of cases brought to trial. The settlement amounts could provide some information if the other determinants were accounted for. The data, though, are not available. In any event, if there were no change in the law or rules, it would not be possible to determine the effect of one alternative or another, since the effects of the existing environment would have been incorporated by the parties in their ex ante calculations.

Consumer Welfare and Fairness
The data required to measure these important considerations are not available and in all likelihood will never be available. Hence legislators will have to decide whether and how to change the rules on the basis of logic and the limited amount of empirical evidence available, including the reported experiences of defendants, plaintiffs, and their attorneys.

6.11 Conclusions

Treble Damages
The damages multiplier ought to be that which makes the intentional violator's expected benefits from violating the law less than the expected costs. To overcome the less than unitary probability that a violation will be discovered and successfully prosecuted, it seems clear that the actual damages should be increased by some multiple so as to compensate for the less than certainty of having to pay damages.

The analysis presented in section 6.7 revealed that failure to include interest explicitly on the damages is likely to increase significantly the benefit to violators of the antitrust laws. It is difficult to conceive of an objection to compensating the injured parties for the opportunity loss on their funds and to charging the perpetrator for the full costs of the damage inflicted. Consequently one recommendation is that interest be included from the date the damage is demonstrated to have occurred.[44]

There also is reason to believe that the estimated amount of damages tends to be overstated. Accounting numbers do not include the opportunity benefits from plaintiffs' using their resources in alternative ways nor the reductions in prices and profits as coconspirators undercut each other in ways that are not readily monitored. Hence it is doubtful that long-term conspiracies result in the damages that often are claimed. Were intentional violators the only defendants in an action, this concern would not be very important. However, the analysis indicates that unintentional violators and innocent bystanders are likely to be charged with antitrust law violations. Hence increasing damages has the dual effect of deterring intentional violators while restraining others from making desirable investments and punishing innocent firms that are caught in the plaintiffs' net. Furthermore the prospect of inflated damages give plaintiffs incentives to pursue defendants even when there is only a small probability of success. The consequence is a waste of resources and unreasonable incentives for risk-averse defendants to settle meritless cases.

Class Action Suits
Class action suits increase the probability that intentional violators will be charged with the damage they do. The evidence does not indicate that these actions have resulted in excessive burdens to defendants or to the courts. However, there is reason to be concerned that the funds obtained for the class might be dissipated in attorneys' fees and expenses. The courts could control for this potential abuse by having auditors rigorously examine and validate the amounts claimed by the attorneys and settlements they obtain. The auditors should report to the courts and be paid by the class.

Additional recommendations for making class action suits more effective are beyond the scope of this paper but can be found in Coffee (1983).

Joint and Several Liability, Contribution, Claim Reduction, and Individual Responsibility
The joint and several liability rule should result in very few conspiracies with more than a few equally sharing firms (see analysis in section 6.7). Smaller firms would not be included because the risk that they will be liable for the entire conspiracy's damages gives them considerable incentives to sell out the conspiracy. The plaintiff's incentives reinforce this result.

It seems likely therefore that plaintiffs that charge large numbers of defendants with being coconspirators have either mistakenly or deliberately included innocent firms. Joint and several liability (particularly when combined with class action suits and overmeasurement of damages) has the effect of extorting settlements from innocent defendants, particularly those that are risk averse. This result is contrary to concerns for consumer welfare and fairness.

Contribution offers the disadvantage of eliminating the benefits to defendants from settling. This would appear to place too great a burden on plaintiffs, particularly when they have to finance their actions out of the proceeds of settlements.

Claim reduction, though, does appear to be in the public interest. This rule would result in defendants' being responsible for the damages they are found to have imposed. While some intentional violators still could count on selling information to plaintiffs for a reduced settlement, they would have to contend with the plaintiffs' lower incentives to settle. With claim reduction, plaintiffs will not be able to replace the damages due to the intentional violator with claims against the other defendants, some of which may not be guilty of violating the law.

Individual responsibility also would be in the public interest. With firms held responsible only for the damages they cause, the crime and its punishment would be joined. This rule would reduce the necessity of innocent firms' settling rather than facing the prospect of being held responsible for damages they did not (and in many cases, could not) impose on the plaintiffs. It also would reduce the plaintiffs' incentives to include all possible defendants because they will have to prove damages against defendants individually. This greater precision would permit (in the sense of fairness) an increase of damages allowed because these would be more likely to be imposed on intentional violators.

Deterrence, Consumer Welfare, and Fairness

The analysis indicated that increasing the damages for antitrust violations leads to possible increases in deterrence that are likely to be offset, to an unknown degree, by reductions in consumer welfare and greater unfairness. The misallocation of resources engendered by antitrust violations should be measured against the misallocations when firms forgo beneficial investments and practices that might give rise to charges of antitrust violations. The resources used for protecting against and prosecuting legal proceedings also should be considered as a reduction of consumer welfare. Finally, although it is unfair for consumers to bear the costs of antitrust law violations, it is similarly unfair for innocent firms to be forced to transfer funds to plaintiffs. The probability that the latter has occurred is not small, as indicated by the large numbers of firms that are included as defendants and the extent to which plaintiffs' actions are dismissed and their litigated cases are lost.

Notes

I am indebted to Lawrence White for helpful suggestions.

1. The damage amount plus legal and related expenses are deductible as business expenses (Internal Revenue Code § 162 g). If the defendant previously was not criminally convicted, or pleaded guilty or nolo contendere, the punitive (trebled) damages are deductible (IRS § 162 a).

2. See Landes (1983), who emphasizes the efficiency benefits that can accompany an antitrust collusion.

3. See Posner (1975) for a discussion of the social costs of acquiring and maintaining a monopoly.

4. The mnemonic symbols are formed with the first letter of the relevant words in the description.

5. On the assumption that the cartel is not a discriminating monopolist and that I's marginal unit costs are constant, the damage benefits per period from price fixing are

$$D = p_2 q_2 - p_1 q_2 = (p_2 - p_1)q_2,$$

where

p_2 = collusion increased price,

p_1 = precollusion price,

q_2 = collusion quantity purchased.

This is the amount usually assessed against losing defendants in price-fixing cases (see Page 1980, 479: "the courts have uniformly held that the proper measure of damages in price-fixing cases is the overcharge, the difference between the cartel price and the competitive price, variously defined"). However, the gross damage (before benefits from other resources saved and used) inflicted on the economy is the consumer surplus forgone, which is equal to the integral of the area under the demand curve over the quantity no longer purchased ($q_2 - q_1$, where q_1 = the precollusion quantity), the "monopoly triangle." As Elzinga and Breit (1976), Page (1980), Landes (1983), and many others point out, this amount is the social loss from monopoly. The damage amount, D, does not represent a social cost, since it is only a shift of resources from consumers to producers. It is, however, a private cost, and hence the basis for legal damages.

6. This rationale is given by Posner (1979) in analyzing *United States* v. *United States Gypsum Co.*, 438 U.S. 422 (1978).

7. Among others, see Posner (1976), Bork (1978, chaps. 13, 14, and 15), Block and Sidak (1980), and Reich (1980) and references therein to other authors and cases.

8. However, Sullivan (1983, 61) believes that:

it is unlikely that 'unwitting' violators frequently exist.... In antitrust cases, oriented as they are towards large businesses with hugh cadres of lawyers, the totally unwitting defendant will be a rarity. In the typical situation the defendant will have had knowledge of possible illegality and have taken a chance on the outcome. The fact that the judgment as to legality may have been reasonable when made does not detract from the fact that the defendant knew or should have known of the risks and chose to assume them in return for the business benefits which resulted. (note omitted)

9. Sullivan (1983, 40) reaches a different conclusion. He cites six countervailing factors. These include (1) the investment of plaintiff in terms of costs and attorneys' fees, (2) the risk of plaintiff's being assessed defendant's attorneys' fees if bad faith is proved, (3) the likelihood that plaintiff's attorney will be subject to disciplinary sanctions and assessment of defendant's costs for bringing such an action, (4) the possibility of plaintiff's triggering a counterclaim, (5) the specter that defendants, though normally risk averse, will react nonrationally to being "held up" and refuse to settle, and (6) the possibility that defendants will view litigating particular suits as a necessary investment to prevent groundless suits from routinely being brought.

However, the opportunity cost to the plaintiff of including more defendants once a case is filed is very small, as long as the charge is not made in obvious bad faith. For example, several cement company representatives testified that almost every company in the industry was charged in the *Cement and Concrete Antitrust Litigation*, MDL 296 (D. Ariz.), including one company in South Carolina that never sold any cement in Arizona, its maximum shipping distance from its sole plant being 300 miles (Craigmyle 1981–82, 406).

10. These and the other legal and other antitrust related expenses and benefits probably are positively related to the amount of expected damages, though the relationship probably is not linearly proportional.

11. As noted earlier, this is an important reason for the Supreme Court's decision to limit standing to sue for damages to direct purchasers.

12. Elzinga and Breit (1976, 84) suggest a

"perverse incentives effect" ... [in that a victim] will not attempt to alter his customary purchasing practices to avoid being overcharged because he believes reparations will be forthcoming should he be found to be dealing with an antitrust violator. Moreover, the possibility of receiving more than the actual amount of damages magnifies the perverse incentives effect, since an individual has an incentive not only to neglect seeking out substitutes or finding ways of avoiding damages, but also even to suffer damages in order to benefit from the collection of threefold the amount of damages actually sustained.

Easterbrook (1985, 451), however, argues that "the efficiency loss of an antitrust offense arises because purchasers faced with a higher price switch to substitutes that are less desirable, are produced at higher real cost, or both." Consequently he considers purchasers' decisions to continue buying the price-fixed goods a benefit rather than a "perverse effect." As Landes (1983, 673) puts it: "efficiency usually requires compensating the victim of an intentional tort to prevent him from spending resources to avoid the tort." In any event Sullivan (1983, 35) argues that "potential plaintiffs are unlikely to incur unnecessary damages in the hope of future treble recovery. The treble damages, after all, must be discounted by the chances of not prevailing on the merits and of having an *in pari delicto* or mitigation defence applied." See cases cited in Page (1980, 487–488) that support Sullivan's argument.

13. However, Coffee (1983, n. 18) mentions two cases in which "the government's action appears to have been based on earlier detective work undertaken by a private enforcer." He cites *United States* v. *United States Gypsum*, 438 U.S. 422 (1978), and In re *Gas Meters Antitrust Litigation*, 500 F. Supp. 956, 957 (E.D. Pa. 1980). Tydings (1982, p. 26), a plaintiffs' lawyer, also states that "sometimes that knowledge [of the liability and damage issues in a case] is gained because you have been beating your head against the wall with the Department of Justice for two years and the Federal Trade Commission for two or three years trying to get them to initiate a government action. Frequently, despite your educational efforts, they will not move and ultimately you are forced to file a plaintiff's class action." See Kauper and Snyder (chapter 7) for evidence on this question.

14. See Coffee (1983, 239 ff.) for an excellent description and discussion. Also see Herzel and Hagan (1981), and Lattimer (1982, 1575–1579), among many others.

15. See Shavell (1982) for an analysis of the effects on the probability of a suit's being filed of alternative rules for allocating legal costs.

16. Present values are ignored on the assumption that the discount rate and expected time of events after pretrial settlement are the same for the defendant and plaintiff. Legal and other expenses to the pretrial settlement (LS) in equation (3.1) are not included because these are sunk costs. (As noted earlier, the forgone benefits from settling, BS, are included as a cost in subequation 3.2.)

17. Present values are not shown as explained in the previous footnote.

18. The relationship increases at a decreasing rate, since

$$\frac{\partial(g_{PD} - g_d)}{\partial(TD)} = -\frac{TBS}{(TD)^2},$$

where TCT_D and TBT_{PD} net out to zero.

19. The relationship increases at an increasing rate, since

$$\frac{\partial(g_{PD} - g_d)}{\partial TBS} = \frac{1}{TD},$$

where TCT_D and TBT_{PD} net out to zero.

20. As equation (4) shows, the optimal settlement amount is less than total damages because (1) there is a less than certain probability that the plaintiff will win, (2) there would be a delay in receiving the damages, and (3) legal costs would have to be incurred.

21. Easterbrook, Landes, and Posner (1980) conclude that joint and several damages leads to an increasingly greater probability of settlement. They say: "as more and more defendants settle, the expected liability of each remaining defendant grows; defendants therefore compete not to be left out of the settlement round; and a plaintiff can exploit this competition to obtain a larger aggregate recovery than he would expect to receive if all of the defendants litigated" (p. 354). This conclusion is drawn from a simplified model, which leads them to conclude that "in the multiple-defendant case, it is always possible to find positive settlement values, no matter how trivial, that make the plaintiff and at least $n - 1$ defendants better off compared to their expected trial outcomes" (p. 357). They do not show why the probability of settlement changes over time—indeed, their model and example (p. 358) indicates that all defendants should settle immediately or not at all.

22. H.R. 1242 ("A bill to provide for contribution of damages attributable to an agreement by two or more persons to fix, maintain, or stabilize prices under section 4, 4A, or 4C of the Clayton Act, and for other purposes"), January 23, 1981; and S. 995 (same title as H.R. 1242), February 16, 1981.

23. Landes and Posner (1980) similarly draw this conclusion.

24. The Senate and House bills appear to call for this situation, since they provide: "(d) Nothing in this section shall affect the joint and several liability of any person who enters into an agreement to fix, maintain, or stabilize prices."

25. This point is discussed at length and formally by Breit and Elzinger (1973), Polinsky and Shavell (1979), and Breit and Elzinga (1985), among others.

26. Stephen Susman (1982, 1525), lead counsel in the Corregated Antitrust Litigation, speaking on partial settlements, advised:

Plaintiffs would do well to give a substantial discount for meaningful cooperation [by defendants], such as the right to informally interview witnesses and the waiver of corporate and individual privileges. Despite the fact that corporate counsel tells you that they cannot force any individual executives to waive any privileges, they can if the price is right and will do so. . . . In approaching plaintiffs for settlement defendants would do well to overcome the code of honor among thieves and consider the possibility of offering substantial assistance as a means of reducing the price tag.

In fact, International Paper, a felony indictee with the largest market share (8.3 percent), settled second for $1 million a market share percentage (point). Thereafter the settlement price increased to $2 million a point through $6.5 million a point. (The first corporation to settle, St. Regis Paper Co, was unindicted and settled for $0.5 million a point, or $1,980,000.) (Civiletti, 1982, 330)

27. Presented by Civiletti (1982, 330).

28. Net income could not be obtained for the following companies (all of which were unindicted): Dura Container; Longview Fibre; Willamette Industries; Menasha Corp.; U.S. Corregated; and Green Bay Packaging. Stock market data also could not be obtained for Champion and MacMillan-Bloedel.

29. *Hanover Shoe* v. *United Shoe Machinery Corp.*, 392 U.S. 481 (1968), and *Illinois Brick Co.* v. *Illinois*, 431 U.S. 720 (1977). See Landes and Posner (1979) for an early analysis leading to this conclusion and Benston (1986) for an extension and review of the subsequent literature.

30. See Kauper and Snyder (chapter 7).

31. See Salop and White (chapter 1). Also see Parker (1971) for a discussion and numerical demonstration showing the effect of nominal interest rates on increasing the net benefit from price fixing and Parker (1973) for a similar illustration for bid-rigging on a state highway project.

32. Parker (1971, 486–487) states that "[t]he courts have rejected arguments that the 'time interval' between the date the injury was sustained and the date damages are awarded is an element to be included in damage computations." Giving citations, he reports: "The Court concludes that it is *not* necessary to include interest or an adjustment for inflation in order for plaintiff to recover full indemnification for defendant's violation" (p. 487, emphasis in original). However, Page (1980, 476) states that "[t]he trebling of damages . . . was never intended to be a discounting factor, and scarcely serves this function." He supports this conclusion with the following footnote (47): "The trebling provision was imported from the original Statute of Monopolies, 21 Jac. 1, c. 3 (1624)."

33. This concern supports legislative action to repeal the *Illinois Brick* rule. See Benston (1986) for a summary of the arguments and citations to the literature, and a review of the empirical evidence.

34. See Hoyt, Dahl, and Gibson (1976) and Weinberg (1976) for discussions of the court-accepted methods of computing damages, with citations to the relevant decisions.

35. For example, the plaintiffs' economic expert in the Fine Paper Antitrust Litigation insisted that a price-fixing conspiracy had taken place because an index of fine paper prices had increased considerably over the period in question, despite the fact that the consumer and producer price indexes had increased by almost the same amount at the same time. (*In Re Fine Paper Antitrust Litigation* (ten cases), finding for defendants in U.S. District Court for the Eastern District of Pennsylvania, affirmed on appeal to the U.S. Court of Appeals, Third Circuit, 685 F. 2d 810 (1982)).

36. They do not discuss the situation where the total benefits exceed the total costs, nor do they consider the implications of their reasoning for the existence and composition of conspiracies.

37. Block and Sidak (1980) make this point very well, as follows: "Judges and prosecutors will always mischaracterize some competitive or efficiency-enhancing costs that are impossible to

reduce by trading higher penalties for lower enforcement efforts. If managers are risk averse, then even if the expected penalty for all antitrust enforcement is held constant, increasing the damage multiple while reducing enforcement efforts will always increase the cost of a given error rate" (p. 1138).

38. Block and Sidak (1980) cleverly and ironically speak to this issue with the subtitle of their article, "Why Not Hang a Price Fixer Now and Then?" They emphasize judicial error rather than suits against innocent bystanders.

39. For example, the average amount of damages before legal and distribution costs that might have been claimed by indirect final consumers (had they standing to sue for damages) in 13 major antitrust settlements between June 1977 and June 1983 is $1.13 per capita or $2.58 per household for consumer goods, and $424 per housing unit for construction materials (Benston 1986, table 1).

40. *State of New York* v. *Dairylea Cooperative, Inc. et al.*, No. 81 Civ. 1891 U.S.D.C. Southern District of New York, Slip Opinion, June 26, 1985.

41. However, an audit revealed that about 75 percent of the initial claims were not justified. Had all claims been accepted, consumers would have received only 10 cents on the dollar (King 1977, 68).

42. In re *Fine Paper Litigation*, 98 F.R.D. 48 (E.D.Pa. 1983). The settlements in this case totaled $50,650,000, of which the plaintiffs' attorneys (41 firms and state attorneys general) claimed $21,000,000 in fees and expenses (41 percent). After bickering among the attorneys about who was to get what, objections were filed, and a report on the attorneys' claims was commissioned by some of the larger company plaintiffs. The report, submitted by Weil, Gotshal & Manges detailed what appeals court Judge Becker characterized as "unjustified claims for travel, lodging, and meal expenses, numerous items of needless duplication of effort, and a plethora of other meritless requests." (In re *Fine Paper Litigation*, 751 F.2d.562 (1984), p.601 n. 1) After a week of hearings, district court Judge McGlynn reduced the claims to $4.3 million in fees and $1.1 million in expenses. Ten firms with total claims of $8.1 million appealed the reduction of their claims to $1.7 million. The Second Circuit Court of Appeals upheld the district court's total disallowance of $114,507 claimed by one firm and, as to the other appellants, reversed and remanded the case for redetermination "in a manner consistent with this opinion" (p. 601). Judge Gibbons' opinion, however, details and (at least to this reader) virtually fully supports the action of Judge McGlynn.

43. The audit disallowed about 75 percent of the amounts claimed, a large portion of which were voluntarily withdrawn when it became known that the claims would have to be substantiated.

44. See Patell, Weil, and Wofson (1982) for a comprehensive analysis of the appropriate rate of interest. They conclude that the defendant's debt rate is the correct rate to use.

References

Baumol, William J., and Janusz A. Ordover. 1985. Use of Antitrust to Subvert Competition. *Journal of Law & Economics* 28: 247–265.

Baxter, William. 1979. The Political Economy of Antitrust. In Robert D. Tollison, ed. *The Political Economy of Antitrust*. Lexington, Mass.: D.C. Heath, pp. 3–49.

Benston, George J. 1986. Indirect Purchasers' Standing to Claim Damages in Price-Fixing Antitrust Actions: A Benefit/Cost Analysis of Proposals to Change the *Illinois Brick* Rule. *The Antitrust Law Journal* 55: 213–249.

Bernstein, Roger. 1978. Judicial Economy and Class Actions. *Journal of Legal Studies* 7: 349–370.

Block, Micael K., and Joseph G. Sidak. 1980. The Cost of Antitrust Deterrence: Why Not Hang a Price Fixer Now and Then? *Georgetown Law Review* 68: 1131–1139.

Bork, Robert H. 1978. *The Antitrust Paradox*. New York: Basic Books.

Civiletti, Benjamin R. 1981–82. Prepared Statement of Benjamin R. Civiletti. In *Antitrust Damage Allocation*. Hearings before the Subcomittee on Monopolies and Commercial Law of the Committee on the Judiciary, House of Representatives, Ninety-Seventh Congress, First and Second Sessions, October 21, 1981, March 3, 18, June 9 and September 9, 1982, pp. 308–330.

Craigmyle, Robert. 1981–82. Prepared Statement of Robert DeR. Craigmyle. In *Antitrust Damage Allocation*. Hearings before the Subcomittee on Monopolies and Commercial Law of the Committee on the Judiciary, House of Representatives, Ninety-Seventh Congress, First and Second Sessions, October 21, 1981, March 3, 18, June 9 and September 9, 1982, pp. 406–407.

Coffee, John C., Jr. 1983. Rescuing the Private Attorney General: Why the Model of the Lawyer as Bounty Hunter is Not Working. *Maryland Law Review* 42: 215–288.

Dewees, Donald N., J. Robert S. Prichard, and Michael J. Trebilcock. 1981. An Economic Analysis of Cost and Fee Rules for Class Actions. *Journal of Legal Studies* 10, 155–185.

DuVal, Benjamin S., Jr. 1976. The Class Action as an Antitrust Enforcement Device: The Chicago Experience (I) and (II). *American Bar Foundation Research Journal*: 1023–1106, 1273–1358.

DuVal, Benjamin S., Jr. 1979. The Class Action as an Antitrust Enforcement Device: The Chicago Study Revisited. *American Bar Foundation Research Journal*: 449–463.

Easterbrook, Frank H. 1985. Detrebling Antitrust Damages. *Journal of Law & Economics* 28: 445–467.

Easterbrook, Frank H., and Daniel R. Fischel. 1983. Antitrust Suits by Targets of Tender Offers. *Michigan Law Review* 80: 1155–1178.

Easterbrook, Frank H., William M. Landes, and Richard A. Posner. 1980. Contribution among Antitrust Defendants: A Legal and Economic Analysis. *Journal of Law & Economics* 23: 331–370.

Elzinga, Kenneth G., and William Breit. 1973. Antitrust Penalties and Attitudes toward Risk: An Economic Analysis. *Harvard Law Review* 86: 693–713.

Elzinga, Kenneth G., and William Breit. 1976. *The Antitrust Penalties: A Study in Law and Economics* New Haven: Yale University Press.

Gould, John P. 1973. The Economics of Legal Conflicts. *Journal of Legal Studies* 2: 279–300.

Hoyt, Richard C., Dale C. Dahl, and Stuart D. Gibson. 1976. Comprehensive Models for Assessing Lost Profits to Antitrust Plaintiffs. *Minnesota Law Review* 60: 1233–1256.

King, Benjamin F. 1977. Auditing Claims in a Large-Scale Class Action Refund—The Antibiotics Case. *Antitrust Bulletin* 22: 67–93.

Landes, William M. 1983. Optimal Sanctions for Antitrust Violations. *University of Chicago Law Review* 50: 652–678.

Landes, William M., and Richard A. Posner. 1979. Should Indirect Purchasers Have Standing to Sue under the Antitrust Laws: An Economic Analysis of the Rule of *Illinois Brick*. *University of Chicago Law Review* 46: 602–635.

Latimer, Hugh. 1980. Damages, Settlements and Attorneys' Fees in Antitrust Class Actions. *Antitrust Law Journal* 40: 1553–1580.

Page, William H. 1980. Antitrust Damages and Economic Efficiency: An Approach to Antitrust Injury. *University of Chicago Law Review* 47: 467–504.

Parker, Alfred L. 1971. Treble Damage Action—A Financial Deterrent to Antitrust Violations? *Antitrust Bulletin* 16: 483–505.

Parker, Alfred L. 1973. The Deterrent Effect of Private Treble Damage Suits: Fact or Fancy? *New Mexico Law Review* 3: 286–293.

Patell, James M., Roman L. Weil, and Mark A. Wofson. 1982. Accumulating Damages in Litigation: The Roles of Uncertainty and Interest Rates. *Journal of Legal Studies* 11: 341–364.

Polinsky, A. Mitchell, and Steven Shavell. 1979. The Optimal Tradeoff between the Probability and Magnitude of Fines. *American Economic Review* 69: 880–891.

Polinsky, A. Mitchell, and Steven Shavell. 1981. Contribution and Claim Reduction among Antitrust Defendants: An Economic Analysis. *Stanford Law Review* 33: 447–471.

Posner, Richard A. 1975. The Social Costs of Monopoly and Regulation. *Journal of Political Economy* 83: 807–827.

Posner, Richard A. 1976. *Antitrust Law: An Economic Perspective*. Chicago: University of Chicago Press.

Posner, Richard A. 1979. Information and Antitrust: Reflections on the *Gypsum* and *Engineers* Decisions. *Georgetown Law Review* 67: 1187–1203.

Priest, George L., and Benjamin Klein. 1984. The Selection of Disputes for Litigation. *Journal of Legal Studies* 13: 1–55.

Reich, Robert B. 1980. The Antitrust Industry. *Georgetown Law Review* 68: 1053–1073.

Rosenfield, Andrew. 1976. An Empirical Test of Class-Action Settlement. *Journal of Legal Studies* 5: 113–120.

Schwartz, Warren F. 1980. An Overview of the Economics of Antitrust Enforcement. *Georgetown Law Review* 68: 1075–1102.

Shavell, Steven. 1982. Suits, Settlement, and Trial: A Theoretical Analysis under Alternative Methods for the Allocation of Legal Costs. *Journal of Legal Studies* 11: 55–81.

Solovy, Jerold S., Terry Rose Saunders, Dennis J. Block, and Alan E. Garfield. 1985. "When the Court Awards Fees." *The National Law Journal*, July 8 Special Section.

Sullivan, Charles A. 1983. Breaking up the Treble Play: Attacks on the Private Treble Damage Antitrust Action. *Seton Hall Law Review* 14: 17–73.

Susman, Stephen D. 1982. Prosecuting the Antitrust Class Action. *Antitrust Law Journal* 49: 1513–1526.

Tydings, Joseph H. 1982. "Settlement of Government and Private Cases: The Plaintiff," *Antitrust Law Journal*, 50, 25–34.

Tydings, Joseph H. 1982. Prepared Statement of Joseph D. Tydings, Esq., Finley, Kumble, Wagner, Heine, Underberg & Casey. Hearings before the Subcommittee on Monopolies, and Commercial Law of the House Judiciary Committee on Antitrust Damage Allocation. Ninety-Seventh Congress, September 9, Serial No. 118.

Weinberg, David B. 1976. Recent Trends in Antitrust Civil Action Damage Determination. *Duke Law Journal*: 485–520.

White, Lawrence J. 1984. Litigation and Economic Incentives. Working paper no. 84-85. New York University Faculty of Business Administration.

Private Antitrust Cases That Follow on Government Cases

Thomas E. Kauper and Edward A. Snyder

7.1 Introduction

Section 4 of the Clayton Act authorizes any person injured in its "business or property by reason of anything forbidden in the antitrust laws" to recover three times actual damages, costs, and reasonable attorney's fees.[1] Injunctive relief to private plaintiffs is authorized by section 16 of the same act.[2] In some instances, private suits—particularly treble damage suits[3]— are based on conduct that is already (or is about to be) the subject of litigation initiated by the Department of Justice or the Federal Trade Commission.

The filing of an antitrust complaint or return of an antitrust indictment by the government signals potential plaintiffs and plaintiffs' counsel that the named defendant many have violated the antitrust laws.[4] Given the extent to which the enforcement agencies are known to review cases before they are filed, and the caution with which they are generally thought to act, the signal is very strong. In simple terms it is widely believed that if the Antitrust Division acts, there must be substantial reason for its action.[5] This signal is likely to trigger the filing of private suits and influence parties' beliefs as to the merit of the subsequent private litigation. As a result conduct of the parties during the litigation and in settlement negotiations can be affected in a number of ways.

The plaintiff gains an additional benefit when the government succeeds in its litigation. As one commentator has put it, plaintiff's counsel can increase its gain "by depending upon the government to undertake 'test runs' of liability in advance"; counsel can then, in his view, "profitably free ride on the government's successes by initiating their own actions once liability has been established."[6] How much plaintiffs can free ride, however, is a matter of some controversy. Competition among plaintiffs' counsel to handle a particular matter or to secure the advantages of being the first to file may drive counsel to file suit long before the outcome of the government case is known, relying only on the signal given by the filing (or even the likely filing) of the government suit rather than the potentially stronger signal given by its outcome.

Along with signaling private plaintiffs, government cases are potentially valuable to private plaintiffs in a variety of legal and practical ways.[7] Section 5(i) of the Clayton Act tolls the statute of limitations otherwise applicable to a private action during pendency of the government case and for one year thereafter if the private case "is based in whole or in part on any matter complained of" in the government action.[8] Thus a potential plaintiff whose cause of action is within the limitations period when the government action is filed may await its outcome before deciding whether to file, without fear that the statute of limitations will run in the interim.

Section 5(a) of the Clayton Act[9] provides that a final judgment in a case brought by the United States "to the effect" that a given defendant has violated the antitrust laws "shall be prima facie evidence" against such defendant "as to all matters respecting which said judgment . . . would be an estoppel between the parties." In addition collateral estoppel may be available to prohibit relitigation of issues.[10] Consent decrees and nolo contendere pleas are exempted from section 5(a), a fact that allegedly causes a significant number of defendants in government cases to use such decrees or pleas[11] when they would not otherwise do so to lessen the risk of treble damage liability.[12] Although there is no doubt that Congress intended that section 5(a) would expedite private follow-on litigation, practitioners disagree over its utility to plaintiffs.[13] The provision has been hard to apply, and the meaning of "prima facie effect" remains unclear.[14] In many cases the identification of those issues to which an estoppel would be raised has proved difficult. Further, even when liability is established, plaintiffs must prove injury as a result of the defendant's action and must support their measure of damages. Nevertheless, section 5(a) undoubtedly confers some advantage on plaintiffs.

A more significant advantage in some cases is the availability to private plaintiffs of data collected by government in the preparation of its case. Court documents are publicly available,[15] and plaintiffs may obtain access to data (and, in some instances, even government staff memoranda) through a variety of formal and informal means. These include formal demands for grand jury data,[16] Freedom of Information Act requests,[17] and use of third party discovery processes against the government. In some instances, government agencies simply release data that have no claim to confidentiality. Not all of these techniques may be useful to plaintiffs in every case, nor will they necessarily be successful. Rules governing grand jury secrecy, protection of material submitted pursuant to Civil Investigative Demands, and Freedom of Information Act exemptions may thwart access to some information. As a result plaintiff's efforts to obtain data may not reduce costs or shorten the private litigation. Substantial sums and considerable time may have been expended in the process of getting access if plaintiff's demands are contested. However, plaintiffs will pursue such demands only to the extent the cost of doing so is more than offset by the benefits gained. Since oftentimes plaintiffs expend considerable resources in gaining access, the practical advantages of following a similar government case appear to be considerable, and so it is commonly believed that a government case not only triggers private litigation but also provides much of its evidentiary support.[18]

In at least one respect, following a government case may put plaintiffs at a disadvantage. Payments by defendants to plaintiffs in private cases that follow a related criminal case in which the defendants were convicted or pleaded nolo contendere or guilty are taxed differently than payments in other treble damage cases.[19] In the latter the entire treble damage award or settlement payment is a deductible business expense; in the follow-on case to a successful criminal case, two-thirds of the damages are not deductible. Whatever the merits of this distinction, nondeductibility of two-thirds of damages may influence litigation and settlement decisions. Defendants in follow-on cases who do not share part of the burden of treble damages with the government may be more likely to litigate than to settle, and may be willing to settle only at lower figures, than are defendants in other private cases. Greater intransigence on the part of defendants may translate into higher costs for plaintiffs and greater expenditure of judicial resources.

Given the overall advantages of following the government, the expectation of some observers—and shared by the Congress[20]—has been that follow-on cases should take less time, use fewer resources, and result in higher awards than comparable private actions lacking the advantages conferred by government enforcement action. In substantive terms, follow-ons should follow the enforcement patterns of the government agencies. There is also a widespread belief that follow-on cases tend to involve more parties and to be more complex factually than the typical private action.

The accuracy of the commonly held beliefs regarding follow-ons is a prime concern of this paper, which investigates the characteristics of both "follow-on" cases and cases that have no contemporary or directly preceding government counterparts. We refer to the latter as "independently initiated."

7.2 Empirical Results

In this section we describe the results of our review and classification of the Georgetown project's sample of 1,935 private antitrust cases filed in five

U.S. District Courts in the period 1973 to 1983. We examined each case to determine whether it was substantially similar to a case filed by a federal enforcement agency. The methodology used in this classification is described in the appendix. Each case was categorized as (1) a "direct follow-on," alleging the same antitrust violation as a government case that preceded it or was substantially contemporaneous with it, (2) an "indirect follow-on," alleging a violation substantially similar to a preceding government case but extending the allegations to different markets, time periods, or defendants, or alleging additional wrongful acts, or (3) "independently initiated," meaning not in either of the first two categories. We also separated "follow-ons" to Department of Justice actions from those related to FTC actions. References simply to "follow-ons" include both direct and indirect follow-ons related to actions of both agencies. Multidistrict litigation cases (MDLs) were excluded from the sample and are discussed separately.

Number and Type of Private Cases in the Period 1973–1983

Of the 1,935 case sample, 171 cases follow government cases, accounting for slightly less than 9 percent of the sample. Of these, 149 cases follow Department of Justice cases, and 22 cases follow Federal Trade Commission actions. The majority of the follow-on cases, 133 of the total sample, are substantially identical to government cases, and so are "direct" follow-ons; 38 follow-ons cite claims that differ in meaningful ways from the government cases they follow, and these are identified as "indirect" follow-ons. Table 7.1 provides the number and type of follow-on cases by year. The exclusion of multidistrict cases from the sample skews the percentage of follow-on cases on the low side, since multidistrict cases are more likely to be follow-ons.

We investigated whether the percentages of follow-on cases vary significantly by district or by year. The data do not reveal significant variations across districts but do reveal important variations over time. It is useful to divide the 11 years covered by the sample into two periods: 1973 to 1977 and 1978 to 1983. In the early period the average annual number of follow-on cases was 24, and they accounted for 11 percent of total cases filed. In the later period the average annual number of follow-on cases dropped to 8.5, accounting for about 6 percent of total cases filed. Of note, the average number of independently initiated cases filed each year also dropped, from 190 in the early period to 162 in the later period.

Several explanations might be offered for this decline in the number and percentage of follow-on cases during 1978 to 1983. Clearly the number of

Table 7.1 Private antitrust cases, 1973–1983

	1973	1974	1975	1976	1977	1978	1979	1980	1981	1982	1983	Total
A. Total cases, all types	205	209	203	233	219	189	164	131	168	132	109	1,935
Independently initiated cases[a]	179	186	188	206	190	174	152	126	163	96	101	1,764
Follow-on cases[a]	26	23	15	27	29	15	12	5	5	6	8	171
Follow-ons to DOJ cases	23	18	11	27	25	13	12	5	2	6	7	149
Follow-ons to FTC cases	3	5	4	0	4	2	0	0	3	0	1	22
Direct follow-on cases	21	15	11	24	21	13	11	5	4	4	4	133
Indirect follow-on cases	5	8	4	3	8	2	1	0	1	2	4	38
B. Horizontal price-fixing cases (primary allegation)[b]	38	32	33	55	29	25	17	18	31	19	32	329
Independently initiated cases[a]	26	21	21	35	14	15	11	16	29	16	26	230
Follow-on cases[a]	12	11	12	20	15	10	6	2	2	3	6	99
Follow-ons to DOJ cases	12	9	8	20	13	9	6	2	0	3	5	87
Follow-ons to FTC cases	0	2	4	0	2	1	0	0	2	0	1	12
Direct follow-on cases	10	9	10	20	13	9	6	2	2	2	3	86
Indirect follow-on cases	2	2	2	0	2	1	0	0	0	1	3	13

a. Refer to the appendix for definitions of independently initiated cases, follow-on cases, and types of follow-on cases.

b. The information regarding primary offenses alleged was obtained from the Court Records Questionnaire, which provided data on 27 specific practices. The survey instructed that only one offense be selected as the primary offense and that other offenses cited be identified as secondary offenses. However, some case records included multiple primary offenses, while others had multiple secondary offenses but no primary offenses. The data reflected here include cases citing other primary offenses, but exclude other cases that did not cite any offense as primary yet cited horizontal price fixing as a secondary offense.

follow-on cases may be expected to fall if the number of government filings falls. But the number of Department of Justice cases did not drop substantially during this period.[21] This suggests an inquiry into the type of government cases filed during the period. Importantly, a large number of cases alleging bid rigging in asphalt paving and electrical contracting industries were filed. A significant number of such cases were initiated in districts covered by our sample. These cases might be likely candidates for follow-on litigation, yet we identified only one of the 171 follow-on cases as a follow-on to these government bid-rigging cases.[22] Putative defendants in many of these DOJ cases were small firms that might have been judgment proof, meaning they lack assets to pay potential plaintiffs. In others, state officials may have been reluctant to sue prominent local businesses. We suspect, however, that state governments, who would most likely file for private damages based on these DOJ filings, used the threat of debarment under state statutes to recover substantial sums from these defendants.[23] Follow-ons thus may have dropped because the most likely plaintiffs had an alternative remedy.

Also relevant to the decline in follow-on litigation, congressional action in 1974[24] to increase criminal penalties may have affected the character of the government cases filed after 1977 when felony penalties began to be applied. Stronger penalties deter violations and encourage efforts to keep violations secret. Therefore the Department of Justice would be expected to detect fewer of the types of offenses to which the felony penalties apply. Further, if the probability of detection rises with the severity of the offense, the increased penalties may have reduced the severity of offenses.[25] If so, criminal cases filed by the Department of Justice after felony penalties became effective might more often be marginal in size or merit.[26] If felony penalties produced such effects, the change in penalties would reduce both follow-on cases and independently initiated cases. However, the deterrent effect of criminal penalties would more clearly manifest itself in reduced numbers of follow-on cases for the following reason: criminal penalties are most often applied to price-fixing conspiracies. As explained later, follow-on cases, more so than independently initiated cases, focus on horizontal price fixing. Further, of those independently initiated cases alleging horizontal price fixing, it is unlikely that many concern "hard-core" price-fixing conspiracies typically subject to criminal prosecution. Therefore, given that the deterrent effects of felony criminal penalties would be focused on hard-core price-fixing cases, the change in penalties would reduce disproportionately the number of follow-on cases.

Another factor may have contributed to the lower percentages of follow-on cases in 1978 to 1983: the 1977 *Illinois Brick*[27] decision, which denies indirect purchasers standing to sue for treble damages, would be most apparent in horizontal price-fixing cases. Such cases are the most common type of cases initiated by the Department of Justice and, as mentioned, are the most common type of follow-on cases. Therefore, like the deterrent effect of higher criminal penalties, the direct purchaser requirement may have had a disproportionate impact on follow-on litigation.[28]

The Filing of Follow-on Cases

The extreme stereotypical view of follow-on cases is that counsel for private plaintiffs rush to file related litigation and often file in the same district. Our sample of non-MDL follow-on cases suggests otherwise. Of the 149 DOJ follow-on cases, only 68 cases were filed in the same district as the government proceeding. The percentage of such cases filed in the same district was the lowest in Chicago (35 percent) and highest in Atlanta (94 percent). These lower than expected percentages may reflect forum shopping or result from the jurisdictional or venue requirements of private plaintiffs.

We also found the intervals between the filing date of the government action and the filing date of the follow-on case were not as tightly distributed as expected. Of the 171 follow-on cases, 44 (26 percent) either preceded the government action or were filed less than 30 days after, 44 (26 percent) were filed in the interval between 30 and 180 days after the government action, and 83 (49 percent) were filed more than 180 days after the government action. Filing interval data appear in table 7.2. The distribution of filing intervals does not vary significantly between those cases following DOJ actions and those following FTC actions. The distributions for direct and indirect follow-ons, however, differ in the percentage of cases filed within 180 days of the government action, with a smaller percentage of indirect follow-ons filed in this interval. The wider distribution of intervals for indirect follow-ons is consistent with the weaker factual and legal relationship between the government action and indirect follow-ons.

We found that intervals for non-MDL differ from MDL follow-on cases. More than half of MDL follow-on cases are filed within 30 days of the government case as compared with 26 percent of non-MDL follow-on cases.[29] The difference most likely reflects the greater value of the plaintiffs' damage rights in MDL cases and possible competition among counsel for private plaintiffs for such rights.

Table 7.2 Interval between filing date of government cases and filing date of private follow-on cases

	More than 30 days prior	0–30 days prior	0–30 days after	31–60 days after	61–90 days after	90–180 days after	More than 180 days after	Total
Follow-on cases[a]	10	8	26	18	7	19	83	171
DOJ follow-on cases	10	8	26	18	7	16	64	149
FTC follow-on cases	0	0	0	0	0	3	19	22
Direct follow-on cases	3	8	19	17	7	18	61	133
Indirect follow-on cases	7	0	7	1	0	1	22	38
Follow-on cases citing horizontal price fixing as primary offense[c]	3	1	9	15	3	12	56	99
MDL follow-on cases (direct follow-ons only)	0	6	0	0	0	0	4	10

Note: Filing dates for cases filed by the Department of Justice are obtained from Commerce Clearing House, Inc., Trade Regulation Reporter, U.S. Antitrust Cases Summaries: Complaints, Indictments, Developments. Filing dates for cases filed by the Federal Trade Commission are obtained from Federal Trade Commission Reports.

a. Refer to the appendix for definitions of follow-on cases and types of follow-on cases.

b. See table 7.1, note b.

Data on Real Dollars Demanded in Private Antitrust Cases

Data on the real dollars (1980 dollars) demanded[30] according to complaints filed are available for 811 cases in the sample, only 30 of which are follow-on cases. We organized demand data in a series of brackets, $0 to $500,000 at the low end and $4 billion to $7 billion at the high end. See table 7.3 for the results. Of the 781 independently initiated cases, 34 percent demanded under $500,000, 71 percent demanded under $5 million, and only 1 percent demanded over $1 billion. Of the 30 follow-on cases for which data were available, 23 percent sought $500,000 or less, 70 percent demanded under $5 million, and none sought damages in excess of $1 billion. While a lower percentage of follow-on cases demanded less than $500,000 than was true for independently initiated cases, virtually the identical percentage demanded $5 million or less.

Therefore we find little difference in our sample of non-MDL cases between the real dollar demands of private plaintiffs in follow-on cases and those filing independently initiated cases. Nor do we find significant differences between DOJ and FTC follow-ons. While these results on non-MDL cases contradict general expectations about follow-on cases, data on MDL cases would more likely be consistent with expectations. A higher percentage of MDL cases are follow-ons, and the dollars demanded in multidistrict litigations (certainly for the total number of cases in each MDL and probably per case) are higher than the non-MDL sample.

Types of Violations Alleged in Private Antitrust Cases

With respect to the practices alleged in the complaint, the Georgetown data identify 28 separate categories ranging from horizontal price fixing to fraud. As explained in the appendix, we regrouped these 28 categories into three categories: horizontal, vertical, and other. In the horizontal category are all cases in which the conduct's immediate competitive impact was allegedly at the competitive level of the defendant. Included in this category are not only actions that involve agreements among competitors (e.g., horizontal price fixing, horizontal mergers) but also those that target competitors (e.g., monopolization, predatory pricing). The vertical category includes restraints between buyer and seller (e.g., vertical price fixing, dealer terminations). Certain practices could fall into either category (e.g., boycotts, price discrimination) and so are placed in the "other" category.

For the 1,935 cases in the Georgetown sample, data on offenses alleged are available for 1,600. Thirty-three percent of the cases alleged horizontal restraints, 45 percent vertical restraints, and 23 percent could not be placed

Table 7.3 Real dollars demanded (1980 dollars) according to complaint information

	$0–$.5M	$.5M–$1M	$1M–$5M	$5–$10M	$10–$50M	$50–$100M	$100M–$1B	$1B–$4B	$4B–$7B	Sub-total	Cases with missing data	Total
A. All cases												
Independently initiated cases[a]	263	93	195	66	116	20	20	5	3	781	982	1,763
Follow-on cases[a]	7	6	8	1	3	3	2	0	0	30	141	171
DOJ follow-on cases	5	4	6	1	2	2	1	0	0	21	128	149
FTC follow-on cases	2	2	2	0	1	1	1	0	0	9	13	22
B. Cases citing horizontal price fixing as primary offense												
Independently initiated cases[a]	21	13	19	9	19	4	3	0	0	88	142	230
Follow-on cases[a]	1	0	2	1	2	1	1	0	0	8	91	99
DOJ follow-on cases	1	0	1	1	1	0	0	0	0	4	83	87
FTC follow-on cases	0	0	1	0	1	1	1	0	0	4	8	12

Note: The Court Records Questionnaire yielded two demand figures: the figure on the court docket sheets and the demand figure in the complaint. This table relies only on the figure in the complaint, and dollar demands are in 1980 constant dollars, deflated by the Producer Price Index. Rf. U.S. Department of Labor, Bureau of Labor Statistics, GNP Deflator Series.

a. Refer to the appendix for definitions of independently initiated cases, follow-on cases, and types of follow-on cases.

b. See table 7.1, note b.

in either category. Of the independently initiated cases, 29 percent were horizontal, 47 percent were vertical, and 24 percent were other.[31] Of the follow-on cases, 76 percent were horizontal, 18 percent were vertical, and only 6 percent could not be classified. Table 7.4 reports these totals, along with yearly data. For independently initiated cases, the percentage of vertical cases ranges from 57 percent in 1973 to 37 percent in 1976. No marked trends are reflected in the data. Follow-on cases reflect greater variation, with horizontal cases ranging from 93 percent in 1975 to 50 percent in 1982 when only six follow-on cases were filed.

Whatever the yearly variations, it is clear that the greatest percentage of independently initiated cases challenge vertical restraints and by far the greatest percentage of follow-on cases involve horizontal restraints. This is hardly surprising, given the emphasis by the enforcement agencies during the past dozen years on horizontal restraints.

Outcomes of Private Antitrust Cases
Outcome data for almost all of the cases in the Georgetown sample are available. Cases were grouped into one of seventeen outcome categories. These results are shown in table 7.5. Of most interest, 15 percent of the total number were voluntarily dismissed by the plaintiff, 40 percent ended in pretrial stipulations, 10 percent were settled, and 9 percent resulted in judgments.

We analyzed follow-on and independently initiated cases using the specific outcome categories and found that outcomes of independently initiated cases do not vary significantly from the entire sample. The pretrial stipulation rate is slightly higher, and the settlement rate is slightly lower. On the other hand, outcomes of follow-on cases do vary significantly from the sample in several respects. Of the 171 follow-on cases, 22 percent ended in pretrial stipulations, 22 percent were settled, and 12 percent were litigated. Thus, as compared with independently initiated cases, a lower percentage of follow-on cases ended in pretrial stipulations, and a higher percentage ended in formal settlement orders.[32] When follow-ons to Department of Justice cases are considered separately, the settlement rate is still higher (24 percent), and the pretrial stipulation rate still lower (21 percent).

The outcome data are more accurately portrayed by eliminating from the universe those cases without true outcomes—that is, cases where the outcome is unknown or still pending—and cases where the only known outcome is consolidation or transfer to another court. We grouped cases in the remaining specific outcome categories into four general groups: dismissed, settled, litigated, and ending in pretrial stipulations. See

Table 7.4 Private antitrust cases, by type of offense, 1973–1983

	1973	1974	1975	1976	1977	1978	1979	1980	1981	1982	1983	1973–1983
All cases												
Total	170	179	171	194	176	164	141	103	128	81	93	1,600
Horizontal	54	62	51	83	59	40	33	31	45	27	38	523
Vertical	92	79	76	64	72	87	72	46	60	30	36	714
Other	24	38	44	47	45	37	36	26	23	24	19	363
Independently initiated cases												
Total	148	160	157	170	153	150	134	101	126	75	86	1,460
Horizontal	39	51	38	61	42	30	27	29	43	24	32	416
Vertical	85	71	76	63	68	85	71	46	60	29	36	690
Other	24	38	43	46	43	35	36	26	23	22	18	354
Follow-on cases												
Total	22	19	14	24	23	14	7	2	2	6	7	140
Horizontal	15	11	13	22	17	10	6	2	2	3	6	107
Vertical	7	8	0	1	4	2	1	0	0	1	0	24
Other	0	0	1	1	2	2	0	0	0	2	1	9

Note: Refer to the appendix for definitions of independently initiated cases, follow-on cases, and types of follow-on cases. Also refer to the appendix for definitions of the three categories of offenses: horizontal, vertical, and other.

Table 7.5 Outcomes of private antitrust cases

	Dismissed pretrial	Pretrial stipulation	Pretrial withdrawal	Judgment for all plaintiffs	Judgment for all defendants	Judgment for some plaintiffs	Judgment for some defendants	Mixed judgment	Settlement
A. All cases	278	763	77	48	115	5	10	1	199
Independently initiated cases[a]	254	725	72	42	101	5	9	1	161
Follow-on cases[b]	24	38	5	6	14	0	1	0	38
DOJ follow-on cases	19	31	4	5	14	0	0	0	36
FTC follow-on cases	5	7	1	1	0	0	1	0	2
Direct follow-on cases	16	29	5	3	13	0	1	0	29
Indirect follow-on cases	8	9	0	3	1	0	0	0	9
B. All horizontal price-fixing cases (primary allegation)[b]	46	104	13	7	22	0	5	0	53
Independently initiated cases[a]	31	84	10	6	10	0	4	0	26
Follow-on cases[a]	15	20	3	1	12	0	1	0	27
DOJ follow-on cases	12	15	3	1	12	0	0	0	27
FTC follow-on cases	3	5	0	0	0	0	1	0	0
Direct follow-on cases	12	19	3	0	11	0	1	0	24
Indirect follow-on cases	3	1	0	1	1	0	0	0	3

Table 7.5 (continued)

	Statistically closed	Missing	Pending	Unknown	Dismissed by court	Remanded to state court	Dismissed for other reasons	Consolidated	Total
A. All cases	15	14	114	53	49	108	34	38	1,921
Independently initiated cases[a]	14	12	104	51	46	86	33	34	1,750
Follow-on cases[b]	1	2	10	2	3	22	1	4	171
DOJ follow-on cases	1	1	8	1	3	22	1	3	149
FTC follow-on cases	0	1	2	1	0	0	0	1	22
Direct follow-on cases	1	2	7	2	0	20	1	4	133
Indirect follow-on cases	0	0	3	0	3	2	0	0	38
B. All horizontal price-fixing cases (primary allegation)[b]	3	2	39	4	6	10	0	15	329
Independently initiated cases[a]	2	2	31	3	5	4	0	12	230
Follow-on cases[b]	1	0	8	1	1	6	0	3	99
DOJ follow-on cases	1	0	6	1	1	6	0	2	87
FTC follow-on cases	0	0	2	0	0	0	0	1	12
Direct follow-on cases	1	0	6	0	0	6	0	3	86
Indirect follow-on cases	0	0	2	1	1	0	0	0	13

Note: Data on outcomes were obtained from the Court Records Questionnaire, pp. 8–10, which yielded 17 specific, mutually exclusive categories. One of these 17 categories is missing, and 14 cases fall in this category. Note that 14 cases in the 1935 case data set had no outcome data available and are not represented. Also two cases of the 331 citing horizontal price fixing had no outcome data and are not represented.
a. Refer to the appendix for definitions of independently initiated cases, follow-on cases, and types of follow-on cases.
b. See table 7.1, note b.

the appendix for details. (We investigated whether pretrial stipulations are dismissals or settlements and concluded that the category includes both types of outcomes, leading us to retain these cases as a separate category.[33])

We analyzed the outcomes of cases in the restricted universe using these four groups, with the results appearing in table 7.6. Of the independently initiated cases in the Georgetown sample, 28 percent were dismissed, 48 percent were resolved on pretrial stipulation, 11 percent were settled, and 11 percent were litigated.[34] The distribution of outcomes of follow-on cases is significantly different: 25 percent were dismissed, 29 percent were resolved on pretrial stipulation, 29 percent were settled, and 16 percent were litigated. When only Department of Justice follow-ons are considered, the dismissal rate falls to 24 percent, pretrial stipulations fall to 27 percent, the settlement rate increases to 32 percent, and the percentage of cases litigated rises slightly to 17 percent. Clearly follow-on cases are dismissed with less frequency, settled more often, and more often litigated than independently initiated cases. Therefore the results support the commonly held view that follow-on cases are more successful than independently initiated cases, at least to the extent that fewer are dismissed and more are settled. The results also support the view that follow-on cases use fewer resources in that more such cases are settled.

We also classified the outcome data referred to in the preceding paragraph by year. The percentage of cases dismissed varies from year to year for both follow-ons and independently initiated cases, but the range of variation for independently initiated cases is not great. The percentage of litigated cases in both categories, however, dropped steadily throughout the period until at least 1981. (For 1982 and 1983 the number of "other" dispositions such as "pending" increases so substantially that the outcome figures for these two years may be unreliable.)

The subset of litigated cases is of special interest. Of the 1,923 cases for which outcome data are available, 179 cases (slightly more than 9 percent) were litigated to the point of judgment.[35] Of these, 158 were independently initiated, with 21 others in the follow-on category. Overall, some or all plaintiffs won in 30 percent, and some or all defendants won in 70 percent. These figures remain virtually the same when independently initiated and follow-on cases are treated separately—that is, independent of whether the cases followed government cases, some or all defendants won 70 percent and some or all plaintiffs won 30 percent of litigated cases. When only those DOJ follow-on cases that were litigated are considered, the success rate of defendants rises to about three-quarters.

Table 7.6 Consolidated outcomes of private antitrust cases

	Dismissed	Settled	Litigated	Pretrial stipulation	Subtotal	Other	Missing[b]	Total
A. All cases	438	199	179	763	1579	112	14	1,935
Independently initiated cases[a]	405	161	158	725	1449[c]	301	14	1,764
Follow-on cases[a]	33	38	21	38	130[c]	41	0	171
DOJ follow-on cases	27	36	19	31	113	36	0	149
FTC follow-on cases	6	2	2	7	17	5	0	22
Direct follow-on cases	22	29	17	29	97	36	0	133
Indirect follow-on cases	11	9	4	9	33	5	0	38
B. All horizontal price-fixing cases (primary allegation)[d]	65	53	34	104	256	71	2	329
Independently initiated cases[a]	46	26	20	84	176[e]	52	2	230
Follow-on cases[a]	19	27	14	20	80[e]	19	0	99
DOJ follow-on cases	16	27	13	15	71	16	0	87
FTC follow-on cases	3	0	1	5	9	3	0	12
Direct follow-on cases	15	24	12	19	70	16	0	86
Indirect follow-on cases	4	3	2	1	10	3	0	13

a. Refer to the appendix for definitions of independently initiated cases, follow-on cases, and types of follow-on cases. Also refer to the appendix for definitions of dismissed, settled, litigated, pretrial stipulation, and other categories of outcomes.

b. Note that for 14 cases in the 1,935 case data set, no outcome data were available, and these are not represented. The same was true for two cases in the 329 case data set.

c. The differences between the distribution of independently initiated cases and follow-on cases among the dismissed, settled, litigated, and pretrial stipulation categories are significant at the 5 percent level. The chi-square statistic for these two groups of cases is 44.9, with three degrees of freedom.

d. See table 7.1, note b.

e. The differences between the distribution of independently initiated cases and follow-on cases among the dismissed, settled, litigated, and pretrial stipulation categories are significant at the 5 percent level. The chi-square statistic for these two groups of cases is 18.2, with three degrees of freedom.

To sum up, we find that follow-on cases are more likely to be selected for litigation, but the outcomes of litigated follow-on cases do not differ from independently initiated cases.[36] Theory yields ambiguous predictions as to whether follow-on cases are more or less likely to be litigated.[37] We expect the beliefs of parties in follow-on cases would converge, which would encourage settlements. However, the presumed lighter burden of plaintiffs in follow-on cases implies a lower marginal cost of litigation and so encourages litigation.[38] Further, the higher aftertax stakes in some follow-on cases mean that smaller divergences in the parties' expectations may encourage litigation. Accordingly our finding suggests that the latter factors are strong enough to overwhelm the effects of the convergence of beliefs in follow-on cases.

The similarity of litigated outcomes of follow-on and independently initiated cases suggests that the presence of government actions is not influential.[39] This finding requires further investigation. As discussed later, we related the outcomes of the government case to the outcomes of litigated follow-on cases. However, the striking similarity in litigation outcomes may point to a dominating factor: the importance of defendant reputations. Defendants who are more likely to be involved in repeat litigation bear additional costs of losing litigated cases insofar as outcomes affect future settlement/litigate decisions. Defendants in private litigation who bear such costs therefore must be more optimistic about their chances in order to litigate. The slightly higher success rate in litigation for defendants in DOJ follow-on cases is also consistent with this point since defendants in these cases most likely are charged with horizontal violations involving substantial treble damage liability.

We analyzed the outcome data by types of offense using the horizontal, vertical, and other categories. These data appear as table 7.7. For the whole sample, outcomes vary remarkably little within the offense categories. The dismissal rate for horizontal cases (27 percent) is similar to that for vertical cases (26 percent), whereas the settlement rate for horizontal cases (17 percent) is higher than for vertical cases (11 percent). If we include all horizontal *price-fixing* cases in the sample for which meaningful data are available, the dismissal rate (25 percent) is lowest and the settlement rate (21 percent) is highest.

For independently initiated cases the dismissal, pretrial stipulation, settlement, and litigation rates remain virtually the same for horizontal, vertical, and other cases. The type of offense alleged seems to have little connection with outcome. In follow-on cases, however, outcomes vary significantly by type of offense alleged. The dismissal rate for horizontal

Table 7.7 Outcomes of private antitrust cases, by category of offense claimed

	Dismissed	Settled	Litigated	Pretrial stipulation	Subtotal	Other	Missing	Total
All cases								
Horizontal	112	70	48	188	418	104	3	525
Vertical	162	70	76	325	633	78	6	717
Other	95	37	26	158	316	43	4	363
Missing	69	22	29	92	212	116	2	330
Total	438	199	179	763	1,579	341	15	1,935
Independently initiated cases[a]								
Horizontal	92	40	32	166	330	84	3	417
Vertical	155	68	74	315	612	74	6	692
Other	91	36	26	155	308	42	4	354
Missing	67	17	26	89	199	100	2	301
Total	405	161	158	725	1,449	300	15	1,764
Follow-on cases[a]								
Horizontal	20	30	16	22	88	20	0	108
Vertical	7	2	2	10	21	4	0	25
Other	4	1	0	3	8	1	0	9
Missing	2	5	3	3	13	16	0	29
Total	33	38	21	38	130	41	0	171

Note: Refer to the appendix for definitions of independently initiated cases, follow-on cases, and types of follow-on cases. Also refer to the appendix for definitions of the three categories of offenses: horizontal, vertical, and other.
a. The differences between the distribution of independently initiated cases and follow-on cases in the horizontal category among the dismissed, settled, litigated, and pretrial stipulation categories are significant at the 5 percent level. The chi-square statistic for these two groups of cases citing horizontal offenses is 35.0, with three degrees of freedom.

The differences between the distribution of independently initiated cases and follow-on cases in the vertical category among the dismissed, settled, litigated, and pretrial stipulation categories are not significant at the 5 percent level. The chi-square statistic for these two groups of cases citing horizontal offenses is 0.7, with three degrees of freedom.

The differences between the distribution of independently initiated cases and follow-on cases in the other category among the dismissed, settled, litigated, and pretrial stipulation categories are not significant at the 5 percent level. The chi-square statistic for these two groups of cases citing horizontal offenses is 2.0, with three degrees of freedom.

follow-on cases is 22 percent, while for vertical cases it is 33 percent. The settlement rate for horizontal cases is 34 percent, while for vertical cases it is 10 percent. The difference between horizontal and vertical follow-on cases is again revealed when DOJ follow-ons are considered separately. Of these, 22 percent of horizontal and 32 percent of vertical cases are dismissed, 21 percent of horizontal and 53 percent of vertical cases are disposed of on pretrial stipulation, and 38 percent of horizontal and 11 percent of vertical cases are settled. Therefore the beneficial impact of following a government case is concentrated in follow-ons alleging horizontal offenses. The data reveal that follow-ons alleging vertical restraints do no better than other private cases alleging vertical restraints.

The outcomes of follow-on cases also may be influenced greatly by the outcomes of the government cases they follow. To investigate further the interaction between the government cases and follow-on cases, for each follow-on case we added relevant data on government cases, including data on the outcome of the government case, the violation alleged, whether the case was filed by the FTC or the DOJ, whether the DOJ case was civil only or involved alleged criminal violations, and whether the government action was successful. Although to date we have not fully exploited our supplement to the Georgetown data, we can report some interesting results on the impact of the outcomes of government cases on the outcomes of private cases, specifically regarding the success of the government case.

We classified government cases as either successful or not successful, weighting separate counts against individuals and corporations equally. If the government succeeded in 50 percent or more of its counts the case was classified as successful. In particular, civil DOJ cases were classified as successful if the case resulted in either a litigated decree or consent judgment. A criminal DOJ case was classified as successful if the result was a nolo contendere plea, a guilty plea, or a guilty verdict. An FTC case was classified as successful if it resulted in a cease and desist order. Using the 50 percent cutoff, about three out of four government cases on which private cases in our sample followed were successful.

The results regarding the importance of success in the government case are reported in table 7.8. We find that all follow-on cases to ultimately unsuccessful government cases were dismissed, disposed of on pretrial stipulation, or litigated. The litigation rate (38 percent) in such cases is very high. Conversely, 35 percent of the follow-on cases to successful government cases were settled. Furthermore the follow-ons to successful government cases were dismissed less frequently (23 percent) than were follow-ons to unsuccessful government cases (38 percent).

Table 7.8 Outcomes of follow-on cases: the impact of the government case outcome

	Dismissed	Settled	Litigated	Pretrial stipulation	Subtotal	Other	Missing	Total
All follow-on cases	33	38	21	38	130	41	0	171
Cases following-on government wins	25	38	13	33	109	37	0	146
Cases following-on government losses	8	0	8	5	21	4	0	25

Note: Refer to the appendix for definitions of dismissed, settled, litigated, pretrial stipulation, and other categories of outcomes. Government wins and losses are defined according to a 50 percent standard of success, where separate counts in government cases are weighted equally. Civil DOJ cases were classified as successful if the case resulted in either a litigated decree or a consent judgment. Criminal DOJ cases were classified as successful if the result was a nolo contendre plea, a guilty plea, or a guilty verdict. FTC cases were classified successful if the case resulted in a cease and desist order or a consent agreement. The differences between the distribution of follow-ons to successful government cases and follow-ons to unsuccessful government cases among the dismissed, settled, and litigated categories are significant at the 5 percent level, using the 50 percent standard. The chi-square statistic for these two groups of cases is 16.6, with three degrees of freedom.

Table 7.9 Litigated outcomes of private antitrust cases: the impact of the government case outcome

	Judgment for some or all plaintiffs	Judgment for some or all defendants	Total
All cases	53	125	178
Independently initiated cases	47	110	157[a]
Follow-on cases	6	15	21[a]
Cases following-on government wins	4	9	13
Cases following-on government losses	2	6	8

Note: Information on outcomes was obtained from the Court Records Questionnaire, pp. 8–10, which yielded 17 specific, mutually exclusive categories. Two categories, "judgment for all plaintiffs" and "judgment for some plaintiffs," are combined. Likewise, "judgment for all defendants" and "judgment for some defendants" are combined. One independently initiated case in the sample was litigated to a mixed judgment, and it is not included in this table.

Government wins and losses are defined according to a 50 percent standard of success, where separate counts in government cases are weighted equally. Refer to the appendix for definition of follow-on cases. Civil DOJ cases were classified as successful if the case resulted in either a litigated decree or a consent judgment. Criminal DOJ cases were classified as successful if the result was a nolo contendre plea, a guilty plea, or a guilty verdict. FTC cases were classified as successful if the case resulted in a cease and desist order or a consent agreement. In classifying government cases as successful or not successful, counts against individuals and corporations were equally weighted.

a. The differences between the distributions of types of litigated cases between the plaintiff victories and defendant victories are not significant at the 5 percent level. Regarding the differences between litigated follow-on cases and litigated independently initiated cases, the chi-square statistic is 0.02, with one degree of freedom.

Regarding the differences between follow-ons to successful government cases and follow-ons to unsuccessful cases, the chi-square statistic is 0.08 using the 50 percent standard.

In our sample of 21 follow-on cases that were litigated, 13 of these followed successful government cases and eight followed unsuccessful government cases. Although proportionately more follow-ons to unsuccessful cases are selected for litigation, we find only small differences in litigated outcomes between these two types of follow-on cases. Table 7.9 reports these results, which support the view that cases selected for litigation are close calls.

The analysis indicates that the government case outcome does influence related private litigation. A limitation is that we do not distinguish between coincidental and consequential effects by investigating those follow-ons cases whose outcomes are determined after the government case is decided. An unsuccessful government case may reveal that the private case is of lower merit and therefore less likely to succeed (a coincidental effect), but if the outcome of the private case is determined prior to the failure of the government case, the consequential effects may be small. Similarly follow-ons to ultimately successful government cases are likely to succeed because the case is revealed to be of higher merit. The particular manner of disposition of the government case may further influence those follow-on cases whose outcomes are determined after the government case is decided. For example, criminal cases are disposed of by a variety of means: nolo contendere pleas, guilty pleas, guilty verdicts, and not-guilty verdicts. Private cases following a government criminal case will benefit most from a guilty verdict since it may create a prima facie case and the government litigation may generate potentially useful information. These comments concerning coincidental and consequential effects also apply to our finding that of those cases selected for litigation and therefore at the boundary, the outcome of the government case does not strongly influence the litigated outcome of the private case.

Length of Private Antitrust Cases
An important issue in assessing private antitrust litigation is the length of cases since length may be a proxy for resources spent. We are interested in the general assumption that follow-on litigation is briefer than independent litigation. We examined the duration of litigation using three different intervals: (1) time to last docket date, (2) time to judgment date, and (3) time to award date. Data using the first measure of length, time to last docket date, appear in table 7.10. The last docket date data are further classified by type of offense, using horizontal, vertical, and other categories (see table 7.11).

Our results show that by each measure of length the percentage of follow-on cases terminated within two years of filing is significantly smaller than the comparable percentage for independently initiated cases. This is true whether or not the data are analyzed by type of offense alleged. A higher percentage (15 percent) of follow-on cases exceeds five years than is the case for independently initiated cases (10 percent). This pattern holds without regard to type if offense alleged, although the lengths of follow-on cases differ from independently initiated cases if the specific offenses alleged are considered. Overall, it appears that on average follow-on litigation is somewhat longer in duration from time of filing to termination than independently initiated litigation. An ordinary least squares regression on the length of cases supports this point (see table 7.12 for the results). We note that the truncated nature of the dependent variable suggests alternative specifications are preferred if more precise coefficients are critical to the analysis.

Table 7.10 Length of case

	0–6 months	6 months– 1 year	1 year– 18 months	18 months– 2 years	2 years– 3 years	3 years– 4 years	4 years– 5 years	Over 5 years	Sub-total	Missing	Total
All cases	377	345	264	201	256	160	97	192	1,892	43	1,935
Independently initiated cases[a]	347	331	248	186	223	138	83	167	1,723	41	1,764
Follow-on cases[a]	30	14	16	15	33	22	14	25	169	2	171
DOJ follow-on cases	25	12	15	14	32	21	11	19	149	0	149
FTC follow-on cases	5	2	1	1	1	1	3	6	20	2	22
Direct follow-on cases	26	9	10	11	28	16	13	18	131	2	133
Indirect follow-on cases	4	5	6	4	5	6	1	7	38	0	38

Note: Length is defined as the number of days between filing date and the date of the last docket entry.
a. Refer to the appendix for definitions of independently initiated cases, follow-on cases, and types of follow-on cases.

Table 7.11 Length of case, by category of offense

	0–6 months	6 months– 1 year	1 year– 18 months	18 months– 2 years	2 years– 3 years	3 years– 4 years	4 years– 5 years	Over 5 years	Sub-total	Missing	Total
Horizontal cases											
All horizontal cases	82	85	59	58	77	55	28	71	515	10	525
Independently initiated cases[a]	69	80	45	49	57	41	16	52	409	8	417
Follow-on cases[a]	13	5	14	9	20	14	12	19	106	2	108
Vertical cases											
All vertical cases	121	134	119	80	98	52	38	62	704	13	717
Independently initiated cases	118	131	119	76	90	49	38	59	680	12	692
Follow-on cases	3	3	0	4	8	3	0	3	24	1	25
Other cases											
All other cases	80	75	52	44	46	25	13	22	357	6	363
Independently initiated cases	79	73	51	43	45	23	12	22	348	6	354
Follow-on cases	1	2	1	1	1	2	1	0	9	0	9

Note: Length is defined as the number of days between filing date and the date of the last docket entry. Refer to the appendix for definitions of the three categories of offenses: horizontal, vertical, and other.

a. Refer to the appendix for definitions of independently initiated cases and follow-on cases.

Table 7.12   Ordinary least squares regression: Length of private antitrust cases

Dependent variable: length of case (from filing date to last docket entry)
Independent variables (t statistics in parentheses)[a]

Follow-on	261.3
	(1.97)
Settled	121.9
	(1.35)
Pretrial stipulation	163.5
	(2.89)
Litigated	646.9
	(7.03)
Horizontal	153.9
	(2.16)
Vertical	43.0
	(0.70)
Atlanta	−328.1
	(3.27)
Chicago	−152.2
	(2.16)
Kansas City	−145.7
	(1.32)
New York	−201.9
	(3.08)
Number of parties	9.6
	(3.26)
Real dollars (1980) demanded ($M)	0.04
	(0.58)
Constant	764.6
R-squared	0.14
Number of cases	737

a. The independent variables are defined as follows:

Follow-on: dummy variable for follow-on cases (equal to one if the case is a follow-on, zero otherwise).

Settled: dummy variable if the case was settled (equal to one if the case was settled, zero otherwise).

Pretrial stipulations: dummy variable if the case ended in a pretrial stipulation (equal to one if the case ended in pretrial stipulation, zero otherwise).

Litigated: dummy variable if the case was litigated (equal to one if the case was litigated, zero otherwise).

Horizontal: dummy variable for cases citing horizontal offense (equal to one if the case was horizontal, zero otherwise).

Vertical: dummy variable for cases citing vertical offense (equal to one if the case was vertical, zero otherwise).

Atlanta: dummy variable for cases filed in the No. Dist. Georgia.

Chicago: dummy variable for cases filed in the No. Dist. Illinois.

Kansas City: dummy variable for cases filed in the West. Dist. Missouri.

New York: dummy variable for cases filed in the So. Dist. New York.

Number of parties: the sum of the numbers of plaintiffs and defendants.

Real dollars demanded: dollar demand of plaintiffs according to complaint information, in constant 1980 dollars, deflated by the Producer Price Index.

The regression omits the following dummy variables: "dismissed" for outcome category, "other" for category of offense, and No. Dist. Calif. for district filed. Hence the dummy variables included measure differences between the categories represented and the omitted categories.

Our results on length of non-MDL follow-on cases contradict the common view. However, we do not conclude from these results that follow-on cases are less efficient and consume more resources than independently initiated cases. Length may proxy for resources used, but in the case of follow-on litigation, delays may conserve resources. It may be optimal that the government case proceed and generate information for the related litigation rather than have both litigations proceed concurrently. Therefore more direct measures of resource expenditure are needed to determine whether follow-on cases proceed more efficiently than do independently initiated cases.

Horizontal Price-fixing Cases Analyzed Separately
The comparisons of follow-on cases with independently initiated cases identify differences and suggest some general conclusions, but our approach can be criticized in that cases in each category are sufficiently different that they cannot be accurately compared. For example, most independently initiated cases alleging vertical restraints may involve specific allegations of dealer terminations, whereas most follow-on cases alleging vertical restraints may involve vertical price fixing. Differences in dollars demanded, outcomes, length, and so on, might be attributable to the type of conduct at issue rather than to follow-on status. Similarly, if follow-on cases are generally more complex than independently initiated cases, complexity might well be the key variable. To control for this, we analyzed the subset of cases alleging horizontal price fixing. Within this category legal and factual issues are relatively similar, including proof of damages, and all such cases involve multiple defendants.

Of the 1,600 cases in the sample for which offense data were available, 329 alleged horizontal price fixing as the primary offense. Ninety-nine of these cases were follow-ons, while 230 were independently initiated (see part B of table 7.1). Most of these cases were filed between 1973 and 1978. Horizontal price-fixing cases were a much higher percentage of follow-on cases (70.4 percent) than of independently initiated cases (22.5 percent).

We examined horizontal price-fixing cases with respect to the real dollars demanded in complaints and for those that follow government cases the intervals between the filing dates. A higher percentage of complaints in independently initiated price-fixing cases sought small dollar amounts and a lower percentage sought large dollar amounts, as compared to complaints in follow-on cases. These results, reported in part B of table 7.3, contrast sharply with the full sample results. However, the number of cases for which data are available is not sufficiently large to draw firm conclusions. With regard to the filing of follow-on cases, plaintiffs were somewhat slower in filing price-fixing cases than other follow-on cases, with over half filed more than 180 days after the government action was initiated (see table 7.2).

In reviewing outcomes, we again eliminated cases that did not involve true outcomes (pending, consolidated, remanded, missing), leaving 176 independently initiated cases and 80 follow-on cases. Of the independently initiated cases, 46 (26 percent) were dismissed, 84 (48 percent) were ended on pretrial stipulation, 26 (15 percent) were settled, and 20 (11 percent) were litigated (see part B of tables 7.5 and 7.6). These percentages for independently initiated horizontal price-fixing cases reflect a slightly lower dismissal rate and slightly higher settlement rate, than do comparable figures for all independently initiated cases (table 7.6). Of the follow-on horizontal price-fixing cases, 19 (24 percent) were dismissed, 20 (25 percent) were ended on pretrial stipulation, 27 (34 percent) were settled, and 14 (18 percent) were litigated.[40]

A comparison of follow-ons alleging horizontal price fixing with their independently initiated counterparts confirms that follow-on cases derive benefits from a government case. We find follow-ons alleging horizontal price fixing are less likely to be dismissed, more likely to settle, and more likely to be litigated. The percentage figures are virtually the same as those for follow-on cases alleging offenses within the general category of horizontal restraints. Although the higher percentage of litigated cases may be interpreted as a negative, this result in part reflects that fewer of these follow-on cases are dismissed. Of interest, we note that of nine horizontal price-fixing cases following FTC actions, three were dismissed, five were ended on pretrial stipulation, none was settled, and one was litigated. Therefore our review of horizontal price-fixing cases reveals that private plaintiffs derive benefits from following the Department of Justice, but not necessarily from following the Federal Trade Commission.

Finally, within the horizontal price-fixing classification, follow-on cases on average take longer to termination than independently initiated cases, confirming the findings based upon examination of the sample as a whole (see table 7.11).

Multidistrict Litigation

Detailed data on multidistrict litigations (MDLs) were not collected for the Georgetown sample. Thus cases organized in MDLs that were heard by judges within the sample districts, as well cases filed within the sample districts but consolidated as part of an MDL docket outside these districts, are not reflected in our results. Although some data were collected for 19 of the 29 MDL dockets in the sample districts, these data are not comparable to those collected for other private cases and therefore could not be integrated with the balance. As a result the basic data may be somewhat skewed in several respects.

The MDL dockets represent a large number of individual cases, about 485 by our count. Not all of these cases were filed within the five sample districts, and of those that were, not all cases in the 19 MDL dockets were filed within the time period of the Georgetown sample. Thus even in terms of numbers of cases the MDL data are not fully comparable with those in the Georgetown sample for non-MDL cases.

The exclusion of the MDL cases would be of little consequence if they reflected the same basic patterns as the cases for which data were collected, but this does not seem to be the case. MDL cases appear to involve larger sums demanded, a relatively higher settlement rate, and a higher percentage of follow-ons than other litigation. The absence of comparable data for MDL cases thus may cause inaccuracies in the analysis of the sample data, particularly as it relates to follow-ons.

Of the 29 antitrust MDL cases in the sample districts during the relevant time period, no data were available for ten cases. One follow-on case[41] is still pending, and little data were collected for it. Nine of the 18 remaining MDL cases follow government actions,[42] a much higher percentage than in the sample cases. This is also true of all MDL case nationwide. Although we have not been able to classify all MDL cases as follow-ons or independently initiated, at least 42 of the 123 MDL cases nationwide that were primarily antitrust cases (as of January 1, 1985) were follow-ons. Thus of all MDL antitrust cases at least 34 percent were follow-ons.

The ten follow-on MDL cases represent a total of 403 cases. The other nine MDLs for which we have data represent a total of 82 cases. If we add all cases represented by the nineteen MDLs to the Georgetown sample, the total number of cases increases to 2,420, and the total number of follow-ons rises to 574. The resulting percentage of follow-ons (24 percent) is biased upward, given that (1) a number of cases within the MDL dockets were filed before the sample time period and (2) the districts included in the sample attracted a significant number of cases in the MDL dockets filed in other districts, a number greater than the number of cases filed with the sample districts but consolidated as MDLs in other districts. Since cases in each MDL docket are closely related, their inclusion on a numbers-of-cases basis overemphasizes their significance. Nevertheless, the 24 percent figure is probably a closer approximation to the true pattern of follow-on cases than the 9 percent figure derived from the basic data base from which MDL cases are excluded.

Of the 19 MDL dockets for which data are available, eight are comprised of horizontal price-fixing cases.[43] Seven of these follow DOJ cases.[44] These eight MDL dockets represent 341 of the approximately 485 cases in all 19 dockets. Within this limited sample, 70 percent of the MDL docket cases were horizontal price-fixing cases. Two of the 18 MDL cases in the sample districts involved only two cases each, while one represented 122 cases.[45]

In at least ten of the MDL dockets, there was a settlement in favor of at least some plaintiffs. In four of these, settlements exceeded 50 million dollars, with a high of $218 million.[46] Three of these four were follow-ons; in the remaining case the government returned an indictment shortly after the settlement was reached.[47] Although the data are unclear in some cases, it appears that the average time between filing of the first case in the MDL docket and termination of the entire MDL proceeding is approximately 6.1 years. The average elapsed time for MDL follow-on cases was 5.7 years; for other cases it was 6.4 years. As we noted earlier, the intervals between the filing of the government case and MDL follow-ons tend to be much shorter than non-MDL follow-ons; half of the MDL follow-ons were filed within 30 days.[48]

7.3 Conclusions

We offer some tentative conclusions based on the results presented in this chapter. If all private antitrust actions were follow-ons to *successful* government actions, the policies underlying the treble damage remedy would be confined almost exclusively to victim compensation and the imposition of a large enough penalty to deter misconduct by the convicted miscreant and, more important, by others.[49] If some additional cases followed *unsuccessful* government cases, we might conclude that absent concerns over judicial error there was little justification for such cases at all. On the other hand, if all private cases were independently initiated, the rationale for a treble damage remedy encompasses not only the policies of compensation and penalty but also the need to provide private incentives to detect and prevent continuing violations. Where, as is currently the case, private actions are a mixture of follow-on and independently initiated cases, it is important to judge the significance of each category if alternatives are to be adequately evaluated.

Our study indicates that follow-on cases represent a relatively small fraction of all private antitrust actions filed. In 1965 a commentator examining the relationship between public and private antitrust actions concluded that about 75 percent of all treble damage actions filed before 1960 were initiated after, and in reliance on, similar government enforcement actions.[50] Although there may be disagreement over the precise figures to be drawn from the current study, the percentage of follow-on cases filed (including MDL cases) as compared to all private actions filed during 1973 to 1983 does not, we believe, exceed 24 percent and is probably less. The percentage is still declining. A reassessment of the treble damage remedy must begin therefore with recognition that 80 percent or more of the private cases filed are not follow-ons.

The decline in the percentage of follow-on litigation from the pre-1960 period to the 1973–1983 period does not mean the number of follow-on cases has declined. The most obvious explanation for the change in percentages is not a decrease in follow-on cases but an increase in independently initiated cases. Public enforcement activity held at relatively steady levels through the 1960s and 1970s, so follow-ons could not increase significantly. However, the same period was marked by dramatic increases in the number of independently initiated cases.[51] The number of follow-on cases of course may be expected to vary somewhat with the type of cases filed by government agencies; merger actions did not spawn follow-on cases, whereas price-fixing cases generally did. The large price-fixing cases of the mid-1970s resulted in a large number of follow-on cases.[52] The bid-rigging cases of the 1980s brought few follow-on cases. There is no simple correlation between the number of government cases filed and the number of follow-ons. However, the number of follow-on cases cannot rise in large numbers without an increase in public enforcement activity.

We have no reason to believe that the total number of follow-on cases either increased or decreased from 1960 through 1977. However, our data reflect a steady decrease in the number of follow-on cases and their percentage of the total, beginning in 1978. This decline cannot be attributed to a sharp drop in public enforcement actions. *Illinois Brick* may be responsible in part. More likely, the cause is the nature of the cases filed. The largest number of government cases involved rigging of bids to public purchasers. Because the Department of Justice often returns indictments on a bid by bid basis, damages in each case may have appeared small. Moreover state purchasers are able to use threats of debarment to extract settlements from indicted contractors without initiating antitrust litigation and so have an effective, alternative remedy that other plaintiffs lack. During this period few large price-fixing cases were filed, and the government's success rate in such cases fell.[53]

Despite the recent decrease in the number of non-MDL follow-on cases, follow-on litigation remains a significant element in antitrust litigation, more significant than simple numbers suggest. Many of the largest recoveries in the past ten years are the result of follow-on cases (often in MDL dockets). Although we find little difference in dollars demanded in complaints between independently initiated cases and follow-on cases in the Georgetown sample excluding MDL cases, with the inclusion of MDL cases we believe that follow-on cases on average involve significantly larger amounts.

Further, follow-ons are far more likely than independently initiated cases to focus on horizontal price fixing, the most egregious and economically significant antitrust violation. Because the government in recent years has placed primary emphasis on price fixing, it is not surprising that follow-on cases do the same. Our study shows that independently initiated cases lack the same focus. The data offer little explanation as to why this is so. Several factors play a role, however. First, price fixing is difficult to detect. Private litigants lack the resources and compulsory process available to government. In many cases private litigants may be unable to proceed without the signal and assistance provided by government prosecution. Second, independently initiated cases are more likely to focus on conduct that is visible and has a clear "victim"; both of these conditions are far more likely to be present when vertical restraints are at issue. Whatever the explanation, however, it seems clear that follow-on litigation is critically important in dealing with horizontal price fixing.

The prototypical non-MDL follow-on case involves horizontal price fixing. Contrary to the perception of some, it is not filed precipitously; a relatively small percentage of cases in the non-MDL sample were filed within 30 days of the initiation of the government action, and only about 40 percent within six months. It does appear, however, that in large price-fixing cases (as reflected in MDL data), follow-ons are filed more quickly. And it is more likely than not that the follow-on was filed in a district other than that where the government action was filed.

The finding that intervals between the filings of government cases and non-MDL follow-ons are often lengthy may be important. Given the low cost of filing a follow-on damage claim, the delays may indicate that the value of private treble damage rights in many cases is not as great as is normally believed. Plaintiffs may find filing to be worthwhile only after the government case proceeds, either clearing hurdles that make the rights more valuable or by generating information about who is most likely to succeed in recovering damage awards. The finding may also indicate that competition among counsel to establish themselves in the event of multiple filings may not be so severe. Alternatively, treble damage rights may be more well defined than is commonly believed. The point that intervals for MDL cases are shorter, aside from merely reflecting the greater value of these rights and the competition for them, tempers these points. On the other hand, the MDL and non-MDL cases are themselves a subset of a larger set that includes potential claims arising from government cases that are not filed. Recent research suggests that a significant number of government cases are not followed by treble damage claims.[55] Future research using the data on intervals may be able to distinguish along potential theories.

What of the belief that follow-ons use fewer resources, take less time, and are more successful for plaintiffs than independently initiated cases? We have little direct data on costs. The case length data suggest that follow-on cases generally take longer than independently initiated cases even when relevant factors such as type of offense alleged, numbers of parties involved, and ultimate disposition are accounted for in the analysis. On the assumption that our tentative conclusion is accurate, the explanation may simply be that follow-ons are more complex. It may also be that resolution of issues relating to the relationship of the government and private cases, and contests over the availability of data supplied to the government, actually add to the length of the litigation. We do not believe that this is necessarily cause for concern.

The outcome data are the most revealing. A higher percentage of follow-ons was litigated than was true for independently initiated cases. Of the cases litigated, plaintiffs in follow-ons were no more successful than plaintiffs in independently initiated cases.[54] These results are inconsistent with common perceptions, but based on outcomes as a whole, follow-on cases were more likely to be litigated because fewer were dismissed. Settlement rates were significantly higher for follow-ons than for other cases. Thus, overall, follow-on plaintiffs met with greater success, as measured in terms of lower dismissal and higher settlement rates. These results on outcomes suggest an explanation for the somewhat greater length of follow-on litigation: follow-on cases are less likely than independently initiated case to be settled or dismissed quickly. Fewer follow-on cases are likely to result in summary judgment for defendants. The average length of follow-on cases would therefore be longer than the length of independently initiated cases, where early dismissals are more common.

We cannot determine whether this greater success rate for plaintiffs is attributable to the signal by the government or to the legal and practical benefits it confers on private plaintiffs. But for the findings on litigated outcomes the results are consistent with general beliefs, although not as strongly in plaintiffs' favor as we might have thought.

Our results on the relationship between outcomes of follow-on cases and the related government cases are also revealing. We find that if the government loses, follow-on cases are more likely to be dismissed or litigated. Of the 27 follow-ons to unsuccessful government, only one resulted in a settlement. In contrast, the outcome of the government case has virtually no impact on outcomes of litigated follow-on cases. Therefore the government litigation provides important information concerning the merit of the private case and thus affects the boundary between those cases that are dismissed and those that are not. However, the government case is apparently irrelevant to the outcome of these cases selected for litigation.

7.4 Appendix: Data Description and Methodology for Classification of Cases

Data Description

On behalf of the Georgetown private litigation project, the Cambridge Research Institute (CRI) collected three data sets. The first set, which was used for the bulk of our analysis, consists of docket information from the files of all private antitrust cases filed in the 11-year period 1973 to 1983 in five U.S. district courts: the Southern District of New York (New York City), the Northern District of Illinois (Chicago), the Northern District of California (San Francisco), the Eastern District of Missouri (Kansas City), and the Northern District of Georgia (Atlanta). One hundred and thirty variables suggested by a ten-page questionnaire were extracted from each docket file. Over 3,200 cases were filed in the five districts in this time period. The completed data set contains 1,935 cases. The balance falls into three categories: cases consolidated into other cases in the same district, cases consolidated in other districts (multidistrict litigations), and cases for which substantial docket data were not available.

A second data set collected by CRI includes information on 19 multidistrict litigations, which consolidated approximately 600 individual cases. The data received includes some information on about one-half of the individual cases. The MDLs include a large portion of follow-on cases and many of the most significant private cases filed, such as the *Alton Box Litigation* and the *In Re. Sugar Institute Litigation*. The third data set collected by CRI includes responses to questionnaires sent to attorneys representing plaintiffs and defendants in all cases. We did not attempt to integrate these data into our analysis.

Classification of Cases as either Follow-ons or Independently Initiated Cases

A major part of our work involved classifying cases as follow-ons or independently initiated. Follow-on cases allege roughly the same violation as a government case that usually, but not always, precedes its filing. We used indexes for DOJ and FTC reporters to match defendant names. (The FTC index was compiled by eliminating nonantitrust cases from the full FTC index. The antitrust index is overinclusive to the extent that some purely procedural matters appeared to be substantive and is underinclusive for the opposite reason.) We then used a variety of screens to determine if matched private cases actually followed a government case: violation alleged, statutory authority relied on, time of the violation, product market, relationship of the plaintiff to the defendant, timing of the private suit, and the filing district. We thank Robert McGuckin and Jon Joyce of the Antitrust Division for providing data that match private follow-on cases to DOJ criminal section 1 cases over the period 1969 to 1980. Their data, which match cases according to defendant name and filing dates, were helpful in confirming some of our classifications.

We noted answers to the docket survey question (P.5, Q. # 13), "Were these practices the subject of other legal proceedings, e.g., a government investigation or suit, other private law suits, or previous related suits (Y/N)? Give dates, full citations, and outcomes." However, since "yes" responses could refer to private actions, the "yes" responses are not reliable. We discovered among case records of clear follow-on cases, docket information indicating a "no" response to this question. Accordingly, these responses were not used in classifying the data.

We further distinguished follow-on cases as direct or indirect follow-ons to account for differences in the extent to which the private case correspond in the violation alleged to the related government case. Virtually all follow-on cases diverge in at least a minor way from the government case with respect to the specific practices alleged, the product and geographic markets cited, the time period covered, the names of defendants, and so on. We classified as direct follow-ons those private cases that essentially duplicate the theory of the government case. We classified as indirect follow-ons those private cases that significantly extend the government case by alleging additional practices that differ from those alleged by the government, expanding the time of the conspiracy, or expanding the alleged practices to different markets. Typically a private case alleging an additional, but similar, charge (e.g., adding refusal to deal to a vertical restraint case) was classified as a direct follow-on. However, if the private case alleging a practice that was not similar to that alleged in the government case (e.g., adding predatory pricing and monopolization to a horizontal price-fixing case), then the case was classified as an indirect follow-on.

Two points are worth noting. First, we could not identify private cases that follow government action short of a complaint or indictment, even though we believe private cases follow, for example, grand jury investigations. Second, questions concerning classification arose. We considered adding an "uncertain" category but rejected this option because of the difficulty in drawing the additional boundary.

Methodology for Classifying Outcomes of Private Cases

The docket survey sought a variety of information concerning outcomes of cases. The data set includes a categorical variable with 17 mutually exclusive possible outcomes. We collapsed this information on the primary outcome into five broad categories: dismissed, settled, litigated, pretrial stipulation, and other..

The "dismissed" category consists of the following outcomes: dismissed pretrial on motion, pretrial withdrawal, dismissal by court, dismissal by other means. The "pretrial stipulation" category consists only of outcomes identified as pretrial stipulation and order. The "settled" category consists only of outcomes identified as settled. The "litigated" category consists of the following outcomes: judgment for all plaintiffs, judgment for some plaintiffs, judgment for all defendants, judgment for some defendants, judgment for some plaintiffs and some defendants. The "other" category consists of the following outcomes: statistically closed, consolidated, file missing, transferred or remanded to state court, outcome unknown, and pending.

The pretrial stipulation category raises important questions, especially given our finding that a much lower percentage of follow-on cases result in pretrial stipulations. It is likely that this category mixes dismissed and settled cases. We suspect that when pretrial stipulations involve some payment to the plaintiff, the dollar amounts are small. In this sense cases ending in pretrial stipulations are likely to be of lower merit than are settled cases. Regression analysis of the length of cases indicates that cases ending in pretrial stipulations end significantly earlier than dismissed cases, which in turn end earlier than settled cases (see table 7.12). Of some interest, 44.1 percent of cases ending in pretrial stipulations end within one year, suggesting these cases differ from both other dismissed cases and from settled cases. Specifically, 22.8 percent of settled cases and 33.0 percent of dismissed end within one year. For the reasons noted, we considered categorizing pretrial stipulations as dismissals. However, our cross-check of cases ending in pretrial stipulations and data on whether cases ended with or without prejudice suggested some of the pretrial stipulations are settlements.

Methodology on the Classification of Offenses

Information regarding primary offenses alleged was obtained from the Court Records Questionnaire, which provides data on 27 specific practices (e.g., horizontal price fixing). The data are coded as follows: 1 identifies the primary offense, 2 identifies the secondary offenses, and blanks denote that the specific offense was not among those alleged.

We classified the 1,600 cases for which offense data are available into three major groups: horizontal, vertical, and other. The "horizontal" group consists of the following specific practices: horizontal price fixing, merger/joint venture, asset accumulation, predatory pricing, and monopolization. The "vertical" group consists of the following specific practices: vertical price fixing, resale price maintenance, vertical price discrimination, exclusive dealing or tying, territorial restrictions, dealer termination, and refusal to deal. The "other" group consists of these following practices: inducing government action, breach, slander, fraud, restraint of trade, bribes, unfair competition, license and trademark practices, boycott, interference, misrepresentation, conspiracy, boycott, confidential information/trade practices, and price discrimination.

The survey instructed that only one offense be selected as the primary offense and that other offenses cited be identified as secondary offenses. However, some case records included multiple primary offenses, while others had multiple secondary offenses but no primary offenses. We used a simple algorithm to classify each case uniquely according to primary offense alleged when more than one primary offense was listed.

Methodology on the Classification of Plaintiff's Business Relationship to Defendant

The information regarding plaintiff's business relationship to defendant was obtained from the Court Records Questionnaire, which provides data on 18 specific categories (e.g., competitor) with the data coded as follows: 1 identifies the primary relationship, 2 identifies the secondary relationship, and blanks denote that the specific relationship did not apply.

We classified the 1,592 cases for which business relationship data are available into six categories: competitor, customer, dealer, supplier, licensee/franchisee, and other. These categories are defined as follows. The "competitor" category consists of these business relationships: competitor–same product, competitor–similar or substitute product, and other competitor. The "customer" category consists of final customer or end user, defendant supplier to plaintiff. The "supplier" category consists of only the supplier business relationship. The "dealer" category consists only of the dealer, agent, or distributor business relationships. The "licensee/franchisee" category consists of the licensee and franchisee business relationships. The "other" category consists of these business relationships: employee, state or local government, labor union, stockholder, lessee, trade association, and other business relationship.

As with the offenses alleged, the survey instructed that only one relationship be identified as primary. However, a few case records identified more than one relationship as primary. We used a simple algorithm to classify uniquely according to plaintiff's business relationship when more than one primary relationship was identified.

Notes

We thank Kurt Braun, Krista Kauper. Todd Miller, and Jane Phifer for expert research assistence. Edward Snyder acknowledges financial assistence provided by the University of Michigan Graduate School of Business Administration's summer research program.

1. 15 U.S.C. Sec. 15 (1982)

2. 15 U.S.C. Sec. 27 (1982)

3. A few private suits seek only injunctive relief.

4. Indeed, the mere fact that the government has investigated the matter may send such a signal, albeit a weaker one. See Kohn, Evaluation of an Antitrust Claim, Prospective Cost of Litigation, Standing to Sue and Preparation of Suit, 38 Antitrust L.J. 7, 10–11 (1968).

5. See, e.g., Lerman, Settlement of Government and Private Cases: The Defense, 50 Antitrust L.J. 17 (1980). Compare Reich, The Antitrust Industry, 68 Geo. L.J. 1053, 1065 (1980).

6. Reich, The Antitrust Industry, supra note 5, at 1065.

7. For general discussions on the advantages of prior government actions, see Collen, Procedural Directions in Antitrust Treble Damage Litigation: An Overview on Changing Judicial Attitudes, 17 Antitrust Bull. 997, 1011–1016 (1972); Symposium on Government Enforcement and Private Actions, 42 Antitrust L.J. 209–243 (1972); Symposium on Relationships Between Government Employment Actions and Private Damage Actions, 37 Antitrust L.J. 823–871 (1968); Seamans. First Aid to the Plaintiff, 32 Antitrust L.J. 41 (1966).

8. 15 U.S.C. Sec. 16(i) (1982). This provision has been held applicable to Federal Trade Commission proceedings as well as to proceedings initiated by the Department of Justice. See Minnesota Mining and Mfg. Co. v. New Jersy Wood Finishing Co., 381 U.S. 311 (1965).

9. 15 U.S.C. Sec. 16(a) (1982). There is some doubt concerning the applicability of section 5(a) to Federal Trade Commission orders. The issue was left unresolved in Minnesota Mining, *supra* note 8. Lower courts have applied section 5(a) to such orders where the Commission is enforcing the Sherman and Clayton Acts but have generally refused to apply it when the Commission is acting to implement its broader authority under section 5 of the Federal Trade Commission Act. *See* P. Areeda, Antitrust Analysis 92, n. 160 (3d ed. 1981).

10. Section 5(a) of the Clayton Act was amended in 1980 to ensure that it was not construed to impose any limitation on assertions of collateral estoppel. 15 U.S.C. Sec. 16(a) (1982).

11. Most government actions are settled by consent decree or by nolo contendere plea. *See*, *e.g.*, Posner, A Statistical Study of Antitrust Enforcement, 13 J. Law & Econ. 365, 375, (1970) (75 percent from 1890–1969); McDavid, Saankbeil, Schmidt, & Brett, Antitrust Consent Decrees: Ten Years of Experience under the Tunney Act, 52 Antitrust L.J. 883 (1983). (In the period 1955–73, 80 percent of Department of Justice civil actions were terminated by consent decrees. Since 1973, 92 percent of such cases have been terminated in such a manner.)

12. *See*, *e.g.*, Collen Procedural Directions in Antitrust Treble Damage Litigation: An Overview on Changing Judicial Attitudes, n. 7 *supra* at 1013. *See also* Kramer, Subsequent Use of the Record and Proceedings in a Criminal Case, 38 Antitrust L.J. 300 (1968). *Cf.* H.R. Rep. No. 874, 96th Cong., *reprinted in* 1980 U.S. Code Cong. & Ad. News 2752, 2756 n. 4.

13. *Compare* Breit and Elzinga, Private Antitrust Enforcement: The New Learning, 28 J. Law & Econ. 405, 413 (1985), and Wheeler, Antitrust Treble–Damage Actions: Do They Work?, 61 Cal.L.Rev. 1319, 1326 (1973) with Korman, The Antitrust Plaintiff Following in the Government's Footsteps, 16 Vill.L.Rev. 57, 68–69 (1970); Blecher, The Plaintiff's Viewpoint, 38 Antitrust L.J. 50, 57 (1968). Section 5(a) may be of greater utility since the 1980 Antitrust Procedural Improvements Act amended sec. 5(a) to permit a collateral estoppel, rather than merely a prima facie effect, to previous government judgments in appropriate cases. *See supra* note 10. The amendment is discussed in detail in H.R. Rep. No. 874, 96th Cong., *reprinted in* 1980 U.S. Cong. & Ad. News 2752, 2756. For discussion of the advantages of collateral estoppel, *see*, *e.g.*, Shores, Treble Damage Antitrust Suits: Admissibility of Prior Judgments under Sec. 5 of the Clayton Act, 54 Iowa L.Rev. 434, 445 (1968). See also Note, The Use of Government Judgments in Private Antitrust Litigation: Clayton Act Section 5(a), Collateral Estoppel, and Jury Trial, 43 U.Chi.L.Rev. 338 (1976).

14. *See* 2 P. Areeda and D. Turner, Antitrust Law 117–188 (1978); Korman, The Antitrust Plaintiff Following in the Government's Footsteps, *supra*, note 13 at 63–70; H.R. Rep. No. 874, 96th Cong., *reprinted in* 1980 U.S. Code Cong. & Ad. News 2752.

15. In addition to documents and testimony in the public court record, the Publicity in Taking Evidence Act, 15 U.S.C. Sec. 30 (1982) provides that deposition proceedings in Department of Justice cases seeking equitable relief shall be open to the public. The plaintiff may also find assistance in the competitive Impact Statement that the Department of Justice must file with the court when a consent decree is to be entered. *See* Dramatization: The Pros and Cons of Settlement, 48 Antitrust L.J. 165, 176 (1979).

16. The practical problems of securing grand jury data are discussed in detail in all the authorities citied in *supra* note 7.

17. 5 U.S.C. Sec. 552 (1982). The act contains a number of exceptions. Requests therefore may involve substantial time and money, particularly if the agency asserts that some or all of the material requested is in an exempt category.

18. *See*, *e.g.*, Korman, The Antitrust Plaintiff Following in the Government's Footsteps, 16 Vill.L.Rev. 57, 70–77 (1970); Kohn, Evaluation of an Antitrust Claim Prospective Cost of Litigation, Standing to Sue and Preparation of Suit, 38 Antitrust L.J. 7, 11 (1968); Loevinger, Handling a Plaintiff's Antitrust Damage Suit, 4 Antitrust Bull. 29, 43–44 (1959).

19. United States Internal Revenue Code Sec. 162(g); Treas. Reg. Sec. 1.162-22 (1972). *See generally* Wright, A Tax Formula to Restore the Historical Effects of the Antitrust Treble Damages Provisions, 65 Mich.L.Rev. 245 (1966).

20. *See, e.g.*, H.R. Rep. No. 874, 96th Cong., *reprinted in* 1980 U.S.C. Code Cong. & Ad. News 2752, 2754.

21. The following table represents the total number of antitrust cases filed by the Department of Justice for each fiscal year from 1974 through 1985:

1974	1975	1976	1977	1978	1979	1980	1981	1982	1983	1984	1985
66	43	75	65	82	66	88	103	112	107	114	58

The figures for fiscal years 1974–1981 are taken from M. Handler, H. Blake, R. Pitofsky, and H. Goldschmid, Trade Regulation 124 (2d ed. 1983). The balance are derived from the case summaries of Department of Justice filings in 4 Trade Reg. Rep. (CCH) 45,081 *et. seq.* For the filings of the Department of Justice in the Years 1890–1969, *see* Posner, A Statistical Study of Antitrust Enforcement, note supra, at 366.

22. Kaiser Cement Corp. v. Fischbach & Moore Inc., filed September 2, 1983 (N.D. Cal.). This case follows a criminal case filed by the U.S. on June 8, 1983, United States v. Fischbach & Moore, Inc., 4 Trade Reg. Rep. (CCH) 45,083 (W.D. Wash. 1983), alleging bid rigging of primary electrical contracts in the State of Washington.

23. It is also possible that a few state damage claims were filed by states under their own antitrust statues.

24. Antitrust Procedures and Penalties Act, 88 Stat. 1706 (1974). The act increased individual and corporate fines and raised the maximum jail sentence from one to three years. Violations became felonies rather than misdemeanors.

25. If the probability of conviction depends on the severity of the offense, then the deterrent effects of penalties include reductions in both the total number of offenses and the severity of offenses committed. *See* Block, Nold, and Sidak, The Deterrent Effect of Antitrust Enforcement, 89 J. Pol. Econ. 429 (1981).

26. Snyder investigated the effects of the 1974 increase in criminal antitrust penalties and found that (1) the number of cases alleging horizontal conspiracies fell, (2) higher potential penalties (criminal penalties and exposure to treble damage penalties) encouraged defendants to plead not guilty, (3) of those cases alleging horizontal conspiracies that were litigated, the government's success rate fell significantly, and (4) the real volume of commerce in such cases won by the government fell. Edward A. Snyder, "Defensive Effort" and Efficient Enforcement, Ph.D. dissertation, University of Chicago, 1984.

27. Illinois Brick Co. v. Illinois, 431 U.S. 720 (1977).

28. The *Illinois Brick* decision and the *Hanover Shoe* decision [Hanover Shoe, Inc.v. United Shoe Machinery Corp., 392 U.S. 481 (1968)] effectively transferred some treble damage rights from indirect to direct purchasers. According to two recent studies the transfer of rights alone did not reduce the number of private follow-on cases filed if the number and type of government cases filed is taken into account. Joyce and McGuckin found that the number of follow-on cases to nonhighway bid-rigging cases increases after the *Illinois Brick* decision. Snyder used a time series/cross-sectional analysis of the legal rules employed by district courts from 1963 to 1982 to investigate the effects of the combined *Hanover Shoe* and *Illinois Brick* rules. He found, accounting for changes in the numbers of government cases, that the rule had a neutral effect on the number of private antitrust cases filed. Joyce and McGuckin, Assignment of Rights to Sue Under Illinois Brick: An Empirical Assessment, EPO Discussion Paper No. 85-6, Antitrust Division, U.S. Department of Justice (April 9, 1985); Snyder, Efficient Assignment of Rights to Sue for Antitrust Damages, 28 J. Law & Econ. 469 (1985).

29. The interval for MDL follow-ons is defined as the time between the filing dates of the government case and the first private case in the MDL. Our review indicated that most of the other underlying cases are filed shortly after the first.

30. The Producer Price Index was used to deflate the dollar demand data.

31. The 1979 study of 352 private antitrust cases filed in the Southern District of New York between 1973 and 1978 conducted by National Economic Research Associates, Inc. (NERA) found that 73 percent of these cases involved vertical relationships. *See* National Economic Research Associates, Inc., A Statistical Analysis of Private Antitrust Litigation: Final Report (1979); Melican, The Treble Damage Case: Fact and Fiction, 49 Antitrust L.J. 981 (1980). The differences between these figures and ours may reflect variations in classification, time periods or the nature of the sample, which was confined to one judicial district. See also, Posner, A Statistical Study of Antitrust Enforcement, *supra* note 11, at 409, table 32.

32. There was one other striking dissimilarity: 13 percent of all follow-on cases were remanded to state court. Nothing in these data explains this counterintuitive finding.

33. We examined length data, award data, and data on whether cases were dismissed with or without prejudice to aid in determining whether pretrial stipulations are dismissals or settlements. We concluded that this category includes both types of outcomes. Length of case data reveal that dismissed cases are shorter than settled cases. We looked at cases ending in pretrial stipulations for an indication as to whether they, in this respect, resemble either category. We found, other factors held constant, that cases ending in pretrial stipulations are significantly shorter than dismissed cases. This ranking alone suggests settlements. We also reviewed available data on whether cases ending in pretrial stipulations were disposed of with or without prejudice. If a case is settled, defendant will require that the settlement ends the dispute, meaning that the disposition is with prejudice. The docket questionnaire asked for these data with questions distinct from those extracting data on specific outcomes. An analysis of the prejudice data and the outcome data indicates that approximately the same percentage of cases in the settled and pretrial stipulation categories ended with prejudice, suggesting many cases ending in pretrial stipulations are settlements. Award data, however, do not indicate that pretrial stipulations usually involve payments.

34. The 1979 NERA study, *supra* note 31, examined outcomes in 209 cases in the Southern District of New York. The study did not differentiate between follow-on and independently initiated cases. Of the 209 cases studied, 81 percent were voluntarily dismissed or settled. Only 16 percent were decided on motion for summary judgment or went to trial. See also Posner, *supra* note 11, at 383, table 13.

35. Outcome data in the sample were placed in categories showing judgment for all plaintiffs, judgment for all defendants, judgment for some plaintiffs, judgment for some defendants, and mixed judgments. We have treated the total number of cases in these five categories as "litigated to judgment." Because some summary judgments are within these categories, "litigated"—as we have defined it—does not mean that these cases involved actual *trial* time.

36. This result is consistent with a recent theoretical and empirical analysis by Priest and Klein, who examine the selection process of cases for litigation (as against settlement). Under certain conditions the proportion of plaintiff victories will converge toward 50 percent, but that proportion will adjust to the decision criteria of the parties. Our finding suggests that defendants have stricter decision criteria; that is, they must believe that their probability of success is greater than that of plaintiffs, most likely because they are more concerned with the effect that a given litigated outcome—especially a loss—will have on their reputations. Underlying this point is a presumption that defendants are faced with more potential litigants and therefore are more concerned with their reputations. Priest and Klein, The Selection of Disputes for Litigation, 13 J. Legal Stud. 1–57 (1984).

37. For a detailed analysis of the factors that influence the decision to settle or litigate and their relevance to differences between follow-on cases and independently initiated cases, *see* Kauper and Snyder, The Outcomes of Private Antitrust Cases: A Legal and Economic Analysis, 74(4) Geo. L. J. (April 1986).

38. This would seem particularly true after the 1980 amendment to section 5(a) of the Clayton Act, discussed in *supra* note 13. The effect of the amendment cannot be evaluated with the data in the Georgetown sample.

39. Refer to table 7.9 for results on litigated outcomes of follow-on and independently initiated cases. Defendants win about 70 percent of cases in each category. This finding is consistent with Priest and Klein's (1984) hypothesis that only cases where plaintiff's proba-bility of success is within a small range will be selected for litigation. Priest and Klein expect, and their empirical findings support, that the range is 50 percent independent of the standard of law, whether judges are hostile, and so on. Importantly, theirs is a one-period model in which defendant's potential loss is symmetrical to plaintiff's potential gain. They demonstrate when this is not the case—for example, when defendants suffers a loss of reputation if plaintiff prevails—the proportation of plaintiff victories will diverge from the 50 percent range. In the example of potential defendant reputation loss, the percentage of plaintiff victories will fall since defendants must be more confident of their success to forego settlement. Priest and Klein, *supra* note 36.

40. When these figures for horizontal price-fixing cases are classified more specifically by outcome, as shown in table 7.6A, it is apparent that the most significant differences between follow-on and independently initiated cases are with respect to pretrial stipulations (36.7 percent for independently initiated cases, and 20.0 percent for follow-ons) and settlement (18.1 percent for independently initiated cases, and 27.0 percent for follow-ons). Interestingly, in litigated price-fixing cases, plaintiffs are somewhat more successful in independently initiated cases.

41. *In re* Potash Industry Antitrust Litigation, MDL #272 (N.D. Ill.).

42. *In re* Sugar Antitrust Litigation (West Coast), MDL #201 (N.D. Cal.); *In re* Chicken "Broiler" Antitrust Litigation, MDL #237 (N.D. Cal.); *In re* Folding Carton Industry Antitrust Litigation, MDL #250 (N.D. Ill.); *In re* Armored Antitrust Litigation, MDL #318 (N.D. Ga.); *In re* Airport Car Rental Antitrust Litigation, MDL #338 (N.D. Cal); *In re* B.F. Goodrich Passenger Tire Antitrust Litigation, MDL #386 (N.D. Cal); *In re* Ocean Shipping Antitrust Litigation, MDL #395 (S.D. N.Y.); *In re* Shopping Carts Antitrust Litigation MDL #451 (S.D. N.Y.); *In re* Coconut Oil Antitrust Litigation, MDL #474 (N.D. Cal.). We did not include *In re Holiday Magic*, MDL #124 (N.D. Cal.) because it is not primarily an antitrust case.

43. *Gypsum Wallboard, Sugar, Broiler Chicken, Folding Carton, Armored Car, Ocean Shipping, Shopping Carts,* and *Coconut Oil.*

44. All the MDL cases in *supra* note 43 are follow-ons except *Gypsum Wallboard.*

45. *In re* International House of Pancakes Litigation, MDL #77 (W.D. Mo.) and *In re* Amerada Hess Litigation, MDL #127 (S.D. N.Y.) both involve two cases. The *West Coast Sugar* proceeding, *supra* note 42, involves 122 cases.

46. Out settlement figures are somewhat uncertain, and in several cases different amounts appear in different places in the data. With this caveat the settlements referred to are in *In re* Gypsum Wallboard Industry Antitrust Litigation, MDL #14 (N.D. Cal.) ($75 million); *In re* Folding Carton Industry Antitrust Litigation, *supra* note 42 ($218 million); *In re* Ocean Shipping Antitrust Litigation, ($51 million); *In re* Sugar Industry Antitrust Litigation, *supra* note 42 ($60 million).

47. *Folding Carton, Ocean Shipping*, and *Sugar* are follow-on cases. In *Gypsum Wallboard* indictment followed settlement of the private case.

48. One striking fact about the follow-on MDL cases for which data were available is the relative speed with which they were filed. This may reflect competition among counsel to be the first to file.

49. There is a burgeoning literature on the policies supporting the treble damage remedy, the best means for achieving deterrence in cases where deterrence is desirable, and the choice between public and private enforcement. Much of this literature is discussed in other papers in this volume. *See generally* W. Breit and K. Elzinga, The Antitrust Penalties: A Study in Law and Economics (1976); Breit and Elzinga, Private Antitrust Enforcement: The New Learning, 28 J. Law & Econ. 405 (1985); Schwartz, An Overview of the Economics of Antitrust Enforcement, 68 Geo. L.J. 1075 (1980).

50. Comment, Consent Decrees and Private Actions: An Antitrust Dilemma, 53 Calif. L. Rev. 627, 628 n.7 (1965). *Compare* Guilfoil, Private Enforcement of U.S. Antitrust Law, 10 Antitrust Bull. 747 (1965), discussed, *infra* note 53, where the precentages of follow-on cases through 1963 are somewhat lower than this 75 percent estimate, but far higher than in the Georgetown sample.

51. See the statistical breakdown in M. Handler, H. Blake, R. Pitofsky, and H. Goldschmid, Trade Regulation 129 (2d ed. 1983).

52. *See, e.g., In re* Folding Carton Industry Antitrust Litigation, *supra* note 42.

53. Snyder's analysis indicates that after the change from misdemeanor to felony penalties, which was complete in 1978, the success rate of the Antitrust Division in all criminal cases alleging Sherman Act section 1 violations fell significantly as did its success rate in litigated case of this type. Edward A. Snyder, "Defensive Effort" and Efficient Enforcement, Ph.D. dissertation, University of Chicago, 1984.

54. This conclusion is similar to that drawn in Guilfoil, Private Enforcement of U.S. Antitrust Law, 10 Antitrust Bull. 747 (1965). Guilfoil examined all *reported* treble damage actions from 1890 through 1939, and 1940 through 1963. During these periods relatively high percentages of *reported* cases were follow-ons. In the period 1940–1963, 94 percent of horizontal price-fixing cases were follow-ons, with the percentages less in other violation categories. Yet his study clearly showed a low degree of correlation between the successful outcomes of government cases and the awarding of damages to private plaintiffs. The Guilfoil study is of course likely to be skewed because its focus solely on reported cases omits many cases that were dismissed or settled without report, as he notes.

55. See Joyce and McGuckin, supra note 28, and Howard P. Marvel, Jeffry M. Netter, and Anthony M. Robinson, Price Fixing and Civil Damages: An Economic Analysis, Ohio State University Working Paper, August, 1986.

Comment: Settlement Incentives and Follow-on Litigation

Roger G. Noll

One benefit of a new data set is that in using it, scholars think through more carefully their fundamental understanding of the phenomena to which the data pertain. Whereas an efficient data-gathering exercise must be guided by theory to ensure that it provides answers to sensible questions, inevitably the attempt to use the data raises new theoretical issues. The Georgetown project on antitrust litigation illustrates this point. Much of the new information does no more than confirm and quantify widely held views. The data show that the vast majority of antitrust complaints are dropped, dismissed, or settled before litigation is terminated and that a significant fraction of private cases are follow-ons to federal cases. Neither of these findings is a surprise. Nevertheless, the papers in this compendium, in attempting simply to exposit these results and to examine their implications, address several new conceptual issues.

This comment draws together in a simplified, integrated format many of these ideas, and especially the material contained in the chapters by George Benston, Jeffrey Perloff and Daniel Rubinfeld, Thomas Kauper and Edward Snyder, and Stephen Calkins. Benston's paper (chapter 6) sets up a very complex theoretical model to analyze the consequences of two legal institutions—class actions, and joint and several damages—on decisions to litigate. The paper by Perloff and Rubinfeld (chapter 4) also contains new theoretical material, but its focus is the effect on settlement of the fact that the outcome of a current case may alter the decisions of other potential plaintiffs to pursue similar litigation against the defendant. In this circumstance the stakes of the defendant in any given case are larger than the stakes of the plaintiff. Calkins (chapter 5) investigates the characteristics of cases that are likely to give rise to dismissal or summary judgment, whereas Kauper and Snyder (chapter 7) examine the follow-on litigation to antitrust suits filed by the federal government.

My purpose is to provide a simple, stripped-down theoretical model that incorporates both the choice between settlement and litigation and the follow-on consequences of present cases. It can serve as introductory material to facilitate some of the more complicated theoretical analysis, as a conceptual framework for interpreting empirical studies, and as a basis for suggesting additional research.

The basic verbal story that describes the sequence of decisions in litigation is as follows: First, plaintiffs sue because they expect a lawsuit to produce net benefits. These benefits may be simply a change in the behavior of the defendent, but most likely they consist primarily of monetary awards to compensate the plaintiff for the defendant's bad acts. Second, defendants fight back because the costs of resisting are expected to be smaller than the benefits. Two forms of benefits may accrue to the defendant. Resistance may lead to victory, may reduce the plaintiff's damage award, or may raise the costs and lower the benefits expected by potential plaintiffs who may base future decisions to file suit on the outcome of the present case. Third, the case can be settled; thus both sides can avoid some litigation costs, and the defendant can avoid whatever spillover effects are created by litigating to a clear decision. Fourth, as litigation proceeds and new information is developed, either side may revise its expectations about the eventual outcome. This may lead to settlement, dismissal, or summary judgment in the middle of litigation. Fifth, either party can make a serious mistake, leading also to summary judgment or dismissal before litigation is completed. Because the presence of these kinds of mistakes is detected before the end of litigation, the failure of motions for summary judgment or the absence of a dismissal by defendant's motion can be important information to both parties about the likely outcome of the case and hence can alter settlement chances by narrowing the issues on which the parties are likely to disagree.

Here I present these core ideas in a very simple mathematical model that abstracts from most of the complexities of the other papers but that should be comprehensible to those who initially may be discouraged by the more complex versions. The model is an extension of a theory of settlement initially developed by William Baxter.[1] The beginning assumption is that both parties to a case are self-interested, risk-neutral actors. Specifically, each seeks to maximize his or her expected value of the litigation, calculated as the probability of each possible outcome times the net benefit should that outcome come about. To formalize this idea, we need first to define a few key terms. These are shown as follows:

P_d, P_p = subjective probability held, respectively, by the defendant and the plaintiff that the plaintiff will win,

D_d, D_p = estimates of the defendant and the plaintiff, respectively, as to the damages that will be awarded if the plaintiff wins,

C_d, C_p = costs of the defendant and the plaintiff, respectively, to litigate the case rather than settle,

m = damage multiplier,

a = share of the plaintiff's costs that the plaintiff must pay even if the plaintiff wins,

E_d, E_p = net expected effects of litigating the case to conclusion, measured as costs for the defendant and benefits for the plaintiff,

$K(mD_d)$ = defendant's estimate of the costs of follow-on litigation should the plaintiff win the current case,

S = defendant's estimate of the spillover cost of settlement.

The plaintiff's net benefits of litigating to conclusion can be calculated as follows:

$$E_p = P_p mD_p - P_p aC_p - (1 - P_p)C_p. \tag{1}$$

If there is no settlement, the plaintiff will litigate to conclusion, rather than drop the case, if E_p is positive, which requires that

$$mD_p > C_p \left[a + \frac{(1 - P_p)}{P_p} \right]. \tag{2}$$

As relation (2) makes clear, each of the following increases the likelihood that a plaintiff is willing to litigate to conclusion: (1) an increase in the damage multiplier, (2) an event that makes the plaintiff think that the damage award will be larger (as might occur if a similar case is decided against the same defendant), (3) an event that increases the plaintiff's chance of winning (e.g., a decision in a similar case against the same defendant), (4) a reduction in the fraction of the legal costs that the plaintiff must pay if the defendant loses the case, and (5) a reduction in the plaintiff's costs of litigation (e.g., as might occur if another case produces evidence that the plaintiff can use at a lower cost than if the evidence had to be developed independently).

This simple formulation of the decision to pursue litigation provides some key insights about private follow-on suits. Suppose a firm has engaged in a practice over which there is considerable disagreement about its legality and/or economic consequences. Among all of the potential plaintiffs, the first to litigate will be the one that is most optimistic—that is, that has a relatively high expected net damage award. If this firm loses, further litigation is unlikely. The remaining firms were initially more pessimistic, and further bad news will make them even more so. Even a win may not generate further litigation if the damage award is low, for the same reason. But a win with a large damage award is more likely to generate further litigation: it may make others less pessimistic and lower their litigation costs.

Follow-on suits from government cases are more complicated. The outcome of the government case will cause potential private plaintiffs to revise their probabilities of winning but will have less effect on damage estimates because government cases do not produce damage awards. The government case will reduce the cost of subsequent litigation, but perhaps not as much as a private case, again because of the absence of a damages phase of the trial. Nevertheless, the results are qualitatively similar to follow-on litigation to private cases. If damage expectations are unaffected by the government case, expression (2) has the following implications. If the government wins the first case, C_p declines and P_p increases; hence (2) is more likely to be satisfied, and the chance that a plaintiff will drop a private complaint over the same matters will decline. If the government loses, P_p presumably declines, but so does C_p. The net effect is indeterminate, although normally the effect on the chances of winning exceeds the effect on litigation costs. If so, the loss of a government case should increase the chance that a private follow-on will be dropped.

The effect of a filed complaint on the defendant can be represented in much the same way as (1) depicts the outcome for the plaintiff. The defendant's expected cost of litigation is as follows:

$$E_d = P_d[mD_d + C_d + (1 - a)C_p] + (1 - P_d)C_d + P_dK(mD_d). \qquad (3)$$

The spillover costs in the last term in (3) incorporate two possible disadvantageous effects of losing the case. First, the outcome of one case can cause potential litigants to revise their expectations about follow-on litigation and therefore file more suits or hold out for better settlements. The defendant's best guess as to this effect is the change in the estimate of the defendant's expected cost (E_d) of all possible subsequent cases. Second, the loss of a case could have an undesirable effect on future business relations of the firm. Henceforth we will focus exclusively on the first type of spillover.

Settlement can occur only if it is in the interest of both parties. No defendant will offer a settlement larger than E_d in (3); however, no plaintiff will accept less than E_p in (1). Thus a necessary condition for settlement is that $E_p \leq E_d$. Even when this is satisfied, settlement is problematic because the parties may not discover through negotiations that settlement is really in their mutual interest, as discussed by Perloff and Rubinfeld.

The necessary condition for settlement is as follows:

$$C_d + C_p \geq m(P_pD_p - P_dD_d) + (P_p - P_d)(1 - a)C_p - P_dK(mD_d). \qquad (4)$$

From this relation the forces for and against settlement are quite clear. Spillover effects promote settlement: the smaller is K, then the less is the chance that the total litigation costs will exceed the right-hand side of (4). Settlement is also likely if the parties agree. Agreement means that $P_p = P_d$ and $D_p = D_d$; hence the first two terms on the right side of (4) are zero. Because litigation is costly, agreement means that (4) is always true. Thus spillover effects are unnecessary to motivate settlement unless the parties disagree sufficiently to make spillovers important. Specifically, if (4) is not satisfied, the first two terms must be positive; that is, the plaintiffs must expect to win substantially more than the defendants expect to lose. Thus settlement is likely to occur unless the defendants honestly believe that they did not break the law (e.g., P_d is low) and/or that they caused relatively little damage (e.g., D_d is small), while the plaintiff strongly disagrees. Even then settlement may still occur if the spillover effects are sufficiently large.

Perloff and Rubinfeld posit a theory of settlements that is not explicitly incorporated in expression (4). Their model is a theory of bargaining inefficiencies: a greater gap between the stakes of the two sides causes a higher probability of settlement. Hence a larger spillover effect unambiguously increases the chance of settlement. By widening the gap in stakes between the defendant and the plaintiff, spillover effects reduce the likelihood of a negotiating mistake that precludes a mutually beneficial settlement.

Expression (4) enables us to reconcile conflicting views about the effect of the damage multiplier on the prospects for settlement. Some, like Perloff and Rubinfeld, contend that an increase in the damage multiplier unambiguously increases the proportion of cases that are settled. Others, like Benston, argue that an increase in the damage multiplier unambiguously has the opposite effect. Perloff and Rubinfeld base their argument on the possibility that the defendant perceives an expected loss that exceeds the expected gain of the plaintiff, and they cite as an example the possibility of spillover litigation.[2] Benston emphasizes the other side, believing that plaintiffs are more likely to have high estimates of expected damages than are defendants. Thus Perloff and Rubinfeld focus on the case in which the right-hand side of (4) is negative, whereas Benston focuses on the case where it is positive. The general case of course admits both possibilities. At one extreme, an increase in the damage multiplier makes settlement more likely if both parties agree on the expected damages and spillover costs are significant. At the other extreme, if spillover effects are relatively small and the plaintiff expects to win more than the defendant expects to lose, the right-hand side of (4) will be positive and will increase if the damage multiplier is increased. This would reduce the prospects for settlement.

Expression (4) provides a starting place for examining settlement prospects in a progression of antitrust cases against the same defendant, as discussed by Kauper and Snyder. Assume that settlement has a spillover cost for the defendant that is less than the spillover effect of losing the first case. This is incorporated into (4) as follows:

$$C_d + C_p \geq m(P_p D_p - P_d D_d) + (P_p - P_d)(1 - a)C_p - [P_d K(mD_d) - S]. \quad (5)$$

The last term on the right side of (5) is now the expected net spillover cost of litigating to conclusion. An increase in S lowers the spillover saving from settlement and thus makes settlement less likely.

Each case in the pipeline has three separate effects on subsequent cases. The first is on litigation costs. Cases litigated to conclusion should reduce litigation costs more than cases that are settled, for the latter presumably will produce less evidence and legal argument. The second effect is on expectations. After each case ends, subsequent plaintiffs and the defendant will update their estimates of the probability that the plaintiff will win and of the size of the damage award. In general, expectations in future cases should grow closer together whenever a case ends in a litigated outcome. This will not necessarily be true, however, for settled cases, for settlement produces less information than does a litigated outcome. The third effect is on subsequent spillover costs. In general, as one move down the pipeline, spillover effects will tend to decline. Each case influences a smaller number of remaining cases. In addition the spillover effect of a case will depend on the outcome of previous cases. For example, suppose the defendant loses the first case. This may cause the defendant to revise P_d upward, which would increase the expected spillover effect of a second loss. But working in the opposite direction is the fact that a second loss would provide relatively little new information for subsequent litigants. The damage to the defendant has largely been done by the first loss. Consequently the expected spillover cost of the second—beyond the effects of the first—is not likely to be very large. By the same line of argument, the spillover effect of a settlement of the second case, once the first is lost, is also likely to be small.

If the defendant wins the first round, the only factor affecting the net spillover effect in subsequent rounds is the revision of expectations about outcome probabilities and damage awards. On balance, the effect should be for both sides to revise expected future damages downward, which should also reduce $P_d K(mD_d)$. The spillover effect of a settlement, however, should not be so affected, for the willingness to settle round two after a defendant's win in round one will be a strong signal that the defendant is vulnerable in subsequent rounds, despite the early victory. Consequently the effect of a win by defendant should be to increase the size of the net spillover term in (5) for subsequent rounds, which works against settlement.

This analysis enables us to reach some conclusions about the likelihood of settlement in follow-ons to private litigation. First, if the first round is settled, the primary effect on subsequent rounds is the convergence of expectations. Costs will stay about the same. Spillover effects will decline, with the magnitude depending on how many subsequent cases are in the pipeline. Moreover, given that the most optimistic plaintiff will litigate first, even before expectation convergence the right-hand terms in (5) should be smaller for the second round than the first. Thus, once settlement occurs, subsequent cases should also be settled with very high probability.

Second, suppose the defendant loses the first round. This will reduce the costs for subsequent rounds, the differences of opinion between plaintiff and defendant, and the expected spillover effects. These three factors do not work in the same direction, so that the likelihood of a settlement in the second round is ambiguous. If the drop in litigation costs is small, settlement is likely; however, if litigation costs are very low, the result could go the other way.

Third, suppose the defendant wins the first round. Essentially the same effects occur as in the previous case. The primary difference is that the spillover costs of settlement remain high, discouraging settlement. Hence settlement should be rarer when the defendant wins the first round than when the plaintiff wins or the case is settled.

The conclusions are similar for follow-on cases to federal litigation. The sources of difference are that federal cases may have less effect on costs and the convergence of opinion because damages are not awarded and that a defendant who loses a federal case faces a higher damage multiplier. Specifically, damage awards imposed on a defendant who has lost a federal antitrust case are not tax deductible. The effect is to drive a wedge between the damages faced by the defendant and those collected by the plaintiff. Suppose that the damage multiplier for the defendant is M, which is larger than m. Then the term $-(M - m)P_d D_d$ must be added to the right side of (5). In addition the spillover effect from a loss is greater as $K(MD_d)$ replaces $K(mD_d)$ in (5). Both effects unambiguously increase the prospects for settlement. Thus private suits that are follow-ons to successful federal cases should have a higher probability of being settled than follow-ons to successful private cases.

The primary lesson from this discussion is as follows: even in a very simple formulation of the settlement process, the conclusions about the effects of prior cases or changes in the damage multiplier are ambiguous. They turn on comparisons of empirical phenomena that work in opposite directions. Hence, the value of comprehensive data about case outcomes is very high. We need such data not simply to confirm logical conclusions about how the world works but more fundamentally to figure out the direction of change that can be expected from a change in institutions.

The Georgetown data, and the first empirical work that uses them, thus assume considerable importance. Nevertheless, additional effort to refine the data could reap significant dividends by enabling scholars to address questions raised by the theory of settlement and litigation. Specifically, the numerous ways in which litigation can end need to be classified more carefully. For example, some dismissals are settlements that amount to a victory for the plaintiff, while others are involuntary terminations in the view of the plaintiff. Some are dismissals on plaintiff's motion whereby the plaintiff simply gives up, which are like settlements in which the negotiated payment in zero. Because events in other cases or new information in the case at hand can cause the plaintiff's expectations to become more pessimistic, some dismissals ought to be predicable within the framework of the settlements model even if they are not technically settlements. For example, a win by plaintiff in another case may cause an excessively optimistic revision of expectations by other potential plaintiffs, which then are dashed by the reality of follow-on litigation. Some summary judgments may be the result of spillover information from other cases. In any event the various categories of outcomes other than litigation to conclusion probably can be modeled in a fashion quite similar to settlement theory.

Notes

I am indebted to William Baxter and Thomas Campbell for very useful comments on the initial presentation and first draft of this paper.

1. William Baxter, "The Political Economy of Antitrust," in Robert D. Tollison, ed. *The Political Economy of Antitrust*, Lexington, Massachusetts: Lexington Books, 1979.

2. They also assume that litigation costs rise with the stakes in the case, so that a higher damage multiplier causes higher litigation costs, which would increase the left-hand side of (4).

Comment

Charles B. Renfrew

The three issues of special interest to me are (1) the role of private antitrust enforcement in the overall enforcement of antitrust laws, (2) the role of the jury in antitrust trials, and (3) the role of deterrence, one of the significant goals of antitrust policy.

As to private antitrust enforcement and its role in the overall antitrust enforcement in this country, I would like to refer to the rash of recent antitrust cases dealing with the forest products industry. In the last 15 years no industry has been affected by antitrust enforcement as much as the forest products industry with respect to the number of cases, the commerce involved, the amount of settlements, and the judicial and legislative battles that ensued.

These cases all stemmed from a private antitrust enforcement action arising in the Northern District of California. A private treble damage action filed in San Francisco (which was ultimately settled) led to the convening of the grand jury in the paper label cases, which resulted in indictments and pleas of nolo contendere. In the course of that grand jury investigation evidence was uncovered that led to the convening of the grand juries in the *Folding Carton*, *Corrugated Cardboard*, and *Fine Paper* cases, which in turn were followed by private treble damage actions.

As to the use of the jury in antitrust cases, I do not at this time intend to enter the debate as to whether juries should be used in antitrust cases. But, since juries are being used in antitrust cases, we should ensure that the juries are given assistance so that they may do their job as effectively as possible. Too often at the present time, we handicap juries by refusing to let them take notes and failing to explain adequately what is expected of them and how to evaluate the evidence and many other matters, and then we criticize their performance after we have unnecessarily handicapped them. Until we have given juries every benefit, it may be unfair to judge their effectiveness and ability to handle complex cases.

Finally, all of the papers agree that one of the goals of an effective antitrust policy is to deter antitrust violations. No one has mentioned the deterrence effect of the criminal sanction, which I think is significant, nor has an effort been made to interview those who have been found guilty of antitrust violations to see whether their conduct was the result of rational economic behavior—that is, measuring the anticipated gains of an activity against its anticipated costs. Further there is the question whether the persons who engage in the unlawful activity were those likely to be affected by the deterrent effect of treble damages. I suspect that often middle-level managers engage in antitrust violations for the purposes of meeting marketing quotas and goals but are not immediately affected by the treble damages ultimately imposed, since that hits the shareholders and the overall corporate performance.

We have heard a great deal about the need to fine-tune the damage remedy. Mitchell Polinsky urged that the damage remedy be decoupled so that the portion used for deterrence or retribution could be separated from that used for compensation or incentive for the private plaintiff to pursue a treble damage action. But still, what empirical evidence do we have that it is the amount of the damages, rather than the speed of apprehension, trial, and punishment, that affects deterrence? In short, I feel that we have talked a great deal about deterrence without a real understanding of how we can deter the actual actors involved in violations, of the effect of the amount of the damages on the actual deterrence, and of the factors or considerations that have led to violations of the antitrust laws.

A great deal has been said about the recent decline in important government price-fixing cases. Some attribute this to a lack of interest or effectiveness of the Antitrust Division; others see it as evidence that we need to add even greater multiples of damages to give further incentives to private plaintiffs. All agree that deterrence is one of the main goals of our antitrust policy. We recently have had a significant number of criminal cases followed by immense treble damage cases with settlements in the hundreds of millions of dollars, all of which received tremendous publicity. There have also been enormous efforts on the part of corporations to avoid those adverse consequences by developing and following antitrust compliance programs. Under these circumstances could not the reduction in the number of government price-fixing cases today reflect the fact that we may have deterred at least some antitrust violations?

Lawrence A. Sullivan

The Kauper-Snyder paper (chapter 7) dramatizes both the potentials and limitations of an enterprise like this one. The authors did with ease and competence precisely what they were invited to do; they mined the data and even supplemented it with an empirical investigation of their own. Where they encountered problems (ambiguities in the data; small numbers problems) they made credible judgment calls. Even so, there was a disjunction between the data they were given and the task they were assigned. The data is broadly descriptive; the questions they were asked to explore are quite specific. The circumstances in which empirical material can be used to answer specific policy questions are limited. The policy must be predicated on some factual assumption or hypothesis. That hypothesis must be capable of being specified with enough particularity. And the empirical investigation must be designed to yield a statistically significant affirmation or negation of the proposition. These desiderata were not present here.

To say this is not to be dismissive of this paper, which I admired. It is to put the whole Georgetown study in its place. This paper, and several others, make interesting observations—several with policy implications. But few gain great force from the underlying data. The relationship between policy and data remains rather cloudy—which is perhaps inevitable, given that the policy issues are multifaceted and the data intractable.

Even so, this paper yields some interesting results. For one, it shows that in nonmultidistrict cases the follow-on process is working reasonably well, even if not precisely as we might have supposed. The Kauper-Snyder observations, moreover, seem consistent with an important observation made by other authors and commentators—namely, that once you get out of the top decile, private antitrust cases, whether follow-on or not, are just cases. They are not discernibly more complex, nor do they chew up more resources than do other cases that make their ways through the federal courts.

If the Kauper-Snyder paper demonstrates some of the tentativeness that must be involved in drawing conclusions from the Georgetown data, the Benston paper (chapter 6) demonstrates some of the rocks on the other shores; it purports to develop refined policy proposals without an eye for data at all. Benston simply ignored the empirical material. He wrote a quite conventional, theoretical paper. The most convincing thing in it has been expressed before by Judge Frank Easterbrook and others—that joint and several liability increases the incentive to settle private cases.

Benston is on far weaker ground when he argues that joint and several liability gives plaintiffs an incentive to name "bystanders" as defendants. If one were looking for a model of problems to be concerned about in relying on theoretical work, the Benston treatment of that issue would serve. The exercise presupposes, first, that the categories used are functional—that one looking at the real world of business and litigation could fit economic actors into the Benston categories—and, second, that the Benston assumptions about information, motivation and responses have some useful relationship to reality. I find neither in the paper nor in my experience any basis for indulging either presupposition.

Benston also argues that incentives to settle are higher in class actions than in other cases because in class actions attorneys are in control. The underlying and somewhat cynical assumption is that lawyers representing a class can be expected to act solely, or predominately, in the interests of maximizing their own per hour fees. Apparently that cynicism is suspended when Benston theorizes about decisions by lawyers (and corporate executives) representing, not classes, but particular corporations, whether plaintiffs or defendants.

I must regard with a certain skepticism an analysis that assumes that one set of agents will be routinely faithful to their trust, and that another set will be routinely devoid of fealty. My own experience suggests that class action lawyers, lawyers for individual plaintiffs and defendants, and corporate officers all are arrayed as to fealty, integrity, and ability in a distribution that resembles the classic bell curve. Some are smarter or more able than others. Some are more honorable than others. Some have good judgment. Some do not. Most of them are aware of both their own career interests and the interests of the entity they represent. They may confuse the two sets of interests at times. But most of them try most of the time to serve the interests they represent in sensible and decent ways.

If we turn from these two papers to the Georgetown study as a whole, what are the likely impacts on the policy debate? I do not see that much is changed. We now have data that will clarify some factual issues to a degree and that may require some backing and filling in dealing with some of the shared assumptions earlier bolstered only by armchair assertion. But none of the conventional arguments for or against the treble damage system or contribution are either foreclosed or greatly enhanced.

Inevitably policy debate is largely about values. It is often set against indeterminate facts. If one takes the antitrust tradition seriously and focuses on the importance of an effective system of deterrence, the data tend to support, rather than to refute, the usual arguments for leaving the treble damage system intact. This is especially true if, in the face of all the uncertainties, one gives an edge to the status quo and places even a small burden of persuasion on the proponents of change. This is conventional for a lawyer. Stare decisis has some weight even in legislative matters. Past ways of doing things have more than random value. One who seeks change ought to be able to be quite convincing about why change is needed.

Of course there are ways to work some of the Georgetown data into credible arguments for fine tuning—for moving to arrangements like judicial discretion as to the size of the damage multiple. But anyone attempting such fine tuning probably should think of private litigation not as one system, but at least as two. Evidence of serious problems is limited to a few large cases and predominantly multidistrict cases.

The paradigmatic "horrible" entails exposure of upward of $100 million and joint and several liability in a case predicated almost solely on parallel conduct (aided perhaps by a paranoid imagination). Cases like that no doubt can make prudent managers shake and quake even if they conclude that the risk of liability is, say, less than 5 percent. If ever there is a basis for claiming "settlement blackmail," it is in situations like this.

How might such problems be handled? Detrebling, or making treble damages discretionary, or applicable only to cartelization might be little more than a Band-Aid. More to the point might be fine tuning of liability rules, like those concerning when the trier of fact may infer that parallel conduct is conspiratorial.

We are all aware of the direction in which antitrust has been moving. Yet one ought to be slow to predict how fast or far the trend will take us. The views of Congressman Peter Rodino, for example, are probably as potent an influence on the direction of antitrust as are those of William Baxter, or those who have replaced him. And although the judiciary has been changing over the past several years, the changes do not all move in a direction that makes antitrust more responsive to Chicago School economics. When one mentions judicial appointments to an antitrust audience one thinks of course of Judges Robert Bork, Frank Easterbrook, and Richard Posner. But there are some new court of appeals judges and several new district court judges who might well be described as conservative populists— people who value small business, the wide dispersion of economic power, and the tradition of local control.

Indeed, some of our new judges may be more likely to turn to the epistles of St. Paul than to quantum mechanics for the metaphors they apply to antitrust issues. They may take an organic view of issues having impacts on market structure and conduct. They may see participants in the economy as parts of one body, each with its own contribution to make: consumers and producers, large firms and small, stockholders and managers, workers in the provinces, managers at the hub. They may find in the long-established antitrust tradition the kind of balance that is needed to keep a complex system functioning. If so, they will regard Chicago theory not as a new canon but as what properly it is, one of several alternative styles of economic analysis that, like other approaches, can at time offer useful insights.

Comment

Thomas B. Leary

The discussions of deterrence and potential violators' risk evaluations ignore the fact that often the people who violate the antitrust laws are not those who actually pay the damages. Damages may be paid by shareholders who knew nothing about the conduct, and violations may be perpetrated by individuals with an agenda of their own. This complication suggests that we should not talk so glibly about sextuple or octuple damages. It also suggests possible alternatives. Suppose that a judge had the discretion to detreble damages on a showing that a corporate defendent had made a good-faith effort to get its employees to comply with the law and that the case involved the actions of a renegade. Deterrence might not be any weaker if this discretion were allowed; it might encourage greater compliance efforts than we see today.

Further the character of the substantive law can affect compliance. Predicatability enhances compliance, and rules of per se *legality* are just as useful as rules of illegality. The "confetti" approach to the rule of reason, to which Judge Frank Easterbrook referred in his oral remarks at this conference, makes predictions very difficult; compliance should be improved to the extent that the rule of reason is structured and empowered by theory.

A third important issue is the impact of different rules for different industries, different litigants, or different jurisdictions. From personal experience, I believe that respect for the law and compliance with the law is undermined when clients are told that the rules may be different, depending on whether they are sued by the government or by a private party. In addition it can be difficult to comply with the law of one jurisdiction when there is another jurisdiction, with conflicting laws, that has a substantial connection with the matter. A pending bill, S. 397, authorizes single damages or even outright dismissals in international antitrust cases depending on the seriousness of these conflicts.

I recognize that not all of these public policy considerations can be discussed here, but I offer them as examples of issues that could usefully be addressed in the future.

Finally, there may have been the mistaken impression that the study overlooked the really big cases. Paul Teplitz's paper (chapter 2) and oral remarks have made clear that this is not so. We recognized from the start that the study could not do everything, and we decided that it would be useful first to get a broad overview of private damage cases—and on the basis of that overview people could decide which areas might justify a closer examination. We never thought the study would answer everybody's questions, and we certainly did not think that it would end debate on these matters.

In fact the most useful thing that may come out of this conference is the stimulation of further inquiry and debate. The 1972 Airlie House conference on "Industrial Concentration" did not yield startling factual revelations, and no consensus was reached. But that conference marked the beginning of a revolution in the way people viewed antitrust issues.

This conference may not spark a similar revolution, but it is important, and it could well lead eventually to results that may not be immediately obvious.

IV

POLICY IMPLICATIONS

8

Policy Implications of the Georgetown Study

George E. Garvey

The Georgetown study's most important contribution to antitrust analysis is conceptual. Narrowly focused examinations of the private antitrust action have produced complex and elegant analytical models. The private antitrust suit is but one variable in a complex body of evolving and interacting substantive and procedural law. Even when viewed in isolation, the treble damage action consists of numerous elements, including the damages multiple, litigation costs, and liability rules. Each element affects private decisions to violate the law, pursue litigation, and settle disputes before, during, or after suit.

Decisions to engage in potentially illegal activities, commence antitrust suits, and settle litigation are analyzed as would be any other economic judgments. A business will engage in desired activities if the expected gains exceed the expected costs, including the potential for detection and prosecution. The optimal enforcement system must therefore ensure that potential violators attach a negative expected value to the illegal conduct. The treble damage multiple promotes this goal by compensating for the likelihood that an offense will be undetected. As a generalization it will be excessive in some instances and too small in others.

The decision to sue also involves a balancing of costs, risk, and probable returns. The victim's injuries are, in economic terms, "sunk." The decision to litigate therefore is based on the expected value of the suit. The prospective value of litigation is a function of the probability of success and the likely amount of damages if the case is won. When the present value exceeds the probable costs, suit will pursued by a rational risk-neutral party. Treble damages increase the likelihood that private antitrust suits will be brought by increasing the expected value.

Settlement is a function of the relative expected values of the parties. Whenever a defendant's expected costs of a suit exceeds plaintiff's positive expectations, the suit should settle. The voluntary resolution of suits does not merely simplify the judicial task, nor is it a one-sided benefit to plaintiffs or their attorneys. A well-considered settlement is beneficial to both parties: plaintiffs receive more than they would accept if the cause of action could be sold, and defendants pay less than would be required to have another assume the risks of the suit. Settlements also allow process costs to be diverted to other productive uses. A system that facilitates reasonable settlements therefore is both fair and efficient.

The analyses identify several factors that are often ignored. The "stakes" of a suit, for example, have substantial effects on the resources expended in litigation and on the manner and stage of resolution. Risk and uncertainty also have significant impact and should be minimized in an efficient dispute resolution system. Finally, the time value of money may prolong litigation, particularly in highly inflationary periods.

The fact that plaintiffs are generally smaller than defendants exaggerates the consequences of risk aversion. A multibillion dollar corporation, for example, will be less averse to the risk of losing several million dollars than a small firm may be to the loss of $100,000. This disparity in aversion gives large firms a bargaining advantage unrelated to the merits of litigation. Reducing the damages multiple would exaggerate the wealthy defendants' advantage in private suits.[1]

Future analysis may also profitably consider agency costs. Agents making decisions to violate the antitrust laws may not be maximizing their principals' interests. An officer responsible for sales, for example, may perceive a contemplated antitrust violation to be the alternative to dismissal for lost sales or diminished profits. The expected value of the violation to the agent (job security) will exceed his expected costs. Subsequent antitrust liability imposed on the firm will then be an extraordinary agency cost. If such activity occurs frequently, the prospect of substantial corporate liability may be essential to induce antitrust compliance programs and adequate monitoring to minimize violations.

Finally, the settlement equation should account if possible for intraparty negotiating processes in complex litigation. Negotiations and agreements among the plaintiffs, as well as defendants, regarding the conduct of litigation complicate the settle/litigate decision. Intraparty transactions and game playing may delay and raise the costs of the overall litigation.[2]

The analyses of the factual data have generated new and important information about treble damage actions, but many of the questions that prompted the study remain unanswered. Several factors account for the somewhat limited value of the empirical data. As Teplitz (chapter 2) concluded, antitrust litigation functions as a "two-tiered market."[3] The "big cases" of antitrust lore represent a small portion of private antitrust suits, but they account for a substantial percentage of the costs and benefits of treble damage actions. For example, according to Teplitz, 10 percent of plaintiffs receiving monetary judgments accounted for 98 percent of the aggregate amounts awarded. Stated more starkly, only 2 percent of the total monetary awards represented in the study were divided among 90 percent of successful plaintiffs. Given this "two-tiered" litigation market, it is difficult to identify problems, or suggest solutions, that are universally applicable. Remedying problems inherent in the "big cases," for example, may have untoward effects on the great bulk of antitrust litigation.

Calkins's analysis (chapter 5) of changes over time in the frequency and success of motions for summary disposition convincingly demonstrates the impact of major antitrust developments on private treble damage actions. Although precise measurement is impossible, Calkins has established the fact and direction of judicial responses to some significant precedents. Not surprisingly, for example, there was an increase in the number and success rate of defendants' motions for summary judgment in 1978—the year after the Supreme Court issued several landmark decisions.[3]

More information about the relationship between significant antitrust developments or decisions and the quantity and nature of litigation may yet be developed. Unfortunately some of the most significant decisions likely to have impact on private suits are too recent to permit analysis with the Georgetown data. Several very important decisions affecting substantive and procedural antitrust law have been decided in the past few years, including *Associated General Contractors*,[4] *Jefferson Parish*,[5] *Spray-Rite*,[6] and *Northwest Wholesale Stationers*.[7] The impact, if any, of these decisions will not be statistically apparent for years.

A more detailed comparison with data from earlier studies may also provide further insights into the evolution of private litigation. A quick look at the NERA study[8] suggests some significant changes in the nature of antitrust suits. Cases alleging horizontal price fixing, for example, were relatively rare in the NERA sample (5 percent of allegations).[9] As Teplitz (chapter 2) points out, it is the most frequently alleged violation in the Georgetown data (17 percent).

The same comparison shows a striking change in "dealership termination" cases. During the survey period of the NERA study (1973 to 1978), dealership termination was the single most frequently alleged primary basis for suit.[10] The Georgetown data, which include the judicial district and time period of the NERA analysis, show a substantially smaller portion of suits represented by dealer termination cases (Teplitz, chapter 2). Moreover Calkins (chapter 5) shows that courts are increasingly willing to grant summary relief in such cases. This significant change shows that antitrust not only seeks a sound equilibrium by adjusting one variable (e.g., standing) to compensate for error elsewhere (e.g., substative rules), it also abandons precedents and policies found over time to be unsound.

Much of the information gathered for the Georgetown study confirms earlier studies.[11] The rapid growth of private suits experienced in the 1960s and 1970s has been reversed. Treble damage suits are not, by and large, inordinately lengthy.[12] Nor do the legal costs appear excessive, given the stakes in antitrust litigation.[13] Although most cases settle (about 88 percent of the sample), determined defendants generally prevail when suits are pursued to judgment, and despite the *Poller* decision's caution against summary judgments in antitrust cases,[14] defendants are relatively successful when pretrial dismissal is sought.

Most antitrust suits are brought by competitors or "downstream" distributors, parties likely to experience the consequences of illegal conduct. The majority of claims arose under the Sherman Act and alleged some form of price fixing or exclusionary practice, such as refusals to deal, exclusive dealing, and tying arrangements.

If we exclude exceptionally large cases, the average levels of the damages awarded by court order, settlements, attorneys' fees, and costs do not seem particularly high. The data, however, are limited, and certain important relationships remain unknown. The nexus between settlements and actual damages and culpability, for example, is not developed. The amounts of known settlements, however, do not suggest that exorbitant payoffs are the norm.[15]

Some significant new facts have been developed. Kauper and Snyder (chapter 7) have provided substantial new information, some of it counterintuitive, about suits that follow-on government cases. They show that the number of follow-on suits has dropped dramatically since 1978, accounting for only three percent of non-MDL cases filed in 1981. These cases are less likely to be dismissed than non-follow-on suits and more likely to settle. A very high percentage (approximately 70 percent) of such cases allege horizontal price fixing. Surprisingly, despite the egregious nature of the offenses and the benefits to plaintiffs of prior government actions, follow-on suits take longer on average to resolve and are litigated as frequently as other suits. Moreover defendants are as likely or perhaps more likely to prevail.

Perloff and Rubinfeld (chapter 4) provide valuable statistical information, particularly about suits requesting class actions. Class suits generally allege classic violations, namely, horizontal price fixing, and are brought by small plaintiffs against more substantial defendants. Plaintiffs are also most frequently customers of defendants. This information suggests that the class action is an efficient antitrust enforcement tool, one not likely to generate the error costs often associated with certain types of antitrust litigation.

The Georgetown study has provided significant factual data and produced major developments in the conceptual analysis of private antitrust enforcement. The results, however, carry no clear message about the need for, or consequences of, treble damage reform.

One of the most important messages of this exercise is that uncertainty generates significant error and process costs. Cases that should be quickly settled or summarily resolved in either party's favor are extended by questions about the applicable substantive laws and procedural rules. Imperfect and asymmetrical factual knowledge naturally complicates the dispute resolution process. Applicable legal rules should therefore be as predictable as justice and efficiency will allow.

Prominent proposals for treble damage reform—such as discretionary treble damages or multiples that vary with the offense or parties—would increase the unpredictability of antitrust litigation. A variable would be added to the already complex equation; one of the few constants of antitrust law would be eliminated. The addition of one more probability factor (under current law the probability of trebling is 1) would have ripple effects on decisions to violate, sue, and settle. Rational change therefore may require countervailing adjustments to limit adverse consequences. Unfortunately this study has shown that many of the relevant factors are incapable of identification and measurement.

Recent judicial developments make this a particularly inopportune time to increase the uncertainty of the antitrust enforcement calculus. The classic formulation of the rule of reason, Justice Brandeis's oft-quoted guidance from *Chicago Board of Trade*,[16] is unmanageable. Yet the Supreme Court in *GTE Sylvania* opted to apply this standard when vertical nonprice restraints are at issue.[17] The multifaceted standing test of *Associated General Contractors*[18] also lacks precision and has spawned some confusion in the lower courts.[19] In short, antitrust law is in a dynamic and somewhat confused state. The need for, and effects of, new remedial provisions could be predicted with greater certainty after the law has had an opportunity to settle.

The general thrust of the substantive law is sound. The move away from excessively rigid per se rules was justified. The consequence of this development, however, has been excessive uncertainty. Analyses presented at this conference have demonstrated the intimate relationships between substantive laws, procedural rules, and liability standards. They suggest that the entire system will operate best if the substantive law is sound and stated with reasonable clarity.

One change in antitrust rhetoric and analysis would foster the development by the judiciary of more predictable rules. The fiction that there are two discrete rules of analysis—per se and the rule of reason—should be abandoned. Per se rules represent generalizations about the utility of certain activities. Some announced per se rules proved over time to be insensitive to legitimate and beneficial practices. They have therefore been modified or rejected. The classic rule of reason, on the other hand, permits no generalizations. Each case depends on its own facts, with consideration given to the circumstances prompting a restraint, defendants' motives, and the ultimate effect on competition. The result is uncertainty, which the analyses prompted by the Georgetown study have demonstrated to be undesirable.

The balance between certainty and flexibility is shifting in favor of flexibility, but some generalizations—though not as gross or rigid as during the height of the per se era—are necessary to achieve both administrative efficiency and the economic benefits of predictability. The principal tools available to the courts are legal presumptions and shifts in the burden of proof. Rather than characterizing a complex combination of relationships and conduct as subject to an amorphous per se rule, courts should attempt to identify clearly those factors that create legal presumptions, the nature of those presumptions (conclusive or rebuttable), and placement of the burden of proof.[20] The result over time would be a reasonably coherent and administrable body of substantive law, not promising the certainty of the per se rules but also not guilty of the unpredictability of the rule of reason.

One very important, counterintuitive result of Salop and White's analysis (chapter 1) is that treble damages may be more appropriate for rule of reason cases than for those judged by the per se rule. The damages multiple will, they argue, increase the resources committed to litigation, which will reduce error in such cases. Per se cases involve egregious behavior, and erroneous decisions are unlikely. The complexity of a reasonableness inquiry, however, may result in error if the facts are not fully developed. This insight challenges the widely held belief that treble damages should be reserved for per se violations.

Proposals to detreble damages in rule of reason cases must also be viewed in light of the diminishing role of per se analysis. If, as some cases imply,[21] per se condemnation extends little further than the decided case, treble damages would be a limited form of punitive damages reserved for egregious cases. Generally, the threefold limitation, however, is too low under such circumstances. Economic analysis suggests that covert activities that are manifestly anticompetitive and lacking in redeeming value should prompt substantially higher multiples to deter would-be violators.

Two years ago Chairman Peter Rodino of the House Judiciary Committee commissioned me to compile and analyze existing literature regarding treble damage actions. Having considered numerous bills to modify the private action for specific industries or circumstances, the committee wished to determine if more sweeping reform was in order. The study found the available facts and scholarship inadequate to reach a firm conclusion.

The Georgetown study has probably generated all of the factual information economically available and has certainly produced a wealth of related scholarship. It does not show that comprehensive reform is clearly necessary or desirable. The consequence of any significant change is unclear— regardless of whether it reduces, increases, or adds flexibility to the existing remedy.

The analytical frameworks presented in the principal papers do provide lawmakers and enforcers with valuable tools to analyze specific proposals. Reducing the damages multiple, for example, is one way to induce business to engage in more of a specific activity that may be problematic under the antitrust laws. All else remaining equal, the expected benefits of the conduct will increase relative to the expected costs. It is unlikely that Congress will often want to induce such questionable activities, but the National Cooperative Research Act of 1984[22] represents a reasoned judgment that the likely benefits of more joint research outweigh the potential harm.

This study has identified several other issues that merit further consideration. The failure to provide prejudgment, market rate interest to prevailing plaintiffs can increase the likelihood of violations and have adverse effects on the efficient resolution of antitrust disputes. The application of joint and several liability in substantial class actions may have undesirable consequences, although beneficial effects have also been identified.[23] Very large antitrust cases, although representing a small percentage of the total number of suits, account for a substantial portion of the costs and awards of private antitrust litigation. Each of these issues may merit further analysis and should certainly be considered if comprehensive modification of the treble damage remedy is contemplated.

The Georgetown study has essentially confirmed Frank Easterbrook's conclusion that "[t]here is no right answer to the sanctions problem"[24]— the optimal solution is unascertainable. Any change from the present system will simultaneously produce beneficial and harmful results, and the net gain or loss remains largely a matter of conjecture. Fifteen years ago the antitrust laws demonstrated an occasionally striking insensitivity to the benefits of efficiently organized business. The multiple damages provision magnified the problem. Over the past decade or more, however, the law has adjusted in many areas to accommodate the legitimate goals of business. Moreover restrictive standing rules and the freer use of summary judgments have minimized the likelihood that unwarranted suits will be brought or successfully pursued by plaintiffs. In the present climate therefore the case for a comprehensive change in the structure of the private damage remedy is not compelling.

Notes

1. In response to an earlier draft of this paper, Mitchell Polinsky has correctly noted that a damages' multiple may result in a *relative* disadvantage for plaintiffs by increasing the size of the risk. As potential damages increase, smaller, and presumably more risk-averse, plaintiffs will likely be willing to settle for a smaller percentage of the probable larger recovery. Such plaintiffs, however, will remain *absolutely* better off because the settlement amounts should exceed those likely with a lower or no multiplier.

2. For an example of the application of game theory to litigation in the United States, *see,* P'ng, Strategic Behavior in Suit, Settlement, and Trial, 14 Bell J. Econ, 539 (1983).

3. Continental T.V. Inc. v. GTE Sylvania, Inc., 433 U.S. 36 (1977); Brunswick Corp. v. Pueblo Bowl-O-Mat, Inc., 429 U.S. 477 (1977); Illinois Brick Co. v. Illinois, 431 U.S. 720 (1977).

4. Associated General Contractors of California, Inc. v. California State Council of Carpenters, 459 U.S. 519 (1983).

5. Jefferson Parish Hospital District No. 2 v. Hyde, 104 S. Ct. 1551 (1984).

6. Monsanto Co. v. Spray-Rite Service Corp., 104 S. Ct. 1464 (1984).

7. Northwest Wholesale Stationers, Inc., v. Pacific Stationery & Printing Co., 105 S. Ct. 2613 (1985).

8. National Economic Research Associates, Inc., Statistic Analysis of Private Antitrust Litigation: Final Report (Oct. 30, 1979). (hereinafter cited as NERA Study)

9. Id. at 28.

10. NERA Study, *supra* note 9 at table B6. Dealer terminations and boycotts combined represented 26% of the primary alleged violations in the NERA Study.

11. *See* summary in Garvey, Study of the Antitrust Treble Damage Remedy, Report of the Committee on the Judiciary, U.S. House of Representatives, 98th Cong., 2d Sess. 14–15 (1984).

12. The average cases lasted slightly more than two years, the median less than a year. Salop and White (chapter 1).

13. Salop and White (chapter 1) estimated that the average cost to individual parties is $75,000 per case and the average cost per case is $200,000–$250,000.

14. Poller v. CBS, Inc., 368 U.S. 464 (1962).

15. The median settlement ranged from $23,997 to $50,000 depending on the source of the data. The *average* settlement figures confirm the "two-tiered" nature of antitrust litigation. The average settlement was approximately $450,000.

16. "The true test of legality is whether the restraint imposed is such as merely regulates and perhaps thereby promotes competion, or whether it is such as may suppress or even destroy competition. To determine that question, the court must ordinarily consider the facts peculiar to the business to which the restraint is applied; its condition before and after the restraint is imposed; the nature of the restraint, and its effect, actual or probable. The history of the restraint, the evil believed to exist, the reason for adopting the particular remedy, the purpose or end sought to be attained, are all relevant facts." Chicago Board of Trade, v. U.S., 246 U.S. 231, 237 (1918).

17. Continental T.V., Inc. v. GTE Sylvania, Inc., 433 U.S. 36 (1977); *See* Rill, Non-Price Vertical Restraints Since Sylvania: Market Conditions and Dual Distribution, in Antitrust Policy in Transition: The Convergence of Law and Economics 384–85 (Fox & Halverson, eds., 1984).

18. Associated General Contractors of California, Inc. v. California State Council of Carpenters, 459 U.S. 519 (1983).

19. Prior to the recent entry by the U.S. Supreme Court into the development of standing rules, the several courts of appeals had adopted divergent standards. *See* Berger & Bernstein, An Analytical Framework for Antitrust Standing, 86 Yale L.J. 809 (1977). By acknowledging the validity of all of these standards, the Supreme Court in Associated General Contractors perpetuated some of the preexisting confusion.

20. Judge Frank Easterbrook has called for the use of "filters" to identify those cases where careful analysis is appropriate. Such filters would be the legal counterpart to the economist's presumption. Easterbrook, The Limits of Antitrust, 63 Tex. L. Rev. 1, 9–17 (1984).

21. See United States v. Jerrold Electronics Corp., 187 F. Supp. 545, 556 (E.D. Pa. 1960), *aff'd per curriam*, 365 U.S. 567 (1961); Cf. Broadcast Music, Inc. v. Columbia Broadcasting System, Inc., 441 U.S. 1, 8–10 (1979).

22. 15 U.S.C.S. §§ 4301–05 (Cumm. Supp. June 1985).

23. *See*, H. Hovenkamp, Economics and Federal Antitrust Law 376–78 (1985); Polinsky & Shavell, Contribution and Claim Reduction among Antitrust Defendants: An Economic Analysis, 33 Stan. L. Rev. 447 (1981); Easterbook, Landes, & Posner, Contribution among Antitrust Defendants: A Legal and Econimic Analysis, 23 J.L. & Econ. 331 (1980).

24 Easterbrook, *Detrebling Antitrust Damages*, 28 J. Law & Econ. 445, 446 (1985).

9

The Georgetown Study of Private Antitrust Litigation: Some Policy Implications

Ira M. Millstein

For years there has been a growing consensus among antitrust practitioners, scholars, and policymakers that our antitrust remedies system needs to be reformed.[1] The desirability and scope of specific reform proposals have been the subject of intense debate. The Georgetown study of private antitrust litigation is an ambitious effort to gather and analyze empirical data on the costs and benefits of our antitrust remedies system. The Georgetown study sheds important new light on these issues by confirming some of the basic suppositions that many have long held about how our antitrust remedies system works. The data collected are not perfect and do not provide answers to all of our questions. But no one effort ever will, and the importance of what has been done should not be diminished by assertions that more research is still possible. In my view more research might shed a few more rays of light, but I doubt that it will disclose enough to warrant delaying the policy determinations that are needed if there is to be reform.

9.1 What Do the Georgetown Data Tell Us?

Supposition No. 1: Most private antitrust cases do not allege hard core violations such as horizontal price fixing.
According to the data, horizontal price fixing was a primary allegation in only 17 percent of the non-MDL cases studied (Teplitz, chapter 2). By contrast, at least 42 percent of the cases involved alleged refusals to deal, exclusive dealing or tying, price discrimination, dealer terminations, and miscellaneous vertical offenses—practices that many economists would argue are likely to be procompetitive and economically desirable.[2] Thirty-six percent of the cases involved complaints brought by competitors of the defendants, the category of cases in which there is the greatest danger that the antitrust laws may be misused to suppress, rather than promote, competition.[3] And another 25 percent involved cases brought by dealers, agents, and distributors, complainants who often take a contract, tort, or termination dispute and dress it up in antitrust clothing (Elzinga-Wood, chapter 3).[4] Summing up the data, Elzinga and Wood concluded that "over

three-fourths of the treble damage litigation was of an economic character where economists potentially would not expect efficiency-enhancing characteristics if the plaintiffs prevailed."

The message for antitrust remedies reform is clear: whatever rules are fashioned should take into account the broad array of economically ambiguous behavior that is routinely subject to private antitrust challenge. The antitrust remedies system was developed at a time when policymakers and scholars were far more confident of (or less concerned about) their substantive footings, than they are today. Although horizontal price fixing and other hard-core per se offenses are important, they are a minority of the cases brought. There is therefore a serious danger that penalties that seem warranted for horizontal price fixing could result in economically ambiguous behavior's being penalized or deterred when applied across the board.

Supposition No. 2: A critical determinant of private litigation's adding to the deterrence of horizontal price fixing is government enforcement.

This proposition, which has long been the view of many experienced antitrust practitioners, is strongly supported by the Georgetown data. Thus the data show that though the greatest percentage of "independently initiated" private actions challenged vertical restraints, more than three-quarters of the follow-on cases to government suits involved hard-core price fixing and other horizontal violations (Kauper-Snyder, chapter 7). Even more significant, of the seven MDL dockets studied involving horizontal price fixing (some 336 separate cases), six of these dockets were follow-ons to Department of Justice actions. Reviewing all of the data, Kauper and Snyder found that follow-on litigation was more likely than non-follow-on litigation to focus on horizontal price fixing, more likely to involve the largest damage amounts, and more likely to result in successful outcomes for plaintiffs. Of course this "more horizontal price-fixing" aspect of follow-on litigation can be accounted for by the fact that the government brought more price-fixing cases; but the "more successful plaintiffs" aspect of the data remains to show that follow-on litigation is extremely important to the deterrence of price-fixing behavior.

The key to the effectiveness of private litigation in deterring horizontal price fixing would thus appear to lie with aggressive government enforcement. Unfortunately the Georgetown data suggest that such government enforcement has been on the wane. Since 1978 there has been a significant decline in the number of private follow-ons to government actions. Why? Because the Antitrust Division's enforcement efforts during this period shifted away from major price-fixing complaints to more narrow bid-rigging actions involving state government contracts. Kauper and Snyder found that these cases generated only one private follow-on case that they could identify. Unless we believe that there has been a dramatic decline in price fixing outside of the bid-rigging area, an important step that can be taken to increase the successful use of private litigation against price fixers would be to increase government enforcement activities.

Supposition No. 3: Most private antitrust cases adjuticated to a conclusion are won by defendants.
The Georgetown data show that approximately 70 percent of the cases adjudicated to judgment are won by defendants. Moreover, when defendants file motions to dismiss or for summary judgment, such motions are granted more than 50 percent of the time (Calkins, chapter 5; Teplitz, chapter 2). Indeed, even in cases in which damages are awarded, defendants receive such an award almost as often as plaintiffs.

All of this suggests that a number of the private treble damages actions being brought may be without merit. Why should we care about such cases if the defendants ultimately win them? Three reasons come to mind. First, the costs involved in adjudicating a meritless case to conclusion are not insubstantial (Elzinga-Wood). This is particularly true, given the fact that some of the cases least likely to bring about a procompetitive result are the most costly to litigate (Teplitz). Second, for every meritless case that defendants win, there may be a score that are settled because of the uncertainty and litigation costs involved. Third, the filing of large numbers of meritless treble damage actions can have an in terrorem effect on other companies fearful of engaging in economically productive behavior that may lead to burdensome lawsuits by their competitors, distributors, or suppliers.[5]

Supposition No. 4: Most private antitrust actions are settled.
The Georgetown data show that an astonishing 88 percent of those cases reaching final disposition ended with a settlement (Salop-White, chapter 1). Moreover the settlement figure was 90 to 100 percent for cases involving a large defendant (Perloff-Rubinfeld, chapter 4).

This enormously high rate of settlement suggests that antitrust remedies must be fashioned to take into account the dynamics of the settlement process. The danger, as Salop and White suggest, is that such high rates of settlement may reflect a "blackmailer's paradise." Multidefendant cases would appear to merit particular scrutiny, since it is in such cases that the coercive effect of treble damages and joint and several liability would appear to be particularly severe.

Supposition No. 5: The "average" private antitrust case entails significant litigation costs, but not of an enormous magnitude, whereas most litigation costs are concentrated in the largest cases.

The Georgetown data indicate that although the "average" private antitrust litigation is more costly than other types of civil litigation, it is not enormously so (Salop-White; Elzinga-Wood). Thus, although Elzinga and Wood have concluded that it costs at least 60 cents of legal fees to distribute a dollar's worth of damages, such costs would seem tolerable if we had a high rate of confidence that the "average" case brought had economic and legal merit. However, the Georgetown data also indicate that most of the costs incurred are concentrated within the top 10 percent of cases filed each year (Teplitz). These large cases, which number in the hundreds at any one time, may have a disproportionately adverse effect on the economy, rendering the use of averages and medians of little utility in assessing the overall cost impact of private antitrust litigation.

9.2 Policy Implications

By bringing to the fore the great "middle range" of private antitrust actions, I believe the Georgetown Study confirms that, for all of its warts, the private treble damage action serves a useful and important function. Although there appear to be a substantial number of bad cases and results that should be weeded out of the system, there also appear to be a number of meritorious cases that would never have been brought by the government and do not cost as much as many critics have feared.

This is not to say that reform is not required in the antitrust remedies area. The private antitrust action, though durable, is also dynamic and has been substantially altered by the haphazard rush of procedural and substantive developments that have led to many of the undesirable consequences we see in the Georgetown data.

So what is to be done? I would advocate the following reforms.

Individual Treble Damage Responsibility

As many of you know, I have been supporting S. 1300, a bill introduced by Senator Strom Thurmond and a bipartisan majority of the Senate Judiciary Committee, which would rectify what I consider to be the most serious unfairness in the antitrust remedies system—the combination of joint and several liability with treble damages.[6] When members of the plaintiffs' antitrust bar tell us, as they have at this conference, that they would rather have joint and several liability than treble damages, it ought to tell us something about coercion. Joint and several liability in antitrust cases is coercive and unfair, and everyone knows it.

S. 1300 would make defendants in antitrust actions individually, rather than jointly, responsible for treble the amount of damages attributable to their violations. Under current law each defendant in such an antitrust action, regardless of size, degree of culpability, or market share, can be held liable for an entire industry's treble damages. Joint liability permits an antitrust plaintiff to determine arbitrarily how much to seek from each alleged coconspirator, and it can coerce defendants into settling for substantial amounts, regardless of the merits of the claim. S. 1300 would eliminate these abuses, while still ensuring that the plaintiff is made whole if a defendant is unable to pay its treble damages or is beyond the jurisdiction of the U.S. District Courts.

To the extent that the Georgetown data tell us something about joint and several liability, they tend to support the premises of S. 1300. Specifically, though the data do not directly examine the type of fundamental unfairness present in such cases as the *Corrugated Container* litigation, they do indicate that the potential for settlement abuse is not uncommon. The settlement rate in antitrust cases is over 80 percent. Many settlements are for substantial dollar amounts, and the larger the defendant, the more likely the case is to settle. There is also a positive correlation between the number of defendants in a case and the settlement amounts received by plaintiffs (Perloff-Rubinfeld). These statistics may reflect the fact that some companies who believe in their innocence are being coerced into settlements by the onerous combination of treble damages, joint and several liability, and uncertain standards of proof.[7]

Even more significant, the Georgetown data highlight the lack of any empirical evidence that would suggest that S. 1300 would lessen deterrence by reducing the incentive for private actions against horizontal price fixing.[8] Rather, the data suggest that the level of government antitrust enforcement is the far more important factor determining the deterrent effect of private litigation in the horizontal price-fixing arena. The best deterrence that the Antitrust Division could undertake in this area therefore would be to bring more horizontal price-fixing actions outside of the bid-rigging area. By contrast, there is simply no convincing evidence that S. 1300 would significantly affect deterrence one way or the other, suggesting that fairness should be the primary concern in enacting this reform.

Reconsidering the Treble Damage Remedy in Rule of Reason Cases

Although I do not believe that the damage multiple should be reduced for price-fixing actions, modifying the rule for other offenses would appear to be worthy of consideration. The Georgetown study demonstrates that the substantial majority of cases brought involve economically ambiguous offenses subject to the rule of reason. Moreover the identity of the majority of plaintiffs as competitors and distributors strongly suggests that some of these cases are being filed for coercive reasons or to suppress competition. The response to the argument of Salop and White that treble damages may be necessary to encourage plaintiffs to bring complex, difficult to prove, rule of reason cases, is that these do not appear to be the types of cases we want to encourage from an economic standpoint.

In my view the case for reconsidering treble damages in non-price-fixing cases has been made. Now the policy debate should focus on where to draw the line. The position that I took with my partner Jeffrey Kessler two years ago in the *Legal Times* appears amply justified today: The law is too uncertain in the rule of reason area, and the possibility of deterring pro-competitive activity too great, to justify mandatory treble damages across the board.[9]

9.3 Conclusion

In sum, although the Georgetown data do not supply all the answers, they do provide us with as much information as we are likely to have for some substantial time to come. The subject of antitrust remedies reform has now been on the policy agenda since at least 1955, when the Attorney General's Committee recommended discretionary detrebling.[10] As William Baxter once stated, "[l]ooking at whole pictures is a slow and laborious process which sometimes never comes to an end."[11] I now believe that in the area of antitrust remedies, it is time to stop looking and time to start making the necessary policy determinations—and acting.

It is predictable that some will now argue for a comprehensive package of remedies and reforms plus substantive changes in the antitrust laws. In my view such an approach is almost certain to lead to the creation of every legislator's favorite Christmas tree and to endless debate, resulting in such confusion as to make any concrete reform more unlikely. As Congressman Peter Rodino observed at this conference, the political outlook for substantial and precipitous change in the antitrust laws is not promising at this time. While the political debate continues on more comprehensive packages, I believe that we would clearly be better off, both pragmatically and substantively, selecting those few, moderate and carefully tailored reforms—such as S. 1300—that can be supported by consensus on their own merits.

Notes

I would like to thank my partner, Jeffrey L. Kessler, and my associate, Shelley E. Harms, for their assistance in the preparation of this paper.

1. *E.g.*, Global Competition, The New Reality, Report of the President's Commission on Industrial Competitiveness, Vol. I at 58, Vol. II at 192, January 1985; I. M. Millstein and J. L. Kessler, Integrated Reform Suggested for Antitrust Remedies, Legal Times, June 27, 1983 at 29, col. 1; K. Elzinga and W. Breit, The Antitrust Penalties, A Study in Law and Economics 1976; Report of the Attorney General's National Committee to Study the Antitrust Laws, 379 (1955).

2. *See, e.g.*, R. Posner, The Next Step in the Antitrust Treatment of Restricted Distribution: Per Se Legality, 48 U. Chi. L. Rev. 6 (1981); R. Bork, The Antitrust Paradox, A Policy At War with Itself (1978).

3. *See* F. Easterbrook, The Limits of Antitrust, 63 Tex. L. Rev. 1 (1984).

4. Thus the paralegals who reviewed the dockets in the Georgetown Study concluded that 22 percent of the "antitrust" cases studied did not involve significant antitrust issues at all (Teplitz, chapter 2).

5. *See* Calvani, Non-Price Predation: A New Antitrust Horizon, 4 Trade Reg. Rep. (CCH) ¶ 50,475 (July 9, 1985) (discussing the anticompetitive effects of predatory litigation).

6. S. 1300, 99th Cong., 1 st Sess., 131 Cong. Rec. S8365–66 (1985).

7. *See* Benston (chapter 7).

8. *See* Testimony of Charles F. Rule before the Senate Judiciary Committee, Hearing on S. 1300, July 29, 1985.

9. I. M. Millstein and J. L. Kessler, *supra* note 2.

10. Report of the Attorney General's National Committee to Study the Antitrust Laws, 379 (1955).

11. Testimony of William F. Baxter, Hearings before the Subcomm. on Monopolies and Commercial Law, House Comm. on the Judiciary, 97th Cong., 1st Sess., March 3, 1982; *reprinted in* Serial No. 118 at p. 57.

10

Private Antitrust Enforcement: Policy Recommendations

Donald F. Turner

10.1 Introduction

While the statistical information gathered in the Georegetown study does not provide a clear answer, in my opinion there is little reason to doubt that a substantial number of private antitrust cases are ill-founded, brought in hopes of obtaining substantial cash settlements from defendants seeking to avoid the costs of litigation and the risk that bits of evidence—such as damaging employee statements—will lead to adverse jury verdicts. The mandatory treble damages rule magnifies the incentives of plaintiffs to bring weak cases and of defendants to settle them.

The simple solution would be to eliminate all private rights of action or limit private enforcement to equitable proceedings. However, I do not believe a persuasive case has been made for such a radical change.

In addition to revision or clarification of substantive rules, there are several steps that may be taken to reduce the excessive scope of private actions.

First, the courts should continue the trend toward expanded use of summary judgment. Summary judgment in a case alleging conspiracy is clearly appropriate where the behavior complained of is consistent with independent self-interest and there is no evidence indicating that conspiracy was more probable than not. I believe the same test—more probable than not—should be applied to cases resting on claims of unlawful intent.

Second, standing to sue should be narrowed, drawing, among other things, on the *Brunswick* principle; namely, that in order to have standing, a plaintiff must show injury or threatened injury causally related to the basis on which the alleged conduct would be held unlawful. *Brunswick Corp.* v. *Pueblo Bowl-O-Mat*, 429 U.S. 477 (1977).

I shall now discuss more fully two additional proposals: (1) elimination of jury trials in private antitrust cases to the extent constitutionally permissible and (2) reducing the scope of treble damages.

10.2 Elimination of Jury Trials

There would be several significant advantages from eliminating jury trials in private antitrust actions. First, it would reduce the private and public costs of antitrust litigation. Among other things, trial to judges would facilitate narrowing of issues put to full trial and also facilitate summary judgment.

More important, elimination of juries would increase the probability of accurate results. The nature and complexity of the factual and legal issues raised in most antitrust cases are beyond the competence of most jurors to understand and to reason through to a rationally based conclusion. Consequently there is a high likelihood that jury decisions will be influenced by emotional and other irrational factors, thus inviting distorted case presentation and legal argument.

Moreover, unlike judges, who are or typically feel obligated to spell out the reasons behind their fact findings and ultimate conclusions of law, juries, even when required to submit special verdicts, do not have to explain how they reached their results. As a result corrective appellate review would be facilitated by eliminating jury trials. Full district court opinions and the greater scope of appellate review would lead to greater clarification and rationalization of substantive antitrust rules and to greater consistency of results.

The problem with this proposal of course is raised by the Seventh Amendment to the Constitution, which provides that "[i]n suits at common law, where the value in controversy shall exceed twenty dollars, the right of trial by jury shall be preserved." Although the language is limited to common law actions, the Supreme Court expanded its coverage to actions enforcing statutory rights "if the statute creates legal rights and remedies, enforceable in an action for damages in the ordinary courts of law" (*Curtis v. Loether*, 415 U.S. 189, 194, 1974). However, the Court has opened the door by indicating that the right to jury trial hinges, among other things, on "the practical abilities and limitations of juries" (*Ross* v. *Bernhard*, 396 U.S. 531, 538 n. 10, 1970). Although this test was offered with reference to issues, not cases as a whole, there have been a few lower court decisions denying jury trial in antitrust cases of high complexity. And the Third Circuit has held that the Seventh Amendment is overridden by the Due Process clause where

the complexity of a suit [is] so great that it renders the suit beyond the ability of a jury to decide by rational means with reasonable understanding of the evidence and applicable legal rules .... (*In re Japanese Electronic Products Antitrust Litigation*, 631 F.2d 1069 3d Cir. 1980)

Moreover, since antitrust law is a vitally important national public policy, and private rights of action were created not merely to enable recovery of damages but also to supplement governmental enforcement, it seems to me that a strong argument can be made that a congressional statute eliminating jury trial of private antitrust actions would be constitutional, given the importance to antitrust policy of accurate results, clarification of the law, and minimizing disincentives to procompetitive behavior. In the *Atlas Roofing Co.* case (430 U.S. 442, 1977), the Court upheld a statute creating new private rights to protect employees from death or injury due to unsafe working conditions and providing that they be adjudicated by an administrative agency. Given that holding, I do not see why the Court should insist that there be jury trials of statutory rights of action committed to courts of law, where important public policies are at stake and there is good reason to believe that juries are incapable of functioning satisfactorily in such cases.

10.3 Treble Damages

Treble damages is a more complex issue than that of jury trials because the mandatory treble damage action does serve certain useful functions. By providing a powerful financial incentive for injured parties to detect and sue for violations of antitrust law, treble damages increase the likelihood that a violator will pay heavily and thereby discourages illegal conduct.

On the other hand, mandatory treble damages has the countervailing adverse effects of encouraging baseless or trivial suits brought in hopes of coercing settlements and of discouraging legitimate competitive behavior in the gray "rule of reason" areas of the law. Moreover mandating treble damages over the whole range of antitrust law is inconsistent with the customary standards for punitive damages, which are similar to those applied to criminal sanctions.

Although I have not had the time to study the issue closely, assimilate all the literature, and formulate a complete set of guidelines, it seems perfectly clear to me that treble damages should not be mandatory in all cases. At a minimum, damages should not be trebled where liability rests on a change in the law, an expansion of the scope of an existing substantive rule, or a new rule not clearly indicated by precedents. I believe we should go further and limit treble damages to cases where the violation is clear, either a per se offense or a non per se case in which there plainly was no justification for the conduct concerned—such as a nonancillary restraint in a joint venture or other cooperative agreement. I recognize that this would tend to discourage complicated suits in the rule of reason areas, where there are potential efficiency or procompetitive defenses, but that would not lead to significant consumer harms and would lower the disincentives to economically beneficial behavior.

Comment: The Policy Implications of the Georgetown Data Set

Most of us are understandably dissappointed that the data set yields compelling answers to no questions and suggestive answers to few. Still, a conclusion that the data set is useless would be premature. Further work may well prove rewarding. Work that focuses on the change in the tax laws seems the most promising.

The data set at present permits observation to be made cross-sectionally, comparing those cases where damage awards are fully deductible by the defendant with the "follow-on" type of cases where they are not and hence where the effective damage multiple is substantially higher. Further work that concentrates on that classification will be useful, but it will be hampered by the fact that the tax difference is not the only difference that separates the two categories.

If it proves to be possible to extend the data set in any respect, serious consideration should be given to extending it backward in time so as to create a sample of follow-on and non-follow-on cases that antedated the change in the tax law. That would make possible both before and after cross-sectional observations and also follow-on and non-follow-on time series observations. That appears to me to represent the best opportunity for ascertaining the consequences of varying damage multiples.

Researchers in the future are likely to find still other ways, not now obvious to us, to mine the data set. We should preserve the value of this project by preparing cleaned-up versions of the data in machine-readable form and adequately documented so as to facilitate future work.

Although these data are unlikely to change the priors with which anyone arrived at this conference, one of the reasons for this is that the data do not paint a picture of a system running wildly amuck. And, with one exception to which I will return, this suggests that the great attention focused on the damage multiple does not indicate concern about the distortions to which multiple damages give rise so much as it is symbolic of our unease about the nature of the substantive rules that we enforce with those strong remedies. Our principle effort in the future should be a continuing assault on the inane substantive rules that the courts continue to apply to sensible and efficient business arrangements that happen to be susceptible to characterization as tie-in sales, collective refusals to deal, or vertical price constraints.

The exception to which I alluded a moment ago involves the large, multidefendant, class action case. We must do something about the problem to which the rule of joint and several liability and the practice of serially negotiated settlements give rise. In the interests primarily of fairness (rather than efficiency) there is a compelling case for eliminating the present randomness and arbitrariness over where damage liability comes ultimately to rest, whether the solution takes the form of contribution, carve out, or a straightforward attack on the underlying liability rule.

Let me offer one final observation on a point that bears importantly on the total costs of administering the private remedy system. Those of us who have been working for years to rationalize antitrust have allowed our patterns of speech to be co-opted: we tend to speak of getting rid of per se rules, and of leaving conduct subject to the rule of reason. That formulation is regrettable. It is of great importance that we do not move from one extreme of arbitrary rigidity to a totally amorphous and unstructured inquiry of the kind that Justice Brandeis seems to have had in mind when he wrote his Chicago Board of Trade opinion. When everything is relevant, then nothing is dispositive. Disposition of cases by motions to dismiss or through summary judgment procedures is rarely possible. Discovery and trial are potentially endless. It is important that as we shed the per se rules, we move to a system of structured inquiry—a context in which the plaintiff must first prove A, B, and C, whereupon the burden of proof shifts to the defendant to show either D or E, and so forth. The general structure of the restatement of torts is indictive of the patterns I have in mind. The possibility of summary disposition exists only when there is sufficent clarity about a particular party's evidenciary obligations to allow a confident conclusion that the obligation has not been carried.

Comment on the Policy Implications of the Georgetown Study

Harvey J. Goldschmid

Overview of Policy Implications

Even after acknowledging the clear imperfections in the data base of the Georgetown study,[1] I am greatly comforted by what has been put before us. Indeed, since I approached the Georgetown study expecting to find more of a problem, my fundamental conclusion is that the data present a powerful picture of a private antitrust enforcement system that is working surprisingly well. To their collective credit, Garvey, Millstein, and Turner have recognized the basic validity of this conclusion. Their respective policy prescriptions are appropriately narrow and problem oriented.

My hope is that the Georgetown study will effectively end serious debate about radical solutions. For example, although I understand the value judgments that move Ernest Gellhorn to urge the abolition of private antitrust actions—or the abolition of treble damages as a second-best solution—I see nothing in the Georgetown data to support his conclusions.

Nevertheless, at the margin I would support some change in the treble damage remedy. I am particularly concerned about the vagueness and malleability of various antitrust rules and the danger of liability of potentially disastrous proportions for relatively innocent defendants. My ameliorating approach is to eliminate mandatory trebling when a judge finds—in a non per se case—that a defendant "reasonably believed" that a given act or transaction would not violate the antitrust laws.

The idea of course is to provide only single damages when, for example, liability is created by a change in, or expansion of, present law. The dispensation from treble damages would also cover, for example, a restrictive covenant that was held to be unreasonably restrictive, but was just over—and understandably so under the circumstances—what we know is sometimes a murky gray line. In addition, to ameliorate hardship to consumers and the United States in areas where the present antitrust damage scheme may not be rigorous enough, I would recommend that in egregious circumstances (e.g., where defendants knowingly conspired to produce serious anticompetitive effects) that a five times damage penalty be made available and, in general, that the United States be permitted to sue for treble damages.

The Nature of the Alleged Treble Damage Problem

I approached the Georgetown study with two basic policy concerns about treble damages: First, do mandatory treble damages create excessive deterrence—particularly in vague, rule of reason areas—and discourage efficient conduct? Second, are a substantial number of weak cases brought, containing large damage claims that (particularly when fueled by fears of juries, and/or "untutored" judges, and/or procedural hurdles[2]) lead to unwarranted, large settlements? To put the second concern graphically, since few lawyers will tell a defense client that he has better than a 90 percent chance of success in court (even if the lawyer believes a case is basically meritless), do significant numbers of innocent but profit-maximizing clients, facing treble damage claims of $30 to $100 million in such circumstances, settle cases by paying at least a few million dollars? The policy concerns with respect to this second category are obvious. I am worried about unfairness, waste, and long-term disrespect and distaste for the law.

Turner's paper (chapter 10), in effect, addresses my concerns and answers "yes" to each of the questions posed. Most significant, Turner asserts that "ill-founded" cases are brought in "large number[s] . . . solely in hopes of obtaining substantial settlements."

As indicated, I believe that there may be some excessive deterrence in rule of reason areas, and in any event, certain outcomes may be unfair to those who reasonably believed in the lawfulness of their acts. Beyond this, however, I am skeptical about the validity of Turner's answers. In particular, I believe that his assertion about large numbers of "ill-founded" cases being brought "solely in hopes of obtaining substantial settlements" is suspect. Though such cases are undoubtedly filed, I believe that this is much less of a problem—in terms of magnitude. Moreover, Calkins paper (chapter 5) indicates that judges are now using the summary dismissal route to diminish greatly any remaining problem.

The data produced by the Georgetown study do not provide answers to the questions about "excessive deterrence" or "unwarranted settlements." Nevertheless, for me these are the principal policy concerns. I am simply not very intrigued by the issue (discussed at some length in this volume) of whether double damages instead of treble damages would produce more or fewer settlements. The issue of pivotal concern is how the considerable advantages of deterrence associated with treble damages balance against perceived, but unproved, imperfections in the *quality* of outcomes. These outcomes of course come largely by way of settlements.

In terms of work in the future, I recommend that priority be given to a study of selected cases with the purpose of evaluating the *quality* of settlements. After settlements are made and finalized, it may be possible with proper guarantees of confidentiality to obtain relatively contemporaneous reactions from judges, magistrates, and opposing counsel. It should be remembered that even defendants under the gun of large exposures have countervailing incentives to litigate fiercely and to prove—with long-term profitability in mind—that they are not easy touches. Why would these defendants, with their resolve buttressed by the availability of summary dismissals, consistently settle meritless cases for millions of dollars? Why would not plaintiffs and their lawyers be discouraged from bringing large, but meritless, cases by the prospect of a fierce fight to the finish (at least some of the time) and by the new willingness of courts to grant summary dismissals?

Evaluation of Proposed Policy Prescriptions

Use of Summary Dismissal Motions

I share Turner's enthusiasm for the increased use of summary dismissal motions. Calkins's paper is very encouraging in this regard. Although the data set forth in Calkins's study are imperfect (particularly, because one cannot accurately distinguish between "procedural" and "substantive" dismissals), the study presents substantial evidence that judges are increasingly using summary disposition motions to weed out the meritless case before an unwarranted settlement is entered into. In my opinion summary dispositions represent a far better way of ridding the legal system of meritless antitrust cases than the alternative of giving up the benefit of treble damages in situations where additional deterrence is often needed.

The Treble Damage Remedy

Millstein (chapter 9) recommends that "rule of reason cases should be subject either to actual damages, or at most discretionary trebling, with perhaps a discretionary interest factor added from the time of suit." I agree with Millstein that adding interest from the time of suit would weigh against use of dilatory tactics. I believe, however, that his "per se–rule of reason" distinction is much too crude. Is, for example, the exchange of price and customer information among firms in a tightly concerntrated market (probably not a per se offense[3]) less bad than formal price fixing among a large number of small competitors? Similarly under Ira's approach airtight territorial and customer restraints imposed by a dominant firm under egregious circumstances would result in the payment of only actual damages, or at most, in discretionary trebling. Given detection and other problems, Ira's approach would send potential wrongdoers the wrong message.

Let me note that too much space in this volume is devoted to deterrence in the context of incentives for litigation. It is the deterrence incentives leading to proper corporate counseling and compliance programs that I find truly compelling. In this respect I believe Millstein's approach—particularly if only actual damages were applicable to rule of reason cases—would greatly diminish deterrence in a number of highly significant areas.

About as far as I would go in terms of "detrebling" is to create a dispensation from treble damages if a judge finds in a non-per se case that a defendant "reasonably believed" that a given act or transaction did not violate the antitrust laws.[4] As indicated, this "reasonable belief" test would allow for single damages when the law has changed or been expanded, or simply when a defendant with a reasonable belief (that turned out to be incorrect) wandered just beyond a far-from-bright line. I would readily concede that proof and certainty problems raise questions as to whether my game is worth the effort. But my approach does provide a fair solution to a real problem and meaningful protection for the relatively innocent. To balance my approach, I would also recommend that a five times damages penalty be made available to judges where defendants have knowingly conspired to commit serious anticompetitive acts in egregious circumstances. In addition the United States should be permitted to sue for treble damages.

Notes

1. My major concerns about the data base relate to ambiguous categories, bias of various types, the problem of small numbers, and the use of paralegals for analysis.

2. I have in mind, for example, Millstein's concerns about joint and several liability.

3. See United States v. United States Gypsum Co., 438 U.S. 422 (1978).

4. The term "reasonably believed" is intended to have both an objective and a subjective content. A defendant would have to believe that an act or transaction did not violate the antitrust laws, and he would have to be reasonable in having such a belief. The absence of such an affirmative belief—for example, because the lawfulness of an act or practice had not been considered at all—would not create a dispensation from treble damages.

Comment: Proposed Changes in Private Antitrust Enforcement, Policy Implications

Emory M. Sneeden

Before undertaking reform of private antitrust actions, we must first answer the basic question: "What purposes do private actions serve?" The response has three primary elements: First, private actions compensate the victims of antitrust violations for economic injury. Private actions also serve to deter violations of antitrust law. Any reform proposal must therefore retain for the victim of a violation the incentive to sue, while preventing a tip of the balance that would make violations of antitrust laws profitable.

Finally, the private antitrust suit may be used offensively. The private suit is sometimes used as a tactical maneuver to restrain competition. The prospect of a treble damage verdict may prompt the abandonment of some business decisions that could have resulted in enhanced competition.

Broad economic goals must also be considered before measures are attempted. Reform must benefit the consumer and positively serve the economy. It is within this framework that we seek solutions to problems in current antitrust law.

The Value of the Data

The value of the data gathered in the Georgetown study has been criticized. Complaints range from the sample size to the labels attached to the data. Although the data gathered may not be perfect, the study clearly provides valuable insights. For example, the study further explodes myths concerning the nature of antitrust suits.

The suggestion of more study and more data is always enticing. I am not persuaded, however, that any organized effort such as this will be initiated soon. Furthermore new information is certain to arise in time. Individual scholars will look on the data with different points of view, and new insights will emerge. Probably we will see expansion of the data base by those who will be enticed to explore particular areas further. Others may add to the data pool during congressional hearings. Thus the information we now have will likely serve as a catalyst to prompt the acquisition of additional data.

I assume therefore that the Georgetown study provides us with important new information. The study has also generated proposals to improve current antitrust law. I will specifically address the suggestions to reform treble damages.

Trebling

It has been suggested that detrebling should be accomplished in private antitrust cases through the mechanism of judicial discretion. I have no quarrel with this approach. However, the question of which types of cases will be subject to judicial discretion is immediately raised.

Detrebling should not be discretionary in cases in which a violation of the law is clearly intended. Conduct of this nature strikes at the heart of antitrust law. Deterrence of this kind of activity, which usually involves intentional criminal conduct, is obviously needed. The treble damages penalty is therefore most appropriate for offenders. Also evidence indicates that Congress may be very reluctant to give judges the discretion to detreble damages in certain types of antitrust cases.[1]

In many areas I favor detrebling. I have not approached the problem in detail, nor have I investigated standards or guidelines in the various subareas of the antitrust law. However, I find myself in basic agreement with Turner (chapter 10), who writes: "[I]t seems perfectly clear to me that treble damages should not be mandatory in all cases. At a minimum, damages should not be trebled where liability rests on a change in the law, an expansion of the scope of an existing substantive rule, or a new rule not clearly indicated by precedents. I believe we should go further and limit treble damages to cases where the violation is clear ... "

I would, however, go beyond Turner's suggestions. We must remove as much of the gray area in antitrust law as possible. There should be very few exceptions to the types of violations for which the treble damages remedy is reduced to actual damages, reasonable attorneys' fees, and litigation costs. If corporate decision makers are provided with legal certainties when evaluating their alternatives, competition will be enhanced. When making decisions, industry and business leaders should not have to speculate as to the risks of suits for the treble damages. Business risks should be taken on the basis of competition.

It is time to take another look at our national antitrust policy to ascertain whether it is appropriate for the era in which we live. Laws must be relevant in today's world. If this proposition is accepted, then we must consider whether change is appropriate in the area of antitrust law.

When the treble damage remedy was introduced in private antitrust actions, it served to encourage domestic competition. Though it may have been appropriate ten years ago, the remedy may well be outdated today. The shoe, steel, and textile industries are struggling to compete with foreign competitiors, some of whom are unconstrained by antitrust laws. Detrebling to remove legal uncertainty may be one way to boost the competitive posture of these industries. History teaches us that protectionism is not the sole salvation of our ailing industries. These troubled industries may be made more competitive in the marketplace, however, by adjusting domestic antitrust law.

The path to enacting legislative improvements will not be easy—nor should it be. Antitrust law has served our nation well for many years. Congress will be in no rush for change. This conference is but a first step. Viewpoints on all sides of the issue of detrebling in antitrust cases should be received and carefully considered by Congress. Hopefully a consensus can be reached. A need for reform is present.

Note

1. Middleton, "New Antitrust" Era Takes Shape, The National Law J., Jan. 13, 1986 at 1, 8.

Let's Fix Only What's Broken: Some Thoughts on Proposed Reform of Private Antitrust Litigation

Peter W. Rodino, Jr.

Let me offer three general observations about the current debate over private antitrust litigation. First, this debate, though perhaps more sophisticated than earlier versions, is not original. Most of the underlying issues were visited during the debates leading up to passage of the Sherman Act in 1890. Second, although the private enforcement suit did not immediately rise to prominence, it has done so over the last 40 years to the point that it is now the body and soul of our antitrust enforcement system. Finally, although improvements in the private enforcement system should always be sought, precipitous or one-sided changes in the system are unwise and—in all likelihood—politically unacceptable. As in the 1890 debate Congress is likely to tread a careful and pragmatic path between extremes.

History, we are often told, is cyclical. Certainly this has been the case with respect to antitrust enforcement. Current suggestions that the private antitrust remedy be abolished altogether, limited in application, reduced in measure, or transformed into a purely restitutionary device are echoes of debates heard on the House and Senate floors in the years 1888 to 1890.

It should not be a surprise that then—as now—the antitrust enforcement debate tended to reflect a larger debate between two basic schools of thought. In 1890 the economic Darwinists wanted no federal intervention in the marketplace. They believed that any economic practice that persisted over time must be efficient and therefore beneficial to society. The populists, on the other hand, believed that trusts were destroying the economic and social fabric of American life. They wanted large combinations destroyed at any cost.

Today the modern counterpart of this debate continues. Adherents of one school push for an unrestrained marketplace that, in their view, will most efficiently allocate the nation's resources. The modern-day populists continue to urge strong and unyielding proscriptions on undue concentrations of power. In between are those who respect the workings of the free

This is an edited version of Congressman Rodino's address to the Conference on November 8, 1985. The full text of Chairman Rodino's address is available from the House Committee on the Judiciary.

market but concede the need for an active federal presence, perhaps including more coordinated industrial planning.

Senator Hoar is credited with adding the treble damage provision in 1890 as a modification of the double damages provision in Senator Sherman's original bill. Though he accepted a federal role in enforcement, he argued strongly for a self-policing mechanism:

A man knows when he is hurt better than an agency or government can tell him. Make it worth his while—as the triple damage provision is intended to do—and injured members of the business community can be dependent upon to police an industry.[1]

If the good senator believed that private suits would eventually become the mainstay of our antitrust enforcement system, he had good future vision. In the first 50 years after the Sherman Act was enacted, private actions were no more numerous than cases brought by the federal government.[2] But beginning in 1940, and accelerating subsequently, there has been a dramatic growth in private suits. Today the private action is truly the heart of our antitrust enforcement system. Over the last decade well over 90 percent of antitrust cases filed in the federal courts have been private suits.[3] Although a few cases filed by the federal government have made headlines— the AT&T case is a prime example—they no longer dominate judicial developments.

Another clear sign of the eclipse of federal government enforcement and the rise of private enforcement is the Supreme Court's docket of antitrust-related cases. In the 1960s federal government-initiated antitrust actions remained roughly at the same levels as private suits on the Supreme Court's antitrust docket. Thereafter government-initiated suits dropped sharply, virtually disappearing from the Supreme Court's docket in some years. In 1984, none of the Supreme Court's 24 reported antitrust decisions (including denials of certiorari) came in a case initiated by the federal government. The result is the same if we look at the major antitrust opinions of the Supreme Court. Over the last two years, eight of the Court's nine significant antitrust rulings came in suits initiated by private parties.[4] The government has limited itself to filing amicus or intervenor briefs in these cases.

To be sure, the key role now being played by private suits may be due in large part to the conscious choice of the current administration to de-emphasize antitrust enforcement. Bolstered by their ideological conviction that the marketplace sweeps away most inefficient restraints, the Justice Department and FTC have largely abdicated enforcement efforts in what they have termed noncartel areas.

To many of us, the private suit takes on even greater importance at a time when the enforcement agencies have not fully carried through on their mandated responsibilities. No better example exists than the area of retail price maintenance. Despite repeated and very specific signals from Congress affirming the per se rule against vertically imposed price restraints,[5] neither federal enforcement agency has brought an enforcement action in this area during the last five years. What is far more disquieting, this administration has persisted in efforts to undermine that rule. In particular, the Justice Department has intervened in private enforcement suits in support of elimination—or more limited interpretation—of the per se rule. And in January of this year the Department issued Vertical Restraints Guidelines whose undisguised goal is to limit in various ways the scope of the per se rule.[6]

I am aware, of course, of those among us who believe that vertical restraints—even vertical price fixing—should generally be condoned. I disagree. But the point is that until Congress changes the law, it remains the enforcement mandate. And private enforcement, though not a fully satisfactory substitute, will help to tide us through periods of indifferent or hostile attitudes by public enforcement officials.

This leads me to my last observation: substantial and precipitous change in the private antitrust enforcement mechanism is unwise at this time. The political outlook for such proposals is, fortunately, not promising.

A number of experts have suggested changes in the treble damage remedy. These proposals warrant careful study. For example, some have suggested that liability in rule of reason cases might be limited to actual damages. Strong arguments can be made that this change would discourage litigation in marginal cases brought under the rule of reason standard. But this proposal raises troubling questions.

Many rule of reason cases are not marginal—serious anticompetitive injury may be occurring. And as some of this conference's contributors suggest, rule of reason cases are likely to be more expensive to try than cases subject to the per se rule. Detrebling the damage award could eliminate any chance that such cases will even be brought. With little or no deterrent from private enforcement, and a lax federal enforcement policy toward most rule of reason cases, business self-discipline could disappear. This result is particularly disturbing at a time when the Justice Department has urged that more types of antitrust conduct be judged under the rule of reason standard.

Another more general danger in tampering with the damages multiple is the likely ripple effect on substantive law. Again, some of the papers presented here document that changes in procedures or remedies inevitably affect the courts' interpretation of substantive law. We cannot ignore such ripple effects in assessing the various reform proposals. If we are troubled by potentially counterproductive types of private suits, we should address directly the substantive law doctrines that allow recoveries in these cases.

History tells us that major legislative initiatives in the antitrust field succeed only when they enjoy broad, bipartisan support. This was certainly true for the Sherman Act in 1890. In my era, it has been true for the Celler-Kefauver Act in 1950, the Hart-Scott-Rodino Act in 1976, and, most recently, for two bills that I shepherded through the Congress: the National Cooperative Research Act (joint research and development) and the Municipal Antitrust Act.

Recently, under the banner of improving U.S. industrial and trade performance, some high administration officials have called for precipitous repeal of section 7 of the Clayton Act and—insofar as it applies to acquisitions—of section 1 of the Sherman Act. All of this is very disquieting to me.

I have watched the evolution of the antitrust laws in the Congress since 1948. I saw the Celler-Kefauver amendments of 1950 eliminate troublesome loopholes in section 7. I participated in the crafting of the Hart-Scott-Rodino Act of 1976 that established our highly successful premerger notification system. All of this—and much more—would be discarded under these hastily concocted recipes for bolstering U.S. industrial performance. Antitrust, it would seem, is once again being made the "whipping boy" for everything from record trade deficits to the perceived loss in U.S. technological leadership.

These remedies will not work. If there is any connection between the antitrust laws and these seemingly intractable economic problems, it would be that more vigorous competition—not less enforcement—is needed.

All of this should not suggest that further inquiry and debate are not useful. I welcome the continuing discussion of the purposes and goals of antitrust policy. As economic understanding increases, it will—as it has in the past—affect our interpretations of antitrust laws and improve our policymaking. But we have, as yet, not arrived at a point where economists even agree on macroeconomic policy for managing our fiscal and monetary affairs, let alone the optimal antitrust enforcement approach. As Nobel Laureate George Stigler has noted, the science of economics is sufficiently imprecise that "there is no position ... which cannot be reached by a competent use of respectable economic theory." [7]

Economics, in the end, does not "win" or "lose" a debate that subsumes more than mere economic goals; it informs that debate. In 1884 Henry Lloyd, in his famous article "Lords of Industry," observed that there were "two outstanding tendencies" in the distinctly American economic system: "the tendency to combination," on the one hand, and the "tendency for social control," on the other. Lloyd concluded that the "first promotes wealth while the second promotes citizenship."[8] He added that for the welfare of the nation, we need both. I must agree.

In conclusion, the private antitrust enforcement suit, though sometimes criticized, has become the heart of our enforcement system. At a time when public enforcement efforts are diminished, I do not see the Judiciary Committee's embracing any proposal that would substantially undercut the private remedy. The Judiciary Committee will continue its efforts, however, to gather more information on the strengths and weaknesses of private enforcement and to examine particular problem areas. Our undertaking will be substantially advanced by the careful and scholarly work of this conference.

Notes

1. 2 G. Hoar, Autobiography of Seventy Years, 363 (1903).

2. Posner, A Statistical Study of Antitrust Enforcement, 13 J. Law & Econ. 365 (1970).

3. House Committee on the Judiciary, 98th Cong., 2d Sess., Study of the Antitrust Treble Damage Remedy (Comm. Print 1984), at 14.

4. Aspen Skiing Co. v. Aspen Highlands Skiing Corp., 105 S.Ct. 2847 (1985); Copperweld Corp. v. Independence Tube Corp., 467 U.S. 752 (1984); Town of Hallie v. City of Eau Claire, 105 S.Ct. 1713 (1985); Hoover v. Ronwin, 466 U.S. 558 (1984), *rehearing denied*, 467 U.S. 1268; Jefferson Parish Hospital District No. 2 v. Hyde, 466 U.S. 2 (1984); Mitsubishi Motors Corp. v. Soler Chrysler-Plymouth, Inc., 105 S.Ct. 3346 (1985); Monsanto Co. v. Spray-Rite Service Corp., 465 U.S. 752 (1984), *rehearing denied*, 466 U.S. 994; National Collegiate Athletic Association v. Board of Regents of the University of Oklahoma, 468 U.S. 85 (1984). In the sole government-initiated case considered by the Supreme Court in 1984, the Court did not adopt the position advanced by the Department. Southern Motor Carriers Rate Conference, Inc. v. United States, 471 U.S. 48 (1985).

5. Beginning with fiscal year 1984, and for each subsequent fiscal year, the House Judiciary Committee has added a rider to the Department of Justice's authorization bill prohibiting the expenditure of funds for any Departmental activity that would seek in the courts a reversal of the per se rule against resale price maintenance. Identical language was approved as a provision in the DOJ appropriations bill for fiscal 1984 (H.R. 3222). (Subsequent to the delivery of these remarks, the Congress included, and President Reagan signed into law, the same provision in the Department of Justice's appropriations bill for fiscal year 1986, H.R. 2965, P. L. 99-180).

6. Subsequent to delivery of these remarks, Congress declared its sense that the vertical guidelines do not accurately reflect existing law, shall not be accorded the force of law, and should be withdrawn by the attorney general. This language was included in the State, Justice, and Commerce appropriations bill for fiscal year 1986, H.R. 2965, P. L. 99-180. See H. Rep. No. 99-399, 99th Cong., 1st Sess. (1985).

7. G. Stigler, The Politics of Political Economists, *Essays in the History of Economics* 63 (1965).

8. H. Lloyd, Lords of Industry, 138 Am. Rev. 535–53 (1884).

Conference Participants

William F. Baxter	Stanford University
Edward R. Becker	U.S. Court of Appeals, Third Circuit
George J. Benston	University of Rochester
Maxwell M. Blecher	Blecher, Collins & Weinstein
John DeQ. Briggs	Howrey & Simon
Joseph F. Brodley	Boston University
Stephen Calkins	Wayne State University
Thomas J. Campbell	Stanford University
Kenneth G. Elzinga	University of Virginia
George E. Garvey	Catholic University
Ernest T. Gellhorn	Jones, Day, Reavis & Pogue
Harvey J. Goldschid	Columbia University
Thomas E. Kauper	University of Michigan
Thomas B. Leary	Hogan & Hartson
Ira M. Millstein	Weil, Gotshal & Manges
Roger G. Noll	Stanford University
Jeffrey M. Perloff	University of California, Berkeley
Robert Pitofsky	Georgetown University
A. Mitchell Polinsky	Stanford University
Charles B. Renfrew	Chevron Corporation
Peter W. Rodino, Jr.	U.S. House of Representatives
Daniel L. Rubinfeld	University of California, Berkeley
Steven C. Salop	Georgetown University
F. M. Scherer	Swarthmore College
Walter A. Schlotterbeck	General Electric Corp.
Richard L. Schmalensee	Massachusetts Institute of Technology
Warren F. Schwartz	Georgetown University
Joe Sims	Jones, Day, Reavis & Pogue
Emory M. Sneeden	McNair Law Firm

Edward M. Snyder	University of Michigan
Lawrence A. Sullivan	University of California, Berkeley
Stephen D. Susman	Susman, Godfrey & McGowan
Paul V. Teplitz	Boston Research Corp.
Donald F. Turner	Wilmer, Cutler & Pickering
Lawrence J. White	New York University
William C. Wood	Bridgewater College

Legal and Corporate Donors to the Georgetown Project

Law Firms and Corporate Legal Departments That Contributed Paralegal Time

New York
Weil, Gotshal & Manges
Mobil Oil Corporation
Winthrop, Stimson, Putman & Roberts
Exxon Corporation
Paul, Weiss, Rifkind, Wharton & Garrison

Chicago
Bell, Boyd & Lloyd
Sidley & Austin
Winston & Strawn

San Francisco
McCutcheon, Doyle, Brown & Enerson
Pillsbury, Madision & Sutro
Heller, Ehrman, White & McAuliffe
Morrision & Foerster
Blecher, Collins & Weinstein (Los Angeles)
Thelen, Marrin, Johnson & Bridges

Kansas City
Shugart, Thomson & Kilroy
Mobil Credit Card Center

Atlanta
King & Spalding
Bondurant, Miller, Hishon & Stephenson

Corporate Donors

Aetna Life and Casualty Foundation
Alcoa Foundation
Bank of America

The B. F. Goodrich Company
Boise Cascade Corporation
Bristol-Myers Company
Champion International Foundation
Chevron Corporation
The Coca-Cola Company
The Continental Group, Inc.
CPC International, Inc.
Dart & Kraft Foundation
Deere & Company
E.I. Du Pont De Nemours & Co., Inc.
Exxon Corporation
FMC Corporation
Ford Motor Company Fund
Freeport-McMoran, Inc.
General Electric Company
General Motors Corporation
Georgia-Pacific Corporation
Green Bay Packaging, Inc.
The Hammermill Foundation
Hercules, Inc.
International Business Machines Corporation
International Minerals & Chemical Corporation
ITT Corporation
Thomas J. Lipton Foundation, Inc.
The Mead Corporation Foundation
Miller Brewing Company
Minnesota Mining and Manufacturing Corporation
Mobil Corporation
Owens-Illinois, Inc.
J.C. Penny Company, Inc.
Pepsico, Inc.
Pfizer, Inc.
Pizza Hut, Inc.
The Procotor & Gamble Company
Scott Paper Company
Union Camp Corporation
Westvaco
The Weyerhaeuser Company

Index

Adickes v. *S.H. Kress and Co.*, 204
Agency costs, 390
Albrecht v. *Herald Co.*, 195
Alton Box litigation, 361
American Medical Int'l., Inc., 249
Ames v. *American Telephone & Telegraph Co.*, 198
Antibiotics antitrust litigation, 313–314
Antitrust rules. *See* Legal standard
Areeda, P., 45, 186–187, 190–192
Arnold, Thurman, 143
Aspen Skiing Co. v. *Aspen Highlands Skiing Corp.*, 192
Associated General Contractors of California, Inc. v. *California State Council of Carpenters*, 199, 202–203, 211, 229, 249, 391, 393
Atlantic Refining Co. v. *FTC*, 188
Atlas Roofing Co., 409
Attorneys, in class action suits, 283–284
Attorneys' fees, 121–131
   in class action suits, 313–314, 320
   deregulation of, 138
   plaintiffs' gains and, 123–124
   settlements and, 247
Austin, Arthur D., 137–138
Automatic fee shifting. *See* Fee shifting
Averch, Harvey, 138
Award. *See* Damages multiple; Relief granted; Treble damages

Baldridge, Malcolm, 249
B.A.T. Indus. Ltd., 249
Baumol, W. J., 274
Baxter, William, 11–12, 272, 317, 372, 383, 404
Beckenstein, A. R., 46
Becker, Gary, 88–89
Benston, George J., 371, 375, 381–382
Berkey Photo, Inc. v. *Eastman Kodak Co.*, 191
Bernstein, R., 310
Bigelow v. *RKO Radio Pictures, Inc.*, 37, 198
Block, D. J., 314
Block, Michael K., 139

Blue Shield of Virginia v. *McCready*, 202, 249
Bok, Derek, 97–98
Bork, Robert, 383
Bose Corp. v. *Consumers Union of United States, Inc.*, 228
Brandeis, Louis, 393, 411
British rule. *See* Fee shifting
Brunswick Corp. v. *Pueblo Bowl-O-Mat*, 229, 249, 259, 407
Bubar v. *Ampco Foods, Inc.*, 249
Burger, Warren, 186–187
Business relationship
   alleged illegal practices and, 7–9
   classification of, with follow-ons, 364–365
   goals of litigation and, 131–134
   litigation costs and, 111–112, 118–119
   motions for dismissal and, 208, 217, 220, 222
   settlement and, 41, 164–165
   strategic behavior and, 131–134
   summary judgment and, 209, 217, 221–222

Calderone Enterprise Corp. v. *United Artists Theatre Circuit*, 198
Calkins, S., 240–241, 246, 248, 257–258, 371, 391, 401, 413–414
Calvani, Terry, 190
Cantor v. *Detroit Edison Co.*, 197
Celler-Kefauver Act, 422
Champion Paper Co., 299
Chicago Board of Trade v. *U.S.*, 393, 411
Christian Schmidt Brewing Co. v. *G. Heileman Brewing Co.*, 248
Chrysler Corp., 132
Chrysler Credit Corp. v. *J. Truett Payne Co.*, 228
City of Lafayette v. *Louisiana Power & Light Co.*, 197
Claim reduction rule, 250
   deterrence and, 306
   fairness and, 315–316
   public interest and, 321
   settlement and, 292–293

Class action suits
  attorneys' fees and, 320
  consumer welfare and, 310–311
  cost reduction and, 271
  as enforcement tool, 392
  joint and several liability and, 411
  lawyers in, 283–284
  legal resources, 111
  litigation costs and, 118
  plaintiffs' attorneys and, 283–284
  plaintiffs in, 283–284, 293–294, 303
  probability of settlement and, 166–167
  serially negotiated settlements and, 411
  summary dispositions and, 227
  treble damages remedy and, 197
Clayton Act, 7, 250, 252–253, 274, 320,
    329–330, 422
Coffee, J. C., Jr., 283, 320
Competitor suits
  protectionism and, 133, 257–259
  social cost and, 132–134
Compliance, 385
Conley v. Gibson, 201
Consent decrees, 330–331
Consumer welfare
  deterrence and, 308–311, 321
  and policy changes, 240, 242–243
  treble damages and, 240
Continental T. V., Inc. v. GTE Sylvania,
    Inc., 103, 195, 393
Contract claims, 45
Contribution rule, 250, 292, 306, 315–316,
    321
Copperweld Corp. v. Independence Tube
    Corp., 250
Corregated Container antitrust litigation,
    297–300, 303, 379, 403
Costs. See also Litigation costs; Private
    costs; Public costs
  components of, 30, 45–46
  in Georgetown project data, 13–15, 73,
    78–79, 107–148, 261–262
  intraparty transactions and, 390
  of legal error, 30–31, 34
  and policymaking, 30
  procompetitive benefits and, 131–134
  for protection, 274–275
  types of, 30
  unintentional violator and, 279
Cost/settlement ratio, 13, 41–43, 126–127
Countersuits, 44, 222

Criminal sanction, 379–380
Cross-claims, 222
Curtis v. Loether, 408

Damage claims, 43–44
Damages awards. See also Damages
    multiple; Treble damages
  amounts awarded, 392
  calculation of, 31–32
  vs. violator's benefits, 301–303
Damages multiple. See also Decoupling;
    Detrebling; Treble damages
  breakdown of settlement and, 154–160
  changes in, 48, 151, 168–170, 254
  cost of errors and, 34
  dangers in change in, 421–423
  detection of violations and, 32
  discretionary, 34–35, 48, 247, 250–251,
    412, 414–415, 417–418
  double damages and, 151–160
  interest and, 36, 252–254, 263
  Laffer curve of litigation and, 20
  likelihood of suit and, 33
  nuisance suits and, 150
  probability of trial and, 170
  reform proposals and, 393
  rule of reason cases and, 33–34, 393–394,
    404
  settlement and, 26–27, 150–151, 168–170,
    176–181, 246, 375
  single damages and, 99–101, 412
  taxation and, 254, 263, 331
  trial expenditure and, 160–161
  underdeterrence and, 32–33
  variable, 34–35, 48
Dealer-agent suits, 132–134
Decoupling, 35, 47–48, 87–94, 380
  price changes and, 92–93
  vs. detrebling, 87, 89–93
Defendants, 271
  in Georgetown project data, 5–7
  gross benefits to, 19, 272–275
  legal costs for, 275–280
  liability for legal expenses and, 271, 278
  litigation activity of, 71
  numbers of, and size of payoff, 79
  ratio of losses for, 124–126
  settlement and, 163, 284–290
  summary relief prospects for, 210
  win rate for, 401
Desu, M., 117

Deterrence
  benefits and costs of, 307
  change in damages multiplier and, 154
  civil penalties and, 16–18
  claim reduction and, 306
  class action plaintiffs and, 303
  compliance programs and, 46
  consumer welfare and, 308–311, 321
  contribution rule and, 306
  criminal sanctions and, 379–380
  determinants of, 300–308
  employee violations and, 385
  government suits and, 32, 400–401
  individual responsibility rule and, 306
  innocent bystanders and, 306–307
  joint and several liability rule and,
    304–305, 307–308, 403
  Laffer curve of litigation and, 19–21
  price-fixing cases and, 380
  quality of outcomes and, 413–414
  settlement and, 318–319
  unintentional violators and, 271–272,
    306–307
Detrebling, 240, 246, 395, 415, 417. *See also*
  Damages multiple; Treble damages
  dangers in, 421–423
  tax factors and, 254, 263
  vs. decoupling, 87, 89–92
Dewees, D. N., 303, 314
Discretionary multiple. *See under* Damages
  multiple
Dismissals. *See also* Summary disposition
  circumstances of granting, 207–208, 210
  in class actions, 227
  conventional wisdom and, 200–203
  countersuits and, 222
  follow-ons and, 363–364
  frequency of granted motions in, 210–211
  in jury suits, 227
  over time, 211–213
  prevalence of, 317
Duration of case. *See* Length of case
DuVal, B. S., Jr., 206, 310, 317–318

E.I. Du Pont de Nemours & Co. v. FTC,
  189, 190
Easterbrook, F. H., 274, 305, 310, 315,
  382–383, 385, 395
Eastman Kodak Co. v. *Southern Photo
  Materials Co.*, 192
Effort at trial, model of, 171–173

Eichlin Mfg. Co., 249
Elzinga, K. G., 240–242, 245–247, 253,
  255–257, 399–400, 402
Enforcement
  costs of, 256–257, 259–263, 411
  economic theory of, 88–89, 92, 383–384
  executive branch policy and, 248
Equilibration tendencies, 185–200, 246
Executive branch policy, 102, 248–249
Expected value, likelihood of litigation and,
  18–19
Export Trading Act, 196, 254
Extortion. *See* Frivolous suits

Fabricated claims, 255–256
Fact issues, vs. issues of law, 203–204
Fairness, 311–316, 403, 411
Fashion Originators' Guild of Am. v. *FTC*,
  194
Federal Trade Commission Act, section 5,
  188–191
Federal Trade Commission standards vs.
  antitrust law, 188–191
FTC v. *Brown Shoe*, 188–189
FTC v. *Motion Picture Advertising Service
  Co.*, 188
FTC v. *Sperry & Hutchinson Co.*, 189
Fee shifting, 27, 35–36, 47
Fine Paper litigation, 141, 314, 379
First National Bank v. *Cities Service Co.*,
  205
Fischel, D. R., 274
Folding Carton litigation, 96–97, 379
Follow-on cases
  advantages to plaintiffs, 329–331
  classification of, 362–363
  costs and, 360
  decision to sue in, 374
  filing of, 335–336, 374
  number of, over time, 312–335, 392
  price fixing and, 352, 354–355, 359,
    400–401
  real dollars demanded in, 337–338
  settlement and, 371–378
  statute violations alleged in, 337, 339–340
  type of, 332–335
Fortner Enterprises, Inc. v. *U.S. Steel Corp.*,
  195
Freedom of Information Act, 330
Frivolous suits, 27–28, 35, 150, 222
Full fee shifting. *See* Fee shifting

Garfield, A. E., 314
Garvey, George E., 412
Gellhorn, Ernest, 412
Georgetown project data
 ambiguous categorization in, 85–86
 awards in, 12, 79–80
 biases in, 84–85
 cases in, 7–8, 61, 66–75
 characteristics of parties in, 66, 68–70
 civil cover sheet information and, 66–67
 confidential data set, 121–127
 costs/payoffs analysis and, 75–80
 damage claims in, 75, 77–78
 data collection process, 61–65
 defendents in, 5–7
 follow-ons analysis and, 361–362
 legal costs summary, 78–79
 linkage with economic performance
   indicators, 96–98
 litigation effort measures in, 71–73
 natures of suits in, 66, 68–70
 outcomes in, 10–13, 16
 overall assessment and, 241
 plaintiffs, 5–7
 process aspects in, 8–10
 settlements in, 75, 77–80, 161–170
 small numbers problem and, 82–83
 sources of variability in, 65
 and summary motions findings, 207–227
 value of, 416–417
Governmental subsidy. See Decoupling
Government cases. See also Follow-on
   cases
 consent decrees and, 330–331
 deterrence and, 32, 400–401
 interval before follow-ons, 359
 nolo contendre pleas and, 330–331
 outcomes of follow-on cases and, 347–350
 plaintiffs and, 359–360
 statute of limitations and, 330
Grossman, J. B., 12, 45
Guy, Ralph, 198–199
Gypsum litigation, 313

Harlan, John, 197, 206
Hart-Scott-Rodino Act, 422
Havoco of America, Ltd. v. Shell Oil Co.,
   202
Hawaii v. Standard Oil Co. of California,
   193, 199
Heterogeneity, 117

Hoar, G. F., 420
Horizontal price fixing. See Price fixing
Horizontal restraints, 192–194
Hospital Bldg. Co. v. Trustees of Rex
   Hospital, 201
Hospital Corp. of America, 249

IBM, 97, 135, 141, 213
Illegal practices, alleged
 classification of, for follow-ons, 364
 costs and, 113, 119, 128–131
 decision to engage in, 389
 in Georgetown project data, 6–7, 69–70
 measures of legal resources and, 113
 settlement data and, 41
 summary procedures and, 208–209, 222,
   225–226
 trends in suit frequency, 37–40
Illinois Brick Co. v. Illinois, 132, 199, 211,
   222, 229, 249, 335, 358
Incentives
 to settle, 23–26, 154–160, 290–296, 382
 to sue, 17–23, 151–154, 283, 372–374
 to violate, 17–23, 390
Individual responsibility rule, 293, 306,
   315–316, 321
Innocent bystander
 costs and, 280
 deterrence and, 306–307
 gross benefit to, 274–275
 incentives to settle and, 296
 joint and several liability and, 382
In pari delicto defense, 197
Intentional violator
 costs and, 279
 deterrence and, 307
 gross benefit to, 273
 incentives to settle and, 294–295
Interest
 damage award and, 36, 252–254, 263
 delaying tactics and, 36, 414
 perverse incentive hypothesis and,
   253–254
 to plaintiffs, 395
Interference cases, 119
International Paper Co., 297, 299
Intervenors, 5

Japanese Electronic Products antitrust
   litigation, 408
Jefferson Parish Hospital District No. 2 v.

Hyde, 391
Johnson, Leland L. 147
Joint and several liability rule. *See also*
    S. 1300
  in class actions, 284, 395
  consumer welfare and, 310, 320–321
  deterrence and, 271, 304–305, 307–308
  fairness and, 315–316, 320–321
  innocent bystanders and, 382
  settlement and, 290–292, 382
  treble damages and, 402–403
Joyce, Jon, 362
Judges' rulings, litigation costs and, 112,
    118
Judgments
  plaintiff win rates and, 40–41
  vs. settlement, 318
Judicial interpretation, 37, 48, 248
Judiciary
  misinformation effect and, 137, 248
  as party to litigation, 37, 48
  policy trends and, 383–384
Jurisdictional reach, 195–196
Jury trials
  elimination of, 247, 250, 407–409
  juror knowledge of awards and, 245, 247,
    250, 379
  legal resource costs and, 111, 118, 139–140
  role of jury and, 245, 250
  summary dispositions and, 227

Kane, M., 205–206
Kauper, T. E., 95, 317, 318, 371, 376, 381,
    392, 400–401
Kelly, K. K., 13
Kessler, Jeffrey, 404
King, Benjamin F., 313–314
Klein, B., 12, 25, 41, 272, 318
Klor's Inc. v. *Broadway-Hale Stores, Inc.*,
    194

Laffer curve of litigation, 19–21
Landes, W. M., 88–89, 305, 310, 315
Large cases. *See* Megacases
Latimer, H., 313–314
Lee, E., 117
Lee-Desu test, 117–119
Legal error. *See* Costs, of legal error
Legal fees. *See* Attorneys' fees; Costs;
    Legal resources; Litigation costs
Legal resources. *See also* Attorneys' fees;

Costs; Litigation costs
  allocation of, 262–263
  in class action vs. non-class action cases,
    111
  juries and, 111, 139–140
  in jury vs. nonjury trials, 111
  kind of case and, 110–116
  measures of, 108, 110–111, 113–117, 241
  misinformation effect and, 137
  ordinary litigation and, 142
  price-fixing cases and, 140–141
  relief granted and, 115
  relief requested and, 116
  statute allegedly violated and, 114
Legal standard, 21, 29–31, 36, 188–191
Length of case, 8–10, 15, 119.
  follow-on case and, 350–354
  jury trials and, 118
  probability of truth and, 97
  size of payoff and, 79
Lessig v. *Tidewater Oil Co.*, 192
Liability. *See* Decoupling; Joint and several
    liability rule
Litigation costs, 78–79, 402. *See also*
    Cost/settlement ratio; Legal resources
  aggregate, 15, 261–262
  alleged illegal practices and, 113, 119,
    128–131
  attorney's fees and, 120–121
  class action cases and, 118
  court awards and, 120–121
  damages multiple and, 33–34, 160
  determination of, 28–29
  economizing on, 22–23
  estimation of, 129–130
  in judge vs. jury trials, 118
  Laffer curve of litigation and, 20–21
  magistrates' rulings and, 112, 118
  settlement and, 23–24, 154–160
Litigation effort, measures of, 71–73
Litigation process
  economics of, 150–161
  interdependent strands in, 149–150,
    171–176
  static model of, 171–176
Litton v. *AT&T*, 12
Lloyd, Henry, 423
Local Government Antitrust Act, 196, 422
Lockheed Corp., 190
Lodestar method. *See* Attorneys fees,
    in class action suits

Lorain Journal Co. v. *United States*, 191
Lupia v. *Stella D'Ori Biscuit Co.*, 206

McCloskey, Donald N., 127–128
McGuckin, Robert, 362
McLauchlan, William, 204–206
Magistrates' rulings, 112, 118
Marshall, Thurgood, 197
MDL. *See* Multidistrict litigation
Mead Corp., 299
Megacases, 141–142, 240–241, 385–386,
    390–391
Mergers and acquisitions, 248–250
Miller, A., 200, 205–206
Millstein, Ira M., 412, 414–415
Misinformation effect, 136–138, 248, 255
Monfort of Colorado, Inc. v. *Cargill, Inc.*,
    248
Monopolization, 191–192
Monsanto Co. v. *Spray-Rite Service Corp.*,
    85, 194, 229, 250, 391
Motions to dismiss. *See* Dismissals
Multidistrict litigation, 4, 63
    awards and, 359
    follow-on cases and, 335–336, 355–357

National Cooperative Research Act, 196,
    254, 395, 422
National Economic Research Associates
    (NERA), 206–207, 391
*National Independent Theater Exhibitors,
    Inc.* v. *Buena Vista Distribution Co.*,
    249–250
Net expected value, 18–19
Nolo contendre pleas, 330–331
Non-class actions, 111
Nonclass plaintiffs, 283, 293–294
Northwest Wholesale Stationers, Inc. v.
    Pacific Stationery & Printing Co., 391
Nuisance suits. *See* Frivolous suits

Official Airline Guides, Inc. v. *FTC*,
    189, 192
Ordover, J. A., 274
Outcomes
    in follow-on cases, 339, 347–350, 363–364
    intermediate, 71, 74–75
    measures of, 10–12, 75–76
    quality of, 413–414
    truth and, 95–98
    by type of offense, 345–346

Out Front Productions, Inc. v. *Magid*, 250
Overdeterrence, 32–33

Perloff, J. M., 240–242, 246–247, 258, 371,
    374–375, 392, 401, 403
Perma Life Mufflers, Inc. v. *International
    Parts Corp.*, 197
Per se rules, 210, 394, 411
Perverse incentives, 135–136, 248, 253–255
Pick-Barth doctrine, 193–194
Plaintiff. *See also* Class action suits,
    plaintiffs in; Incentives, to sue; Nonclass
    plaintiffs
    awards and settlements, 79–80
    benefits and costs and, 280–282
    decision to sue and, 135, 151–154,
        175–176, 282–284
    in follow-ons, 329–331, 360–361
    in Georgetown project data, 5–7, 68
    government cases and, 329–331
    incentives for, 135, 150–151, 282–290
    net expected value for, 18–19
    ratio of fees to gains for, 123–124
    settlement patterns and, 163
    summary relief and, 210
Plaintiff win rate, 11–12
    cost/settlement ratio and, 41–43
    follow-ons and, 360–361
    influences on, 24–26
    settlement patterns and, 16, 40–41, 163
Plywood litigation, 141
Policy change, basic principles for, 46–48
Polinsky, A. M., 27, 293, 305, 380
Poller v. *Columbia Broadcasting System*,
    185, 200, 205–207, 392
Posner, R. A., 88–89, 139–140, 203, 305,
    310, 315, 383
Predatory pricing, 38
Price fixing, 7, 392
    cases, costs of, 140–141
    customer relationships and, 134
    damages vs. violator's benefits and,
        302–303
    dealer suits and, 132
    deterrence of, 400
    duration of case and, 119
    follow-on cases and, 352, 354–355, 359,
        400–401
    frequency as violation, 70, 399
    horizontal, 37–38, 334–335, 345, 354–355
    joint and several liability rule and, 290

legal resource costs and, 140–141
vertical, 38, 337
Prichard, R. S., 303, 314
Priest, G. L., 12, 25, 41, 272, 318
Private costs, 261–262
Profitability, 95
Protectionism, 133
Public costs, 259–261

Radiant Burners, Inc. v. *People Gas Light & Coke Co.*, 194
Reagan, Ronald (U.S. president), 102, 248–249
Refusal to deal cases, 7, 119
Reich, R. B., 12
Reiter v. *Sonotone Corp.*, 202
Relief granted
  breakdown of costs by, 115, 120
  factors in size of, 79–80
  legal resource measures and, 115
Relief requested, 116
Remedial law, 197–200
Reparations costs, 138, 248, 255
Reputation, settlement rate and, 156
Restraint of trade cases, 119
Reuben H. Donnelly, 190
Rie v. *Barry & Enright Productions*, 250
Risk aversion, 26, 283–284, 293, 390
Robinson-Patman claims. *See* Clayton Act
Rodino, Peter, 244, 383, 395, 404
Rosenfield, A., 313–314
Ross v. *Bernhard*, 408
Royal Drug Co., Inc. v. *Group Life and Health Ins. Co.*, 250
Rubinfeld, D. L., 27, 240–242, 246–247, 258, 371, 374–375, 392, 401, 403
Rule of reason cases, damages multiple and, 33–34, 393–394, 404

St. Regis Paper Co., 297
Salop, Steven C., 83–84, 87, 95, 97–98, 132, 143, 172, 257, 261, 317–318, 394, 401–402, 404
Saunders, T. R., 314
Schwartz, Warren, 89
Schwarzer, William, 213
Settlement
  amounts of, 317–318
  attorney's fees and, 123–127, 247
  benefits of, 389–390
  broad vs. narrow definition of, 11, 40, 42

business relationship and, 164–165
claim reduction rule and, 292–293
class vs. nonclass plaintiffs and, 293–294
contribution rule and, 292
damage claims and, 43–44
damage multiplier and, 33, 156–160, 168–170, 240, 375
empirical study of, 161–170
factors in breakdown of, 24–26, 154–160, 164–166
factors in size of, 79–80, 296–300
fee-shifting rules and, 27, 35–36
follow-on litigation and, 371–378
in Georgetown project data, 12–13, 161–170
incentives for, 23–26, 284–290, 371–378
liability and, 290–293
models for, 164–166, 173–181, 375
plaintiff win rates and, 40–41
policy implications and, 26–27
prevalence of, 317, 401–402
probability of, 166–170, 176–181, 316–317
in progression of same-defendant cases, 376–377
risk aversion and, 293
size of firms and, 162–164
spillover effect and, 376–377
uncertainty and, 26
vs. damage claims, 75, 77–78
Settlement blackmail, 383
Settlement gap, 156–160, 164–166, 168–170, 247
Shavell, S., 272, 293, 305
Sherman Act, 7, 38, 120, 252, 420, 422
Shipping Act, 196
Silver v. *New York Stock Exch.*, 194
Snyder, E. A., 95, 317–318, 371, 376, 381, 392, 400–401
Soft Drink Interbrand Competition Act, 196
Solovy, J. S., 314
Spiller, P. T., 36
Spillover effect, 376–377
Stakes, 43–44, 390
Standing decisions, 198–200
Standing test, 393
Statute violations, alleged, 6, 68
  breakdown of costs by, 114, 119–120
  in follow-on cases, 337, 339–340
  settlement data and, 41
  size of payoff and, 80

Statute violations (cont.)
  summary procedures and, 222–224
  trends in suit frequency, 38
S. 1300, 250, 402–403, 405
Stigler, George, 88–89, 422
Strategic behavior, 131–138, 161
Substantive standards, 188, 191–197, 393,
  421–422
Sugar Institute litigation, 361
Suits, temporal pattern of, 37–40
Summary disposition, 401, 411. *See also*
  Dismissals; Summary judgment
  appeals and, 227
  court activity and, 213, 215–216
  by demand damages, 213, 217–219
  by jurisdiction, 213, 215–216
  over time, 211–214, 391
  treble damages and, 227–230
Summary judgment
  circumstances of granting, 207, 209–210,
    401
  in class actions, 227
  conventional wisdom on, 200, 203–207
  frequency of granted motions, 210–211
  in jury suits, 227
  over time, 211, 213–214
Susman, Stephen, 213
Sutliff, Inc. v. *Donovan Cos.*, 203

Taxation, damage multiple and, 254, 263,
  331
Telex Corp. v. *IBM*, 191
Teplitz, P. V., 385, 390–391, 399, 401–402
Thurmond, Strom, 402
Theatre Enterprises Inc. v. *Paramount Film
  Distrib. Corp.*, 194
Tort claims, 45
Trebilcock, M. J., 303, 314
Treble damages. *See also* Damages
  multiple; Detrebling
  complex litigation and, 29
  decision to sue and, 16–17, 389
  deterrence and, 271
  economic costs and, 135–138
  efficiency and, 31–34, 247–248
  elimination of, 19
  follow-on cases and, 358, 360
  interest and, 252–254, 319–320
  liability and, 402–403
  litigation expenditures and, 28–29
  middle range actions and, 402

misinformation effect and, 136–138
monopolization and, 191–192
nonprimary antitrust cases and, 45
number of suits and, 19–21
in pari delicto defense and, 197
perverse incentives and, 135–136
procedural law and, 197–200
proof of damages and, 198
quality of outcomes and, 413–414
remedial law and, 197–200
rule of reason cases and, 404
scope of, 409
strategic behavior and, 135–138
substantive standards and, 191–197
summary dispositions and, 227–230
vs. single damages, 99–101
Triple M Roofing Corp. v. *Tiemco, Inc.*, 249
Trubek, David M., 142
Truth, outcomes and, 95–98
Tunis Bros. Co. v. *Ford Motor Co.*, 250
Turner, D., 45, 186–187, 190–192,
  412–414, 417
Two-tiered market, 80, 390–391

Uncertainty
  damages multiple and, 32–33, 35, 246–247,
    393–394
  likelihood of suit and, 17–18, 21–22
  settlement-trial decision and, 157
Underdeterrence, 32–33
Unintentional violator, 274, 279, 295,
  306–307
United Air Lines, Inc. v. *CAB*, 189–191
United States v. *Aluminum Co. of America*,
  191
United States v. *Arnold, Schwinn & Co.*, 195
United States v. *Calmar, Inc.*, 249
United States v. *Empire Gas Corp.*, 192
United States v. *Griffith*, 191
United States v. *Grinnell Corp.*, 191
United States v. *Sealy, Inc.*, 193
United States v. *Topco Assocs., Inc.*, 193
United States v. *United Shoe Machinery
  Corp.*, 192
United States v. *United States Gypsum Co.*,
  186–187

Vertical restraints, 38, 194–195, 248, 250
Von Kalinowski, J., 206

Weller, Dennis, 139

Weyerhaueser Co., 249
White, Lawrence J., 83–84, 87, 95, 97–98,
    132 , 143, 172, 257, 261, 317–319, 394,
    401–402, 404
Willing victimization, 255
Wood, W. C., 240–242, 245–247, 253,
    255–257, 399–400, 402
Wright, C., 200–201, 205–206
Wyzanski, Charles, 192